Communication in Political Campaigns

This book is part of the Peter Lang Media and Communication list.
Every volume is peer reviewed and meets
the highest quality standards for content and production.

PETER LANG
New York • Bern • Berlin
Brussels • Vienna • Oxford • Warsaw

William L. Benoit

Communication in Political Campaigns

Functional Analysis
of Election Messages

PETER LANG
New York • Bern • Berlin
Brussels • Vienna • Oxford • Warsaw

Library of Congress Cataloging-in-Publication Data

Names: Benoit, William L., author.
Title: Communication in political campaigns: functional analysis of
election messages / William L. Benoit.
Description: New York: Peter Lang, 2022.
Includes bibliographical references and index.
Identifiers: LCCN 2021013719 (print) | LCCN 2021013720 (ebook)
ISBN 978-1-4331-8807-7 (paperback)
ISBN 978-1-4331-8796-4 (ebook pdf) | ISBN 978-1-4331-8403-1 (epub)
Subjects: LCSH: United States—Politics and government. | Communication in
politics—United States. | Campaign speeches—United States. | United
States—Politics and government.
Classification: LCC JK2281 .B46 2022 (print) | LCC JK2281 (ebook) |
DDC 324.7/30973—dc23
LC record available at https://lccn.loc.gov/2021013719
LC ebook record available at https://lccn.loc.gov/2021013720
DOI 10.3726/b18545

Bibliographic information published by **Die Deutsche Nationalbibliothek**.
Die Deutsche Nationalbibliothek lists this publication in the "Deutsche
Nationalbibliografie"; detailed bibliographic data are available
on the Internet at http://dnb.d-nb.de/.

© 2022 Peter Lang Publishing, Inc., New York
80 Broad Street, 5th floor, New York, NY 10004
www.peterlang.com

All rights reserved.
Reprint or reproduction, even partially, in all forms such as microfilm,
xerography, microfiche, microcard, and offset strictly prohibited.

Table of Contents

Preface vii

Chapter One The Nature of Political Campaigns 1
Chapter Two The Functional Theory of Political Campaign Discourse 33
Chapter Three The Role of Medium in Campaign Discourse 69
Chapter Four The Role of Source in Campaign Discourse 115
Chapter Five The Role of Context in Political Campaign Discourse 141
Chapter Six Non-Presidential, Non-U.S. Campaign Discourse 165
Chapter Seven News Coverage of Political Campaigns 185
Chapter Eight Voters: Campaign Messages and Election Outcome 229
Chapter Nine Conclusions 267

Appendix 1 271
References 279
Index 315

Preface

This book investigates the nature and function of political campaign communication. I begin by justifying the importance of this topic (why are political campaigns worth discussing?) and presenting a model for understanding the flow of information in political campaigns. This book takes an explicitly communicative approach to understanding political campaigns: Elections are inherently and essentially communicative in nature. Some would probably argue that money is what is essential to political campaigns. It is certainly true that today it is impractical to run for higher elective office (president, U.S. Senate and House, governor, and others) without money. However, the money raised and spent by political candidates is devoted largely to conveying the candidates' *messages* to prospective voters as well as potential donors; campaign donations are wasted if the candidate does not send messages to voters. Donald Trump rewrote the "rules" for presidential primary campaigns in 2016. Two key elements of his success were (1) his use of Twitter and Facebook and (2) his repeated highly controversial statements (many made in tweets) and the intense media attention he attracted. So, communication served as the basis for his success. Political campaigns use messages to persuade voters to support a given candidate.

This book adopts the perspective offered by the Functional Theory of Political Campaign Communication, so Chapter Two will explain that theory. Then it will turn to an investigation of three communication factors that influence the production (invention, creation) of political campaign discourse: medium, source, and context. I have argued (1994, 2000a) that these factors influence the nature of messages, along with the persuader's purpose, which is represented here as the desire to win elective office and manifested in the three *functions* of political campaign discourse. The fact that the messages analyzed here, political campaign messages, have the same purpose means they should have some similarities. However, these messages also have noteworthy differences which means that they are not completely identical. First, messages that are created for one medium will differ in some respects from messages created for another medium. For example, campaign statements made in debates will have some differences from statements made in television spots or on television talk shows. Second, messages created by certain sources will differ in certain ways from messages created by other sources. Messages produced by the candidates have systematic differences from messages supporting that candidate which are produced by surrogates such as other politicians, PACs (Political Action Committees), and others. Third, persuasive messages created in one kind of situation will be somewhat different from messages produced in other situations. For example, messages in the primary phase of the campaign have clear differences from messages from the general election campaign. Therefore, this book will focus on medium or message form (Chapter Three), source (Chapter Four), and the context or situation of presidential campaign discourse (Chapter Five). Although important differences are revealed in each of these areas, it will become obvious that campaign messages produced in diverse media, by different sources, and in varied contexts also share important similarities.

The remaining chapters address other important topics. Chapter Six will reach beyond presidential campaigns to examine other kinds of political campaign discourse: non-presidential and non-U.S. campaign messages. Most election research to date has focused on presidential campaigns, particularly those in the U.S. These races appear more important: The actions taken by Presidents affect citizens across the entire country, as well as our relations with the rest of the world, so presidential campaign messages naturally receive more publicity than messages from candidates for lesser offices. Nevertheless, campaigns for other offices besides the president deserve consideration, and some research has examined political campaign discourse created for other races. Furthermore, some research is available on political campaign messages in other countries. In additional to messages from the candidates, voters also learn about the candidates and their positions on the issues from the news. Recall that Donald Trump relied heavily on the media coverage about him. Chapter Seven will discuss news coverage of political campaigns because information about the candidates reaches voters through the news media as well as from the candidates directly. Chapter Eight will examine voters, the ultimate audience for campaign messages. asking how they use the information from candidate messages, the news, and other sources of election information to make vote choices? Chapter Nine will offer concluding observations.

This book is designed around theory. It is a good thing when theory can be tested by data; the Functional Theory of Political Campaign Discourse is well-supported by data. These data come from a multitude of election campaigns, spanning decades, encompassing many elective offices and multiple countries, a large variety of media or message forms, and literally hundreds of candidates. This widespread support is important because a few kinds of messages, a few candidates, or an unusual year can be misleading. Using the amount and kind of data available for testing Functional Theory provides a better understanding of election campaign messages than looking at any one kind of message, one candidate or group of candidates, or even one election cycle. It is also important to realize that a good theory does something data cannot: explain why things happen, why the data look like this.

It may appear that some tables report conflicting data. For example, some tables combine primary and general data whereas other tables report these groups separately. Furthermore, because defenses are uncommon (even in debates), Functional Theory does not investigate the topics of defenses. This means acclaims+attacks+defenses do not equal policy+character.

This edition has been revised and updated in several ways. Social media have been added to the media discussed in the first edition. New data have been added from campaigns held after the first edition and from media not examined in the first edition. New topics, such as a discussion of the balkanization (fragmenting) of media and audiences and an analysis of how voters process information in messages, have been added. New illustrative examples from recent campaigns have replaced many of the older examples. The number of tables have been reduced and most statistical analyses are reported at the end of chapters after the table they concern.

I would like to thank my wife Pam Benoit and my daughter Jen Benoit-Bryan for their support (as it turns out, I have published articles related to political campaigns with both!). Second, my coauthors on various political communication research projects – David Airne, Julie Berman, Andy Billings, Joe Blaney, Brian Bough, LeAnn Brazeal, Sumana Chattopadhyay, Sooyoung Cho, Yun Son Choi, Jordan Compton, Venita Cooper, Steve Croucher, Ulises Cruz, Heather Currie, Corey Davis, Jeff Delbert, Jessica Furgerson, Mark Glantz, Jayne Henson Goode, Glenn Hansen, Allison Harthcock, Julio Herrero, Lance Holbert, Andrew Klyukovski, Cho Lee, Glen Leshner, Sheila Maltos, John McGuire, John McHale, Mitchell McKinney, Laura Paatelainen, John Petrocik, Anji Phillips, Bryan Phillips,

Penni Pier, Steve Price, Bryan Reber, Leslie Rill, Sarah Sargardia, Tamir Sheafer, Ivy Shen, Jennifer Seifert, Yonghoi Song, Kevin Stein, Mike Stephenson, Leigh Anne Sudbrock, Rebecca Verser, Courtney Vogt, David Webber, Bill Wells, John Wen, Sheri Whalen, Jessica Wilson-Kratzer, and Jack Yu – have helped me work on these ideas. The students who have taken my classes helped by asking questions and giving feedback about what I found in my research. I have also benefited from the advice of editors and reviewers of my work over the years. The University of Missouri, through its Research Council, granted me a Research Leave for 2003–2004, which allowed me to focus on this project. My Department Chairs during this time period, Pam Benoit and Michael Kramer, have also supported my work. The University of Alabama at Birmingham has given me an opportunity to spend a good deal of my time on research and writing.

CHAPTER ONE

The Nature of Political Campaigns

America is a country of elections. Political candidates seek a wide variety of elective offices including president, governor, mayor, city council, congress (state and federal), senate (state and federal), and in some jurisdictions, judgeships and dog catchers. The federal government has 537 offices (president, vice president, senators, representatives). Voters elect candidates to 18,749 positions in state government. Local (city, county) governments hold elections for another 500,396 elected officials. The U.S. enjoys – or endures – campaigns for almost 520,000 elective offices (Lawless, 2012). Campaigns have imperfections (e.g., candidates can be deceptive, campaign donations and special interests can corrode the process of democracy, and too many voters are apathetic), but nevertheless elections are an integral part of contemporary society and our democracy and better than other forms of government.

Presidential candidates lavish large amounts of money on their political campaigns. Over $2.6 billion was spent on the 2012 presidential election (Center for Responsive Politics, 2012). In 2016 candidates, political parties, and outside groups spent $6.5 billion on presidential and congressional campaigns (both primary and general elections are included; Ingraham, 2017). Democrat Hillary Clinton spent heavily on TV spots. Her opponent, Republican Donald Trump, aired considerable fewer ads in both the Republican primary and the general election (as discussed in Chapter Three, Trump relied heavily on Twitter and

Facebook in his campaign). Still, literally billions of dollars are spent on presidential campaigns in the U.S. and millions are spent on races for other offices here and in other countries.

This incredible amount of money purchases a huge amount of broadcast time. The Wesleyan Media Project (2012) reported that "over 915,000 presidential ads have been aired on broadcast and national cable television since June 1. This is a 44.5 percent increase from the 637,000 ads aired through October 21 in 2008." So, the number of presidential TV spots rose greatly over time. In 2016, the nominations for both political parties were contested (in some years only one party had meaningful primaries: for example, in 2004 no one challenged President George W. Bush, in 2012 President Barack Obama's nomination was uncontested, and no one challenged President Trump for the 2020 Republican nomination). During the 2016 presidential primaries, Democratic presidential candidates bought over 230,000 ads ("Number of ads aired," 2016); Republicans aired almost 230,000 spots ("Number of ads aired," 2016). PACs (Political Action Committees) ran almost 130,000 political commercials in the 2016 Republican presidential primaries ("Number of ads aired for outside groups," 2016). Political advertising is an important medium in contemporary political campaigns.

Today, it is simply not possible to campaign for national election without spending millions of dollars. However, money is not everything. Lau and Pomper (2004) note that "It is not just money but *how* candidates choose to spend their campaign funds that influences the outcome of an election" (p. 46, emphasis original). In the Democratic primary of 2004, Howard Dean raised the most money by a wide margin in 2003: $40.9 million. The eventual Democratic nominee, John Kerry, accumulated only $22 million (Drinkard, 2004, p. 5A). However, Dean had won no primaries or caucuses by the time he dropped out; Kerry, with barely half of Dean's funds, won all but two races. Wesley Clark, who had raised barely one-third of Dean's money, won the Oklahoma primary. In the 2016 general presidential election Hillary Clinton spent $768 million whereas Donald Trump expended far less: $398 million (Ingraham, 2017); nevertheless, Trump won the electoral college and the Oval Office (although Clinton received more of the popular vote). Even though the Democratic candidate received more votes, she spent almost twice as much as the GOP candidate but did not win anywhere near twice the votes as the GOP candidate (Ingraham, 2017; Allison, Rojanasakul, Harris, & Sam, 2016). Money, unless used to disseminate effective messages, is no guarantee of electoral success.

The "rulebook" for political campaigns was completely shredded by Donald Trump in the 2016 Republican presidential primary. Trump was well-known to most voters as a business magnate and television personality before he announced his candidacy on June 16, 2015. Many of his statements during the campaign were perceived as outrageous by many. Such comments guaranteed perpetual media coverage for Trump; combined with his heavy reliance on Twitter, he had no need to spend as much money as other candidates on his primary campaign. Donald Trump expended $18.5 million on television advertising in the 2016 Republican primary campaign. Four other Republican candidates spent more (and lost): Marco Rubio: $72.7 million: Jeb Bush: $66.9 million; Ted Cruz: $37.6; and John Kasich: $18.9 (Estimated Cost of Ads, 2016). In the general election campaign, Clinton devoted $332.1 million to advertising while Trump spent only $18.7 million (Associated Press, 2016; keep in mind that the Democrat and Republican National Committees also spent money on ads, as did outside groups). For comparison, Barack Obama and Mitt Romney each spent over $400 million on spots in 2012 ("Mad Money," 2012). Despite four years of inflation, Trump won the Electoral College in 2016 by spending less than 4% of what Romney spent in his loss in 2012. Television advertising will continue to be an important component of political election campaigns – just as older media such as radio ads and direct mail advertising are still used by candidates today – but TV spots may not be as important in future campaigns as they were in the past. Trump's campaign benefited greatly from his use of social media (discussed in Chapter Three), a medium growing rapidly in importance. However, the situationed when President Trump started campaigning for re-election: Between January 1, 2019 and February 23, 2020 the Trump campaign spent over $17 million despite running unopposed for the Republican nomination (Wesleyan Media Project, 2020). It seems likely that his ad spending in 2020 will far outstrip his 2016 effort.

Obviously candidates also employ other kinds of messages besides television spots. For example, 21 primary debates, three presidential debates, and one vice presidential debate were held in 2016 (as in several earlier campaigns). Presidential candidates employed other messages including speeches (e.g., candidacy announcement speeches, nomination acceptance addresses, speeches at campaign rallies), campaign webpages, and direct mail brochures. They appeared on television talk shows. Social media, such as Facebook and Twitter, have emerged as very important avenues for candidates to reach voters (see Benoit & Glantz, 2020). Political candidates rely on a variety of messages to reach voters and the donors who fund their campaigns.

The 2016 presidential campaign reached millions of voters. The first Republican primary debate of the 2016 presidential campaign was watched by 24 million people, "making it the highest-rated primary debate in television history" (Stelter, 2015). The three general election debates between Clinton and Trump attracted over 222 million viewers; the Kaine-Pence vice presidential debate was watched by

37 million people (Nielson, 2017). Debate have the potential for important effects because of the sheer size of the viewing audience.

Campaigns Matter

This chapter will begin by addressing the basic question of whether political campaigns influence voters. It will argue that many campaigns are necessarily conducted mainly in the mass media. Then I will discuss obvious and subtle influences on vote choice.

Mass Media in Election Campaigns

In 2016, 226 million Americans were eligible to vote (Pew Research Center, 2016; this figure excludes those who are ineligible to vote: non-citizens; people in prison, on probation, or on parole). More people were eligible to vote in 2020 (239 million; Voter turnout, 2022). Because the populace is so huge, the number of voters who could decide how to vote based on their *personal knowledge* of candidates is negligible. Voters must rely on information obtained from the mass media or on discussions with other voters, who had themselves learned about the candidates from the mass media. Ralph Nader, who ran unsuccessfully for president in 2000 as the Green Party nominee, explained that "You cannot reach in direct personal communication even one percent of the eligible voters. In essence you don't run for president directly; you ask the media to run you for president or, if you have the money, you can pay the media for exposure" (p. 155).

Even in races for offices with fewer constituents than the president, the mass media is vital for reaching voters. The Census Bureau (2011) reports that the average congressional district contains about 711,000 constituents (Wyoming, the state with the smallest population, has 544,000 residents and one member of congress). The size of the average congressional district increased after the 2020 census (to over 761,000). Similarly, many mayoral elections are also conducted mainly via mass media: Over 30 American cities have populations over half a million (World Population Review, 2020) and TV spots are important in smaller cities as well. Table 1.1 shows how many voters say they learn about political campaigns from various media. Campaigns matter because they educate our citizens and offer them the opportunity to make informed voting decisions.

Chapter Three discusses the fact that the advent of the Internet and social media have fragmented the mass media into many "audiences" who learn from different content sources (e.g., some voters get news from CNN and others from

Table 1.1. Most useful sources for news about the 2016 presidential election campaign.

Media	Percent
Cable TV news	24
Social media	14
Local TV	14
News website/app	13
Radio	11
Network nightly news	3
Local paper in print	3
National paper in print	2
Issue-based group webpage/app/email	2
Candidate or campaign group webpage/app/email	1

Gottfried, Barthel, Shearer, & Mitchell (2016).

FOX; these sources convey quite different visions of the world and the people and events in it, which means they are likely to have sharply contrasting attitudes; Benoit & Billings, 2020).

Campaigns Have Both Obvious and Subtle Effects

It is important at this point to keep in mind that campaigns have both obvious and subtle effects. Obvious effects include (1) the conversion of vote choice from one candidate to another and (2) the decision to vote for a candidate by a previously undecided voters. Less obvious is the fact that election messages can solidify a voter's existing candidate preference. This solidification effect would not be apparent in public opinion polls – which ask which candidate you lean toward, not how certain you are in this preference. However, strengthening a voter's preference for a candidate increases the likelihood that this voter will (1) donate to a candidate, (2) try to persuade friends, family, and co-workers to prefer this candidate, (3) resist the persuasive efforts of, and on behalf of, opposing candidates, and (4) be more likely to actually go to the polls and cast a vote for that candidate. Chapter Eight will discuss the resurgence of party-driven voting; it is important to realize that campaign messages can have other important effects in addition to conversion.

Next, I will discuss the Limited Effects Model of mass media and other influences on voters (political party affiliation, current events). Then it will argue directly for the effects of campaigns on voters and discuss the two main sources of campaign information, candidate messages and news media.

Limited Effects Model

The People's Choice is a classic study of the effects of presidential campaigns on voters. Lazarsfeld, Berelson, and Gaudet (1948; see also Berelson, Lazarsfeld, & McPhee, 1954) conducted a panel study of voters in Erie County Ohio during the 1940 presidential election. They concluded that two main effects of campaigns on voters were "activation," or "bringing their latent political attitudes to the surface," and "reinforcement," or "telling them what they wanted to see and hear" (p. 94). The voters who experienced a third effect, "conversion," or change in preference from one candidate to another, were "few indeed" (p. 94, italics omitted). Lazarsfeld, Berelson, and Gaudet also found that voters reported more political discussion among family, friends, and co-workers than exposure to radio or print messages. Keep in mind that this study was conducted in 1940 and CBS did not begin television broadcasting until 1941 (WSIU, 2002). Their investigation led them to propose the "two-step flow of communication," in which "ideas often flow *from* radio and print *to* the opinion leaders and *from* them to the less active sections of the population" (p. 151; emphasis original). Although they acknowledged that campaigns can influence citizens' vote choice, Lazarsfeld, Berelson, and Gaudet concluded that such effects are minimal.

In another classic work, *Voting*, Campbell, Gurin, and Miller (1954), studied the 1948 and 1952 presidential elections. They argued for three primary influences on voting behavior: political parties, issues, and candidate evaluations. They argued that it is likely that "the respective weights each of these three factors has would vary from election to election" (p. 183). They were particularly interested in situations in which these three factors would conflict, where there were cross-pressures (e.g., liking one candidate but preferring another candidate's policy positions). These three factors are still important today and I will return to them in Chapter Eight. The relative importance of these three factors not only varies from campaign to campaign but also varies from one voter to another voter. These books are generally considered *sociological* approaches because demographic variables were thought to be very important in vote choice.

The American Voter (Campbell, Converse, Miller, & Stokes, 1960) conceptualized party identification as a relatively long-term attitude, stressing the electorate's "pervasive sense of attachment to one or the other of the two major parties" (p. 541). They emphasized the voters' perceptions, writing that

> By casting a vote the individual acts toward a political world whose objects he perceives and evaluates in some fashion; the view he has formed of the presidential candidates, of the two major parties, and of various political issues and politically active groups has a profound influence on his behavior. (p. 39)

It is important to realize that voters base their decisions on their *perceptions* of the world (e.g., state of the economy) and the candidates, but these perceptions might not necessarily be an accurate reflection of reality. For example, it seems likely that perceptions of a weak economy in 1992 contributed to President Bush's loss. It may be that the economy had already started to improve at that time, but as long as voters *perceived* or believed that the economy was weak, Bush had an important obstacle to overcome. Notice too that campaign messages are capable of influencing voters' perceptions. This approach is considered to be psychological because of the importance of voters' beliefs and ideas in vote choice.

Converse (1966) developed the concept of the "normal vote." He observed that we can divide the vote in any election into two parts: "(1) the normal or 'baseline' vote division to be expected from a group, other things being equal; and (2) the current deviation from that norm, which occurs as a function of the immediate circumstances of the specific election" (p. 11). Thus, over time many voters tend to show a relatively stable pattern of votes. In other word, some citizens cast their votes consistently over time (e.g., the votes of Democrats or Republicans who never defect). However, other votes are influenced by short-term factors, such as the state of the economy or the qualifications or issue positions of the particular candidates running in a given election (and their campaign messages, of course, which state campaign themes over and over). In a sense, the normal vote is not really "in play"; campaigns are decided by the deviations from the normal vote in any given election.

Klapper (1960) argued that mass media are most likely to reinforce existing attitudes and less likely to convert people from one viewpoint (or candidate) to another: "Persuasive mass communication functions far more frequently as an agent of reinforcement than as an agent of change" (p. 15; echoing Lazarsfeld, Berelson, & Gaudet, 1948). Klapper attributed these limited effects in large part to selective exposure (people tend to expose themselves to messages which agree with their attitudes, not to messages that disagree with their attitudes), selection perception (people tend to interpret stimuli, including messages, based on existing attitudes), and selective retention (information that agrees with one's attitudes is likely to be remembered longer than discrepant information). Voters with less interest in the campaign typically have less knowledge about the candidates. Thus, the voters who are most susceptible to persuasion (those with less knowledge) are less likely to pay attention to the campaign. Campbell (2000) recognized the "minimal effects conundrum": "Those who are most attentive to campaign information are the least open to persuasion by it and those who are most open to persuasion by campaign information are the least likely to be attentive to it" (p. 12, emphasis omitted). Zaller (1997) elaborated this idea.

> The least aware rarely change their attitudes because, although likely to accept whatever they receive, they pay so little attention to politics that they rarely receive any new communication; the most aware receive new communication but are too critically inclined to accept its message, and so they maintain their attitudes unchanged; this leaves moderately aware citizens most susceptible to influence – they pay enough attention to politics to get net information but are not sufficiently astute to be able to react critically to it. (p. 299)

Of course, those who are moderately aware may be less committed to their own political attitudes (it may not be simply a lack of knowledge that makes them more persuadable). Thus, early work on mass media generally and political campaigns in particular tended to minimize the effects of messages on voters and concluded that changing attitudes was much less common than activating or reinforcing attitudes.

Finkel (1993) renewed the argument that the most likely effects of campaigns are reinforcement and activation of existing attitudes. His data indicated that the votes of 81% of citizens in 1980 "could be predicted correctly based solely on ethnicity of voters and the June values of party identification and presidential approval, i.e., without taking into account any attitude changes during the campaign whatsoever" (p. 11). He acknowledged that "the *potential* does exist for campaigns to move individuals away from their vote dispositions" (p. 18, emphasis original), and he reported that conversion (changing vote preference) did occur in some voters. However, these effects occurred for both candidates with little net change in the campaign he studied (e.g., some voters who started out favoring Reagan shifted to Carter by the end of the campaign and others moved in the opposite direction). Any model that can explain as much as 81% of voters' behavior should command our attention. On the other hand, we need to keep in mind that no recent presidential election has been decided by anywhere close to 19% of the vote (19% of the vote is unexplained by Bartels' model). This approach may explain how *most citizens vote*, but it cannot explain how *elections are decided*.

Campbell (2000) developed the theory of the Predictable Campaign. He begins by observing that several factors tend to reduce the potential impact of election campaigns and the messages that constitute them. First, many voters are relatively stable partisans (who are likely to vote for their own party's nominee). Second, many voters (presumably including many of the partisans just mentioned) decide how to vote relatively early in the campaign (which of course that information from the remainder of the campaign cannot influence these voters). A third factor is the state of the economy, which is known by voters before the campaign. Finally, another factor which exists prior to the campaign is incumbency. Often the president seeks a second term in office or the vice president tries to ascend to the presidency. Less common (but occurring in 1952, 2008, and 2016) is an "open" presidency, with neither a sitting president nor vice president running for office. Chapter Four discusses the potential advantages of incumbency, which are especially large in House and Senate elections.

Campbell also advances the argument that presidential election races are highly competitive: "American presidential politics are very competitive. Usually the two major party candidates are relatively well known. Both are relatively well financed. Both receive a good deal of media coverage. Both are taken as serious options by the voters" (p. 22). The result of highly competitive campaigns for the White House is a "leveling effect": "Campaigns should generally have the effect of narrowing the difference between candidates" (p. 23). This analysis identifies key variables in presidential elections which tend to limit the importance of the campaign – as well as to make it likely that the gap between the Republican and Democratic candidates is likely to narrow, rather than widen, during the course of the campaign.

Sides and Vavrek (2013) offered a useful metaphor for understanding the apparently limited effects of election campaigns. They compared presidential campaigns to "a game of tug-of-way. Both sides are pulling very hard. If for some reason, one side let go – meaning they stop campaigning – the other side would soon benefit" (p. 9). Individual messages may not appear to have huge effects, but candidates are unwilling to risk losing ground to opponents by failing to campaign actively. The competitive nature of presidential campaigns tends to obscure the very real effects of election campaigns.

Campbell (2001), looking for shifts in support that occurred during campaigns (post-convention polls to election day) argues that two campaigns, 1948 and 1960, were decisive, meaning that the candidate leading after the conventions lost the election after the general election campaign. He also indicated that three other campaigns (1976, 1980, and 2000) may have been decisive. He also concluded that there were significant shifts in support during nine other elections (1952, 1956, 1964, 1968, 1972, 1984, 1988, 1992, 1996), "but not enough or in the direction to have changed what appeared to be the electorate's pre-campaign preference" (p. 446). So, Campbell provides evidence that voting preferences do shift during the campaign, and that these shifts may be large enough in some years to change the outcome of the election.

Another important approach to understanding voting adopts an *economic* metaphor to voting. Downs' (1957) *Economic Theory of Democracy* argues that "each citizen casts his vote for the party he [or she] believes will provide him with more benefits" (p. 36). Downs believed that it was easier to evaluate the performance of the party in power (in the recent past) than to speculate about how that party would do if kept in office. Importantly, many voters may not believe that their individual future outcomes will be significantly improved if they devote much time and effort to become highly informed about their vote choice; they may rely on information short-cuts (see Chapter Eight) to make informed guesses about how to vote. The term *retrospective* voting has been coined to mean the process of deciding how to vote by looking back to the past at the incumbent's record. If a voter believes that the country is doing well – a strong economy, no serious foreign policy problems – that voter may decide that the incumbent candidate or party is doing OK and should be kept in office. On the other hand, if a voter thinks things are not going well (e.g., increased unemployment or inflation or significant military action), he or she may blame the incumbent party and vote for a change in the party occupying the White House. The assumption is that the incumbent's record in office is a good indication of how he (all U.S. presidents so far have been male) will do if given another term in office. Campbell et al. (1960) add that the electorate is "more likely to punish an incumbent party for its mistakes than to reward it for its successes" (p. 556). Note that some years do not offer a true incumbent: Vice Presidents Nixon (1960), Humphrey (1968), Bush (1988) and Gore (2000) ran as a part of the incumbent administration, but none were sitting presidents when they ran in these campaigns. President Gerald Ford, who ran in 1976, was never elected to the Oval Office; he was appointed Vice President after Spiro Agnew resigned; then Ford became President when Richard Nixon resigned over Watergate and related issues. In 2008 neither Barack Obama nor John McCain had served in the White House before the campaign; this was true in 2016 as well as neither Hillary Clinton nor Donald Trump had served as president or vice president.

The other approach to voting is called *prospective* voting, which means deciding how to vote based on speculations (guesses) about how candidates would perform as president if elected. Notice that both of these approaches to voting rely on information obtained largely from the mass media: Voters who engage in retrospective voting need to know whether things are going well or poorly; voters who rely on prospective voting need to know about the candidates' campaign promises (policy proposals) and their likely effectiveness if implemented (Benoit, 2006).

Other Influences on Vote Choice

If, as the limited effects model holds, mass communication has relatively little effect on voters, this raises the question of which other factors *do* influence voters and election outcomes. Three other explanations are commonly proposed for presidential election outcomes. First, political party membership is often cited as an explanation for voting behavior. Republicans tend to vote for the Republican candidate just as Democrats are likely to vote for the nominee of their political party, although "vote defections" when a member of one party votes for a candidate of the other party do occur. Second, consistent with retrospective voting, current events, and particularly economic conditions, are frequently touted as responsible for election outcomes (e.g., Key, 1966; Fiorina, 1981). When things are going well, we may not want to "change horses in the middle of the stream"; however, if the situation is bad, we may wish to "throw the rascals [who are responsible for bad times] out" of office. This explanation for election outcomes clearly assumes that many voters engage in retrospective voting. I will consider both of these factors (political party and current events) and argue that there is still reason to believe that campaign messages are an important influence on voters.

Political Party Membership

Political scientists often study the effects of political party affiliation on voting behavior (see, e.g., Campbell et al., 1960). Kirkpatrick, Lyons, and Fitzgerald (1975) explained that

> The emphasis on partisan identification has long been paramount in electoral research – it is viewed as a long-term stabilizing force, as the most important single variable in explaining the vote (Campbell et al., 1960; Campbell & Stokes, 1959; Converse et al., 1969; Converse, 1972) and as the central force around which individuals arrange their political beliefs. (Converse, 1964, p. 252)

It would be a mistake to ignore the role of political party identification in elections. However, one limitation on the effects of political party affiliation is that party affiliation cannot explain the outcome of the primary phase of the campaign. In 2020, for example, being a Democrat was no help to voters who needed to choose between Vice President Joe Biden, Senator Bernie Sanders, Mayor Mike Bloomberg, Mayor Pete Buttigieg, Senator Elizabeth Warren, Senator Amy Klobuchar, or one of the other Democrats contesting the nomination. In 2016, in the Republican presidential primary, party membership was not an effective way to help Republicans choose among the Republican candidates, such as Donald Trump, Jeb Bush, Ben Carson, Chris Christie, John Kasich, Ted Cruz, or Marco Rubio. Primary campaigns have not attracted the same amount of scholarly attention as general election campaigns but we ignore the primary at our peril.

Given the fact that some general campaigns feature particularly vulnerable presidents (e.g., Gerald Ford in 1976, Jimmy Carter in 1980, or George Bush in 1992), it is quite possible that in those years the primary campaign in the challenging party ultimately determined the outcome of the general election, by deciding who wins the opportunity to face (and presumably defeat) the weak opponent. That is, in 1976 Carter might not have been the only Democrat who could have defeated President Ford. Similarly, other Republicans besides Ronald Reagan might have been able to turn President Carter out of office four years later. In 1992 Bill Clinton may not have been the only Democrat capable of beating President Bush. But because these three candidates won their party's nomination in contested primaries, they were the only ones who had the right to face a vulnerable opponent in the general election. Political party affiliation cannot explain primary campaign outcomes, and this phase of the election campaign can be extremely important.

Some scholars have also argued that campaign messages influence voter preferences in primary campaigns. Martel (1983) argued that primary debates in 1976 and 1980 made a difference:

> It is doubtful that Jimmy Carter could have risen from a 2 percent recognition factor to win the Democratic nomination without his performance in the 1976 candidates forums. Similarly, John Anderson's campaign might never have gotten off the ground in 1980 had he not distinguished himself in the Iowa Republican forum. (p. 52)

Similarly, Denton (1998) explained that in 1996 that Forbes made effective use of television spots in the primary:

> the Forbes campaign did not attempt to build grassroots organizations in primary states. Instead, the campaign relied upon television ads to generate support. ... [H]e bombarded the airwaves with harsh, negative attacks on Dole. ... The media strategy worked. By the beginning of 1996, Forbes had tied all candidates but Dole in the polls. (p. 31)

There is no question that Trump's social media messages, as well as news coverage of his frequently controversial statements, contributed to his success in 2016. Thus, campaign messages have the potential to influence voters during the primary phase of the campaign, a potentially important campaign phase that is not influenced by political party affiliation.

Even when looking at the general election campaign, a moment's reflection demonstrates that political party membership can not determine election outcomes. Consider the simple fact that we have witnessed many swings in the party occupying the White House over the last five decades:

Republican in 1952 and 1956
Democratic in 1960 and 1964
Republican in 1968 and 1972
Democratic in 1976

Republican in 1980–1988
Democratic in 1992 and 1996
Republican in 2000 and 2004
Democratic in 2008 and 2012
Republican in 2016
Democratic in 2020

Each of these shifts in the party controlling the White House were not preceded by huge swings in political party affiliation among voters. But if political party affiliation determined election outcomes, those swings in control of the Oval Office should have been occurred after large shifts in political party affiliation. In fact, considering the fact that Republicans have never outnumbered Democrats in the last half century, how could a Republican party candidate ever have won the presidency if political party determined election outcomes? Political party affiliation does influence many *voters*, but the repeated shifts in the party in the White House (the outcome of the election campaign), along with the distribution of voters between the two major political parties, make it clear that partisanship does not determine election *outcomes*.

One limitation on the influence of political party affiliation is that party membership has dwindled over time (see, e.g., Figure 1.1 and Wattenberg, 1991, 1998). In recent years, many voters do not affiliate with either the Republican or the Democratic Parties. For example, in November of 2016 31% of voters were Democrats and 27% of the electorate were Republican. Independents comprised 36% of the electorate (Gallup, 2017). The National Election Study (2003b) data reveals that the percent of voters who consider themselves Republicans has remained relatively stable over time, but Democratic party affiliation has decreased significantly over time as the number of Independents increased. Kirkpatrick, Lyons, and Fitzgerald (1975) offer evidence that from 1952 to 1972 the effect of party image on the vote has declined as the importance of candidate image increased. Although political party affiliation is an important factor, there are important limitations on this factor. Wattenberg (1991) argued that as presidential candidates became more independent from political parties, this has shifted the "focus of the campaign from long-term to short-term issues" and that "How the candidates have performed in the recent past [retrospective voting] and what they promise for the not-so-distant future [prospective voting] have taken on increased importance" (p. 21).

Bartels (2000) has argued that the decline in partisanship has been overstated by some scholars. Some voters who are Independents lean toward the Republican or Democratic parties and usually vote in accordance with their leanings. Political parties are important because of their ability to raise funds, to help candidates to organize their campaigns, and to coordinate turn-out-the-vote campaigns has grown over time. Political parties also run all of the primaries and caucuses. Evidence indicates that the electorate has become more polarized in recent years. The current ideological divide is clearly shown in President Donald Trump's approval ratings. In July of 2020, Trump's approval among Republicans edged up from 85% to 91%; the president's approval among Democrats dipped from 5% to 2% (Jones, 2020). An approval rating gap of 89% illustrates the extreme polarization in our country.

It is important to realize that the importance of political party membership and voting has increased recently. Research found that "A growing proportion of Americans dislike the opposing party more than they like their own party" (Abramowitz & Webster, 2016, p. 21). As this negative partisanship increased, between 1968 and 1988 split-ticket voting, in which one votes for at least one candidate from each political party, increased (as "straight-ticket" voting declined; Sabato, Kondik, & Skelley, 2016). See Figure 1.1 for these data. We also know that "During the 1970s and 1980s … about a quarter of voters split their tickets–voting

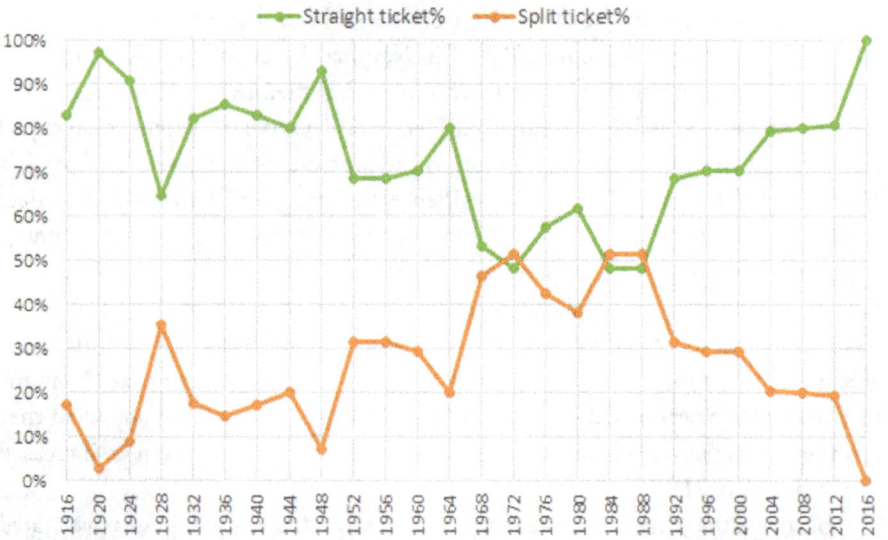

Figure 1.1. *Straight-ticket versus split ticket voting*
Source: Sabato, Kondik, & Skelley (2016)
http://centerforpolitics.org/crystalball/articles/16-for-16/

for presidential and congressional candidates for different parties. In recent elections, only about one voter in ten has cast a split-ticket ballot" (Abramowitz & Webster, 2018, p. 120). The focus on election campaigning has shifted recently from focusing mainly on swing voters to primarily encouraging supporters to go to the polls and vote.

Voters can engage in straight-ticket voting (voting for all candidates from the same political party) or split ticket voting (voting for at least one candidate from the two major parties). Looking just at candidates for President and Senate, in 1920 98% of votes were straight-ticket (Phillips, 2016). In 1972, 1984, and 1988 straight ticket dropped to a low of 49%. However, in 2016, 100% of states elected a Senator and a President of the same party. Split ticket voting is a mirror image straight ticket voting (low in 1920; high in 1972, 1984, and 1988; and a low of 0 in 2016). Stroud (2011) offers convincing evidence that, with so many media choices available today, people gravitate toward media that reflect their own attitudes and this has created more polarization in the electorate. Still, political party affiliation does not determine election outcome.

As American increasingly was divided ideologically, it also became geographically divided. For example, between 1998 and 2008, 100 million Americans moved (Bishop & Cushing, 2008). Sometimes people moved to another residence in the same neighborhood or city. However, some people moved from one state to another. As a result, most states are "becoming even more Democratic or Republican. As Americans have moved over the past three decades, they have clustered in communities of sameness, among people with similar ways of life, beliefs, and, in the end, politics" (Bishop & Cushing, 2008, p. 5). This geographical separation has a variety of implications. One obvious result is that, in general, Republicans are more likely to live in smaller, rural states; Democrats are prone to live in larger metropolitan areas. Of course, exceptions exist, but this is the trend. Examining data divided by counties, research has shown that "much of nonmetropolitan USA has becoming increasingly dominated by Republican party candidates, whereas the large metropolitan central cities remain dominated by the Democrats" (Johnston, Manley, Jones, & Rohla, 2020). Today America is divided by ideology and geography (of course, other divides exist as well, such as racial or income divides).

Holbert, Benoit, and McKinney (2002) found that prior to watching the first presidential debate of 2000, ideology and party ID were the two most important variables discriminating Bush supporters from Gore supporters. However, *after* watching the debate (which in fact provided viewers with information about the candidates' policy positions), the most important factors discriminating between supporting one candidate or the other were Bush's and Gore's positions on the issues; in fact, ideology and party ID were no longer significant discriminators between the candidates' supporters after watching the debate. This reinforces the idea that party affiliation (or ideology) can serve as a shortcut, a basis for citizens to develop an initial vote preference. However, when people obtain information from the campaign, that new information can become the basis for vote choices. This does not necessarily mean that voters have a different vote choice (although some may), but that they have a different basis for that choice, and that new basis is created information obtained from campaign messages.

NES data (2003c) show that the percentage of voters who report that they decide their vote for president during the nominating conventions – when the two political parties decide or announce their nominees – has dropped significantly over time while the number of voters who decide in the final two weeks of the campaign has increased significantly over time. Rasmussen (2018) reported that 26% of voters made up their minds about how to vote in the last week and 10% decided on election day. Thus, in recent years campaigns have a greater potential to influence voters because more citizens wait until at or near the end of the campaign to make their vote choice rather than rely only on party ID.

These limitations on the ability of political party affiliation to determine election outcomes are particularly important because many campaigns have been decided by relatively slim margins:

> In 1960, John Kennedy beat Richard Nixon by about 100,000 popular votes. This is a fraction of a percentage (0.2%) of the total vote. In 1968, Nixon defeated Hubert Humphrey by 500,000 votes (0.7%). In 1976, Jimmy Carter won by less than 2% of the popular vote. Polls in late September of 1976 showed an unusually large number of undecided voters (Reinhold, 1976). In 1980, Ronald Reagan beat Carter by less than 10% of the popular vote, yet two weeks before the election, 25% of the voters were still undecided. (Zakahi & Hacker, 1995, p. 100)

Of course, the 2000 and 2016 presidential races underscore this point dramatically. In 2000 Vice President Gore won the popular vote by half a million votes (Duchneskie & Seplow, 2000), but the outcome of the election turned on Florida's 23 electoral votes. At one point Bush and Gore were separated by about 300 votes in Florida; when Florida Secretary of State Kathleen Harris certified Florida's vote on November 26, fewer than 600 votes separated the two candidates. In 2016, Trump won the electoral college (306 to 232) while Clinton received 2.8 million more votes (*New York Times*, 2017).

As the electorate became increasingly polarized (indicated by the resurgence of straight-ticket voting), campaign strategies have shifted from the traditional emphasis on persuading independent and undecided voters (swing voters) to a dual emphasis, working on both persuading independent voters and on mobilizing their base to vote on Election Day. Dowd explained the increased emphasis on base motivation: "nobody had ever approached an election that I've looked at over the last 50 years, where base motivation was important as swing" (2005). Activation and reinforcement (Finkel, 1993) are becoming increasingly important to modern campaigns.

Current Events

Conventional wisdom, exemplified in the concept of retrospective voting, holds that the state of the economy (or a looming foreign policy crisis) can be an important factor in determining election outcomes. For example, it was widely perceived that the poor economy was an important factor in the losses of Gerald Ford in 1976, Jimmy Carter in 1980, and George Bush in 1992. Kramer (1977) revitalized interest in the effects of the economy on voting (for reviews, see Kiewet & Rivers, 1984; Monroe, 1979). Kramer observed that "to some extent, at least, an individual's vote in a national election represents a choice or judgment between alternative governing 'teams'" (p. 133). However, many voters do not avidly seek out information about platforms and policy proposals, recent legislation, and policy outcomes. Instead, voters' impressions of "the past performance of the incumbent party in particular gives some indication of what it would do if returned to office, and of the effectiveness of its policies and personnel" (p. 134). Using data from 1896 to 1964, Kramer found a positive relationship between incumbent party vote share and income (the more a person earns, the more likely he or she is to voter for the incumbent). There was a negative relationship between incumbent party voter and inflation (the higher the rate of inflation, the fewer votes received by the incumbent party). Kramer did not, however, find the effects he expected for unemployment. Similarly Fair (1978) found that presidential vote was responsive to changes in real Gross National Product (GNP) per capita and the unemployment rate (see also Fair, 1982, 1988, 1996a, 1996b, 2002). Erikson (1989) argued that "the state of the economy and the electorate's evaluations of the candidates together but independently drive presidential election outcomes" (p. 570; cf. Lewis-Beck & Rice, 1984). When current events appear unfavorable to voters, the incumbent candidate usually receives fewer votes. Notice that these findings tend to support the idea that many voters rely use retrospective voting, looking at record during the incumbent party's most recent term in office.

Other current events include wars and terrorism. President George W. Bush's approval ratings soared among members of both political party after the tragic events of 9/11. In September of 2001, President Bush received "the highest presidential job approval rating ever measured by Gallup since it began asking the public for its evaluation of presidents over six decades ago" (Moore, 2001). Current events can enhance as well as detract from the perceptions of a politician.

Besides attempting to identify which variables (income, inflation, unemployment, GNP) research also investigated the question of how far back voters "look" when making a retrospective evaluation of incumbent party performance. Fair (1988) argued that "voters look about between six and nine months regarding the real growth rate and about two years regarding the inflation rate" (p. 177). It is possible some voters are more likely to rely on retrospective voting than others. Weatherford (1978) claimed that "working class citizens are more severely affected by economic cycles" and provided evidence that they "provide the bulk of the electoral response to economic recession" (p. 917). Although there is some variance across this research, generally these studies provide evidence that the state of the economy does relate to presidential vote.

Granting that the state of the economy does influence the way some citizens vote, the key question is how voters become aware of current affairs. Remember that vote choice is influenced by voters' *perceptions* of the economy, which may or may not be accurate. Fair (1978), for example, makes a point of using *updated* or *revised* data on the state of the economy. In other words, his research uses *information that was not available to voters during the election*. He explained that "I have always used the latest revised data in this context, based on the view that voters look at the economic conditions around them – how their friends and neighbors and employers are doing – and not at the numbers themselves" (1996a, p. 94). Some voters probably learn about their economy from "how their friends and neighbors and employers are doing," but this is simply not the only way voters become informed about the state of the economy. Although Markus (1988) found "provided support for the 'pocketbook' model of voting," he made it clear that his conclusion "is *not* that campaigns are 'irrelevant'" (p. 151, emphasis original). He observed that "the campaign is undoubtedly an important vehicle for heightening voter awareness of prevailing economic conditions and the electoral relevance thereof" (p. 152). There is no question that such topics as the current state of the economy (or military involvement in other countries) are addressed in political campaign discourse.

For example, this quotation from the first presidential debate in 2016 shows Donald Trump discussing the state of affairs in the United States:

> Our jobs are fleeing the country. They're going to Mexico. They're going to many other countries …. We have gangs roaming the street. And in many cases, they're illegally here, illegal immigrants. And they have guns. And they shoot people … .The Obama administration, from the time they've come in, is over 230 years' worth of debt, and he's topped it. He's doubled it in a course of almost eight years … .In a place like

Chicago, where thousands of people have been killed, thousands over the last number of years, in fact, almost 4,000 have been killed since Barack Obama became president, over – almost 4,000 people in Chicago have been killed.

Candidate Trump hammered the point of problems in America today. His Democratic opponent, Hillary Clinton, also discussed the current state of affairs in the first general election debate but stressed positive aspects of it:

When I was secretary of state, we actually increased American exports globally 30 percent. We increased them to China 50 percent .... .my successor [as Secretary of State], John Kerry, and President Obama got a deal that put a lid on Iran's nuclear program without firing a single shot.

These excerpts clearly illustrate the point that it is possible for voters to learn about current and recent events from candidate campaign discourse (Transcript of First Trump-Clinton Debate, 2016).

Furthermore research has shown that the content of candidate messages is significantly influenced by the state of the economy. The frequency with which presidential candidates discuss inflation and unemployment in their television ads is directly related to the actual rates of inflation and of unemployment: When inflation and unemployment are high, candidates discuss those topics frequently; when they are low, candidates talk about these topics less often (Benoit, 2003c). Clearly, candidate messages have the potential to inform voters about failures or successes in governing.

Evidence suggests that campaign messages may influence political attitudes more than the news (see Chapter Seven for a discussion of news and campaigns). Agenda-setting research (discussed in more detail in Chapter Seven) has confirmed that news emphasis on issues influences public perceptions about which issues are most important (see, e.g., McCombs, 2004; McCombs & Protess, 1991; McCombs & Shaw, 1972; Shaw & McCombs, 1977). Iyengar and Kinder (1987) investigated the sources of public perceptions of the importance of issues. They compared the influence of news stories, actual economic data, and presidential speeches (albeit not campaign speeches). They found that on the topics of energy and inflation (but not unemployment) presidential speeches had *considerably more impact* than televised news stories on public perceptions of the importance of an issue. Perhaps more importantly, reinforcing the vital role of perceptions, the actual figures for unemployment and inflation had *no appreciable effect* on public opinion of the relative importance of these issues. This study clearly demonstrates that citizens' perceptions and attitudes can be influenced *more by what the president says* about current affairs than by what the news media says about those topics – and that presidential messages can influence public opinion *more than the actual economic figures* themselves.

Thus, research shows that the state of the economy (and other current affairs) influences presidential voting behavior. However, candidates discuss economic problems in their campaign messages as does the news media in their stories. Studies indicate that political messages can have a greater effect on voters' perceptions than the actual state of the economy. The fact that some voters engage in retrospective voting does not make campaign messages irrelevant. Voters can learn about the state of the economy from presidential campaign messages.

This section considered other potential influences on election outcomes besides campaign messages. Each factor has limitations on its ability to determine the outcome of elections, and quite often those limitations are related to political campaign messages. Although these factors do play a role in election outcomes, none eliminate the importance of political campaign messages in election outcomes. There can be no doubt that political campaign messages have the potential to influence voters.

Effects of Campaign Messages on Voters

A considerable amount of evidence indicates that campaign messages can, and do, have effects on voters. Most of this research focuses on what are, arguably, the two most important forms of campaign discourse: television spots and debates. These two message forms are important for two quite different reasons. No one but a political junkie would deliberately pay attention to political spots. However, ads are broadcast repeatedly throughout the campaign. Furthermore, literally millions of dollars are lavished not only on purchasing air-time but on honing the succinct messages conveyed in 30 seconds and on producing these messages. As noted above, this money translates into literally hundreds of thousands of televised political advertisements (Goldstein & Freedman, 2002b). The hope is that broadcasting multiple ads during the campaign will reach many voters sooner or later. Candidates also rely on the fact that some voters will see TV spots over and over. Message repetition can enhance persuasion (Benoit & Benoit, 2009). As noted before, after Trump's electoral success in 2016, scholars are sure to focus heavily on social media.

Several studies investigated effects of television spots in elections. McClure and Patterson (1974) reported that in the 1972 presidential campaign, "Exposure to political advertising was consistently related to voter belief change" (p. 16; see also Atkin & Heald, 1976). Of course, candidate messages are inevitably biased and can be vague. Nevertheless, Popkin (1994) explained that "Campaign communications … increased the accuracy of voter perception; mis-perceptions were far more likely on issues that were peripheral to the campaign." In fact, he concluded that "exposure to communication was the strongest single influence on accuracy of perceptions" (p. 39). Brians and Wattenberg's (1996) analysis of 1992 NES data reveals that issue learning is more likely to arise from seeing television spots than from watching television news or reading newspapers: "Recalling political ads is more significantly associated with knowledge of candidates' issue positions than is reading the newspaper or watching political news on television" (p. 185; see also Holbert, Benoit, Hansen, & Wen, 2002). Chapter Three will identify other research which shows that political television spots can inform voters and influence their attitudes.

Turning to debates, Hellweg, Pfau, and Brydon (1992) reviewed the research on debates and concluded that "most studies of debate viewing contributes to considerable learning about the candidates and their positions" (pp. 106–107). Debates also attract the attention of literally millions of voters who often watch more than one encounter. Balz (2012) argued that the Republican primary debates of 2012 made a difference: The debates "certainly mattered during the Republican nomination contest in the winter. Those 20 debates shaped the campaign and the fortunes of many of the candidates. Think Rick Perry," who dropped out of the 2012 Republican primary after badly flubbing an answer. Again, Chapter Three will discuss research showing that debates inform viewers and can change their attitudes toward the candidates.

A very useful argument about campaign effects was developed by Zaller (1999; see also Finkel, 1993; McGuire, 1986). He noted that campaigns are (for most offices) contests between two opposing candidates: Both candidates use campaign messages to persuade voters.

> If, as they do, the mass media routinely carry competing messages, members of the public who are heavily exposed to one message tend to be heavily exposed to its opposites as well. Each message … has its effects, but the effects tend to be mutually canceling in ways that produce the illusion of modest impact. (p. 20)

Recall that Finkel (1993) found little *net* change: some voters who preferred Reagan switched to Carter in 1980 and some Carter supporters switched to Reagan. The campaigns clearly had effects even if those effects canceled each other out. Similarly, in 2000 voters were exposed to a barrage of messages from and about both Al Gore and George W. Bush. Had we received messages from or about only one candidate, rather than both, the effects of campaign messages would have been far more obvious. However, messages from one candidate can make gains which were offset by gains made by the other candidate. This idea is related to Sides and Vavrek's metaphor of campaigns as a tug-of-war (2013), discussed earlier.

Similarly, Shaw (1999b) explains that whereas "campaigning *can* affect voters, influential campaign events may not be detected because (1) they are lumped in with events that do not matter and (2) the effects of different events may balance out" (p. 417; emphasis original). He analyzed the effects of key campaign events (party nominating conventions, debates, speeches, gaffes, and scandals) on voters from 1952 to 1992: "Taken as a whole, presidential campaigning made an impact" (p. 407). Valence (value-laden) statements and vice presidential debates had small effects. Presidential debates and blunders had "substantial" effects on voters. The national party nominating conventions "were the most influential campaign events for both Republican and Democratic candidates." He reported that convention "effects were almost always positive and large, averaging +7.4 points" and that there was "little decay" over time (p. 413). Shaw (1999a) also analyzed data from TV spots and candidate appearances in 1988, 1992, and 1996, concluding that "a candidate's activities in a state were positively correlated with his vote" (p. 357). Again, evidence indicates that campaign events (messages) can influence voters and support for candidates.

Bartels (1993) offered an additional argument for campaign effects. "Positive effects in one period [of time] canceled out negative effects in another period" (p. 275). Shaw argues that evidence suggesting minimal effects from the mass media

> to be due in significant part to inattention to the implications of measurement error, combined with the tendency of previous research designs to focus upon significant short-term opinion change in circumstances where such change is likely to be quite modest. (p. 276).

Therefore, a variety of evidence contradicts the "limited effects" model and indicates that messages conveyed by the mass media are capable of having significant effects on voters.

Fair (2002), whose data show that the state of the economy influences presidential voting decisions, assumes that both candidates campaign to their best ability and, in effect, the opposing campaigns cancel one another out. Although it is reasonable to assume candidates will campaign to the best of their abilities; however, Fair also appears to assume that candidates (and their advisors) always have the same ability to campaign. This assumption makes his task easier, because it means that an economist need not attempt to analyze the quality of presidential campaigns, but it seems unreasonable.

Electoral College rules stipulate that the presidential candidate who wins the most votes in a state will receive *all* of that state's electoral voters (the exceptions are Maine and Nebraska; Glennon, 1993). This means that the candidate who wins a minority of voters (say 40% or even 49.99% in a two candidate race) in a state will gain *no* electoral votes. In other words, losing a state by a landslide is no worse than losing it by a single vote. On the other hand, there is no advantage to winning a state by a 90% margin instead of, say, 60% or even 50.01%. This winner takes all standard encourages candidates to focus their campaigns on so-called "battleground" states, or states in which the outcome is uncertain. A campaign's resources like time and money are wasted *both* by campaigning in states that candidate is sure to win *and* in those he or she is sure to lose. Benoit, Hansen, and Holbert (2004) compared levels of issue knowledge for voters who lived in battleground and non-battleground states in the 2000 presidential campaign. They found that voters who lived in battleground states, where Bush and Gore ran ads, had significantly more issue knowledge than citizens from other states (see also Patterson, 2003). These results suggest that learning ensued from campaigning. Furthermore, Patterson (2003) reported that active campaigning may have influenced turnout in 2000:

> Although the nationwide turnout in 2000 was 2 percentage points higher than in 1996, there was a decline in nine non-competitive [non-battleground] states. On the other hand, turnout rose by 3.4 percent in the closely contested states. (p 142)

Campaigns can have effects on voters even if those effects are not always easy to detect or may cancel each other out.

The "winner take all" rule operating in the Electoral College means that the winner of the Oval Office might not be the winner of the popular vote. This situation has occurred twice in recent memory: Bush vs. Gore in 2000, and Clinton vs. Trump in 2016. No other office in the U.S. has a system like the American presidential Electoral College. A few other countries use a form of electoral college: including "Burundi, Estonia, Kazakhstan, Madagascar, Myanmar, Pakistan, Trinidad and Tobago and Vanuatu" (Wikipedia, 2017), but no major country uses this approach to select their country's leader.

Campaign Messages Influence Voters

Chapter Eight will focus on voters and how they process information, but it is important to understand how campaign messages can affect voters. As noted earlier, Campbell, Gurin, and Miller (1954) argued that three factors influence voters: ideology, issues, and character. With this in mind, there are several ways campaign messages could influence a citizen's vote choice. First, political campaign messages can address policy (issues). Candidates can boast of their own past successes or ridicule their opponent's failures, enabling retrospective assessments of policy. In the first 2016 Republican debate, Jeb Bush declared that

> There's 6 million people living in poverty today, more than when Barack Obama got elected. 6.5 million people are working part-time, most of whom want to work full-time. We've created rules and taxes on top of every aspiration of people, and the net result is we're not growing fast, income is not growing. A four percent growth strategy means you fix a convoluted tax code. (2015)

Similarly, Scott Walker boasted of his achievements as the Governor of Wisconsin: "Before I came in, the unemployment rate was over eight percent. It's now down to 4.6 percent. We've more than made up for the jobs that were lost during the recession. And the rate in which people are working is almost five points higher than it is nationally" (2015). This approach obviously pertains to retrospective voting, or voting based on the record of the incumbent party in office.

Second, campaign messages can fuel prospective voting on the issues. Turning again to the initial presidential debate of the 2016 general election, both candidates discussed what they would do if elected. Clinton said "They've [experts] looked at my plans and they've said, OK, if we can do this, and I intend to get it done, we will have 10 million more new jobs, because we will be making investments where we can grow the economy .... We can deploy a half a billion more solar panels. We can have enough clean energy to power every home. We can build a new modern electric grid." in turn, her Republican opponent touted his plans: "Under my plan, I'll be reducing taxes tremendously, from 35 percent to 15 percent for companies, small and big businesses ... .I'm going to cut regulations ... ." In the same debate, these two candidates criticized their opponent's proposals. Trump declared that "You are going to approve one of the biggest tax increases in history. You are going to drive business out .... You have regulations on top of regulations, and new companies cannot form and old companies are going out of business. And you want to increase the regulations and make them even worse." The Democratic nominee argued against her opponent's proposals: "What you are proposing ... it is trumped-up trickle-down. Trickle-down did not work. It got us into the mess we were in, in 2008 and 2009. Slashing taxes on the wealthy hasn't worked." So, both candidates provided arguments to support prospective voting in their campaign messages (Transcript of First Trump-Clinton Debate, 2016).

Note that policy utterances are capable of influencing voters' perceptions of policy in several ways. First, they can impart knowledge, *creating* or *changing* impressions of the candidates' policy choices (the nature of past policy and future proposals). In 1996 Senator Bob Dole ran against President Bill Clinton.

Before Dole announced his 15% across-the-board tax cut plan in 1996, voters lacked knowledge of his tax policy. After he proposed these tax cuts, voters could compare this policy proposal with Clinton's targeted tax cuts. These messages answer the voters' question, what has a candidate done (or what would a candidate do) on education (or taxation, or national defense, or Social Security). Second, policy messages can change attitudes about which policy is preferable: For example, would it be better to enact across-the-board or targeted tax cuts?

This means that when voters learns a candidate's policy position, that information always helps *voters* (assuming, of course, that more information is likely to lead to better vote decisions), but the new information may not necessarily help the *candidate* who provided that information. Learning a candidate's position on an issue could increase that candidate's perceived preferability for voters who like that particular policy stance, but it could also reduce preferability for other voters who dislike that policy proposal. For example, learning that Mr. Trump planned to build a wall between the U.S. and Mexico could improve his prospects among voters who were worried about immigration. However, this information could reduce his preferability among those who were opposed to building a wall.

The fact that some information can polarize voters can encourage candidates to adopt strategically ambiguous policy stands. Few voters oppose reducing the federal deficit (a vague yet desirable goal); however, some voters would object to increasing taxes and others might reject proposals to cut entitlements (two specific means of reducing the deficit). Alvarez (1998) sounds a cautionary note for candidates, reporting that voters in the elections from 1976 to 1992 reacted adversely to ambiguity in policy stance, "shunning the candidates that they are more uncertain of, and by embracing the candidates they are more certain of" (p. 143). Similarly, Shepsle (1972) concurs that ambiguous issue positions can create problems, particularly with risk-aversive voters. Strategic ambiguity, therefore, has both pros and cons.

Third, campaign messages can attempt to influence the relative importance of issues, an agenda-setting function (see Chapter Seven). For example, in the 2016 election, Trump worked diligently to make illegal immigration an important campaign issue. Campaign messages could also influence the salience of an issue (priming) or the perspective from which candidates and events are interpreted (framing). Clinton's 1996 Acceptance Address worked to frame his opponent Bob Dole as old, more oriented to the past than the future, and perhaps even out of touch, with Clinton's repeated use of the "bridge to the past" metaphor when referring to Dole (Benoit, 2001).

Presidential campaign messages could have some influence on political party affiliation, a fourth potential avenue of influence. Campaign messages could lead some voters to move from Republican or Democrat to Independent, to change from Independent to Republican or Democrat, or it could even lead some voters to switch political parties. Campaign messages might also strengthen existing partisan feelings. For example, It is possible that statements about the dangers of liberalism could have reinforced Republican and/or diminished Democratic partisanship among voters.

Finally, candidates could attempt to alter the relative importance of these three major factors (party, policy, character) through their campaign messages. For example, in 1996 several of Dole's ads attempted to portray Clinton as dishonest. One spot posed the rhetorical question, "Does the truth matter? Does it matter to you?" (Riady 2). It appears as if this ad is attempting to make character generally, and honesty in particular, a more important factor in viewers' voter choice. The point is that campaign messages are capable of influencing the three variables that influence citizens' vote choices, policy, character, and ideology/political party affiliation.

Conclusion

One cannot understand presidential campaigns without understanding the mass media in which these campaigns occur. Indeed, as population grows mass media are increasingly important even for lower levels of office. Election researchers in political science (e.g., Lazarsfeld, Berelson, & Gaudet, 1954) and mass communication scholars (e.g., Klapper, 1960) proposed the "limited effects" model, discussed earlier: Mass communication (including election campaigns) rarely change the attitudes of viewers; effects are more likely to be activation and reinforcement of existing attitudes. Scholars began to investigate more subtle effects, like agenda-setting, priming, and framing. Other scholars posited important effects for political party affiliation (e.g., Campbell, Converse, Miller, & Stokes, 1960) and the economy (e.g., Fair, 2002). However, I agree with Zaller (1999), who argues persuasively that "at least in the domain of political communication, the true magnitude of the persuasive effect of mass communication is closer to 'massive' than to 'small to negligible' and that the frequency of such effects is 'often'" (p. 18). These effects may not be obvious because opponents campaign against each other and the effects of each campaign may cancel each other out (the fact that there is no large *net* effect simply does not mean the campaigns had *no* effects).

Virtually all voters learn about presidential candidates from the media rather than personal contact with those seeking office. The number of media are increasing and access to new media is increasing. It is important to understand that voters use different combinations of media to learn about candidates (and I do not mean to imply that all voters actively seek out information; some information, such as that in television spots, can be difficult to avoid). These media have different qualities and contain different information, so which media a voter uses can make an important difference in how much information he or she has, and what information he or she obtains. These media have direct effects and they have more subtle influences (agenda setting, framing, priming).

Three important factors form the basis for vote choice: political party affiliation, policy, and candidate character (and the importance of political party affiliation has declined as fewer voters affiliate with parties; it also may diminish in importance as voters acquire information about the candidates and their policy positions). Few voters are political junkies; they obtain information as they go through life (e.g., as prices as the gas pump or the grocery store rise, they experience the effects of inflation) and through exposure to the media. Campaign messages generally and candidate messages in particular are an important influence on voters' knowledge and attitudes and, therefore, on their vote choices.

2020 Election Campaign

President Donald Trump sought a second term in office in 2020. President Trump filed with the Federal Election Commission on the day he was inaugurated as president. He announced his re-election campaign the next month in February 2017. A few Republicans announced challenges to his renomination (e.g., Bill Weld, Joe Walsh, Mark Sanford) but the Republican National Committee voted in February 19 to support President Trump, who secured enough delegates to clinch the nomination in March (2020 Republican Party Presidential Primaries, 2020). No Republican primary debates were held in 2020. The Democratic presidential primary in that year attracted a large number of candidates; presumably many thought President Trump might be vulnerable in the Fall. A total of 29 candidates sought the Democratic nomination in 2020; 23 of them participated in at least one presidential primary debate. The Democratic primary debates began on June 26–27, 2019 (the number of eligible candidates was so large that the first two debates were each split into two parts) and finished on March 15, 2019 (2020 Democratic Party Presidential Debates, 2020). Vice President Joe Biden clinched the Democratic nomination on June 5, 2020 (2020 Democratic Party Presidential Primary, 2020). Table 1.2 offers information on Democratic contenders in 2020.

The Covid-19 pandemic threw a huge monkey wrench into the 2020 elections. One question was whether to hold in-person nominating conventions. Both

Table 1.2. Top seven candidates in the 2020 Democratic primary.

Candidate	Announced	Debates	Popular Vote	Delegates
Joe Biden	4/25/29	11	17,596,164	2617
Bernie Sanders	2/19/19	11	9,364,791	1050
Elizabeth Sanders	2/9/19	10	2,780,632	63
Michael Bloomberg	11/7/19	2	2,474,725	51
Pete Buttigieg	4/14/19	10	912,081	21
Any Klobuchar	2/10/19	10	524,353	7
Tulsi Gabbard	1/11/19	4	261,241	2

2020 Democratic Party presidential primaries; 2020 Democratic Party presidential debates; 3979 total pledged delegates.

parties' conventions were held on-line in 2020, with some live video and some pre-recorded video. The Democratic National Convention met from August 17 to 20 and the Republican National Convention was held from August 24 to 27. But other important questions remained for the Fall campaign. Should candidates hit the campaign trail shaking hands and kissing babies (traditionally political candidates kiss babies to appeal to parents)? Should they give maskless speeches in the physical presence of crowds? Should they tell followers who attend campaign rallies to wear masks? Even if they continued to make some public appearances, Covid-19 would surely incline both Biden and Trump to devote more resources to non-person-to-person campaigning (spots, televised town halls, social media) than they would have without the pandemic.

Other questions arose. Should voters stand in line to cast their votes in person during the pandemic? Many urged the use of vote by mail to reduce the threat of Covid-19 spread, but some states were less welcoming to absentee ballots. Concerns emerged about whether Trump's Postmaster General Louis DeJoy had created obstacles to absentee voting. In fact, President Trump said he "opposes funding for the U.S. Postal Service and election security grants in an effort to stymie mail-in voting for the upcoming presidential election" (Montellaro, 2020). The President cited alleged fraud in absentee voting. Note that voting by mail delays election results because some states do not begin counting mail ballots until after election day; and some ballots inevitably arrive after election day.

Covid-19 also became a significant campaign issue. Trump acclaimed his excellent handling of this crisis; Democrats attacked him arguing that his handling of the pandemic was incompetent. On Friday, October 2, 2020, President Trump was taken by helicopter from the White House to Walter Reed hospital after he tested positive for coronavirus (Jackson & Fritze, 2020). Ultimately, 17 others in his inner circle also tested positive for Covid-19. Thursday October 22 and Friday October 23 – less than two weeks before election day – saw new record highs for Covid infections: 77,640 and 79,303 respectively (Wong, Sheeley, & Siemaszko, 2020). In late October, the White House announced that one of President Trump's accomplishments was ending the Covid-19 pandemic: "The White House included ending the coronavirus pandemic on a list of the Trump administration's science and technology accomplishments, despite nearly half a million Americans tested positive for Covid-19 in just the last week" (Kelly, 2020). This was the largest daily infection rates ever for this disease.

The first presidential debate of 2020 between Donald Trump and Joe Biden was held on September 29, 2020. A vice presidential debate featuring Mike Pence and Kamala Harris happened on October 7, 2020. However, the second presidential debate was scheduled for October 15 but cancelled after President Trump's bout with Covid-19 (ironically, Biden and Trump held separate "dueling" town hall events that night at the same time on different networks). The final presidential debate occurred on October 22, 2020 (2020 United States presidential debates, 2020). Because both presidential candidates repeatedly interrupted their opponent in the first debate – Trump more often than Biden (Blake, 2020) – the Commission on Presidential Debates muted each candidate's microphone while the opponent spoke for two minutes uninterrupted during their opening statements for each topic in the debate (Associated Press, 2020). In the history of political campaign debates, a mute button had never been needed.

Spending on political campaign advertising ran rampant in 2020. With a week to go in the campaign Biden had already spent over $582 million on television spots, more than any other candidate for the Oval Office (Wilson, 2020). Of course, millions of dollars were spent by President Trump, pro-Democratic groups, pro-Trump groups, and candidates and groups spending on races for other offices. Total political advertising expenditures were anticipated to reach almost $11 billion in 2020 (Wilson, 2020).

The 2020 election also saw the rise of Political Action Committees (PACs) which attacked candidates of their own political party. For example, both the Lincoln Project (https://lincolnproject.us/video/) and Republican Voters Against Trump (https://rvat.org/) created messages criticizing the Republican nominee, President Donald Trump. Although relatively rare, some politicians opposed the re-nomination of their own political party's president (e.g., Democratic Senator Ted Kennedy challenged Democratic President Jimmy Carter in the 1980 primary; Republican Pat Buchanan opposed Republican President George Bush in 1992). In 2016 some Republicans opposed Donald Trump and became known as "Never Trumpers." However, creation and use of PACs to oppose a political party's sitting president's re-election may well be completely unprecedented. These two anti-Trump PACs took different approaches: the Lincoln Project developed and disseminated slick ads often featuring audio and video from President Trump to attack him. Republicans Voters Against Trump posted video "selfies" of Republican voters who expressed their regret for voting for Trump in 2016 and argued against voting for him in 2020. These selfies were not "slick" and their comparatively amateur approach may have provided authenticity to these messages.

November 3, 2020 was election day. Republicans were more likely than Democrats to vote in person on election day; Democrats were more likely to cast absentee votes than Republicans. As mentioned above, some states do not start counting mail ballots until election day. This situation meant that America experienced a "red mirage" (also called a "blue shift") in 2020. Initial vote counts included more in-person Republican ballots creating a mirage of red (Republican) results. However, as mail-in ballots were counted and added to the total, the results shifted blue (Democratic) because more Democrats voted by mail than Republicans. The election was called on November 7, 2020 (although Trump's legal actions persisted for some time): Joe Biden defeated Donald Trump (Presidential Results, 2020) to become the 46th president of the United States. Biden won the presidency with 306 Electoral Votes and over 50% of the popular vote (US Election Results, 2020). Two heated run-off elections for the Georgia Senate were won by Democrats, giving that party control of the Senate (with the tie-breaking vote from Democratic Vice President Kamala Harris; Senate Results, 2020). Democrats retained control of the House of Representatives but with a narrower margin than 2018 (House Results, 2020). These data are reported in Table 1.3.

Table 1.3. 2020 Federal election results.

	Biden	Trump
Presidential Popular Vote	78,873,252 (51.9%)	73,202,557 (48.1%)
Presidential Electoral College Votes	306 (57%)	232 (43%)
Presidential States Won	25 (50%) Democrats	25 (50%) Republicans
Senate	50	50
House	222	213*

Source: US Election Results 2020; Senate Results, 2020; House Results, 2020.

*One race remained uncalled in January 2021.

The next chapter explains the Functional Theory of Political Campaign Discourse, the theoretical foundation used here. The next three chapters examine presidential campaign discourse from a communication perspective, discussing medium ("channel"), source, and context. Chapter Six extends this analysis to election campaigns for non-presidential offices (Senate, Representative, Governor, Mayor). Chapter Seven explores news coverage of political election campaigns. Next the book examines another key element of communication and political campaigns: voters (receivers). A final chapter concludes this work.

CHAPTER TWO

The Functional Theory of Political Campaign Discourse

This chapter describes the Functional Theory of Political Campaign Discourse (e.g., Benoit, 1999, 2007, 2014a, 2014b, 2015c, 2017a, 2017b, 2017c), which drives much of the research discussed in this book. Then I explain the advantages of this approach to analyzing political campaign discourse.

A functional analysis is especially appropriate for investigating political campaign messages because such discourse is intended as a *means* of accomplishing a *goal*: *messages used* to *win* an election. Political campaign discourse is therefore unquestionably instrumental, or functional, in nature. Of course, some candidates campaign in order to espouse a particular point of view. This is presumably the case for many third party candidates. For instance, in 2016 Senator Bernie Sanders, who made an unexpected strong challenge to Secretary Hillary Clinton's campaign, did not drop out of the Democratic primary race until July 12, about two weeks before the Democratic National Convention, because he wanted to be sure that the issues he cared about were represented at the convention. This is not to say he had not tried to win the Democratic nomination but that he continued to campaign after it was clear Clinton would win. For those who do hope to win the election campaign messages are the means to gaining votes (and thus winning public office). In 2020 Sanders again continued his campaign for some time after it became clear that Vice President Joe Biden would win the Democratic nomination for president.

Assumptions of Functional Theory

Functional Theory is based on five important assumptions, called axioms here. Each of these assumptions will be explained separately in this section.

1. *Voting is a comparative act.*

Citizens face a relatively simple decision in the voting booth: For whom should I cast my vote? This decision is a choice between two (or more) competing candidates and it clearly entails a comparative judgment. We cannot reasonably expect any candidate to be perfect; on the other hand, no candidate is utterly without redeeming qualities. Thus, in any contested election, a citizen's vote choice represents a comparative decision that one candidate appears *preferable* to the other candidate(s) on whatever basis is most important to that voter. Some voters may be so certain that the candidate they prefer is better that they consider this superiority to be a fact rather than a perception. Nevertheless, voters' candidate choices are best understood as perceptions they form on the basis of their beliefs, values, and attitudes (see, e.g., Fishbein & Azjen, 2010). In other words, the goal sought by a candidate, winning elections, is attained by persuading enough voters to believe that he or she is the better candidate in the race.

This idea that voting is a choice between *competing candidates* is becoming increasingly important as political parties declined in influence. As noted in Chapter One, "in an environment of diminishing party loyalty, campaigns and candidates exert a greater influence on voters than they did in the elections of 1940 and 1948" (Popkin, 1994, p. 12; Wattenberg, 1991). Burns and Martin (2016) reported that the Republican leadership did not support Donald Trump in the 2016 primary; the party failed to prevent his success. In earlier contests, the party nominee was often selected at the convention. Patterson (2003) stated that in 1952 Estes Kefauver won:

> all but one of the twelve primaries he entered and was the clear favorite of rank-and-file Democrats in the final Gallup Poll before the national nominating convention. Nevertheless, the party's leaders chose Adlai Stevenson as the Democratic presidential nominee. (pp. 145–146)

Today, of course, delegates won in primaries and caucuses choose the Democratic and Republican parties' nominees. In 1968, there were only 16 Republican and 17 Democratic primaries (Crotty & Jackson, 1985). By 2000, primaries were held in all 50 states as well as Puerto Rico and the District of Columbia. The 2016 Republican presidential primary (along with the Democratic primary) attracted widespread attention, in large part because of Donald Trump's presence in the race. In 2020 we saw a contested Democratic presidential primary contest.

The increasing prominence of primary contests has changed the nature of politics. One important consequence is an increased importance of individual candidates and their campaign advisors. Although many voters cast their votes in the general election for whoever wins their political party's nomination, the individual candidates, and their apparent preferability to voters, play increasingly important roles in election outcomes. Party affiliation cannot help voters decide who to support the primary because all of the candidates seeking that nomination belong to the same party. For example, in 2020 Democrats had to choose between quite a number of candidates who sought the nomination so they could challenge President Donald Trump, including Vice President Joe Biden, Senator Bernie Sanders, Senator Elizabeth Warren, Senator Kirsten Gillibrand, Senator Kamala Harris, Senator Amy Klobuchar, Mayor Mike Bloomfield, Mayor Pete Buttigieg, and over 20 other Democratic hopefuls.

2. Candidates must distinguish themselves from opponents.

The notion that voting is a comparative act, in which the relative preferability of the contenders determines vote choice, leads directly to the second assumption of the Functional Theory: Candidates must appear different from one another. Simply put, voters cannot make a choice, they have no reason to prefer one candidate over another, if all candidates look exactly the same. Of course, it is common for candidates to adopt some similar policy positions: Everyone wants to preserve Social Security, increase jobs, and protect the U.S. from terrorism. However, if the candidates agreed on *every* issue (and projected the same character) there would be no reason to prefer one over another. This means that it is essential for candidates in contested races to develop some distinctions between themselves and their opponent(s). Voters had to have seen some difference(s) between Clinton and Trump in able to decide their vote for president in 2016. Voters also must see some difference(s) between President Trump and Vice President Joe Biden in 2020.

On way candidates can attempt to differentiate themselves by discussing character. One candidate may stress his leadership ability, as George W. Bush told voters in the second debate of 2000, "I've ... been called a uniter not divider." Another candidate may want to create the impression that he or she is honest – or than an opponent is dishonest. In the 2000 primary campaign, McCain promised that he would "always tell you the truth." McCain surely wanted to create the impression that he was honest. In 2020 Vice President Joe Biden declared that "It's time for respected leadership on the world stage—and dignified leadership at home" (https://joebiden.com/joes-vision/). Senator Elizabeth Warren stressed her background: "Elizabeth grew up on the ragged edge of the middle class in Oklahoma" (https://elizabethwarren.com/meet-elizabeth). These excerpts show how candidates accentuate their positive attributes.

Candidates can also use policy to differentiate themselves from opponents. In the 2000 primary campaign, for example, one of Vice President Al Gore's spots declared that he was "The only candidate who protects Medicare and preserves Medicaid." This statement gave voters who cared about Medicare and Medicaid a reason to prefer Gore to other Democratic candidates. In the 2004 campaign, Senator Joseph Lieberman said in a South Carolina primary debate, "I'm the only candidate here on the stage here tonight that supported both the Gulf War and the war against Saddam Hussein, and I wrote the bill on homeland security. So, I think I'll make the American people feel safe as their next president." In 2016 Trump made it clear that he wanted to build a wall between the U.S. and Mexico to halt illegal immigration. In 2020 a primary TV spot for Tom Steyer declared that "Tom Steyer is committed to combating climate change, fixing our government, and, when elected president, putting people, and not corporations, in charge of our democracy" (https://www.tomsteyer.com/meet-tom-steyer/). Political candidates need not differ on every point of comparison, but political candidates must identify some differences in order to enable voters to prefer one contender over another.

Theories of candidate behavior developed in political science have made similar observations. As indicated above, candidates will usually adopt some of the same issue positions. For example, Page (1978) explained that Downs' (1957)

> economic theory of democracy calls for a candidate's policy stands to echo the policy preferences of the public, and many spatial models – especially those of the public opinion variety – predict that the midpoint of public opinion on issues has an important influence upon the stands that a candidate takes. (p. 29)

Page presented evidence from the 1968 campaign that "Across a wide variety of issues, then, both Humphrey and Nixon took positions which corresponded fairly closely with what the average American favored" (p. 47). However, he also found that both Humphrey and Nixon *disagreed* with the mid-point of public opinion on about 15% of the 72 issues he examined. Specifically, Democrat Humphrey took more liberal positions on some issues whereas Republican Nixon adopted more conservative stands on some issues. This result is, generally, what one would expect. Both candidates took similar issue positions on some issues, close to the majority of the public, but each candidate distinguished himself from the majority opinion on other issues, Humphrey (the Democrat) by moving to the left and Nixon (the Republican) to the right of the ideological spectrum. Page also suggested that in 1964 Goldwater may have been more of an ideologue who did not adapt to public opinion; this is a losing strategy (and he lost). More recently, Donald Trump adopted a number of policy positions that did not appear to cluster around the mid-point of American public opinions; he still won both the Republican primary and the Electoral College in 2016.

   3. *Political campaign messages allow candidates to distinguish themselves.*

Once a candidate decides which distinctions to stress to voters, he or she must communicate that information to voters. Citizens must be aware of these differences in order for such distinctions to be able to affect their candidate preferences. As indicated in Chapter One, most voters cannot rely on direct personal knowledge of competing candidates. Chapter Seven argues that citizens cannot should not depend solely on the news media to obtain information about candidates and their policy positions. The news media do provide some information about the candidates for president, but their paramount purpose is to attract readers, viewers, and listeners. The media focus on reporting what is "news": where the candidates are stumping, how much money they are raising, what changes have occurred in campaign staff or strategies. News *may* inform voters, but it may not. Patterson and McClure (1976) reported that learning occurs from candidates' campaign messages:

> During the 1972 presidential campaign, people who were heavily exposed to political spots became more informed about the candidates' issue positions. ... On every single issue emphasized in presidential commercials, persons with high exposure to television advertising showed a greater increase in knowledge than persons with low exposure. (pp. 116–117)

It is clear that campaign messages – such as presidential television and radio spots, speeches, webpages, tweets, and facebook pages – are an important source of political information. Presidential debates are another medium that provides information to voters about the character and policy of the candidates (see Chapter Three).

Of course, we must not assume that presidential candidates offer a thorough or unbiased discussion of every issue. It is in the candidates' best interests to present themselves in a favorable light and to portray their opponents in an unfavorable light. This could lead to omissions, inaccuracies, exaggerations, and/or misrepresentations of the issues. A simple and possibly less risky approach is to focus on ends rather than means: "I favor a balanced budget [but I won't tell you whether I will increase taxes and/or reduce spending to achieve it]." A certain amount of strategic ambiguity may be useful to political candidates; however, keep in mind that Alverez (1998) found that too much ambiguity is undesirable. Furthermore, some ideas, such as the specifics of proposals to save Social Security or to reform taxes, are so complex that discussion of details becomes unwieldy in campaign messages, particularly TV spots and tweets. Nevertheless, campaign messages help candidates establish the distinctiveness among contenders that gives voters a basis for choosing one candidate over another.

4. *Candidates establish preferability through acclaiming, attacking, and defending.*

Of course, it is not sufficient for candidates to be distinctive in their messages, even on the issues that matter most to voters in that election year; a candidate appear different from his or her opponents *in ways that voters favor*. For example, a candidate who declared that "I am the only candidate who will raise taxes 60% for everyone" or "People just work too hard so I will increase unemployment to help them have more spare time" would surely stand apart from opponents, but not in a way that is likely to attract many votes. So, a candidate must appear both different *and better* than his or her opponent; conversely, one can portray the opponent as both different *and worse*. Popkin (1994) explains that "Somehow, candidates manage to get a large proportion of the citizenry sorted into opposing camps, each of which is convinced that the positions and interests of the other side add up to a less desirable package of benefits" (p. 8). Only three kinds of statements or functions of discourse are capable of making a candidate appear *preferable* to opponents. Functional Theory recognizes that establishing preferability can be achieved through three kinds of statements: acclaims, attacks, and defenses.[1]

Acclaims

First, candidates may offer acclaims (Benoit, 1997), statements that stress a candidate's advantages or benefits. Such self-praise can address the candidate's character or policy stands. For example, assuming voters value honesty in a presidential candidate, candidates who persuade voters of their honesty will almost certainly enhance their perceived desirability as candidates. Comments on policy also have the potential to affect a candidate's perceived desirability. For example, during the Republican presidential primaries of 2016, Kasich touted his record as Governor of Ohio and as member of Congress: "I think when they take a look at my record, both in Washington and in Ohio, with the job growth, the wage growth, reforming the Pentagon" voters will support me (*Face the Nation*, 3/20/16). Presumably voters would agree that job growth, wage growth and Pentagon reforms are all desirable accomplishments. During the 2020 Democratic presidential primary, Tom

Styer's campaign webpage informed voters that "In 2013, he founded NextGen America, a nonprofit group that combats climate change, promotes social justice, and increases participation in our democracy through voter registration and grassroots organizing" (https://www.tomsteyer.com/meet-tom-steyer/). Fighting climate change, enhancing social judgments, and increasing participation in democracy are goals that are likely to appeal to many Democrats.

Attacks

Another way to increase one candidate's (net) favorability is to attack or criticize the opponent(s). Stressing an opponent's undesirable attributes or policy missteps should reduce that opponent's desirability. Because voters make a comparative judgment about which candidate is preferable (A1), a successful attack increases the attacker's net favorability by reducing the desirability of an opponent. In a *Face the Nation* program, Kasich asserted that Trump's "done a lot of name-calling and he's created a very toxic atmosphere" (3/13/16). This statement criticizes the business magnate's character. Turnabout is fair play; Donald Trump leveled this criticism on the policy of the Ohio governor (his record in office): "I could tell you about John Kasich. He's done a terrible job in Ohio ... He's losing his businesses. Real estate taxes have gone through the roof. ... His coal industry is dead. And his steel industry is dead" (*Face the Nation*, 3/13/16). Senator Amy Klobuchar attacked the Republican president in the Iowa Democratic debate: "Donald Trump is taking us pell-mell toward another war" (https://www.desmoinesregister.com/story/news/elections/presidential/caucus/2020/01/14/democratic-debate-transcript-what-the-candidates-said-quotes/4460789002/). In the same debate, Tom Steyer declared that "Mr. Trump has no strategy. He is going from crisis to crisis, from escalation to escalation." Senator Elizabeth Warren criticized the sitting president in the same event: "But we have farmers here in Iowa who are hurting. And they are hurting because of Donald Trump's initiated trade wars. We have workers who are hurting because the agreements that have already been cut really donst have enforcement on workers' rights." Because one's vote choice is a comparative judgment, if a candidate can persuade voters of a weakness of an opponent, that attack should create a new increase in the attacker's desirability compared with that of the target.

Of course, some candidates may be reluctant to attack opponents. We know that voters consistently report that they do not like mud-slinging (Merritt, 1984; Stewart, 1975) so some politicians may wish to avoid engaging in character assassination. In 2000, both McCain and Bush promised to run positive primary campaigns. For example, Bush explained that "I'd like to run a campaign that is hopeful and optimistic and very positive." However, both candidates resorted to attacks and then they each ran television spots attacking the other for breaking his promise to run a positive campaign. An advertisement for McCain reminded viewers of Bush's promise to run a positive campaign featuring the passage just quoted from Bush. Then the spot showed video from a second Bush commercial, which attacked McCain, and declared "This is George Bush's new negative ad, attacking John McCain and distorting his position." Similarly, a Bush spot declared that "John McCain promised a clean campaign, then attacked Governor Bush with misleading ads." Candidates may refrain from attacking, attack less often, or even promise to eschew attacks because voters dislike mudslinging. However, because attacks have the potential to reduce the preferability of an opponent, candidates use this function in their campaign messages. In 2016, Trump succeeded at winning the Republican primary and the general election despite the fact that he created derogatory nicknames for opponents (e.g., "Little Marco," "Lyin' Ted," and "Crooked Hillary"). In his re-election campaign he belittled "Sleepy Joe Biden."

Complaints about negative campaigns are fairly common (see, e.g., Ansolabehere & Iyengar, 1995; Jamieson, 1992; Pfau & Kenski, 1990). Kamber (1997), for example, notes that "previous eras saw severe personal attack on political candidates, but they also saw detailed and sometimes inspiring deliberation over the issues. Our present political discourse is nothing but spleen" (p. 4). It was impossible to avoid noticing that Clinton and Trump (as well as other candidates in the primaries) relied heavily on attacks in the 2016 presidential campaign (see Benoit & Glantz, 2020). Gross and Johnson (2016) found that in the Republican primary: "the front-runner and eventual nominee, Donald Trump, sends and receives the most negative tweets and is more likely than his opponents to strike out against even those opponents who are polling poorly." Vicious attacks are uncalled for and false attacks are detrimental to voters, but truthful attacks can provide voters with useful information. Kamber (1997) explained that

> There is an argument to be made in defense of responsible negative advertisements. The voters need to know the whole story, and solely positive arguments do not provide it. A campaign is not going to willingly offer negative information about its own candidate, and yet that is essential information for the voters to make an informed decision. (p. 7; see also Bryant, 2004)

So, accurate criticism of an opponent can be useful for voters who need to consider both the pros and cons of the candidates when making a vote choice. False attacks, or attacks that are malicious in tone, are not justifiable. But legitimate criticism is a form of attack that can help voters make an informed choice.

It is important to realize that just because voters express distaste for attacks does not necessarily mean that attacking messages cannot be persuasive. Candidates use focus groups and public opinion polls to design their messages and they obviously believe attacks can be persuasive. It seems clear that attacks are capable of reducing the desirability of the target of those attacks. However, it is possible that some attacks may also have a backlash effect and thus hurt both the sponsor (because voters dislike mud-slinging) as well as the target. This means the most important question may be who is likely to suffer the most from an attack: the target of the attack or the attack's sponsor?

There is a widespread belief that negative ads have more persuasive impact than positive ads, a meta-analysis (a statistical method of combining results from multiple studies) by Lau, Sigelman, Heldman, and Babbitt (1999) concluded that negative ads are no more powerful than positive ones. Another meta-analysis by Allen and Burrell (2002) concluded that negative ads are slightly more effective than positive ads at changing attitude toward a policy position and reducing the attitude toward the target of attack. However, they also found attacks have an even larger effect of reducing the attitude toward the sponsor of the attacks (a backlash effect). What we can conclude from these two studies is that negative ads are either no more powerful, or only slightly more powerful (with even stronger backlash effects), than positive ads. In any event, attacks are one important option in political campaigns and attacks have the potential to increase the sponsoring candidate's net favorability.

Recently (more recently than these studies) political party members in America have become more hostile to the opposition party. Davenport (2017) reported that in "the early 1970s, party unity voting [straight-ticket voting] was around 60% but today it is closer to 90% in both the House and Senate." Split-ticket voting, in which a citizen votes for at least one candidate from each of the two major parties, had been rising but with party unity voting increasing, split-ticket voting has become much less common. Sabato, Kondik, and Skelley (2016) also addressed recent party unity voting, reporting that every state that voted for Donald Trump elected a Republican senator while every state that voted for Hillary Clinton elected a Democratic senator. Abramowitz and Webster (2016, 2018) indicated that most voters now dislike the opposing party more than they like their own party. This increased hostility toward the opposition could mean that attacks are more effective with partisans than ever before, which could mean that politicians try to exploit this hostility with increasing levels of attacks on opponents.

The topic of the attack may be one important factor in audience response. Johnson-Cartee and Copeland (1989) provide evidence that voters tend to consider policy attacks more acceptable than character attacks. Other studies (Pfau &

Burgoon, 1989; Roddy & Garramone, 1988) indicate that policy attacks can be more persuasive than character attacks. Benoit (2003), analyzing multiple message forms (primary television spots, debates, and brochures; acceptance addresses; general television spots, debates, and brochures) over the last 50 years, found that winners are significantly more likely to attack more on policy, and less on character, than those who lose elections. This does not mean that policy attacks guarantee a win, or even that attacks on character can never be persuasive. It does suggest that it may be prudent to attack more on policy than one's opponent. Donald Trump's insult-laden 2016 campaign may be an exception or a new normal; only time will tell which one is true.

Defenses

The third function of campaign messages that can affect a candidate's preferability is defense. If a candidate is attacked by an opponent – or perhaps it would be more realistic to say *when* one candidate is attacked by another – the recipient of the attack can choose to defend against (refute) that attack in a campaign message (see Bryant, 2004). For example, after Clinton suggested in the third presidential debate that Trump would be Putin's puppet, the GOP nominee responded: "No puppet. No puppet." Political candidates are attacked and often they respond with defenses or refutations of these attacks.

Defense can be important to a campaign because a timely and appropriate defense may be able to (1) prevent further damage from an attack and (2) restore some or all of a candidate's damaged preferability. Defense, then, is the third potential function of campaign discourse. It attempts to restore, or prevent additional damage to, a candidate's perceived preferability.

At times candidates may decide to forgo defenses when they are attacked. Some candidates may not wish to "dignify" an opponent's accusations with a response. This reluctance may be related to the fact that defenses have three potential drawbacks. First, it is possible that presenting a response to an attack could make the candidate sound defensive, appearing reactive rather than proactive. Second, it seems likely that attacks are most likely to strike at the target's weaknesses, so defending against an attack probably takes a candidate "off-message," devoting precious message time to issues that probably favor one's opponent. Third, the only way to respond to a particular attack is to identify that criticism. Mentioning the attack, in preparation for refuting it, could inform or remind voters of the very weakness that the candidate is trying to combat. Defenses therefore have three potential drawbacks (Benoit, 2007).

Political campaign messages can be classified in a variety of ways (e.g., media used, campaign phase [primary versus general], or source of message). Functional Theory proposes two dimensions, functions – acclaims, attacks, and defenses – and topic – policy and character. This means candidates can acclaim on policy, acclaim on character, attack on policy, and so forth. Another important dimension is veracity or truthfulness. Some statements may be opinions rather than statements of fact. Other claims can be verified as true or false; we could also speak of statements the source (candidate) believes to be true or believes to be false. We often think of attacks (mudslinging) as false, but that is not necessarily the case. So, it is important to understand that some attacks are truthful just as some acclaims can be false (Benoit, 2015). Henson and Benoit (2010) compared TV spots with evidence and those without evidence. Evidence is more likely to be found in attacks than acclaims.

Other Discussions of the Functions of Political Campaign Discourse

Smith (1990) acknowledged the role of two of these three functions when he explained that in politics "people pursue and defend jobs by publicly boasting and attacking others" (p. 107). Sabato (1981) made a similar point from the voters' standpoint when he explained that there are a limited number of ways to vote: "for or against either of the party nominees or not voting at all" (p. 324). Scholars who investigate televised political advertising often distinguish between positive and negative spots (see, e.g., Devlin, 1989, 1993; Kaid & Davidson, 1986; Kaid & Johnston, 2001).

Trent and Friedenberg (2000) noted that televised political advertisements can accomplish three basic functions: extol the candidates' own virtues; condemn, attack, and question their opponents; and respond to attacks or innuendos. These clearly correspond to acclaims, attacks, and defenses. Pfau and Kenski (1990) noted that television spots can be categorized in four types: positive, negative, comparative (both positive and negative), and response (defense). "Comparative" sports consist of acclaims and attacks. So, political scholars have recognized that political television spots acclaim and attack–and a few have even acknowledged the existence of defensive or response advertisements. However, apart from research using the Functional approach, this distinction between positive and negative political advertisements is rarely applied to other forms of campaign discourse, such as debates or speeches. Furthermore, only research from the Functional perspective investigates the frequency of defense in campaign messages.

Political candidates and their campaign advisors also recognize the fundamental principle that campaign discourse performs multiple functions. For example, H. R. Haldeman offered this advice on the 1972 re-election campaign to President Richard M. Nixon: "Getting one of those 20 [percent] who is an undecided type to vote for you on the basis of your positive points is much less likely than getting them to vote against McGovern by scaring them to death about McGovern" (Popkin et al., 1976, p. 794n). Thus, Haldeman recognized that the election hinged on the undecided voters and that Nixon could seek their votes by praising himself – acclaiming Nixon's "positive points" – or by attacking his opponent–"scaring them to death about McGovern." Similarly, Vincent Breglio, part of Ronald Reagan's successful 1980 presidential campaign, acknowledged that "It has become vital in campaigns today that you not only present all the reasons why people ought to vote for you, but you also have an obligation to present the reasons why they should not vote for the opponent" (1987, p. 34). So, political campaign advisors, like political communication scholars, recognize that candidates can praise themselves and attack their opponents.

This is precisely why the Functional approach analyzes political campaign discourse into utterances that *acclaim* the preferred candidate, *attack* the opponent, and *defend* the candidate from opponent's attacks. Although these three functions may not be (and in fact are not) equally common in discourse, they constitute the basic options that every candidate has available for use. These functions are very important because they provide voters a reason to vote for a candidate or against an opponent. A complete understanding of political campaign messages should consider all three functions.

Some scholars have developed other lists of functions of political discourse. For example, Devlin (1986; 1987) discusses several functions of political ads. However, the three functions identified here are more basic than Devlin's list. One of the functions recognized by Devlin is raising money. Surely a candidate must acclaim his or her desirable qualities or policies and/or attack his or her opponent in order to convince donors to contribute money to his or her campaign. Furthermore, the money which is raised will be used to produce messages that acclaim, attack, or defend. Another one of Devlin's functions is reinforcing supporters. Surely supporters would be reinforced by discourse which acclaims the candidate's desirable qualities and, quite possibly, which attacks the opponent's undesirable qualities. Gronbeck also identified several instrumental and consummatory functions of presidential campaigning (1978). Some of these functions appear to be uses and gratifications for the audience. Of course, it is important to know how auditors are likely to make use of the discourse produced by political candidates. However, those kinds of functions supplement, rather than compete with, the Functional analysis of political campaign messages. I explicitly privilege the candidate's purposes in this analysis, rather than voters' or reporters' purposes. Thus, these activities – attacking, acclaiming, and defending – are the three *fundamental* functions of political campaign discourse.

One useful way to understand these three functions is to think of them as an informal form of cost-benefit analysis. Acclaims stress a candidate's benefits. Attacks highlight an opponent's costs. Defenses attempt to refute or minimize potential costs. A good vote decision requires an understanding of the pros (acclaims) as well as the cons (attacks, defenses) of the candidates. Therefore, this means that attacks serve a useful purpose, identifying costs – as long as they are neither false nor misleading. Political candidates can inform voters of an opponent's potential costs through attacks. Kelley and Mirer (1974), using survey data from the 1952–1968 presidential elections, found that 82–87% of citizens voted for the candidate for whom they reported the largest number of reasons for liking that candidate and the smallest number of reasons for disliking that candidate (in other words, benefits and costs). This figure may not reach 100% because a a voter could have fewer, but more important, reasons for liking one candidate more than another.

It is important to note that characterizing vote choice as similar to cost-benefit analysis is not meant to suggest that every voter takes a rational approach to voting: gathering, weighing, and integrating as much information as possible to guarantee that they make the most rational decision possible. Nor do voters make mathematical calculations adding or averaging pros and cons. As Zaller (1992) rightly observed, "citizens vary in their habitual attention to politics and hence in their exposure to political information and argumentation in the media" (p. 1). Only political junkies avidly seek out huge amounts of information about the various candidates. As Popkin argued (1994; see also Downs, 1957), many voters use information shortcuts. They do not seek out information about the candidates or they wait until just before the election to do so. They base their voting decisions on the information they happen to encounter, often from television commercials and discussions with friends and family. Voters do not place the information they obtain about the candidates into mathematical formulas (benefits - costs) in order to calculate their votes. Thus, although deciding how to vote is similar to cost-benefit analysis, voters do not do so numerically or even systematically weigh the pros and cons of competing candidates. Acclaims tend to increase a candidate's perceived preferability, attacks tend to reduce an opponent's preferability, and defenses may restore lost preferability. All three functions work to make one candidate appear preferable to another.

We must realize that campaign messages have limitations when it comes to influencing voters. As noted above, too many voters have little interest in political campaigns and are unlikely to watch speeches or debates and may not read or watch political news. In today's fragmented media environment (Benoit &

Billings, 2020) citizens have thousands of options (cable or satellite television, webpages, Twitter feeds, Facebook pages, and other possibilities) to occupy their time if they are not interested in politics.

Some voters who do pay attention to messages from candidates and others may not accept a candidate's, or a surrogate's, or a reporter's statements at face value. Candidates may not always address the most prominent concerns of voters, and that surely would diminish the utility of the message. Furthermore, different voters may interpret a message in different ways. For example, Jarman (2005) investigated the second presidential debate in 2004. He found that "Republicans always rated Bush's comments higher than Democrats, whereas Democrats always rated Kerry's comments higher than Republicans" (p. 229; see also Warner, McKinney, Bramlett, Jennings, & Funk, 2020). A person's beliefs, values, and attitudes (see Fishbein & Azjen, 2010) influence perceptions of messages.

Petty and Cacioppo's Elaboration Likelihood Model (1981, 1986) offers an explanation for this effect. This theory posits that people think about messages they consume, having positive and/or negative thoughts about the message topic. As a person produces more positive thoughts, attitude change increases. Conversely, more negative thoughts yield less persuasion. Pro-attitudinal messages (e.g., a message that is consistent with a listener's attitude) are likely to result in more positive thoughts, fewer negative thoughts, and more persuasion than a counter-attitudinal message. This means that when a Democrat is exposed to a liberal message, that person is likely to think more favorable thoughts, fewer unfavorable thoughts, and experience more attitude change than when that person hears a conservative message. Republicans, upon reading a conservative message, are likely to produce more favorable thoughts, fewer unfavorable thoughts, and have more attitude change, compared with their reaction to a liberal message. Counter-attitudinal advocacy – a Republican exposed to a liberal message or a Democrat confronted with a conservative message – are likely to provoke more unfavorable thoughts and fewer favorable thoughts, limiting the amount of persuasion from such messages. A final limitation of campaign messages is that a single message may have little impact on a voter's attitudes. This is why candidates wage campaigns with multiple messages over time. The messages to which voters are exposed during a campaign gradually shape their perceptions of the candidates' character and issue stands and, ultimately, a citizen enters a polling place and casts a vote based on those perceptions.

Candidates send information to voters information using campaign messages in a variety of channels or media, such as television spots, debates, speeches, direct mail brochures, radio spots, web pages and, in recent years, social media such as Facebook and Twitter (see Chapter Three). Candidates hope to reach whoever happens to be paying attention to that medium at that point in time. Providing a voter information about a candidate's desirable qualities or issue stands should tend to increase that candidate's apparent preferability. Giving information about an opposing candidate's undesirable qualities or issue stands tends to decrease the opponent's apparent preferability. Offering information in the form of a defense should help restore a candidate's apparent preferability. The effects of these three kinds of messages may have more impact on vote choice when they concern topics that are particularly important to a voter. Although the effects of individual messages may be small and depend upon how many voters attend to them, and although some voters may have strong party preferences, the cumulative effect of such information over time has the potential to influence voters' decisions. Undecided and independent voters, as well as potential vote defectors, may be particularly susceptible to these messages.

This analysis also explains why basic themes are, and should be, repeated throughout the campaign. For those voters who pay attention throughout the campaign, repetition serves to reinforce the candidate's message with those auditors. On the other hand, the campaign puts out a relatively constant message in hopes that voters who only pay sporadic attention to the campaign will sooner or later notice the campaign themes. Message repetition can increase a message's persuasiveness (Benoit & Benoit, 2008).

Relative Frequency of the Three Functions

Functional Theory argues that these three functions are likely to occur with different frequencies. Acclaims, if persuasive (if accepted by the audience) can increase a candidate's apparent preferability and have no drawbacks. This means that acclaims should be the most common campaign discourse function.

In contrast, attacks, if persuasive, can increase a candidate's apparent net favorability by decreasing an opponent's preferability. However, the public is known to dislike mudslinging as noted above (Merritt, 1984; Stewart, 1975) so the risk of backlash may encourage candidates to moderate their attacks. Accordingly, Functional Theory expects attacks to be less common than acclaims.

Finally, defenses, if they are accepted by a voter, can help restore a candidate's lost preferability. However, defenses have three drawbacks: They are likely to take a candidate off-message (because attacks are likely to address the target's weaknesses), they risk informing or reminding voters of a potential weakness (a candidate must identify an attack to refute it), and they may create the impression that the candidate is reactive rather than proactive. Thus, Functional Theory makes two predictions about the functions of political campaign discourse:

H1. *Political candidates are likely to use acclaims more frequently than attacks.*
H2. *Political candidates are likely to use attacks more frequently than defenses.*

Note that a third prediction is implicit in these two expectations, that acclaims are more common than defenses.

It is important to realize that Functional Theory concerns reasons rather than causes. It does not state that candidates *must* acclaim more than they attack; candidates have a reason to acclaim more than they attack. Some individual candidates choose to rely most heavily on attacks. Similarly, Functional Theory does not assert that candidates *must* attack more than they defend, just that they have reasons to do so. Research has confirmed prediction F1, that most candidates in fact acclaim more than they attack: overall 71% of statements were acclaims, 26% attacks, and 3% defenses (see Table 2.1). This relationship (acclaims > attacks > defenses) occurred in every medium studied. Of course, a few individual candidates chose to attack most frequently than they acclaimed, but they are clearly in the minority. No message form studied using Functional Theory has relied on defenses more than acclaims or attacks, confirming F2.

Several studies investigate the circumstances under which candidates are more likely to attack or acclaim (see, e.g., Benoit, 2014; Damore, 2002; Elmelund-Praestekaer, 2010; Maier & Jansen, 2015; Shen, 2012; Sullivan & Sapir, 2012). Several potential factors have been studied including incumbency (challengers tend to attack more than incumbents; see Chapter Four), campaign phase (candidates tend to attack more in general than primary campaigns; see Chapter Five), standing in public opinion polls (those behind usually attack more than leaders), being attacked by opponents tends to provoke attacks in response, competitiveness of race (attacking is positively related to competitiveness), and sponsor of advertisement (parties and other sources are usually more negative than candidates; see Chapter Four). Skaperdas and Grofman (1995) add that in elections with three candidates neither of the two leading candidates is likely to attack the least popular candidate who tends to run a positive campaign (see also Benoit & Wells, 1996). Peterson and Djupe (2005), investigating Senate primary races in 1998, indicated that campaigns are most negative at the beginning and end of a campaign. Finally, looking at defenses, Benoit (2007) reported that debates have more defenses than other message forms.

5. *Campaign discourse addresses two topics: policy and character.*

Functional Theory posits that political discourse can occur on two broad topics: *policy* (issues) and *character* (image). These topics concern *what a candidates*

Table 2.1. Functions and topics of presidential campaign messages.

	Functions			Topics	
	Acclaims	Attacks	Defenses	Policy	Character
Announcements (1952–2016)	**6441 (75%)**	2124 (25%)	35 (0.5%)	**4598 (54%)**	2096 (54%)
Primary TV Spots (1952–2016)	**6646 (72%)**	2481 (27%)	62 (0.1%)	**5040 (55%)**	4613 (61%)
Primary Debates (1948, 1960, 1972–2016)	**30710 (65%)**	14337 (30%)	2332 (5%)	**27350 (69%)**	121004 (31%)
Primary Brochures (1948–2004)	**7776 (85%)**	1361 (15%)	7 (0.1%)	**5660 (62%)**	3424 (38%)
Primary TV Talk Shows (2000, 2004, 2016)	**2731 (59%)**	1399 (30%)	539 (11%)	1870 (44%)	**2350 (56%)**
Primary Websites (2000–2008)	**14308 (89%)**	1689 (11%)	12 (0.01%)	**12358 (78%)**	3485 (22%)
Primary Social Media (2008–2016)	**4755 (73%)**	1685 (26%)	57 (1%)	2639 (41%)	3867 (59%)
Acceptances (1952–2016)	**2891 (74%)**	974 (25%)	25 (0.5%)	**2096 (54%)**	1760 (46%)
Campaign Posters (1828–2012)	**1463 (92%)**	134 (8%)	0	314 (20%)	**1283 (80%)**
General TV Spots (1952–2016)	**4076 (53%)**	3478 (46%)	89 (1%)	**4613 (61%)**	2936 (39%)
General Debates (1960, 1976–2016)	**5304 (55%)**	3545 (37%)	859 (9%)	**6320 (72%)**	2490 (28%)
Vice Presidential Debates (1976, 1984–2016)	**3137 (54%)**	2412 (41%)	270 (5%)	**8742 (76%)**	2687 (24%)

Continued

Table 2.1. *Continued*

	Functions			Topics	
	Acclaims	Attacks	Defenses	Policy	Character
General Brochures (1960–2004)	8036 (70%)	3393 (30%)	48 (0.4%)	8742 (76%)	2687 (24%)
General TV Talk Shows (2000, 2004)	1482 (81%)	282 (15%)	62 (3%)	897 (45%)	982 (55%)
General Websites (2000–2008)	9378 (97%)	259 (3%)	22 (1%)	8585 (90%)	941 (10%)
General Social Media (2012–2016)	2968 (52%)	2687 (47%)	56 (1%)	2637 (47%)	3008 (53%)
Total	112102 (71%)	42240 (26%)	4475 (3%)	102461 (67%)	50713 (33%)

Functions: χ^2 (df = 2) = 112648.3, p < .0001. Topics: χ^2 (df = 1) = 11268.09, p < .0001.

Announcements: Benoit, Henson, Whalen, & Pier, 2008; Benoit & Glantz, 2013, 2020.
Primary TV Spots: Benoit, 2014a; Benoit & Glantz, 2020.
Primary Debates: Benoit, 2014b; Benoit & Glantz, 2020.
Primary Brochures: Benoit & Stein, 2005.
Primary TV Talk Shows: Benoit, McHale, Hansen, Pier, & McGuire, 2003; Benoit et al., 2007; Benoit & Glantz, 2020.
Primary Websites: Benoit, McHale, Hansen, Pier, & McGuire, 2003; Benoit et al., 2007; Benoit et al., 2013.
Primary Social Media: Benoit & Glantz, 2020.
Acceptance Addresses: Benoit, Wells, Pier, & Blaney, 1999; Benoit, 2014; Benoit & Glantz, 2020.
Campaign Posters: Benoit, 2019.
General TV Spots: Benoit, 2014a; Benoit & Glantz, 2020.
General Debates: Benoit, 2014b; Benoit & Glantz, 2020.
General Vice Presidential Debates: Benoit & Airne, 2005; Benoit & Henson, 2009; Benoit & Glantz, 2015; Benoit & Glantz, 2020.
General Brochures: Benoit & Stein, 2005.
General TV Talk Shows: Benoit, McHale, Hansen, Pier, & McGuire, 2003; Benoit et al., 2007.
General Websites: Benoit, McHale, Hansen, Pier, & McGuire, 2003; Benoit et al., 2007; Benoit, Glantz, & Rill, 2016.
General Social Media: Shen & Benoit, 2016; Benoit & Glantz, 2020.

does (has done, will do) and *who a candidate is* (Rountree, 1995). In other words, candidates try to persuade voters of their preferability on policy and character. Pomper (1975), in fact, observed that many voters "change their partisan choice from one election to the next, and these changes are most closely related to their positions on the issues and their assessment of the abilities of the candidates" (p. 10). Policy and character are defined this way:

> *Policy* utterances concern governmental action (past, current, or future) and problems amenable to governmental action.
>
> *Character* utterances address characteristics, traits, abilities, or attributes of the candidates.

Thus, these are the two broad topics on which candidates contend over their preferability (Functional theory also subdivides both policy and character utterances into finer subcategories, as discussed later).

Although Functional Theory dichotomizes the two potential topics of political campaign discourse, it acknowledges that policy and character have a complex and dynamic relationship (Benoit, Blaney, & Pier, 1998). First, it is possible that an utterance which focuses explicitly on policy could influence perceptions of the candidate's character. For example, this passage from Bill Clinton's 1996 Acceptance Address discusses his first term successes with the economy:

> Four point four million Americans now living in a home of their own for the first time; hundreds of thousands of women have started their own new businesses; more minorities own businesses than ever before; record numbers of new small businesses and exports .... We have the lowest combined rates of unemployment, inflation, and home mortgages in 28 years. ... Ten million new jobs, over half of them high-wage jobs, ten million workers getting the raise they deserve with the minimum wage law.

Surely this is a policy utterance, for it discusses home ownership, business ownership, exports, unemployment, inflation, mortgages, jobs, and the minimum wage. He acclaimed by recounting these successes, which works to implicitly reinforce Clinton's apparent leadership ability, a character attribute, because they implicitly demonstrate that he possesses the skills necessary to enact legislation. Similarly, a message that touted programs to help the poor or homeless could create or reinforce an impression of that candidate's compassion.

On the other hand, this passage from one of Vice President George Bush's 1988 Republican primary television spots recounted his experience in the military, focusing on his experience and courage: "How does one man come so far? Maybe for George Bush, it began when he became the youngest pilot in the Navy. Or perhaps it began this day in 1944 when he earned the Distinguished Flying Cross for bravery under fire." This passage clearly concerns Bush's character, the personal quality of bravery, not what he will do if elected president. Nevertheless, voters might reasonably infer that this kind of person, a person with this character, is likely to support a strong military.

These two kinds of comments – policy versus character – have distinctly different content. One passage above (from Clinton) explicitly addresses policy and the other (from Bush) explicitly discusses character. These messages tell us more about Clinton's policies than Bush's policies; we can learn more from them about Bush's personal qualities than Clinton's. However, we should not be surprised that voters could form impressions from these passages that are not explicitly addressed in the text (Hacker, Zakahi, Giles, & McQuitty, 2000).

Furthermore, it appears that candidates in some circumstances purposefully attempt to shift the grounds of discussion from one topic to the other. For example, in the first Clinton/Dole debate of 1996, Jim Lehrer posed this question about Clinton's character generally and his honesty in particular: "Mr. President, what do you say to Senator Dole's point that this election is about keeping one's word?" Clinton's honesty (character) was challenged, and he offered this reply:

> Let's look at that. When I ran for president, I said we'd cut the deficit in half in four years; we cut it by 60 percent. I said that our economic plan would produce eight million jobs, we have ten and a half million new jobs. We're number one in autos again, record numbers of new small businesses. I said we'd put, pass a crime bill that would put 100,000 police on the street, ban assault weapons, and deal with the problems that ought to be dealt with with capital punishment, including capital punishment for drug kingpins, and we did that.
>
> I said we would change the way welfare works, and even before the bill passed we'd moved nearly two million people from welfare to work, working with states and communities. I said we'd get tougher with child support and child support enforcement's up 50 percent. I said that I would work for tax relief for middle class Americans. The deficit was bigger than I thought it was going to be. I think they're better off, all of us are, that we got the interest rates down and the deficit down.

Clinton's response shifted the discussion away from the question of honesty (keeping one's word generally) to keeping one's word on *campaign promises*, or policy accomplishments: jobs, autos, crime, welfare, middle-class tax cuts, interest rates, the deficit. He responded to an attack on character by shifting grounds and acclaiming his past successes on policy.

Similarly, some of Clinton's television spots took the same path, altering questions of character into one of policy. For example, in one Clinton spot, President Reagan's former press secretary, James Brady, praises Clinton. Brady was seriously injured during an attempt to assassinate Reagan; now Brady supports the Brady Bill, a form of gun control legislation.

It was over in a moment, but the pain lasts forever. President Clinton stood up and helped pass the Brady Bill. It wasn't about politics. The president had the integrity to do what was right. *When I hear people question the president's character, I say look what he's done.* Look at the lives the Brady Bill will save. (Clinton, "Seconds," 1996, emphasis added)

In this passage Brady explicitly argues that when people question Clinton's *character*, they should look at his *what he has done*, his policy accomplishments.

This process can also work in the other direction, moving from policy to character. For example, in the second debate of 2000, Vice President Gore attacked Governor Bush's record in Texas on the issue of health care.

Gore: I'm sorry to tell you that, you know, there is a record here, and Texas ranks 49th out of the 50 states in health care – in children with health care, 49th for women with health care, and 50th for families with health care.

Lehrer: Governor, did Vice President – are the vice president's figures correct about Texas?

Bush: *You can quote all the numbers you want, but I'm telling you, we care about our people in Texas,* we spend a lot of money to make sure people get health care in the state of Texas, and we're doing a better job than they are at the national level for reducing uninsured.

Lehrer: Is he right? Are those numbers correct? Are his charges correct?

Bush: *If he's trying to allege that I'm a hard-hearted person and I don't care about children, he's absolutely wrong.* We spend $4.7 billion a year in the state of Texas for uninsured people, and they get health care. (emphasis added)

Both times Lehrer pressed Bush about his record of policy failures as Governor of Texas he tried to turn this question into an issue of character. Bush did mention spending in Texas on health care, but there is a clear effort to shift this attack from policy to character: "we care about our people." Bush even responds to an attack that Gore never made, that Bush is hard-hearted, that he does not care about children: "If he's trying to allege that I'm a hard-hearted person and I don't care about children, he's absolutely wrong." Policy and character are distinct concepts but have a complex relationship.

Functional Theory predicts that, particularly in presidential campaigns, policy will be a more frequent topic of campaign messages than character. We elect presidents to run our government, to implement policy. Although some voters believe that they elect positive role models – and surely we all hope our elected leaders are positive role models – the primary duty of our elected officials is to administer policy. Hofstetter (1976) explains that "issue preferences are key elements in the preferences of most, if not all, voters" (p. 77; see also McClure & Patterson, 1976).

Table 2.2. Most important vote determinant: Policy or character.

Campaign	Policy	Character	Poll
2004	66%	28%	CBS News, 2/12–15, 2004
2000	90%	8%	Princeton Survey Research Associates 10/7–11/99
1996	65%	27%	NBC/*Wall Street Journal*, 10/19–22/96
1992	143%*	16%	Harris Poll, 11/3/92
1988	59%	16%	*USA Today*, 1/21–28/88
1994	87%	7%	*LA Times*, 2/4–9/84
1980	59%	34%	*LA Times*, 10/5–9/80
1976	57%	36%	CBS/*New York Times*, 10/24–27/76

*Respondents were allowed to pick the two most important factors in this poll.
"Don't know" and "unsure" responses also occurred.
All polls obtained from Lexis/Nexis Academic Universe on-line.

Furthermore, public opinion poll data from every campaign we have been able to locate (1976–2004) reveals that the majority of voters believe that policy is more important than character in their vote for president (see Table 2.2).

Character does matter, of course. We must trust candidates to work to achieve their campaign promises, and we must trust them to take appropriate action when unexpected problems arise, topics on which they did not take policy stands during the campaign. Still, because most voters consider policy to be more important than character, Functional Theory holds that candidates are likely to respond to these preferences so that policy will be discussed more frequently in presidential campaign messages than character. This leads to a third prediction:

H3. *Policy comments will be more frequent than character comments in presidential campaign discourse.*

As with the previous two predictions, Functional Theory does not assert that candidates *must* talk more about policy than character. It argues that candidates have reasons to emphasize policy over character. Examination of Table 2.1 shows that this prediction is supported overall, with 67% of utterances addressing policy and 33% discussing character, confirming prediction F3. This relationship (policy > character) occurred in most of the campaign media studied; however, some media are exceptions to this general rule: TV talk shows, campaign posters, and social media. I would argue that these media are "personality friendly" and emphasize character more than policy. Accordingly, I offer a prediction about these media:

H3a. *Character comments will be more frequent than policy comments in personality friendly campaign discourse (TV talk shows, campaign posters, and social media).*

Table 2.1 supports this prediction.

Research has also delved further into the nature of policy and character. Trent and her colleagues (Trent et al., 1993, 1997, 2001, 2005) have surveyed citizens and reporters during the New Hampshire presidential primary in several campaigns to discover the traits of the "ideal" presidential candidate. They investigated several characteristics: experience in office, energy and aggressiveness, forceful publish speaking, morality, discussing America's problems, honesty, gender, calm and cautious. Benoit and McHale (2003) took a different approach, classifying the character-related words in presidential television advertising. Their taxonomy of personal qualities includes four main clusters of traits: sincerity, morality, empathy, and drive. They report differences in emphasis by campaign phase (empathy is discussed more in the primary than the general campaign phase), political party of the candidates (Democrats emphasized empathy more than Republicans; Republicans stressed sincerity more than Democrats), and outcome (winners discussed drive more, and empathy less, than losers). Benoit and McHale (2004) then examined primary and general television spots, primary and general debates, and acceptance addresses to see which qualities were most often discussed. Morality was the most commonly discussed candidate character trait (36%), followed by drive (23%), empathy (22%), and sincerity (19%). Table 2.3 shows that morality was the most common personality trait overall and in four of five message forms.

Some studies have investigated specific policy issues (e.g., education, national defense, the economy). Benoit (2003c) investigated two specific policy topics, inflation and unemployment. He found a positive relationship between the rate of inflation and the discussion of inflation in presidential television spots. Similarly,

Table. 2.3. Forms of personal qualities in presidential messages.

	Primary TV Spots	Primary Debates	Acceptances	General TV Spots	General Debates	Total
Morality	639 (29%)	2495 (41%)	721 (28%)	934 (34%)	1526 (38%)	6315 (36%)
Drive	602 (27%)	1021 (17%)	652 (25%)	718 (26%)	1010 (25%)	4003 (23%)
Empathy	528 (24%)	1476 (24%)	774 (30%)	477 (18%)	611 (15%)	3866 (22%)
Sincerity	446 (20%)	1049 (17%)	465 (18%)	583 (21%)	856 (21%)	3399 (19%)

Benoit & McHale (2004).

when unemployment is higher, there is more discussion of unemployment in presidential TV spots. Hansen and Benoit (2002) found that for only 10 of 26 presidential candidates (1952–2000) was there a significant tendency for television advertising to focus most on the policy issues most important to voters. Democrats had larger relationships than Republicans in 10 of 13 elections, as did challengers versus incumbents.

6. *A candidate must win a majority (or a plurality) of the votes cast in an election.*

The last proposition might appear to be so trivial that it is not worth mentioning. However, this proposition implies several key tenets of campaigning. First, there is no need for a candidate to attempt to persuade everyone to vote for him or her. This is extremely important because some policy positions are inherently divisive and will simultaneously attract some voters and repel others. That is, many issues dichotomize the electorate. For instance, one of the distinctions between Bush and Gore in 2000 was that the former proposed private school vouchers and the latter opposed this proposal. Voters who cared about financing elementary and secondary schools probably either favored or opposed vouchers. Bush's position would simultaneously attract one group of voters and repel another group just as Gore's position would tend to attract those voters who were repelled by Bush's policy and vice versa. In 2016 Clinton's supporters tended to reject Trump's policy positions and vice versa. It is unrealistic to expect either candidate to win the votes of every citizen given the existence of divisive issues such as this one. Luckily, however, candidates need not receive all of the votes that are cast to win the election. As noted in Chapter One, the American electorate has become increasingly polarized in recent years, which means voters are more likely than ever to disagree about vote choice.

Second, only those citizens who actually cast votes matter in deciding an election. This means that a candidate does not have to win the votes of *most citizens*, but only of *most citizens who actually vote on election day*. If the supporters of one political party go to the polls in substantially higher percentages than the other party, that party's nominee is more likely to win the election. Ansolabehere and Iyengar (1995) argued that some candidates use negative television advertisements in order to depress voter turnout, hoping that those who do not vote are more likely to favor the candidate's opponent (but cf. Finkel & Geer, 1998). If candidates have used spots for this purpose that would be reprehensible. On the other hand, several candidates have explicitly attempted to encourage turn-out, which seems to be consistent with the ideals of democracy. For example, in 1964 at least seventeen of Johnson's television spots included the statement "The stakes are too high for you to stay home." Thus, it should be possible to enhance a candidate's chances of winning by increasing the turnout of voters who favor that candidate (or, although this seems deplorable, reducing the turn-out of voters who favor an opponent).

Third, presidential elections are peculiar because of the Electoral College. In a presidential election, a candidate only needs to persuade enough of those who are voting in enough states to win 270 electoral votes. This encourages savvy candidates to campaign more vigorously – e.g., spend more money on political television spots, hold more speeches and rallies – in some states than others. The 2000 presidential election underscored the importance of the electoral vote. Al Gore won the popular balloting by a margin of half a million votes, but because Bush won Florida by 537 votes, he won all of its Electoral College votes and the presidency (*New York Times*, 2001). Thus, a candidate only needs to win a majority of votes in enough states to amass 270 electoral votes to win the presidency, and that influences the placement of campaign discourse. The same situation occurred in the 2016 election: Clinton won the popular vote by 2.8 million votes but Trump because president because he won the electoral college 306 to 232 (Kreig, 2016).

Audience analysis – trying to understand an audience's beliefs, values, and attitudes – can assist candidates in making two important decisions in their campaigns (public opinion polls and candidates' private polls are vital here). First, presidential candidates must decide which states to contest. In 1960 Nixon pledged to campaign in every state (White, 1961) and lost the election, a mistake he did not make when he ran again and won in 1968 and 1972. Candidates who use national advertising buys will spend (waste) money in states that he or she is almost certain to carry as well as in states he or she is virtually certain to lose. Bill Clinton used spot media buys in 1992 to maximize his advertising in states where he and Bush were close (Devlin, 1993). In 2000 the general campaign was largely fought in a limited set of "battleground" states. Matthew Dowd, Director of Polling for the 2000 Bush campaign, explained that

> States were the crucial thing. We never put together a plan to win the popular vote. We put together a plan in the states that we targeted based on winning the electoral college vote ... [W]e never conducted a national poll after December 1999. (Jamieson & Waldeman, 2001, p. 45)

Similarly, Bush and Kerry focused their campaigns in 2004 on an even more limited group (18) of battleground states (Arizona, Arkansas, Delaware, Florida, Iowa, Maine, Michigan, Minnesota, Missouri, Nevada, New Hampshire, New Mexico, Ohio, Oregon, Pennsylvania, Washington, West Virginia, Wisconsin), with the number of contested states declining near the end of the campaign as one candidate or the other developed a lead. In 2016, Mahtesian (2016) identified 11 battleground states: Colorado, Florida, Iowa, Michigan, Nevada, New Hampshire, North Carolina, Ohio, Pennsylvania, Virginia and Wisconsin. Targeting the audience by state allows more efficient use of resources.

As noted earlier, the decision to contest only battleground states is fueled by the Electoral College rules, which declare that the candidate who wins a majority of the vote in a state wins *all* Electoral College votes for that state (Maine and Nebraska are exceptions). This means that there is no incentive for a candidate to try to win a state by a "landslide," because no more Electoral College votes are obtained by winning a state by 10 million voters instead of by a thousand. The "winner-take-all" Electoral College rules mean there is no incentive to campaign in states where one is almost certain to lose: a candidate who loses by only a few votes receives no more Electoral College votes than a candidate who receives no votes in a state. Thus, these rules encourage presidential candidates to campaign only in states in which they have a reasonable chance of winning. Research shows that voters who live in non-battleground states are short-changed, with less issue knowledge about the candidates, than voters who live where the candidates actively campaign (Benoit, Hansen, & Holbert, 2003).

Of course, candidates can use audience analysis to shape their primary campaigns as well their general election campaigns. Candidates are likely to focus their time and money on states with primaries or caucuses that will occur in the near future, and they never return to a state in the primary campaign once its primary is over. At times a primary candidate with limited resources will concentrate his or her campaign resources in a few states. For example, in the 2000 primary John McCain chose not to contest Iowa while George Bush (with a much larger campaign war chest) campaigned in both Iowa and New Hampshire. McCain knew that he did not necessarily have to win Iowa to win the Republican nomination. So, given that he had far less money than Bush, he focused his campaign on New Hampshire and won that primary. McCain did not win the nomination but he forced Bush to treat him as a serious contender even though Bush won Iowa. Thus, in both primary and general campaigns, candidates choose which states to contest to maximize the resources they have available.

Voters who lived in states with active campaigns in 2000 paid more attention to the campaign (Patterson, 2003, p. 111). Patterson also reports that data from an Annenberg Center study of the 2000 campaign reported that "residents of heavily contested primary states were 30% more likely to have particular knowledge of the candidates and issues" (p. 112). This is more evidence that campaigns do inform voters, and that voters who are not exposed to campaigns have less knowledge.

Audience analysis helps candidates make a second choice: which topics to emphasize in their messages – as well as what position to take on particular issues (or whether to be strategically ambiguous on a particular issue). Remember that a candidate must persuade a majority of those who are voting that he or she is preferable on the *criteria that are most important to those voters*. The chase for votes runs on public opinion polls and audience analysis, which influence the issues candidates decide to stress or ignore. An audience's preferences could also lead a candidate to decide what position to might take on a give issue, assuming the candidate's ideology or previous statements on that issue have not foreclosed the candidate's options.

Together, these principles suggest six specific strategies candidates can use in an attempt to maximize the probability of winning the election. First, a candidate can attempt to *increase the election day turnout of voters who prefer that candidate*. If a citizen fails to vote, it does not matter which candidate that person prefers. This means that if the same number of people prefer the two leading candidates, but more of one candidate's supporters actually vote, that candidate will win the election (indeed, a candidate with *less* support than a rival could win if his or her supporters vote at a sufficiently higher rate than the other candidate's adherents).

Second, a candidate can *seek the support of undecided voters*. Most Republicans will vote for the Republican nominee and most Democrats will vote for the Democratic nominee (although there are some vote defectors). Thus, a savvy candidate will focus much of the general election campaign on the undecided voters. In 1996, for example, we heard a great deal about the so-called "soccer moms," swing voters who allegedly held the keys to the White House. Chapter Eight will acknowledge that Independents are less likely to vote than partisans; still, the difference between the number of Republicans and Democrats is so small, and the number of Independents is so large, that Independents are important even if a smaller percentage of Independents vote than partisans.

Third, a candidate can attempt to attract *potential vote-defectors from the other political party*. Candidates are unlikely to attract votes from those partisans who are strongly committed to the other political party, but some party members have weaker connections to their party and so are willing to vote for the candidate of the other party (Nie, Verba, & Petrocik, 1999) – *if* they are given an adequate reason to do so in the candidates' campaign messages. This is a surprisingly large group, ranging from 14–27% (Nie, Verba, & Petrocik, 1999). Thus, political candidates can try to poach voters who have only soft support from their opponents.

Fourth, a candidate can attempt to *prevent members of his or her own party from defecting*. As just indicated, political candidates are not likely to lose the votes of strong partisans, but some party members may be open to persuasion from opponents. So, candidates can try to keep partisan supporters from defecting to the opposing party's candidate. We do not know how many partisans considered defecting but ultimately decided not to do so. It could be roughly the same as the number who do defect, 14–27%. As noted earlier, split-ticket voting has decreased sharply in recent years, making vote defection less common.

Fifth, candidates may attempt to *discourage voter turnout from those who support another candidate*. This strategy runs counter to the ideals of democracy and I consider it to be reprehensible, so I would never recommend it to a candidate. However, it is a possible option, and Ansolabehere and Iyengar (1995) have argued that some negative political advertisements are intended to do so.

Forms of Policy and Character

Functional Theory offers more detail on the two topics of campaign messages, policy and character. Policy remarks can be divided into three subforms, past deeds, future plans, and general goals. *Past deeds* concern the outcomes or effects of actions taken by the candidate, usually actions taken as an elected official. For example, in the 2016 Republican primary Governor John Kasich ran a radio ad ("America, Never Give Up") boasting of his record in office: "As Governor, Kasich delivered the largest tax cut in the nation and over 400,000 new jobs have been created in his state through his leadership." Donald Trump had a very different view of Kasich's record in office as this excerpt from a television spot illustrates: "Kasich gave Ohio Obamacare and increased our budget more than any other governor in the US" ("John Kasich - All Talk No Action Politician"). Past deeds can form the basis for acclaims and attacks in political campaign discourse. Note that past deeds should be particularly relevant for voters who engage in retrospective voting.

The second form of policy utterance is *future plans*. Future plans are means to an end, specific proposals for policy action. When Senator Bob Dole proposed a 15% across the board tax cut in 1996 (instead of a more general "tax cut") this illustrates a future plan. Proposing a future plan can suggest that the candidate not only knows what needs to be done, but also knows specifically how to do it. Voters may want to hear specifics rather than glowing generalities; future plans can fulfil that desire. Recall that President Clinton in 1996 attacked Dole's tax proposal as risky, illustrating an attack on a future plan.

The third form of policy utterance is *general goals*. Unlike future plans, goals refer to ends rather than means. Cutting taxes, without specifying which how much or which taxes to cut would illustrate a general goal. In the 2016 Republican primary Senator Ted Cruz declared that "Ted Cruz will. Repeal ObamaCare. Grow jobs. Destroy ISIS. Jobs, freedom, security" without providing any details ("Right"). In another spot ("Tax Plan") Cruz made a very specific proposal, a future plan: "The Ted Cruz plan ends the IRS. Replaced by a simple, fair, 10% flat tax." Both future plans and general goals concern the future, so they facilitate prospective voting, but general goals are less specific than future plans.

Character is divided into three subforms. *Personal qualities* are the personality traits of the candidate, such as honesty, compassion, strength, courage, friendliness. *Leadership ability* usually appears as experience in office, the ability to accomplish things as an elected official. Finally, *ideals* are similar to goals, but they are values or principles rather than policy proposals. These three forms of character can be used to acclaim and attack. Table A.3 in the Appendix illustrates each form of policy and character.

Functional Theory makes predictions for the forms of policy and character:

H4. General goals will be used more often to acclaim than to attack.

As noted earlier, general goals (e.g., reduce the deficit, strengthen Social Security, increase employment, fight world terrorism – but without telling how) are likely to elicit agreement from the audience. Because these goals are likely to appear desirable to most voters, who would oppose creating more jobs or combating terrorism, it is much easier to use general goals to acclaim than to attack. Keep in mind that this theory does not insist that candidates *must* use general goals more for acclaims than attacks, only that they have reasons to do so.

It is easier for a candidate to identify a goal than to develop a specific proposal or future plan to achieve that goal. Ends or general goals should require less time to develop and articulate than future plans. Use of general goals also preserves strategic ambiguity. Fewer voters would be alienated by a general goal of reducing the federal deficit, a general goal, than by specific proposals to increase taxes or decrease spending, both future plans.

Longitudinal data on the functions of general goals in all seven message forms are presented in Table 2.4. General goals are indeed used more often as the basis for acclaims (86%) than attacks (14%), confirming prediction F4. This predicted contrast occurred in every message form. This form of policy is used to acclaim from 56%-98% of the time.

Ideals are similar to general goals in that they concern principles, values, or rights that are generally viewed as desirable. Freedom, democracy, free speech, and other ideals are difficult to oppose. Thus, Functional Theory predicts that, as with general goals:

H5. Ideals will be used more often to acclaim than to attack.

Table 2.4. Functions of general goals and ideals.

	General Goals		Ideals	
	Acclaims	Attacks	Acclaims	Attacks
Announcements (1960–2016)	2243 (92%)	189 (8%)	1626 (john 91%)	160 (9%)
Primary TV Spots (1952–2016)	2136 (90%)	247 (10%)	800 (90%)	90 (10%)
Primary Debates (1948–2016)	14,815 (90%)	1712 (10%)	1757 (76%)	543 (24%)
Primary Brochures (1948–2004)	2834 (96%)	132 (4%)	526 (91%)	49 (9%)
Primary TV Talk Shows (2000, 2004, 2016)	644 (86%)	106 (14%)	184 (84%)	36 (16%)
Primary Webpages (2000, 2004, 2008)	4905 (98%)	103 (2%)	1819 (95%)	86 (5%)
Primary Social Media (2016)	637 (79%)	174 (21%)	551 (81%)	128 (19%)
Acceptances (1952–2016)	916 (89%)	114 (11%)	793 (86%)	131 (14%)
General TV Spots (1952–2016)	1167 (81%)	267 (19%)	400 (84%)	79 (16%)
Campaign Posters (1828–2020)	184 (81%)	44 (19%)	559 (99.8%)	1 (0.2%)
General Debates (1960, 1976–2016)	1149 (85%)	206 (15%)	290 (79%)	79 (21%)
Vice Presidential Debates (1976, 1984–2012)	1042 (81%)	247 (19%)	169 (94%)	11 (6%)
General Brochures (1952–2008)	2553 (56%)	1980 (44%)	438 (80%)	106 (20%)
General Radio Spots (1972–1992, 2000)	42 (69%)	19 (31%)	151 (67%)	74 (33%)
General Webpages (2000, 2004, 2008)	1766 (98%)	31 (2%)	691 (98%)	11 (2%)
General Social Media (2012, 2016)	1259 (63%)	750 (37%)	750 (84%)	144 (16%)
General TV Talk (2000, 2004)	307 (97%)	10 (3%)	131 (98%)	2 (2%)
Total	38599 (86%)	6331 (14%)	11635 (87%)	1730 (13%)

General Goals: χ^2 ($df = 1$) = 23174.36, $p < .0001$. Ideals: χ^2 ($df = 1$) = 7340.74, $p < .0001$.

Announcements: Benoit, Henson, Whalen, & Pier, 2008; Benoit & Glantz, 2013, 2020.

Table 2.4. *Continued*

Primary TV Spots: Benoit, 2014a; Benoit & Glantz, 2020.
Primary Debates: Benoit, 2014b; Benoit & Glantz, 2020.
Primary Brochures: Benoit & Stein, 2005.
Primary TV Talk Shows: Benoit, McHale, Hansen, Pier, & McGuire, 2003; Benoit et al., 2007; Benoit & Glantz, 2020.
Primary Websites: Benoit, McHale, Hansen, Pier, & McGuire, 2003; Benoit et al., 2007; Benoit et al., 2013.
Primary Social Media: Benoit & Glantz, 2020.
Acceptance Addresses: Benoit, Wells, Pier, & Blaney, 1999; Benoit, 2014; Benoit & Glantz, 2020.
Campaign Posters: Benoit, 2019.
General TV Spots: Benoit, 2014a; Benoit & Glantz, 2020.
General Debates: Benoit, 2014b; Benoit & Glantz, 2020.
General Vice Presidential Debates: Benoit & Airne, 2005; Benoit & Henson, 2009; Benoit & Glantz, 2015; Benoit & Glantz, 2020.
General Brochures: Benoit & Stein, 2005.
General TV Talk Shows: Benoit, McHale, Hansen, Pier, & McGuire, 2003; Benoit et al., 2007.
General Websites: Benoit, McHale, Hansen, Pier, & McGuire, 2003; Benoit et al., 2007; Benoit, Glantz, & Rill, 2016.
General Social Media: Shen & Benoit, 2016; Benoit & Glantz, 2020.

Ideals are much more commonly used to acclaim (87%) than to attack (13%). Table 2.4 shows that, as with general goals, this relationship occurs in each message form. This form of character is used in presidential campaign discourse to acclaim between 67% and 99.8%, confirming prediction F5. Again, this theory does not claim that candidates must acclaim more than they attack on ideals, only that they are likely to do so.

Functional Theory views political campaign discourse as the means to an end – convincing voters to cast voters for a particular candidate – which is achieved through three functions: acclaiming, attacking, and defending (on the two topics of policy and character) to create the impression that the source of the message should be considered the preferred candidate in the race. Functional Theory predicts that these functions are not equally likely to be used in campaign messages: Acclaims should be more common, defenses least common. These functions can address two topics, policy and character. Given the fact that more American voters consider policy more important than character, Functional Theory predicts that American presidential campaign discourse will address policy more often than character. Note that if more voters considered character more important than policy, Functional Theory would then predict that character utterances would outnumber policy comments. Functional Theory divides policy and character comments into more specific topics and predicts that acclaims will be more common than attacks when both general goals and ideals are discussed. These predictions are consistently confirmed through content analysis of presidential campaign discourse. Keep in mind that Functional Theory does not assert that candidates *must* conform to these predictions although most of them in fact do so.

Advantages of the Functional Approach

Functional Theory enjoys several clear advantages over other approaches to studying political campaign discourse. Televised political spots may be the most intensely studied form of campaign discourse, so I will begin by contrasting the Functional approach with previous research on political television advertising. This method is consistent with other analyses of televised political advertisements, categorizing statements in spots as negative (attacking) or positive (acclaiming). However, it adds a third function, defense, which is overlooked in most approaches to understanding the nature of televised political spots. For instance, the political action committee New Day for America refuted attacks on Kasich using a statement from Newt Gingrich: "Jeb Bush's super PAC continues to throw mud, this time about John Kasich. Newt Gingrich responded. 'Any suggestion that John Kasich is anti-defense is simply false'" (Newt). So, one advantage of the Functional approach is that it extends analysis of campaign messages to include a third function, defenses. Defenses may not be as common as acclaims or attacks, but they are distinctive utterances and they are capable of reducing perceived drawbacks (costs). Defenses occur most frequently in election debates.

Second, many studies of political television spots classify ads as concerned with policy (issues) or character (image). Functional analysis extends this work by analyzing both policy and character into finer subdivisions than does most current research: the Functional approach divides policy into past deeds, future plans, and general goals; character is divided into personal qualities, leadership qualities, and ideals. A Functional analysis of the 1996 presidential campaign (Benoit, Blaney, & Pier, 1998) revealed that Bill Clinton's television spots were more comprehensive than Bob Dole's TV ads. Clinton's ads stressed four potential ideas: He acclaimed both his own *past deeds* and his *future plans*, and Clinton attacked both Bob Dole's *past deeds* and Dole's *future plans*. However, Dole's ads acclaimed his own *future plans* but rarely praised his own *past deeds* and Dole's spots attacked Clinton's *past deeds* but rarely criticized Clinton's *future plans*. Any analysis that failed to further analyze policy utterances into those addressing past deeds and future plans could not have detected the places where Bob Dole could have acclaimed (his past

Table 2.5. past deeds and future plans in Clinton's and Dole's 1996 general TV spots.

	Past Deeds		Future Plans	
	Acclaims	Attacks	Acclaims	Attacks
Bill Clinton	117	110	44	34
Bob Dole	5	96	26	3

deeds) but rarely did, or where he could have attacked (Clinton's future plans) but rarely did. That is, such reports could only state that of these utterances, (1) 161 of Clinton's and 31 of Dole's statements were positive and (2) that 305 of Clinton's and 130 of Dole's remarks discussed policy (see Table 2.5).

A third advantage of the Functional approach stems from its use of the *theme* (idea unit, argument, claim, assertion) as the coding unit instead of the entire spot. Most previous research on political spots classifies entire spots as positive or negative. However, many television spots contain multiple utterances which may perform different functions, so each theme in an ad is categorized separately. Many political advertisements are mixed, containing both attacks and acclaims and/or policy and character, and that mix is not always 50/50. A few coding schemes add a third type of TV spot, the comparative ad. This adds only a little to the accuracy of content analysis.

Kaid and Johnston (1991) acknowledge that using the entire spot as a coding unit could affect their results: "Our method of dichotomizing the sample into positive and negative ads by determining a dominant focus on the candidate or his opponent is useful for analysis but may understate the amount of negative information about an opponent present even in a positive ad" (p. 62). To illustrate this potential problem, consider this spot for George W. Bush in 2000:

Announcer: *Under Clinton/Gore, prescription drug prices have skyrocketed, and nothing's been done.* George Bush has a plan: Add a prescription drug benefit to Medicare.
Bush: Every senior will have access to prescription drug benefits.
Announcer: *And Al Gore? He says he wants to fight for the people against HMOs, but his prescription drug plan forces seniors into one HMO selected by the federal government. Al Gore: Federal HMO.* George Bush: Seniors choose.

Italicized utterances attack Gore whereas the other remarks acclaim Bush. To describe this entire spot as *either* positive *or* negative clearly ignores or erroneously classifies part of what is being said to voters. Even classifying this as a comparative ad (which implies a 50/50 split) overlooks the fact that about two-thirds of this ad is negative and one-third positive.

Compare that ad, with both acclaims and attacks, with this television spot from the same campaign:

> 2.2 trillion dollars. That's a lot of money: 8,000 dollars for each American. It's our government's projected surplus over the next 10 years. Al Gore plans to spend it all and more. Gore's proposing three times the new spending President Clinton proposed, wiping out the entire surplus and creating a deficit again. Gore's big government spending plan threatens American prosperity.

Unlike the previous commercial, this one is entirely negative. Yet the method of coding the entire spot would "count" these two messages the same way, each one as an attack ad. Coding themes allows the analysis to more accurately represent the content of these messages.

Furthermore, television spots vary in length. Some campaigns used many 20-second spots. In the 1960s, 60-second spots predominated but that shifted in 1976, as 30-second spots became most common (Benoit, 1999). A few 15 second spots have been produced as well as a few 2 minute and 5 minute ads, but these are relatively rare. Clearly, a 60-second spot can present twice as much information as a 30-second spot. This means using the entire spot as the unit of analysis distorts comparisons of the content of spots of varying length.

Finally, using the theme as the coding unit also facilitates comparisons of different campaign messages. For example, if those who content analyze television commercials using the entire spot as the coding unit were to analyze other messages, what would they use as the coding unit? The entire speech? The entire debate? The entire webpage? Using the theme as the coding unit facilitates comparison of different kinds of campaign messages by content analyzing all messages with the same coding unit.

Some research using the Functional approach also identifies the target of attacks in the primary campaign. Benoit, Blaney, and Pier (1998) posit that primary campaign messages can have several different targets. For example, 1996 Republican primary TV spots attacked other Republican candidates, the Washington establishment, and President Clinton. Similarly, in 2000, Republican primary messages also attacked other Republicans, the establishment, and Al Gore and Bill Bradley attacked each another, the establishment, and Republicans. Surely it makes a difference whether, for example, George W. Bush's primary television advertisements attacked Democrat Al Gore or Republican John McCain. Similarly, some of the Republican primary attacks targeted Barack Obama and Hillary Clinton, whereas others criticized a fellow Republican opponent. However, previous research on television spots ignores the target of political attacks in primary campaign messages.

As suggested in the discussion of the advantages of coding by theme, the Functional Approach can readily be applied to a variety of political campaign messages: televised political spots, radio spots, debates, talk radio appearances, television talk show appearances, web pages, and nominating convention speeches. Most political campaign research focuses on television spots and debates; a number of studies also investigate Keynote Speeches and Acceptance Addresses. In recent years a case can be made that TV spots and debates are the most important messages (viewed by the most voters and arguably most influential), candidates use other messages forms (e.g., webpages, direct mail brochures, television talk show appearances) and substantial numbers of voters are exposed to them. It is clear that social media such as Twitter and Facebook will join TV spots and debates in the group of most influential campaign media.

Other scholars have endorsed Functional Theory. For example, Nai and Walter (2015) edited a book on negative campaigning, adopting Functional Theory "as a baseline for defining and measuring negative campaigning" (p. 17). Hrbkova and Zagrapan (2014), studying political leaders' debates, wrote that "The most influential attempt at systematic analysis of political debates based on a specific theoretical construct is the functional theory by William Benoit" (p. 736). Isotalus (2011) wrote that "One of the most used and systematically tested theories in the studies of the content of television debates has been functional theory" (p. 31). Maier and Jansen (2015) explained that:

> We employed Benoit's Functional Theory of Campaign Discourse in this paper for several reasons. First, it has already been shown that this approach works for different campaign messages (e.g., ads, debates, speeches, campaign coverage) and in different countries. Second, Benoit's approach is not only based on a specific definition of negativity but is embedded in a more comprehensive explanation of what the strategic options of candidates are, when candidates choose a particular strategy, and how these strategies should affect voters. Third, Geer (2006: 36) has demonstrated for televised ads aired in US presidential campaigns that the available measures of negativity are highly correlated. (pp. 5–6)

This book focuses on Functional Theory and data it has developed.

Note

1 Other scholars have addressed the functions of political campaigns at different levels of abstraction (e.g., Devlin, 1986, 1987; Gronbeck, 1978). For example, candidates need to raise money to finance their campaigns. Ultimately, though, a candidate obtains donations by convincing potential donors that he or she is preferable to other candidates. Of course, the reasons given to potential donors to convince them to contribute to a given candidate may not be identical to the reasons given to citizens to vote for that candidate. Nevertheless, it appears that the three functions (acclaims, attacks, and defenses) are more basic than other lists of functions.

CHAPTER THREE

The Role of Medium in Campaign Discourse

Lippmann (1922) recognized that almost all of our knowledge of the world is indirect; public opinion is mainly formed from the reports of others. For example, most people have heard of the city "Moscow" but how many have been there to learn about it in person? Most of us have heard about Halley's Comet but few have seen it in a telescope. The idea that we primarily learn vicariously applies to politics as well. Remember that the U.S. population is so large that it is impossible for an appreciable number of voters to learn about the candidates for the presidency and many other elective offices via direct face-to-face contact with candidates. This raises the question of *where* they obtain the information that creates and shapes their attitudes and influences their votes. For example, in the 2016 campaign election Secretary Clinton was well-known (but not universally well-liked) having been First Lady, Senator, and Secretary of State; Republican Donald Trump was widely known as a businessman and media celebrity. However, his political views were largely unknown. Few people outside his home state had heard about Senator Bernie Sanders prior to his entrance into the 2016 Democratic primary; he and his issues were better known in 2020. At the beginning of the 2020 campaign, most voters knew little or nothing about several of the candidates, including Pete Buttigieg, Andrew Wang, Tulsi Gabbard and Tom Steyer. Voters must learn *something* about the candidates in order to cast their votes. We tend to assume that voters learn about presidential candidates from the news and it does provide some information to voters. However, research has shown that the news has significant limitations as a source of voter information (Chapter Seven discusses the news in more detail). Today news media are for-profit concerns (networks were not concerned about their news operations making money in the 1960's and early 1970's) so attracting viewers is nearly always a more important motivation than informing voters.

First, the presidential campaign is but one topic in the news among many (e.g., the news reports on the weather, sports, entertainment, business, scandal, and in the summer of 2020, Covid-19 and Putin's invasion of Ukraine). Unfortunately, the trend in recent years has been for the news to devote even less time to covering the presidential campaign than in the past. Both the number of political news stories (Farnsworth & Lichter, 2003; Steele & Barnhurst, 1996) and the length of political news stories (Hallin, 1992) have decreased over time. This means that news media are devoting a steadily dwindling amount of attention to coverage of the presidential campaign, providing far less opportunity for the news to inform voters about the candidates and their issue positions. As the Internet and social media become more important as sources of our political knowledge, voters rely less on traditional news and so obtain a great deal of information about political candidates from new technology.

Furthermore, as Chapter Seven will discuss in more detail, when the news media does cover the presidential campaign, it has a clear preference for focusing on "horse-race" coverage: Who is leading in the public opinion polls? Which candidate has raised the most money? Who has received the most endorsements? Which strategies are the campaigns pursuing? Patterson (1980) observed that "In its coverage of a presidential campaign, the press concentrates on the strategic game played by the candidates in their pursuit of the presidency, thereby de-emphasizing the questions of national policy and leadership" (p. 21). Farnsworth and Lichter (2003) reported that the tendency of the news media to emphasize horse race coverage of the presidential campaign has increased over time. This focus makes sense because the news media is a business which must attract viewers or readers in order to make a profit. Patterson (1994) explained that

> Policy problems lack the novelty that the journalist seeks. ... The first time that a candidate takes a position on a key issue, the press is almost certain to report it. Further statements on the same issue become progressively less newsworthy, unless a new wrinkle is added. (1994, p. 61)

Rudd and Fish (1989) found that even when the news mentions an issue, it often does not report the candidates' positions on the issue, let alone the reasons for their positions. Research has established that coverage of presidential primary (Benoit, Hemmer, & Stein, 2010) and general (Benoit, Stein, & Hansen, 2005) campaigns discuss the horse race of campaigning more often than questions of policy or character. Furthermore, the press is much less likely to do stories on lower level offices than on the presidential campaign, providing little help to voters on these races. At times the news media provides useful information about the candidates; however, it is a mistake to assume that the news is a good source of information about the candidates and their issue positions.

Media Environment for Political Campaigns

Figure 3.1 presents a simplified version of the flow of information in a political campaign. Information generally moves from left to right, from three principal sources of information – candidates, surrogates (including Political Action Committees and individuals or groups who support a candidate), and the news media – to citizens (see Figure 3.1). Some information reaches voters directly as when a voter watches an election debate or encounters a TV spot on the election (1, 2, or 3 to 5 in the figure). Some information is seen or heard by one person who then passes it along to other voters via political discussion including social media (1, 3, or 3 to 4 and then on to 5). Information from candidates and other sources goes to the news media (1 or 2 to 3) who filter and interpret that information before sending it out to voters (3 to 4 or 5).

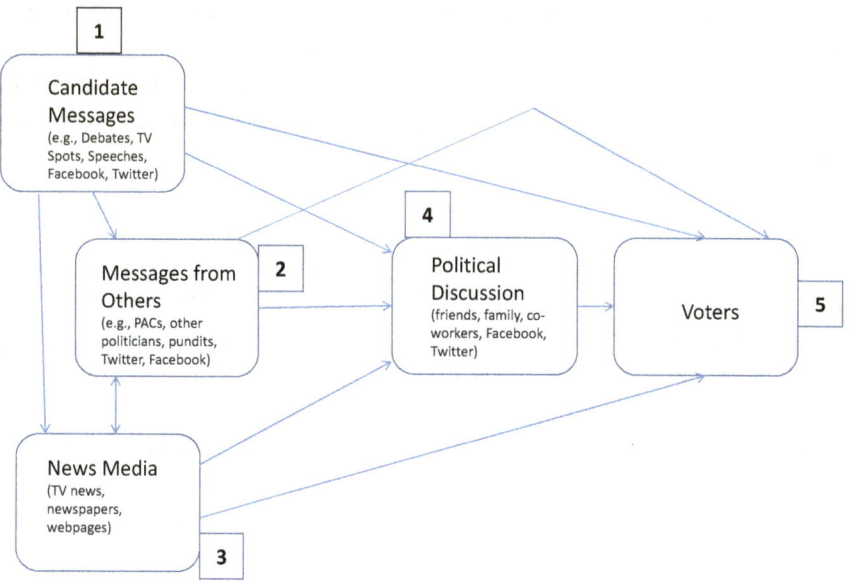

Figure 3.1. Political Campaign Information Flow

In the 1960s and 1970s most people relied on the three broadcast television networks (ABC, CBS, and NBC), sometimes supplemented by newspapers, for their political information. Some people are more interested in question of policy than other voters and people who care most about policy tend to use newspapers more often than other people (Lowden, Anderson, Dosier, & Lausen, 1994). Other voters are more oriented toward candidates' character and they may rely more heavily on television (or in recent years, social media). This situation changed dramatically as cable and satellite television emerged and offered a variety of networks to watch, a change that accelerated with introduction of the Internet and social media (Benoit & Billings, 2020). So today different voters use a different mix of media, each of which offer different pools of information to citizens (some information overlaps across media, but different groups of voters usually acquire some information that others do not possess).

As discussed in Chapter One, some scholars think a relatively small group of opinion leaders passes information along to the rest of voters (Lazarsfeld, Berelson, & Gaudet, 1948). This idea has something in common with the contemporary notion of social media "influencers." Much information does reach voters indirectly, but it is not in general filtered through a very small group of opinion leaders. In Figure 3.1 this idea would basically erase lines from 1 to 5 and 3 to 5, replacing group 4 with a small group of opinion leaders. Discussions about politics among voters does occur, as Figure 3.1 made clear, but information is not only or even primarily passed along by a small number of opinion leaders. In fact, it seems likely that when two voters discuss politics, they exchange ideas, with each person offering some information acquired from various media or from other people that the other person had not known before they interacted. Furthermore, political discussion among friends has become more frequent than ever since the emergence of social media such as Facebook and Twitter (see Amsalem & Nir, 2019).

It should be clear that the media environment in a presidential campaign is extremely complex. In today's environment of on-line resources (including social media) different voters are exposed to different sources (and different messages) and thereby acquire different pieces of information. Each voter receives a patchwork of messages from candidates, other politicians, other public figures (such as business leaders, musicians, or actors), interest groups, news, and other voters during informal discussion. Furthermore, some voters see this commercial, others see that one; some watch every debate, some watch only one, and others watch none; some people watch one network news program and others watch the news on other networks; some read local newspapers, some read a national paper (like *USA Today* or the *New York Times*), some read both local and national papers; some surf the web; some listen to talk radio; and people follow a variety of different

Twitter feeds and visit Facebook pages. Some people use these media regularly, whereas others may use these media sporadically. Even when two people read the same newspaper on the same day they may not both read all of the same stories in that paper (e.g., one reading the sports pages and the other reading the business section). Nor will two people necessarily click on the same stories in their news feeds. For many voters "politics is still far from the most interesting and important thing in life" (Ranney, 1983, p. 11; see also Patterson & McClure, 1976, pp. 123–124), which means they often pay little attention to campaign messages and may in fact actively avoid messages about the campaign. With such an incredible variety of information sources available from traditional media, social media, and the Internet it is certain that different people use some unique sources of information; it is likely that some voters share no common information sources. So, citizens use different media, to varying degrees and thus acquire different clumps of information about the candidates and their policy preferences.

The estimated 235 million Americans who were eligible to vote in 2020 are very diverse. Some are Democrats, some Republicans, and some affiliate with smaller political parties or no party at all. American voters vary by ethnicity, education level, socioeconomic level, religion, and a myriad of other dimensions. Not only is it possible that these groups will not use the same media (e.g., Republicans or conservatives are more likely than other groups to listen to or read books by Rush Limbaugh, watch FOX News, or follow Donald Trump, than Democrats or liberals). Furthermore, voters in these groups can react to or interpret a specific message differently. Jarman (2005) studied the second 2004 presidential debate between Bush and Kerry. Not surprisingly, he found that viewers evaluated their own preferred candidate more favorably than the opponent. So, even when two people do view the same message (e.g., a debate, commercial, news story, or tweet) they can draw different inferences from that message. Today, we see huge contrasts between Republicans and Democrats on their attitudes toward President Trump and other issues. For example, the president's approval rating was 8% among Democrats and 78% for Republicans in late 2019 (Bump, 2019).

Voters can also be divided into other groups that are meaningful for political campaigns besides political party affiliation. Earlier, the importance of battleground states for recent presidential elections was discussed, along with the fact that candidates did not advertise in non-battleground states (and as a result voters who live in those states tend to have less issue knowledge about the candidates). So, geographical location influences voter knowledge. Voters can also be divided according to the issues that matter to them, which sometimes parallels demographic factors. Union members often care about overtime rules, parents are concerned about the quality of education, senior citizens care about Social Security (others care about these topics, but those who belong to these groups are particularly concerned). John Kerry is a Catholic, and in 2004, some argued that the Catholic Church should not give communion to church members who support abortion. This means that voters can be meaningfully considered based on their religious affiliation. Figure 3.1 lumps all voters together for the sake of simplicity, but it is important to keep in mind that the American electorate is a very diverse group and that their backgrounds and interests can influence where they seek information and how they react to information about the candidates. Benoit and Billings (2020) argue that with the advent of cable and satellite TV, the Internet, and social media mass audiences have been "balkanized" or split into many smaller groups who likely use different media and therefore obtain different information. For example, a group of voters watch Fox News (the same idea could begin a group that watches CNN or MSNBC). Some of those Fox News viewers also visit the Breitbart webpage while others view different conservative websites such as RedState or DailyCaller. Some voters watch Fox News, look at Breitbart's webpage, and follow Republican Representative Jim Jordan on Twitter. Some watch Fox News, look at Breitbart's webpage, and follow Senator Lindsey Graham. The possible combinations are endless and each of these conservative voters receives some of the same information as others but also obtains some different information. And they very likely receive different information than most Democrats.

Campaign Media are Dynamic

It is important to realize that this complex media environment has changed in the recent past and continues to evolve today (see, e.g., Johnson, 2021). Shaw (2001) identified three key aspects of campaign media: outlets, access, and receptivity. The sheer number of media outlets available to voters has increased dramatically over the last five decades. The VHS tape recorder was invented in 1976 (WSIU, 2002). VHS, video-tapes (and more recently DVDs), and satellite television provide additional media alternatives that may drain viewers away from other media and messages such as debates. CNN was launched in 1980 (WSIU, 2002). Shaw (2001) pointed to the growth in cable news networks from to include Headline News, CNBC, MSNBC, Fox News, and C-SPAN. These networks are based on broadcast television.

The Internet is an example of a completely new medium brimming with information about candidates and campaign issues. Social media have burst upon the scene and Donald Trump made Twitter a focal point for his campaign for the Republican nomination and for president in 2016. Twitter and Facebook allow people with common interests to connect far more easily and quickly than in the past even if they live far apart. Social media is particularly useful for reaching one's supporters, who often follow the candidate. These changes in the mass media–new technologies and increasing market penetration of technologies – have significant effects on political campaigning.

Overall, television is the medium named by almost half of respondents as the source they turn to most often for news (Shearer, 2018; see Table 3.1). News webpages are the second most frequently used source for news (33%), followed by radio (26%), social media (20%) and print newspapers (16%). Notice that when respondents from 18–29 years old are broken out separately, social media (36%) and news webpages (27%) are most commonly named news as a source of information. Television and radio are chosen for news by only 16% and 13% of this group, respectively. Clearly, preferred sources for news are shifting and vary by age (and other demographic factors).

Consistent with this observation, Benoit and Hansen (2007) have shown that the frequency with which voters use various media to learn about the presidential campaign varies over time. Reported use of newspapers, radio, and debates have decreased significantly over time (1952–2000). Political discussion with friends, family, and co-workers has increased over time. The Internet is a comparatively new medium and use of the world wide web is increasing (Taylor, 2003). Voters use different media to learn about presidential candidates and their issue positions. Note that the word "use" should not be taken to mean that all voters actively seek out information about the campaign; some people "use" media they cannot avoid, such as television spots.

Changes in access can be seen in the increased market share or penetration of these media outlets. In 1940, 80% of US homes had radio (Caslon Analytics, 2003). CBS began commercial broadcasting in 1941 (WSIU, 2002) but even by 1945 only 10,000 homes had television (Caslon Analytics, 2003). By 1956, 71% of households had television sets, a figure that increased to 97% by 1969 (Caslon Analytics, 2003). In 1980 only 1% of US households owned VCRs; VCR

Table 3.1. Which source is used most often to get news.

Source	Total	18–29 years old
Television	49%	16%
News Websites	33%	27%
Radio	26%	13%
Social Media	20%	36%
Print Newspapers	16%	2%

Sherer (2018) Pew Research Center.

penetration surpassed 50% in 1987 (WSIU, 2002). A year later, in 1988, half of all households had cable television but even in 1995 cable penetration was 64%, not quite 2/3 of homes (WSIU, 2002). In 1982, 200 computers were connected worldwide via the Internet; the first Internet browser was not developed until 1991; Microsoft's Internet Explorer was released in 1995 (Caslon Analytics, 2003). Twitter and Facebook, as well as other social media, exploded in popularity recently. Statista reported that in 2016, 78% of Americans had a social media profile. Clearly, access to media has changed dramatically during the last half century. Gottfried, Barthel, Shearer, and Mitchell (2016) found that "91% of U.S. adults learned about the 2016 presidential election in the last week." They also compared several media to see useful in learning about the campaign. Media were considered most useful in learning about political campaigns to a varying extent. For example, cable TV news was ranked highest, followed by social media, local television, and news websites/apps. The evening network news was ranked sixth; print newspapers came in at ninth. Looking at campaign news specifically rather than at news in general, Table 3.2 shows displays the reported usefulness of various news sources for learning about the 2016 election.

Receptivity, or the use of media, is yet a third way media are changing. Benoit and Hansen (2004a) reported significant declines in the percentage of people who reported learning about presidential campaigns from newspapers, radio, and debates. Use of magazines and television did not show a clear trend up or down over time. Political discussion among voters as a source of campaign information

Table 3.2. Relative usefulness of media in learning about the 2016 campaign.

Source	Usefulness
Cable TV News	24%
Social Media	14%
Local TV	14%
News Website/App	13%
Radio	11%
Nightly Network News	10%
Late Night Comedy	3%
Local Print Newspaper	3%
National Print Newspaper	2%
Issue-Based Group Website/App/Email	2%
Candidate or Campaign Website/App/Email	1%

"Percent who name each source type as most helpful." Gottfried, Barthel, Shearer, & Mitchell, 2016.

increased significantly over time. There is no question that the use of Internet and social media to learn about political candidates has skyrocketed.

Benoit and Hansen explained that some of these changes in media use reflect declining audiences. For example, the Newspaper Association of America (2002) reports that daily newspaper readership in 1964 was 80.8% and in 1997 it was 58.3%. The percentage of daily newspaper readers dropped significantly over time. It is not surprising that fewer people report reliance on newspapers when readership is declining substantially. Important changes have occurred in other media as well. An average of 24.4% of the population watched the general election presidential debates between 1960 and 2016. One cannot be informed or influenced by a message one does not see or hear (although it is possible to learn about a message such as a debate second-hand). Again, use of social media to learn about politics has increased substantially in recent years (see Benoit & Billings, 2020). These changes in access and use of media have important implications for citizens (who learn about presidential candidates and campaign issues from media), candidates and their advisors (who must see that their messages reach voters), the news media (whose purpose is to inform voters), and scholars (who seek to understand campaigns and voting).

We should also be aware that just as there are changes in the media environment – and the relative impact of various media – between campaigns, there can be differences within a single campaign. Debates are often held near the end of the general campaign, so this medium cannot possibly inform or influence voters who are forming their opinions in the early part of the campaign. When debates occur, and many voters watch one or more debates, other media probably have less impact as voters who watch a debate cannot the news or surf the Internet while they attend to debates. The "dual screen" phenomenon – e.g., using the Internet on a laptop or smart phone while watching television or using a smart phone along with a laptop – does occur, but there is an inherent trade-off here: The more attention given to the second screen, the less attention is paid to the television and vice versa. We simply cannot pay as much attention to one message when using a second message at the same time as we can when watching only one message (see Benoit & Holbert, 2010; Miller, 1956). Of course, accessing the Internet or social media during a debate will probably provide some information that would not be acquired from watching television alone. Nevertheless, the information obtained from single and dual screening is not the same.

It is also possible that candidates might schedule a last minute blitz of television spots, which could increase the influence of these messages at the end of the campaign. Presidential candidates broadcast a variety of television spots over the course of a campaign. Benoit, Bough, and Hansen (2004) showed that the relative influence of various media shifted during the presidential campaigns in 1992, 1996, and 2000.

Campaign Media Have Key Differences

The idea that different media have different characteristics seems obvious; it is important to understand how they vary. I have argued for two claims about the media: (1) voters are exposed to different media mixes (different voters are exposed to messages from different information sources) and (2) the media environment is dynamic (new media emerge while others decline in importance). These ideas are important because the various media are quite different. This observation may seem so obvious as to be trivial. However, it is important to realize the extent to which the various media differ as well as to understand how they differ. The information provided in the news media overlaps but is not identical.

Obviously, radio has sound, which newspapers lack, although newspapers but not radio can display pictures, graphs, and charts. Television (and the Internet) has written text, sound, and pictures but it can also display video. It is clear that different media can contain different information, which means that people who rely on different media for learning about the world will receive different information. Furthermore, DeFleur et al. (1992), for example, found that information from a news story presented in a newspaper (and on a computer screen) was remembered better than when the same story was presented via television or radio. This means that even when the same information is presented via different media, the impact of information can vary by medium.

Second, diverse media offer voters different information about political candidates in particular. For example, Lichter and Noyes' (1995) study of the 1992 presidential campaign that "The candidate's own speeches actually discussed policy issues far more frequently and in considerably more detail than did either print or broadcast [news] reports" (p. xvii). As mentioned above, research into both presidential primary (Benoit, Stein, & Hansen, 2005) and general newspaper coverage (Benoit, Hemmer, & Stein, 2010) found that news reports mainly focused on the horse race (fund-raising, polls, campaign events) rather than on policy or character. Newspaper articles also reported on attacks more often than the candidates actually make in their campaigns. Newspapers also discuss character (rather than policy) more than the candidates discuss character. Different information sources offer different content to users.

In fact, different messages from the same candidate in different media can offer voters different content. For example, in the 2000 presidential campaign, Benoit et al. (2003) found that both George W. Bush and Al Gore emphasized character twice as much as policy (67% to 33%) on television talk shows; but in every other medium studied (television spots, debates, webpages) these candidates discussed policy much more frequently than character. Furthermore, when presidential candidates discussed policy, specific issue emphases (e.g., education, taxes, Social Security) varied from medium to medium. For example, the three issues addressed most frequently in Bush's TV spots were the economy, health care, and Social Security but in the debates he emphasized national defense, taxes, and education (Benoit et al., 2003). Clearly, when different media provide different information to voters it matters a great deal *which medium* voters use during presidential campaigns.

Second, as Chapter One argued, the various media offer different information to voters. That means that it matters very much *where voters obtain their political information*, because they will obtain different information from different media. I do not want to overstate the case; messages from different media have some overlap in content; it is probably better to say content varies in emphasis across media. However, at times the contrast in content between campaign media can be quite sharp. For example, Benoit, McHale, Hansen, Pier, and McGuire (2003) analyzed five candidate media in the 2000 presidential campaign. One of the categories they investigated was issue topic. Governor George W. Bush did not discuss Social Security on any of his television talk show appearances; Vice President Al Gore mentioned it a single time on one of the three shows. However, the issue of Social Security was mentioned repeatedly in other media. Table 3.4 shows that although every medium studied here acclaimed most and defended least, differences in functions occurred across media. The emphasis on acclaims varied from 63% to 92% in these media. The topic of campaign discourse varied across media: five media stressed policy whereas three emphasized character. Within these two groups of media further differences emerged: policy emphasis in media that stressed policy varied from 56% to 83%. In media that emphasized character, this stress on character varied from 53% to 80%. Furthermore, Chapter

Table 3.3. Number of themes on Social Security in 2000 general campaign.

Medium	Bush	Gore
Television Spots	15	21
Debates	24	25
Webpage	25	74
Television Talk Shows	0	1

Benoit, McHale, Hansen, Pier, & McGuire (2003).

Table 3.4. Functions and topics of major forms of presidential campaign discourse.

	Functions			Topics	
	Acclaims	Attacks	Defenses	Policy	Character
TV Spots 1952–2016	10722 (64%)	5959 (35%)	151 (1%)	9653 (56%)	7549 (44%)
Debates 1948–2016	36014 (63%)	17882 (31%)	3191 (6%)	11980 (67%)	5914 (33%)
Announcements and Acceptances, 1952–2016	9332 (75%)	3098 (25%)	60 (0.5%)	6694 (63%)	3856 (37%)
Direct Mail 1948–2004	15812 (77%)	4754 (23%)	55 (0.3%)	14402 (67%)	7111 (33%)
Social Media 2012, 2016	7723 (63%)	4372 (36%)	113 (1%)	5276 (43%)	6875 (57%)
TV Talk Shows 2000, 2004, 2008, 2016	4213 (65%)	1681 (26%)	601 (9%)	2767 (45%)	3332 (55%)
Candidate Webpages 2000–2008	23686 (92%)	1948 (8%)	34 (0.1%)	20943 (83%)	4426 (17%)
Campaign Posters 1828–2012	1463 (92%)	134 (8%)	0	314 (20%)	1283 (80%)
Total	108965 (71%)	39828 (26%)	4205 (3%)	72029 (64%)	40346 (36%)

Functions: χ^2 (df = 1) = 111266.69, $p < .0001$. Topics: χ^2 (df = 1) = 8932.7, $p < .0001$.

Each medium includes both primary and general campaign messages.
TV Spots: Benoit, 2014a; Benoit & Glantz, 2020.
Debates: Benoit, 2014b; Benoit & Glantz, 2020.
Acceptances and Announcements: Benoit, Henson, Whalen, & Pier, 2008; Benoit & Glantz, 2013; Benoit, Wells, Pier, & Blaney, 1999; Benoit, 2014; Benoit & Glantz, 2020.
Direct Mail: Benoit & Stein, 2005.
Social Media: Shen & Benoit, 2016; Benoit & Glantz, 2020
Campaign Posters: Benoit, 2019.

Four contrasts messages from Democrats and Republicans. Data reported there show that Democrats emphasized "Democratic issues" (e.g., jobs, health care, environment) whereas Republicans stressed "Republican issues" (e.g., national defense, crime, or immigration). However, considering only Democratic candidates, their messages varied in the extent to which they addressed Democratic issues (38% to 73%) just as Republican candidates varied in their emphasis of Republican issues (33% to 72%). Clearly, it matters very much which media a voter uses because there are several differences in the content of messages in different media or from different candidates.

Political candidates use a variety of media to reach voters, including radio and newspaper advertisements, stump speeches at rallies, and bumper stickers. This chapter will discuss several particular campaign media, such as television spots, debates, social media, and acceptance addresses.

Television Spots

The earliest political television commercial, in 1950, was broadcast by Senator William Benton in Connecticut (Wisconsin Public Television, 2001). The first presidential television spots were aired in the 1952 campaign between Democrat Adlai Stevenson and Republican Dwight Eisenhower (and both primary and general campaign messages survive from this campaign). Television spots are usually relatively brief (the two most common lengths are 60 and 30 seconds, although Eisenhower in 1952 broadcast a series of 20-second spots called "Eisenhower Answers America," Wood, 1990). Spots of one minute were most common until 1976; in recent years most television advertisements have been 30 seconds (Benoit, 1999). For a discussion of the history of political television spots, spot, see Benoit (2003a, 2014a), Devlin (1977, 1982, 1987, 1989, 1993, 1997, 2001, 2005), Diamond and Bates (1993), Jamieson (1996) or Levine (1995); for a discussion of negative advertisements in particular, see James and Hensel (1991), Johnson-Cartee and Copeland (1993, 1997), or Procter and Schenck-Hamlin (1996). Kaid (2004) discusses the nature and effects of political advertising.

This kind of message has an important advantage: TV spots are ubiquitous on broadcast television. Other media require some effort on the part of voters: Voters must select the proper channel at the proper time to watch the news on television; they must pick up a newspaper to read about the campaign (and they must look beyond the sports, business, or lifestyle pages); they must select the proper channel, day, and time in order to see a presidential debate. Television spots might be considered stealth messages: It is difficult for voters to avoid them. Spots seek out voters without any effort on the viewers' part. The logic of all advertising, of course, is to buy time on a program that people watch and then hope that the audience does not leave the room or ignore the television until the commercial break is over. Political advertising is no different in strategy for reaching the audience. Patterson and McClure (1976) explain that political "ads seek out the individual. As people sit in front of their television sets in order to be entertained, commercials intrude with political information the viewer has made no effort to discover" (p. 125). This means that ads may have the greatest impact on those who are less interested in, and less well-informed about, the campaign.

Kamber (1997) explained that "Television ads ... are the most effective means of conveying information to the voter, especially those who are relatively uninvolved, those who do not follow politics and are unlikely to seek out candidate information on their own" (p. 42). Patterson and McClure's study of the effects of political spots in the 1972 campaign found that "televised presidential commercials contributed heavily to the political education of the individuals who were least attentive to newspapers" (1973, p. 125). Research shows that television spots do influence voters. Some studies use advertisements created by the researchers, which provides greater control over the message features being studied; ads can be made identical except for the variable being studied by the researcher. Other research uses ads created by politicians, which provides greater realism or external validity. Both kinds of studies report that television spots influence voters. Experimental research using spots developed by researchers (Becker & Doolittle, 1975; Cundy, 1986; Donohue, 1973; Garramone, Atkin, Pinkleton, & Cole, 1990; Hill, 1989; Meadow & Sigelman, 1982; Roddy & Garramone, 1988; Rudd, 1989; Thorson, Christ, & Caywood, 1991) documents ad effects. Similarly, studies which utilize advertisements that were created by candidates (Atkin, 1977; Basil, Schooler, & Reeves, 1991; Christ, Thorson, & Caywood, 1994; Faber & Storey, 1984; Faber, Tims, & Schmitt, 1993; Freedman, Franz, & Goldstein, 2004; Garramone, 1984, 1985; Garramone & Smith, 1984; Geiger & Reeves, 1991; Hitchon & Chang, 1995; Johnston, 1989; Just, Crigler, & Wallach, 1990; Kaid, 1997; Kaid & Boydston, 1987; Kaid, Leland, & Whitney, 1992; Kaid & Sanders, 1978; Lang, 1991; McClure & Patterson, 1974; Merritt, 1984; Newhagen & Reeves, 1991) also confirms effects from these messages. Patterson and McClure (1973) also noted that "the effects of advertising centered almost entirely on people who ignored the newspaper" (p. 125). So, televised political advertising may be most important for those voters who are least well-informed. Again, remember that over the last decade or so, broadcast television has lost many viewers.

As just indicated, a large number of studies have looked at the effects of political advertising. Benoit, Leshner, and Chattopadhyay (2007) conducted a meta-analysis of this literature (meta-analysis is a statistical method of adding together the results of several studies). Ads can significantly increase issue knowledge, influence perceptions of the candidates' character, alter attitudes, alter candidate preference, have an agenda-setting effect and influence voter turnout. Of course, every individual spot does not have all, or even any, of these effects, but ads do influence voters. A given spot may have no effect on the audience but as a group TV spots have substantial effects.

Many people view many ads and they see some particular ads repeatedly. West (2001) noted that "television ads are a major component of political races. In recent presidential campaigns, campaign spots have comprised around 60% of total fall expenditures" (p. 2). Jamieson observed that this investment of campaign budgets allows candidates to reach voters:

> Political advertising is now the major means by which candidates for the presidency communicate their messages to voters. As a conduit of this advertising, television attracts both more candidate dollars and more audience attention than radio or print. Unsurprisingly, the spot ad is the most used and the most viewed of the available forms of advertising. (1996, p. 517)

In the 2000 campaign Goldstein and Freedman (2002b) reported that almost 300,000 presidential television spots were broadcast in the top 75 markets. These messages are important because they reach many voters and they may reach voters who pay little or no attention to other campaign media. The record fund-raising levels in 2004, coupled with the fact that the general campaign essentially began on March 4, insure that new records for ad broadcasting will be set in 2004. Considering all offices, PQ Media estimated that in 2004 over $1.5 billion would be spent on broadcast television political advertising; $676 million was spent in 2000 and $912 million in 2002 (Lieberman, 2004). Combining the presidential candidates, the DNC and RNC, and non-candidate advertising, $580 million was spent on presidential television advertisements in 2004, airing over 675,000 times in battleground states and on cable (Anderson, 2004; see also Devlin, 2005). The television spot has traditionally been an extremely important medium for political campaign messages.

Candidate (and later President) Donald Trump changed political campaigns dramatically. His media preferences shifted from those of past candidates, spending more effort on social media and spending less money on television spots: In 2016, total spending on presidential television advertising dropped for the first time in recent history (still, $2.4 billion dollars were spent on the 2016 presidential primary and general election campaigns; Ingraham, 2017). However, anyone who thinks television spots are irrelevant only needs to turn on the television in 2020 to dispel this idea. Bycoffe (2020) reported that 300 spots had been aired for about $455 million through February 9, 2020. Only one primary or caucus (Iowa) had occurred at this point in time; the general election vote would not occur until almost seven months later.

Of course, the media environment is changing. Now, with DVDs, cable TV, satellite TV, and the Internet many voters can escape most television advertising (advertising can now be found on webpages and social media). Also, the shift to campaigning only in battleground or swing states (see Chapter Five) has influenced which voters are exposed to certain messages: Voters who live in non-battleground states see few or no ads on television and can attend no candidate rallies in their own states. Still, television spots are a means of reaching many voters, some of whom might otherwise be exposed to little or no campaign information in other media.

The relatively short length of television spots is a limitation. There is no question that 30 seconds is a brief message. However, other campaign messages have time limitations as well. The network news is 30 minutes long, but that figure includes commercials and non-campaign topics. The average television political news story in 1988 was 147 seconds (about two and a half minutes), a figure that had fallen from previous years (Hallin, 1992). The length of a sound bite from a candidate quoted in television news dropped to only 9 seconds in 1988 (Hallin, 1992). As mentioned above, the news focuses on "horse-race" coverage rather than on informing voters about the policy proposals or character of the candidates (see also Chapter Seven).

General debates are usually 90 minutes long and primary debates range from 60 to 120 minutes, but this too is deceptive. The time limit includes questions, not just candidate statements, and it can include commercial breaks in primary debates. In a primary debate the total time, often an hour, can be divided between as many as 10 or more candidates. Perhaps more importantly, the candidates' responses to each question are usually limited to between 30 and 90 seconds. The *entire debate* is far longer than a single television spot, but a 60 second answer to a question in a debate about education permits no more detail than two 30-second television spots about education.

Another way to look at this is to compare the total length of messages. If two candidates participate in a general campaign debate, this gives each candidate less than 45 minutes to address voters (90 minutes divided by two candidates; the time for questions and transitions by the moderator will further reduce the time candidates can talk to under 45 minutes). Kaid and Johnston (2001) reported the number of spots created for each candidate. If we focus on the campaigns after 1976, the point at which most spots became 30 seconds long (Benoit, 1999), the average presidential candidate produced 65 spots, which converts into 32.5 minutes of spots. Thus, adding together all of the answers and rebuttals in one general debate is not that much more air time (considerably less than 45 minutes after questions and comments from the moderator are subtracted) than adding together all of the spots produced in a campaign (32.5 minutes). Of course, some voters may see more than one debate – but most television spots are aired repeatedly during a campaign. So, the amount of time in an individual spot is limited, but the limit is not as severe as one might imagine, when limitations of other media are considered.

Diamond and Bates (1993) argue that the typical advertising campaign moves through four phases. First, candidates use ID spots, which "hammer home the candidate's name repeatedly and often show it on screen as well" (p. 297). They also note that, because their names and faces are already familiar to voters, incumbent candidates "frequently turn to the props of the presidency in their ID spots. The Hot Line, Air Force One, and the Oval Office are favorites" (p. 305). The second phase, argument spots, tell us "what the candidate stands for" (p. 306). Most argument spots are not very specific. The third phase is to attack opponents. The last phase identified by Diamond and Bates is the vision spot, which they label "I see an America ..." (p. 339). These four phases are useful concepts, but it must be kept in mind that Diamond and Bates looked for tendencies or emphases; one should not assume, for example, that attacks can only be found in the third portion of the campaign.

Some scholars have argued that negative television advertising has a "demobilizing effect," discouraging some voters from going to the polls (Ansolabehere & Iyengar, 1995; Ansolabehere, Iyengar, Simon, & Valentino, 1994). Others have questioned these studies and provided evidence that attack advertising may mobilize voters and increase turnout (see, e.g., Finkel & Geer, 1998; Kahn & Kenney, 1999; Wattenberg & Brians, 1999). It seems likely that negative advertising probably has different effects on different voters, discouraging some from voting while energizing others who go to the polls to punish the mud slingers. A meta-analysis of the effects of watching positive and negative ads did not reveal a consistent demobilization effect (Lau, Sigelman, Heldman, & Babbitt, 1999).

Finally, some research indicates that attacks in television spots may decrease the percentage of votes received by the attacker (Benoit & Hansen, 2003). Research also suggests that voters detest attacks on character more than attacks on policy (Johnson-Cartee & Copeland, 1989). Candidates whose television spots attack more on character (and therefore who attack less on policy) than their opponents are significantly more likely to lose elections (Benoit, 2003). Thus, negativity in television advertising could influence voter both turn-out and the votes received by candidates (voting will be discussed in more detail in Chapter Eight).

Functions of Political Advertising

Research has investigated the content of political television spots. West (2001), studying a sample of 433 "prominent" spots from 1952 to 2000, found that 44% of the ads were positive and 56% negative. However, his sample was biased toward negative ads: West selected spots mentioned in Jamieson's (1992) book (for 1952 to 1988) and ads broadcast on the *CBS Evening News* (for 1992–2000). However, Jamieson did not intend to select random, typical, or "prominent" ads to discuss in her book. Jamieson, Waldman, and Sherr (2000) observed that West's unusual sampling procedure "biases his analysis toward controversial attack ads" (p. 50; cf. Benoit, 2001b). Kaid and Johnston (2001), who analyzed 1204 presidential television spots from 1952 to 1996, found that 62% of these commercials were positive (acclaimed) and 38% negative (attacked). However, they report that the number of negative ads varied over time: Negative spots spiked at 68% in 1992.

The results of the Functional analysis of television spots summarized here is closer to those reported by Kaid and Johnston than West, which is not surprising, given the non-representative nature of West's sample. Table 3.4 reports the data for presidential television spot functions in both primary and general campaigns, 1952–2016.

Acclaims account for about two-thirds (64%) of the themes in these spots. For example, in the 2020 campaign, a Trump spot (American comeback, 2020) declared that "We've built the greatest economy the world has ever seen." This statement is designed to praise the president's first term accomplishments. About one-third of the statements in television spots (35%) were attacks. For example, Trump created a TV spot that displayed black and white photos of Democrats (such as Bill Clinton, Hillary Clinton, Barack Obama, Nancy Pelosi, and Chuck Schumer) while Trump said "For too long a small group in our nation's capital has reaped the rewards of government while the people have borne the costs" (Forgotten no more, 2020). This constitutes a clear attack on the opposition party. Finally, TV spots used defense in 1% of the utterances. Bush illustrated defense in his 2000 primary spot: "One of my opponents says my tax cut for America is too big, too bold. Another has raised questions about my record. They're both wrong. In Texas, you're only as good as your word. In 1997 I cut taxes $1 billion. In '99, I cut taxes nearly two billion more." This excerpt identifies an attack (two attacks, in fact) and rejects them.

Chapter Four, discussing the influence of source on political campaign messages, contrasts ads sponsored by political parties or non-candidate ads (those sponsored by Political Action Committees or 527 groups [named after a provision in the campaign finance reform law]) with candidate ads. The data reported there indicate that non-candidate groups (political parties, PACs, 527s) are likely to attack more and acclaim less than ads from candidates.

Topics of Political Advertising

The research on the nature of televised political advertising, contrary to what one might expect, tends to report that policy (issues) is discussed more than character (image) in these messages. West (2001), studying 433 spots from 1952 to 2000, reported that 61% mentioned issues. Kaid and Johnston (2001) reported that 66% of spots address issues and 34% image. Geer (1998), analyzing 4177 ads from 1960 to 1992, reported that issues accounted for 50% of ads, personal qualities 21%, and value appeals 21%.

Table 3.4 also displays the results of Functional content analyses of the topics discussed in presidential television spots. These data represent both primary and general presidential television spots from 1952 to 2000. In these campaign messages, policy constitutes almost six of every ten utterances. In 2020, Biden ran an ad (Oppenheim, 2020) showing Trump golfing while a bar graph displaying the increasing Covid-19 deaths in America. This message is clearly an attempt to argue that Trump is relaxing rather than dealing with the pandemic. The president's alleged responsibility for a pandemic is a clear example of a policy topic. Television advertisements also discussed character in 42% of their statements. A spot supporting Biden declared that "no one is more qualified" to be president (Iowa ad, 2020). This messages focuses on his qualifications rather than his policy proposals. So, political television spots discuss both policy and character.

Presidential television spots are an important form of campaign message. Most money is spent on these message forms and they reach millions of voters, including ones who have little interest in seeking out information about the candidates. Voters do learn from spots. Television spots acclaim almost twice as much as they attack and they rarely defend. Television spots focus more on policy than character. Interestingly, Patterson and McClure's (1976) study of the effects of television advertising in the 1972 presidential election found that "advertising image-making had no effect" (p. 111), but that "where image appeals fail, issue appeals work" (p. 116). They explained that "During the 1972 presidential election, people who were heavily exposed to political spots became more informed about the candidates' issue positions" (p. 116). This may not be so surprising if the content of these messages focuses on policy more than character.

Televised Debates

One reason political campaign debates are important is the sheer size of the audience they attract. Stelter offers several comparisons to help appreciate the huge size of primary debate audiences:

> The audience easily exceeded pretty much everything that's been on American television this year, from the finale of "The Walking Dead" to the final episode of David Letterman's "Late Show." The debate was bigger than all of this year's NBA Finals and MLB World Series games, and most of the year's NFL match-ups. It also trumped Jon Stewart's Thursday night's sign-off from "The Daily Show," which averaged 3.5 million viewers. (2015)

The first Republican debate had the largest audience of 2016, but the audience for all debates was very large. Nielson (2016) found that the first six Republican and first six Democratic debates "reached 97 million Americans, with about equal numbers watching the Democratic debates (68 million) as those that watched the Republican debates (67 million)." Nielson also reported the number of viewers for each political party's debates: "about 30.2 million viewers watched only the Democratic debates while roughly 29.2 million viewers only viewed the Republican debates. Additionally, 37.8 million viewers watched both debates" (2016). Notice that on this one dimension (which party's debates did you watch?) the overall primary debate audience is divided into three smaller audiences who were exposed to different messages: watched only Democratic debates, only Republican debates, and debates from both parties.

General election debates also enjoy many viewers. Benoit (2014b) reports that the total audience for American presidential general election debates through 2012 is a staggering 1.7 billion people. The three general election debates between Clinton and Trump attracted over 222 million viewers; the Kaine-Pence vice presidential debate was watched by 37 million people (Nielson, 2017).

One of the earliest and best-known political debates featured Abraham Lincoln and Stephen Douglas. Even though Lincoln and Douglas ran against each other for president in 1860, their debates were not presidential debates. In 1858, a series of seven debates were held between Lincoln and Douglas during the campaign for a U.S. Senate seat from Illinois. Douglas won the election in which these debates occurred, but two years later Lincoln beat Douglas in the presidential election of 1860 (see Benoit & Delbert, 2009).

The earliest presidential debate occurred in a Republican primary campaign in Oregon in 1948 (Kane, 1987). This confrontation featured Thomas Dewey and Harold Stassen. It may be the only debate to feature a proposition ("Should the Communist Party in the United States Be Outlawed?"). Dewey won the Republican nomination but subsequently lost the general election to Harry S Truman. Records for early primary debates are haphazard, but it appears presidential primary debates were held in every campaign since with the exceptions of 1952 and 1964 (Benoit et al., 2002).

The first presidential debate held during a general election campaign involved Vice President Richard M. Nixon and Senator John F. Kennedy (note that months earlier, during the 1960 primary campaign, Kennedy engaged in a debate with Hubert Humphrey in West Virginia; see Berquist, 1960; Stelzner, 1971). Nixon and Kennedy debated four times in the general election campaign and Kennedy won a very close election. Some scholars believe that those who heard Nixon on the radio thought he did better than those who saw him on television, but this idea has been questioned (Kraus, 1996; Vancil & Pendell, 1987).

No general debates were held in 1964, 1968, or 1972, although there were Democratic primary debates in 1968 and 1972. President Lyndon Johnson did not want to debate in 1964 (perhaps he did not want to contribute to the impression that Senator Barry Goldwater had equal status with Johnson). In part due to the fact that he debated Kennedy and lost in 1960, Nixon did not debate in either 1968 or 1972. However, general campaign debates were revived again in 1976 as President Ford wanted to jump-start his lagging campaign. Every campaign since 1976 has included at least one debate between the Republican and Democratic nominees for president. In 1980, Governor Ronald Reagan had one debate with President Jimmy Carter and another one with Congressman John Anderson (who had lost the Republican nomination to Reagan during the primary and was running as an Independent at the time of their debate). Primary debates frequently feature multiple candidates, but the only general debate with more than two contenders occurred in 1992 when H. Ross Perot joined President George Bush and Governor Bill Clinton. Even though Perot ran again in 1996 he was not allowed to participate in those debates (the Commission on Presidential Debates had established criteria for qualifying to debate and Perot did not meet the criteria in 1996). One vice-presidential debate was held in several campaigns (1976, 1984–2016).

Political debates are unlike traditional debates. After the Dewey-Stassen primary debate of 1948, the candidates answered questions instead of giving opposing speeches. Usually questions are asked by a moderator and/or a panel of reporters, occasionally questions are solicited from voters, and sometimes primary debates allow candidates to question each other. Thus, a more apt description than "debate" might be "joint press conferences" (Auer, 1962; Jamieson & Birdsell, 1988).

The fact that political debates are built around questions is very important because those questions constrain the topics candidates can talk about. Candidates do have some freedom to discuss what they wish. Debates may include an opening statement or closing remarks from each candidate. Candidates at times will use part of their time to discuss a topic different form what was asked by a question. President Bill Clinton in 1996 even suggested a topic to the moderator in the first debate of 1996: "Mr. Lehrer, I hope we'll have a chance to discuss drugs later in the program." This suggestion appeared to work because Lehrer's next question was about drugs. At times debates can be characterized as a struggle between the questioner(s) and the candidates for control over the topic of debates. Sometimes a candidate will ignore the question and return to a prior topic. In the November 24, 2003 IA Democratic primary debate, Tom Brokaw asked Governor Howard Dean whether he thought "Saudi Arabia is our friend." Dean replied, "Let me first ... correct an important thing that Dick Gephardt just misinformed us about," concerning legislation authorizing Operation Iraqi Freedom. He ended his interjection by asking, "Now what was the question?" Dean proceeded to address Brokaw's question after it was repeated, but he was determined to refute Gephardt's earlier statement on a different topic. Still, candidates almost always address the topic of the question they are asked.

Sometimes candidates will start with the topic of a question and shift to the message they want to give voters. In that same debate just mentioned, Brokaw asked Representative Dick Gephardt whether he considered Ariel Sharon, prime minister of Israel, to be "a man of peace." Gephardt began by saying that "we can lead to peace in the Middle East." However, he immediately shifted from Sharon, or the Middle East, to a wide-ranging attack on President Bush: "The president's foreign policy is a horrible failure, discussing Bush's policies in the Middle East, on global warning, with the International Criminal Court, and in North Korea." Brokaw reiterated his question, "My question was do you think that Ariel Sharon is a man of peace?" Gephardt said that "the people in Israel, the great majority, want peace," still refusing to answer Brokaw's question. This exchange illustrates the struggle between candidates and questioners about the topics candidates should discuss in a debate. In this case, the candidate said what he wanted and the question went unanswered.

However, it is easy to criticize some of the questions asked in debates. I am not certain that the information which would best help Democrats choose between the Democratic contenders is whether one of them thinks Ariel Sharon is a man of peace (and Brokaw made no attempt to ask other candidates, so voters could not have compared the candidates on this question even if Gephardt had answered it). Arguably a worse question was asked by Robert Maynard of Jimmy Carter in the third 1976 debate: "Can you tell us what caused the evaporation of [your] lead" in public opinion polls (Benoit & Hansen, 2001)? This question treats Carter as a political pundit, asking him to explain the horse race, why Carter's lead had decreased. This question has nothing to do with Carter's qualifications for president or his policy proposals. How can the answer to this question help voters decide whether Carter or Ford would be a better president? Similarly, in the September 9, 2003 Democratic primary debate, Farai Chideya asked the candidates "What's your favorite song?" Is this really the most useful question that could have been asked? Perhaps even more sadly, the candidates appeared to have anticipated this question and had prepared answers ready.

A second criticism is that it appears that some journalists, rather than seeking to enlighten voters with their questions, are attempting to embarrass or show up the candidates. Benoit and Hansen (2001) discuss a question Marvin Kalb asked of President Reagan in the second debate of 1984:

> Mr. President, you have often described the Soviet Union as a powerful evil empire intent on world domination. But this year, you have said, and I quote: "If they want to keep their Mickey Mouse system, that's O.K. with me." Which is it, Mr. President – Do you want to contain them within their present borders and perhaps try to reestablish detente or what goes for detente or do you really want to roll back their empire?

Benoit and Hansen (2001) observe that "Kalb is intent on catching Reagan in a contradiction – forcing him to focus on justifying his statements on policy rather than on explaining his policy or on contrasting his policy with Mondale's alternative .... The voters' interests can be ignored as journalists pursue personal aggrandizement" (p. 138). Matera and Salwen (1996) suggest a motive for journalists other than helping voters make a decision about who should be president: "Journalists whose questions elicit candidates' gaffes are praised by fellow journalists for their tough, penetrating questions" (p. 309). This is surely not in voters' best interests.

Another criticism of the questions journalists ask in presidential debates is that they ignore the concerns of voters. Benoit and Hansen (2001) content analyzed the topic of questions asked in debates by issue (e.g., taxes, jobs, defense) and correlated this with the public opinion poll data about which issues were most important to voters at the time of the debates. If you expect that more questions were asked about the issues which were most important to voters, you would be wrong. There was no relationship between which issues were most important to voters and which issues were addressed most frequently in questions. The results indicate that journalists were not using their questions to enlighten voters on the topics that matter most to voters. McKinney contrasted the town hall debates in

1992 and 2004. Although both debates featured questions written by voters, in the latest debate the moderator selected which questions would be asked. In 1992, there was a significant relationship between the importance of a topic to voters and the number of questions asked about that topic. However, in 2004, when the moderator decided which citizen question would be asked, there was no relationship between a topic's importance to voters and the number of questions asked on that topic.

General campaign debates in 1960 were 60 minutes long; each general debate since then has been 90 minutes. Three election years (1984, 1988, 1996) featured two debates; seven campaigns (1976, 1992, 2000, 2004, 2008, 2012, 2016) had three debates, 1960 had four and 1980 saw one debate (between the Republican and Democratic nominees; Ronald Reagan and John Anderson also debated in 1980 when Anderson was running as a third party candidate). Smith (2015) observed that "the average vote" in elections with debates "was 99 million and the average debate audience was 56 million, so it seems safe to infer that most voters watched at least one debate" (p. 241). Although tens of millions continue to tune in to debates, the number of viewers (and the percentage of voters) who watch them has slipped over time (viewership did increase in 2004).

Debates are important for several different reasons. First, they reach millions of voters. Remember that Nielson (2016) reported that the combined audience for the first six Democratic and Republican primary debates in 2016 had a combined audience was 97 million. Benoit (2014b) said that the total audience for general election debates from 1960 through 2012 was 1.7 billion – and over 222 million watched the Clinton-Trump debates of 2016. Benoit (2014b) also reported that between 1976 and 2012, 418 million watched the vice presidential debates; another 37 million watched the Kaine-Pence vice presidential debate that year. The potential for influence for debates is vast because the audience is so large. Candidates' statements (and non-verbal behavior) are the subject of many news messages, much political discussion, and many social media messages. This extends the potential reach of debates beyond those who watch them.

Debates have important advantages over other media as well. They are particularly helpful to voters because they present the two (or three) leading candidates in the general campaign (or many candidates in the primary campaign). Although candidates display creativity in responding to questions (and previous statements), usually they do address the same topic, allowing voters to directly compare the two candidates on a topic (unlike, for example, television spots). The fact that the candidates are together and speaking live means that it is possible for one candidate to correct misstatements (deliberate or accidental) by an opponent. An advantage for candidates is that debates are free, if you are invited to participate. Nor surprisingly, third party candidates, such as Green Party nominee Ralph Nader in 2000, and their supporters, complain that they are unfairly excluded from debates.

Research has established that debates have several effects on those who watch them (see Holbrook, 1996; McKinney & Carlin, 2004; Racine Group, 2002; Shaw, 1999b). Patterson (2003) reported that according to Vanishing Voter surveys, "Citizens learn more about the candidates during the ninety minutes of an October debate than they do in most other weeks of the campaign" (pp. 170–171). Benoit, Hansen, and Verser (2003) conducted a meta-analysis of the effects of watching presidential debates (a meta-analysis is a way to statistically combine the results from several studies). They found that watching general campaign debates can increase issue knowledge and issue salience (the number of issues a voter uses to evaluate candidates; this concerns the concept of priming discussed in Chapters One and Seven). Debates can change voters' preferences for candidates' issue stands. Debates can have an agenda-setting effect, increasing the perceived importance of the issues discussed in debates. Debates can alter perceptions of the candidates' personality (e.g., honesty, compassion) but they have not been shown to affect perceptions of the candidates' competence (leadership ability). Debates can affect vote preference among viewers. Other research indicates that debates can polarize voters (Warner & McKinney, 2013). Benoit, Leshner, and Chattopadhyay (2007) report that primary debates can also increase issue knowledge, influence perceptions of candidates' character, and alter voter preferences. They also found that the effects from primary debates are larger than for general debates, probably because voters have less information about candidates in the primary than the general campaign. Clearly, debates have effects on the voters who do watch them.

It seems likely that debates will be even more important in non-battleground than battleground states. As noted earlier, presidential candidates since 2000 have limited their campaign appearances and ad buys to battleground states. Although those who live in such states still have access to other media (the Internet, news, social media), they are deprived of the information provided directly by the candidates, and in fact those citizens who lived in non-battleground states had less accurate issue knowledge than those who lived where the candidates actively campaigned (Benoit, Hansen, & Holbert, 2004). This means that debates are even more important sources of information to voters in the states ignored by the candidates.

Functions of Presidential Debates

The Functional approach has content analyzed all of the general presidential debates (and vice-presidential debates) that have occurred in the U.S. though 2016. Unlike

TV spots, other research on debates (not based on the Functional approach) does not content analyze these messages for functions or topics. Combining primary and general debates, acclaims account for 62% of utterances in presidential debates (see Table 3.4). In the 2020 Democratic presidential primary, Elizabeth Warren praised her qualifications:

> I believe the principal job of the commander-in-chief is to keep America safe. And I think that's about judgment. I think it starts with knowing our military. I sit on the Senate Armed Services Committee. I work with our generals, with our military leaders, with our intelligence, but I also visit our troops. I visit our troops around the world. I've been to Afghanistan, to Iraq, to Jordan, to South Korea. I've been to lots of places to talk with our troops. (1/14/20 Des Moines)

She indicates that her experiences mean that she is prepared to be president, a clear example of an acclaim (this is an acclaim on character, leadership ability). Joe Biden called attention to his past work on Iran and nuclear weapons:

> I was part of that deal to get the nuclear agreement with Iran, bringing together the rest of the world, including some of the folks who aren't friendly to us. And it was working. It was working. It was being held tightly. There was no movement on the part of the Iranian government to get closer to a nuclear weapon. (1/14/20 Des Moines)

Most Democratic primary voters would see this as a desirable accomplishment, so it illustrates an acclaim (this acclaim concerns policy).

Attacks comprise 33% of statements in debates. Amy Klobuchar attacked President Trump's withdrawal of troops from Syria: "In Syria, I would not have removed the 150 troops from the border with Turkey. I think that was a mistake. I think it made our allies and many others much more vulnerable to ISIS" (1/14/20 Des Moines). Bernie Sanders also used attack in this debate: "In America today, our infrastructure is crumbling. Half of our people are living paycheck to paycheck. Eighty-seven million people have no health care or are uninsured or underinsured. We got 500,000 people sleeping out on the streets tonight. The American people are sick and tired of endless wars which have cost us trillions of dollars" (1/14/20 Des Moines). Surely his audience would find these conditions unacceptable. These excerpts illustrate attacks in campaign messages and both happen to relate to policy.

In debates, 5% of statements were defenses or refutations of attacks. Reports indicated that Sanders told Warren that a woman could not win the presidential election. Biden responded that "Well, as a matter of fact, I didn't say it .... Anybody knows me knows that it's incomprehensible that I would think that a woman cannot be president of the United States. Go to YouTube today. There's a video of me 30 years ago talking about how a woman could become president of the United

States" (1/14/20 Des Moines). This defense rejects the accusation as false. Warren criticized the health care plans presented by Pete Buttigieg and Biden:

> The problem is that plans like the mayors and like the vice president's is that they are an improvement. They are an improvement over where we are right now. But they're a small improvement. And that's why it is that they cost so much less, because by themselves, they're not going to be enough to cover prescriptions for 36 million people who can't afford to get them filled. (1/14/20 Des Moines)

Buttigieg responded by rejecting this attack: "It's just not true that the plan I'm proposing is small" (1/14/20 Des Moines). Election messages use acclaims, attacks, and defenses.

Maier and Jansen (2015) tackle the question of when candidates attack using data from 46 televised German debates (41 for state offices, 5 for national offices) – "all American-style debates ever held in Germany" (p. 5). They identify four factors that influence the amount of attacks produced in a debate. Challengers attack more than incumbents. Those candidates who are behind in public opinion polls attack more than those who lead in the polls. Debates using a town hall format have fewer attacks than other formats of debates. Attacks occur more often in national than state debates.

Topics of Presidential Debates

Research based on the Functional approach has also investigated the topics of presidential debates. Primary and general presidential debates together address policy in 70% of their utterances. See Table 3.4 for these data. In a Democratic primary debate from 2020, Biden declared that "If I'm elected president, I'll reinstate all the mileage standards that existed in our administration which were taken down. That's 12 billion gallons of gasoline to be saved immediately" (1/14/20 Des Moines). This proposal is likely to be viewed favorably by his audience, the hallmark of an acclaim. When asked about Senate votes on military action in Iran and Afghanistan Biden said that "I was asked to bring 156,000 troops home from that war, which I did" (1/14/20 Des Moines). Moving American troops out of harms way concerns military policy and is likely to be considered desirable by his audience.

In contrast, 29% of debate themes discuss character. In the 2020 Democratic primary, Biden criticized the Republican incumbent: "Donald Trump is corrupt. He is a pathological liar and he is a fraud" (1/14/20 Des Moines). These statements clearly attack the President's character. Amy Klobuchar acclaimed her leadership ability in this debate: "I've been in the U.S. Senate for over 12 years. And I think what you want in a president is someone who has dealt with these life-and-death issues and who has made decisions" (1/14/20 Des Moines). The Senator is clearly touting her qualifications for the Oval Office.

Debates provide voters with an extended opportunity to view the leading candidates side-by-side. Despite declining audiences, debates still attract tens of millions of viewers. Watching debates can affect voters' knowledge of candidates' issue positions and perceptions of their character—as well as their vote choice. More than twice as many utterances in debates concern policy as character and a minority of comments function as defenses. Over twice as many remarks address policy as character. Debates are an important medium for candidate messages.

Finally, research has also investigated the content of vice presidential debates (Benoit & Airne, 2005; Benoit, 2014b, Benoit & Glantz, 2020), which have occurred in ten presidential campaigns so far (1976, 1984–2016). These events attract many viewers (an average of 42 million compared with an average of 50 million watching the presidential debates of the same campaigns). Vice presidents acclaim more than they attack and rarely defend (53%, 41%, 6%) and they discuss policy more than character (67%, 33%).

The Internet and Social Media

This section discusses the Internet and social media as forms of election campaign communication. The Internet emerged in 1970 from a Department of Defense contract for ARPANET (Advanced Research Projects Agency Network). Commercial Internet service providers first appeared in the 1980s (History of the Internet, 2016). The Internet grew rapidly: The amount of information moved via two-way telecommunication using the Internet was 1% in 1993, 51% in 2000, and over 97% in 2007 (History of the Internet, 2016). Statista (2019a) reports that in the United States in 2019 293 million people used the Internet. Overall, Google processes about 70,000 search requests every second or about 2 trillion searches per year (Prater, 2020). The Internet is an incredible resource for connecting people today.

Email was also made possible through the Internet. In 1973 ARPANET developed standards for sending email messages (Email, 2017a). According to Internet Live Stats (2017), over 175 billion emails were sent on February 14, 2017. Lenhart (2015) found that 64% of teens use email to communicate with friends. Contemporary instant messaging began in the 1990s (Instant messaging, 2017). Lenhart (2015) reported that 79% of teens sent instant messages to friends. Statista (2017) predicted that in 2017 28.2 trillion mobile messages will be sent worldwide. Many people seem to be shifting to greater use of mobile messages and less reliance on email.

Social media are widely used to connect people today. 79% of the U.S. population uses social media including 170 unique million monthly Facebook users and 121 million unique monthly Twitter users (Statista, 2019b). The average number of Facebook account friends was 338 in 2019 (Bandwatch, 2019a); the average number of Twitter followers was 707 (Bandwatch, 2019b). Literally millions of people rely on these social media.

The Internet and social media are now a staple of election campaigns (see, e.g., Johnson, 2021). In the U.S., about 25% of candidates had campaign websites in 2001; today, almost all candidates have a webpage (Gainous & Wagner, 2014). According to Twitter, in 2016 one billion tweets (not all from candidates, of course) concerned the election between August 2015 and November 2016 (Coyne, 2016).

Candidate Campaign Webpages

The Internet has quickly become an important medium for contemporary campaigns. Internet penetration has increased rapidly for this new medium. In 1995, only 9% of adults in the United States had Internet access; by the end of 2002 two-thirds could surf the net (Taylor, 2003). Many sites are available on the web, from news organizations, political parties, interest groups, political candidates, and others. This section will focus on the web as a means for candidates to reach voters.

As early as 1996, "campaigns often provided their Website addresses (URLs) in brochures, on the air, and in speeches" (Cornfield, 2004; Bimber & Davis, 2003; Davis, 1999). Of course, not everyone visits the candidates' webpages, but many do. In August of 2000, over three-quarters of a million people had accessed Al Gore's and George W. Bush's webpages ("A Whole New," 2000). During the 2004 Democratic primaries, Governor Howard Dean raised over $3.8 million in only nine days, $3 milllion on the Internet (Yoon & Snow, 2003). The Internet as a campaign communication medium is now well-established.

Benoit and Benoit (2005) identify advantages and disadvantages of the World Wide Web for political campaigning. This medium has eight advantages for candidates. The Internet is a "master medium," which can disseminate information through various media, such as text, pictures, audio, and video. Second is the huge and growing potential audience for this medium. A third benefit is that webpages are less expensive than other media, such as television spots. Fourth, unlike news, journalists and reporters do not filter and interpret the content of a candidate's webpage. A webpage allows for quicker responses to changing campaign conditions or new attacks. Sixth, webpages can provide longer and more complete messages to voters. A seventh advantage is that the Internet (and email) allows precise targeting of audiences. Benoit and Benoit observed that:

> A well-designed Web site can provide information on both the candidate's character and positions on the issues. Voters can decide which information to access when they visit a Web site. Those voters who consider character paramount can spend most, or all, of their time on a Web site learning about the candidate's character. Voters who care more about issues or policy can devote their time to acquiring information about the candidate's issue positions. (p. 234)

In short, candidates can put a great deal of information on their Webpage and, with effective navigation tools, allow voters to select and view only the information that appeals to them; in effect, voters can tailor the candidates' Web messages to suit their own needs and interests. Finally, the Internet opens up the possibility of interactivity with voters.

Benoit and Benoit identify five advantages of the Internet for voters. First, it feeds the public's desire for information, an additional source of knowledge and opinions about the campaign. Second, the Internet is increasingly available to voters (another implication of the fact that increasing Internet penetration creates a larger audience for campaign messages). Third, the Internet allows voters to access information when it is convenient to them. Fourth, as hinted above, unlike other media such as debates or television spots, voters can control which information they view on a Webpage. Finally, the Internet provides voters access to multiple sources (both candidates, news organizations, third parties).

Four disadvantages or limitations of the Internet for candidates were also identified. First, even though Web access is increasing, "some voters are not connected to the Internet" and, furthermore, "many of those who use the World Wide Web do not visit candidates' Web sites" (Benoit & Benoit, 2005, p. 234). Third, although webpages are comparatively inexpensive, their cost will increase as they are used more extensively. Finally, connections to the Internet as well as hardware and software employed by users vary widely (which may particularly impact the quality of video on the web).

Benoit and Benoit also identified three disadvantages or limitations for candidates. First, as suggested before, the potential audience reached by a Webpage is large and growing but candidates cannot hope to reach every voter through this medium. Second, voters must be able to find the candidates' Internet sites. They point out that during the 2000 presidential election, "Gore2000" connected surfers to a webpage selling bumper stickers and campaign buttons rather than the Vice President's campaign webpage. The Internet possess both advantages and disadvantages for the candidates who produce them and the voters who visit them; clearly it is established as a new and important campaign medium.

Wiese and Gronbeck (2005) identified six important developments in cyberpolitics in the 2004 campaign:

Table 3.5. Functions and topics of presidential campaign webpages 2000, 2004, 2008.

	Functions			Topics	
	Acclaims	Attacks	Defenses	Policy	Character
2000 Primary	95%	5%	0.1%	79%	21%
2004 Primary	88%	12%	0.1%	72%	28%
2008 Primary	85%	15%	0.1%	81%	19%
Primary Mean	89%	11%	0.1%	77%	23%
2000 General	98%	2%	0	90%	10%
2004 General	98%	2%	0	75%	25%
2008 General	92%	8%	0	82%	18%
General Mean	96%	4%	0	82%	18%
Overall Mean	93%	7%	0.05%	80%	20%

Sources: Benoit, McHale, Hansen, Pier, & McGuire (2003); Benoit et al. (2007); Benoit et al. (2013); Benoit, Glantz, & Rill (2016).

(1) The introduction of network software and theory....; (2) the move to expand databases functions ... ; (3) the incorporation of coproduction features ...; (4) the entrenchment of Web video and Web advertising ...; (5) the evolution of candidate Web sites into a standard genre ... ; and (6) the introduction of blogs. (p. 221; see also Williams, 2005)

Thus, an important new weapon in the political campaign arsenal is the campaign webpage.

The Functional Theory has investigated presidential candidate campaign webpages from 2000 through 2008 (keep in mind the fact that this sample is more limited than the samples for several other message forms). Candidates in these campaigns used acclaims most often (93%), followed by attacks (7%) and defenses (0.05%). These messages were much more likely to address policy (80%) than character (20%). See Table 3.5 for these data.

Social Media

As noted above, the Internet enables the use of social media, which includes a variety of platforms, including Facebook, Twitter, Instagram, and Snapchat. Instagram, for example, allows uses to share text, pictures, and videos. Snapchat sends video and messages but these are only available online for a limited time. These media are quite distinct from traditional media such as newspapers or television. Traditional media (such as newspapers, television) exemplify mass media in the sense of a source sending a message to many people in the audience. People choose which medium to use and which network or stories to consume. Unless the television program is recorded a person watches from the beginning to the end (or from when they turn on the program to when they turn it off). Newspapers allow consumers a more choice: A reader can choose to read the front page or the business page or the sports page. These traditional media offer little in the way of interactivity or feedback from the audience to the source (although public opinion polls allow newspapers and others to learn something about users). This section will focus on Facebook and Twitter as campaign media.

In sharp contrast to traditional media, Gainous and Wagner (2014) explained that "each individual in a social network chooses whether to read, redistribute, or even add to each stream of information that comes to them" (p. 11). Reliance on newspapers and television and radio news puts the candidates' information under control of the media (gate keepers), who decide what information from candidates to relay to voters – and decide whether to comment favorably or unfavorably on those candidate ideas. Of course, candidates decide which ideas to include in their TV spots and what to say in debates. Auter and Fine (2016) explain that social media allow "politicians to maintain direct control of their messages to potential voters, bypassing the distortive gate keeping function of media. Additionally, unlike costly national campaign tools, social media campaigning is cheap, requiring only the setup and maintenance of a (free) account." Someone does have to create the content, and more elaborate Internet and social media presence requires a larger staff, but they campaign has total control over the content of the candidates' Facebook pages and Twitter feeds. Traditional campaign media often used common content, with the same ideas and often the same words appearing in speeches, debates, and TV spots. But today social media can disseminate that information and make it relatively easy to offers unique content (putting content on social media is quicker and cheaper than, e.g., creating new TV spots).

Facebook

Facebook went online in 2004; it was initially limited to students at Harvard University (History of Facebook, 2017). This early version of social media was opened to other Universities and eventually it was made available generally. This medium allows people to share content (e.g., messages, photos, videos) with one another via the Internet. Users develop Facebook pages with the information they want to share with their friends. Reposting occurs when one Facebook users takes content from one Facebook page (e.g., a candidate's page) and places it on his or her own Facebook page where it can seen by the friends of the reposter. Each piece of information from a candidate's Facebook page that is reposted on another Facebook page extends the reach of the candidate's message. It is also possible to like a post which may increase the post's visibility.

Many people use Facebook: 47% of users got news on Facebook in 2013; by 2015 this had risen to 63% (Lichterman, 2015). Internet Live Stats (2017) reported that on February 2017, Facebook had over 1.8 billion active users. The percentage of registered voters who follow on social media sites such as Facebook and Twitter doubled from 2010 to 2014 (Anderson, 2015). In the 2016 presidential campaign, Donald Trump's Facebook page reported 21 million friends; Hillary Clinton's Facebook page reported 10 million friends. Some of these "friends" are actually fake accounts, but it is clear that millions of people followed the 2016 presidential candidates on Facebook.

Borah (2016) analyzed the Facebook pages of presidential candidates from 2008 (Obama vs. McCain) and 2012 (Obama vs. Romney). Overall, acclaims were more common than attacks (59% to 41%). However, the two Republican candidates (McCain and Romney) attacked more than they acclaimed, while their common opponent – Obama – relied more on acclaims. Obama utilized more appeals to enthusiasm; McCain and Romney relied heavily on fear appeals. She found most posts served to promote the campaigns (e.g., announcing candidate appearances in person or on TV and radio). Policy was the second most common type of post after promoting the campaign; no instances of posts on character were reported here (it is not clear whether Borah looked for posts about character). Shen and Benoit (2016) examined the Facebook pages of Obama and Romney in the 2012 general election campaign. Acclaims were the most common function (60%), followed by attacks (39%), and defenses (1%). Policy was about three times as common as character (76% to 24%). Analysis of Facebook pages in 2016 found that acclaims were most common than attacks in primary but not general pages (Benoit & Glantz, 2020). Contrary to expectations character was more common than policy in both phases of the campaign (Benoit & Glantz, 2020). The Pew Research Center examined links on 2016 presidential Facebook pages: "78% of Trump's links in Facebook posts send readers to news media stories while 80% of Clinton's direct followers to campaign pages" (Pew, 2016). These candidates' pages offered much information to voters.

Auter and Fine (2016) analyzed the Facebook posts of all Senate candidates in 2010. They reported clear patterns of attack. Competitive races produced more attacks than non-competitive races. Candidates who trailed in the polls made more posts than the leading candidates. Posts that attacked addressed issues over twice as much as they discussed character. Competitive races produced more issue attacks than non-competitive canpaigns. Finally, candidates who were behind in the polls were more likely to attack than leading candidates.

Wen (2014) employed Functional Theory to analyze Taiwanese Facebook posts in the 2012 presidential election campaign. He found that both candidates acclaimed most often, attacked second most often, and defended least often. The incumbent acclaimed more and attacked less than the challenger. These candidates discussed policy more frequently than character. These findings are consistent with the predictions of Functional Theory.

Functional Theory has been used to investigate Facebook use in the U.S. in 2008, 2012, and 2016 (and MySpace in 2008). Facebook posts conformed to Functional predictions with 61% acclaims, 39 attacks and 1% defenses. However, this form of social media stressed character (60%) more than policy (40%). See Table 3.6 for these data. The evidence suggests that social media tend to focus more on character than most other campaign media.

Table 3.6. Functions and topics of political campaign social media.

	Functions			Topics	
	Acclaims	Attacks	Defenses	Policy	Character
Facebook					
2008 Presidential Primary	198 (99%)	1 (1%)	0	53 (27%)	144 (73%)
2012 Presidential General	1177 (60%)	754 (39%)	16 (1%)	1471 (76%)	460 (24%)
2016 Presidential Primary	1162 (73%)	416 (26%)	16 (1%)	569 (36%)	1009 (64%)
2016 Presidential General	1165 (49%)	1186 (51%)	24 (1%)	766 (33%)	1575 (67%)
Total Facebook	3702 (61%)	2357 (39%)	56 (1%)	2159 (40%)	3188 (60%)
MySpace					
2008 Presidential Primary	259 (88%)	34 (11%)	3 (1%)	173 (48%)	188 (52%)
Twitter					
2016 Presidential Primary	3136 (71%)	1234 (28%)	38 (1%)	1844 (42%)	2526 (58%)
2016 Presidential General	626 (45%)	747 (54%)	16 (1%)	400 (29%)	973 (71%)
2016 Governor, Senate, House	3193 (68%)	1509 (32%)	18 (0.4%)	2151 (46%)	2541 (54%)
Total Twitter	6955 (66%)	3490 (33%)	72 (0.7%)	4395 (42%)	6040 (58%)
Grand Total	14109 (65%)	7390 (34%)	149 (0.7%)	9678 (45%)	11961 (55%)

Sources: Shen & Benoit, 2016; Benoit & Glantz, 2020; Stein & Benoit, 2021

Twitter

Twitter was launched in 2006 (Gainous & Wagner, 2014, p. 77). This program allows one user to follow another (somewhat similar to being a "friend" in Facebook). A person creates a Twitter feed and those who are interested can choose to follow it (this means the posts from the originator appear on the follower's news feed). Originally tweets were limited to 140 characters (although it is possible to generate several tweets on the same topic) and can include comments, links to webpages, pictures, and other content. In 2017 Twitter doubled the maximum number of characters to 280. 52% of users got news on Twitter in 2013; by 2015 it had increased to 63% (Lichterman, 2015). Internet Live Stats reported that on February 14, 2014 over 475 million tweets were sent this day between over 307 active Twitter users (2017). In 2016 Hillary Clinton's Twitter feed had 13.3 million followers; Trump's feed attracted 25.1 million followers. Again, even though some of these accounts are fake, millions of people followed these candidates' Twitter feeds.

Twitter, like Facebook and other social media, enables users to have a "dual screen" experience: watching one thing (such as a political debate) while tweeting or reading tweets from others. In 2012, "over 50,000 Obama-related tweets per minute were happening" (Gainous, 2014, p. 6). This example the dual-screen phenomenon probably means less attention to the debate but more information from others' tweets. This is different, for example, than the experience voters had when watching a presidential debate before the Internet exploded. One could, of course, read Facebook pages or use other features of the Internet while using media – and some do so – but Twitter's relatively short messages lend themselves more to dual-screening than other social media or Internet sites.

Gainous and Wagner (2014) analyzed tweets from members of congress and leading candidates in the 2010 congressional elections. The most common topic of these message is campaign announcements (44%), followed about equally by character (19%), attacks (18%), and policy (17%). From the standpoint of Functional Theory, these categories raise concerns because attacks can occur on either policy or character. Challengers used Twitter more frequently than incumbents, 66% to 34% (Gainous & Wagner, 2014, p. 82). They also reported that members of the GOP tweeted more than Democrats and candidates for the Senate seats tweeted more often than candidates running for House seats.

In the 2016 presidential campaign, the main candidates used Twitter in quite different ways: "Only Trump tended to include members of the public in his reposts: 78% of his retweets were from members of the public, compared with none of Clinton's and 2% of Sanders'" (Pew, 2016). In 2012, "over 50,000 Obama-related tweets per minute were happening" (Gainous, 2014, p. 6). The GOP candidate's approach could well have had made his followers likely to feel valued (if Mr. Trump retweeted my tweet, it must be important) and feel as if they were part of the campaign, part of the on-going "conversation." Another contrast is that most of Trump's tweets linked to news media stories; the majority of Clinton's tweets linked to her webpage (Pew, 2016). This meant the Democratic candidate's tweets tended to simply repeat other content from her campaign, they were less likely to include new or unique information. Why read Clinton's tweets if they were no different from her webpage?

Data from Functional analyses are available for candidates' use of Twitter in 2016: presidential primary tweets, general presidential tweets, and tweets in non-presidential races (governor, senate, house). As with the other social media discussed above (Facebook), tweets conformed to the prediction for functions (65% acclaims, 34% attacks, and 0.7% defenses) but not for topics (character 55%, policy 45%). These data are displayed in Table 3.6.

At the dawn of campaigning, candidates used speeches and broadsides (posters). To these they added newspaper ads, direct mail pamphlets, radio ads, debates, and television spots. Each added medium simply meant another channel to reach voters with the same message. Early candidate webpages resembled a resume (Benoit, 2000). As time went on, these websites became more sophisticated. Initially, political candidates saw social media as just another way to reach voters. However, candidates and their campaign advisors are finding other uses for social media: connecting with supporters. Traditional media such as debates, TV spots, and speeches do not connect voters with candidates like social media.

Social media allow candidates to reach voters with comparatively little cost; candidates with large budgets may create more lavish posts or tweets, but those with less funds can still reach many voters at little cost. Tweets are arguably easier to consume than Facebook pages because tweets are limited to 280 characters. It is important to realize that voters who consume candidate webpages, Facebook pages, and Twitter feeds are largely self-selected. The news media sometimes reproduce candidate messages from the Internet, and one who does not follow a candidate could encounter that some of that candidate's messages by following someone else who reposted or retweeted the candidate's idea. Still, because friending and following are most likely to occur from those who like the candidate, social media seem better designed to reach supporters than voters who do not support a candidate, better at reinforcing than changing attitudes.

In 2016, Donald Trump relied on Twitter and Facebook (and the free publicity from comments many thought were outrageous) to reach voters. He retweeted and reposted messages from some of his supporters, involving them in his campaign as no presidential candidate had ever done. He relied less on television advertising in 2016 than any recent major party presidential candidate (although President Trump raised millions of dollars and is planning to run ads the second time around, Dawsey & Lee, 2020; Rosenberg & Roose, 2019). Social media use by political candidates will never be the same.

Nominating Convention Acceptance Addresses

The political party nominating conventions once were used to select the party's nominee for president. This lent both drama and suspense to the proceedings. However, protests at the divisive 1968 Democratic Convention in Chicago grew violent and the nation watched in horrified fascination. Some believe this divisive convention hurt Hubert Humphrey's chances to defeat Richard Nixon (see, e.g., Bartels, 1988; Davis, 1997).

Many Democrats were also dissatisfied with the fact that Humphrey became the nominee without campaigning in a single primary. Vice President Humphrey stepped aside during the primary season as President Lyndon Johnson sought the Democratic nomination again. However, Johnson dropped out of the race late in the primary season, almost certainly due to widespread discontent with the Vietnam War, too late for Humphrey to run a solid primary campaign. In order to prevent someone from becoming the nominee without having campaigned in the primaries, both political parties changed their procedures and expanded the system of primary elections. As primaries became more important, nominating conventions became less and less critical.

Today the identity of the nominee is known months in advance of the convention. Instead of *choosing* a nominee the conventions of today *celebrate* the nominee. The convention is oriented toward the television audience rather than to the delegates who are physically present at the convention. Conventions are now viewed as an opportunity to woo voters through free television time and the candidates carefully control what is shown to the public (Patterson, 2003): "Both parties in 1996 and 2000 presented tightly choreographed gatherings that kept any sign of division off the convention floor" (p. 117) and therefore off voters' television sets.

Not surprisingly, given the lack of suspense and the attempt to use them as long commercials, television networks have reduced the coverage of these events. Patterson (2003) reported that "In 1976, each of the major networks – ABC, CBS, and NBC – broadcast 25 hours of coverage of each convention. By 1984, that average had fallen to 12 hours. It was a mere 5 hours in 2000" (p. 119). In 2004, the broadcast networks devoted only 3 hours to each national convention, although cable networks did show more of the conventions. Nor surprisingly, audiences shrank as the number of hours dropped: a "46% decline in convention ratings between 1976 and 2000" (Patterson, 2003, p. 168). The potential influence of the national nominating conventions on the electorate is surely shrinking. In 2020, worries over the covid-19 pandemic threatened the conventions as most government officials promoted social distancing.

Holbrook estimated that about a quarter of the electorate decides how to vote during the party nominating conventions (1996). Data from the NES suggests that the figure may have been closer to 13% in 1996 and 10% in 2000 (2003b). Even though this group probably has decreased quite a bit over time, this is still a large number of voters. Despite changes in the nature and function of conventions, they are still designed to make the nominee's acceptance address the highlight. This makes these speeches worth studying. Note that debates attract viewers from both major political parties. Nomination conventions, on the other hand, may tend to attract more viewers from the political party hosting the convention being broadcast. This could mean that Acceptance Addresses are more likely to reinforce the attitudes of partisans who already support the candidate than to convert undecided voters.

Functions of Acceptance Addresses

Content analysis of every Acceptance Address presented at the party nominating conventions from 1952 to 2000 reveals that 777% of the statements in these messages are acclaims (see Table 3.4). For example, during the 2000 Republican Nomination Convention, Bush told viewers "To the seniors in this country, you earned your benefits, you made your plans, and President George W. Bush will keep the promise of Social Security, no changes, no reductions, no way." Protecting Social Security is an idea that would appeal to most voters. Similarly, Gore told his Democratic audience that "We now have the biggest surpluses, the highest home ownership ever, the lowest inflation in a generation, and instead of losing jobs, we now have 22 million good new jobs, higher family incomes." These accomplishments of the Clinton/Gore administration could serve as a reason to choose Gore as president.

Attacks occur in 23% of utterances in these speeches. Gore referred to earlier years when Republicans controlled the White House (and in fact these Republican administrations included his opponent's father as vice president under President Reagan and then as president): "But let's not forget that a few years ago you were also working hard. But your hard work then was undone by a government that didn't work, didn't put people first, and wasn't on your side." These criticisms, if accepted by the audience, should reduce the desirability of Gore's Republican opponent. Governor Bush observed that the Clinton/Gore record had problems:

> This generation was given the gift of the best education in American history, yet we do not share that gift with everyone. Seven of 10 fourth graders in our highest poverty schools cannot read a simple children's book. And still this administration continues on the same old path, the same old programs, while millions are trapped in schools where violence is common and learning is rare.

These problems, attributed to the Clinton/Gore administration, function as reasons to evaluate Gore more negatively.

Finally, the least common function in Acceptances is defense, which comprises 1% of these speeches. Neither Bush nor Gore used defense in their 2000 Acceptances. In 1992, President George Bush used defense in this passage:

> My opponent says America is a nation in decline. Of our economy, he says we are somewhere on the list beneath Germany, heading south toward Sri Lanka. Well, don't let anyone tell you that America is second-rate, especially somebody running for president. Maybe he hasn't heard that we are still the world's largest economy.

This statement identifies the attack – "my opponent says American is a nation in decline" – and then rejects that attack: "we are still the world's largest economy."

Topics of Acceptance Addresses

The topics of these messages have also been investigated. 55% of the themes in Acceptances concern policy (Table 3.4). For instance, in 2000 Gore declared that "we will fight for affordable health care for all, so patients end ordinary people are not left powerless and broke. We will move toward universal health coverage, step by step, starting with all children." Health care is clearly a policy topic. In the Republican Acceptance, Governor Bush stated that:

> I will use this moment of opportunity to bring common sense and fairness to the tax code. And I will act on principle. On principle, every family, every farmer and small-business person should be free to pass on their life's work to those they love, so we will abolish the death tax. On principle, no one in America should have to pay more than a third of their income to the federal government, so we will reduce tax rates for everyone in every bracket.

Taxation, discussed by Bush here, is another clear example of a policy topic.

Acceptance Addresses devote 45% of their themes to character. Bush promised that he would be trustworthy: "If you give me your trust, I will honor it." This utterance does not concern any particular policy; it addresses the candidate's character. Similarly, Gore offered this statement in his Acceptance: "My parents taught me that the real values in life aren't material, but spiritual. They include faith and family, duty and honor and trying to make the world a better place." Thus, presidential candidates discuss both policy and character in their Acceptance Addresses. These speeches are meant to showcase the nominee, the candidate, so it is not surprising that character comments account for almost half of the themes in these messages.

Acceptance addresses are viewed by millions of voters and are considered the highlight of the carefully orchestrated party nomination conventions. These message forms contain over three times as many acclaims as attacks and few defenses. They provide a fairly balanced treatment of topic, with a slight emphasis on policy. Given the fact that the nominating conventions focus on the party's *nominee*, the fact that these speeches emphasize character more than do spots or debates is readily understandable.

Direct Mail

Little research has investigated direct mail advertising, sometimes referred to as pamphlets, brochures, or flyers. Pfau, Kenski, Nitz, and Sorenson (1990) explained that "Targeted or direct mail has a relatively long history dating back to 1914 when Woodrow Wilson sent out more than 300,000 pieces of campaign mail" (p. 26). Brochures remain a popular medium for communicating with voters. PQ Media (Lieberman, 2004) estimated that direct mail advertising would be the second largest expenditure, after broadcast television advertising, during the 2004 election season (all races combined). In 2012, Obama and Romney "spent nearly twice as much on old-fashioned fliers, get-out-the-vote cards and other forms of direct mail as they have on Internet advertising" (Eggen, 2012). According to the US Postal Service, "in 2012 2.8 billion political mail pieces were sent." Reliance on direct mail advertising continued in the 2016 presidential primaries. For example, Hillary Clinton was "the target of $768,000 in reported direct mail attacks by conservative groups" through January 2016 (Vogel, 2016). Jaye (2016) observed that direct mail advertising is "a growing medium, and this election cycle is likely to see the most political mail in USPS history." This media merits our attention.

Trent and Friedenberg (2000) identify two potential advantages for direct mail advertising, compared with other media. First, it is easy to target specific groups of voters with this message form (assuming one can obtain the mailing addresses). Second, brochures allow longer messages (compared with, for example, spot advertising). Shea (1996) explained the advantages of this medium in modern times:

> More than any other political technology, direct mail has changed dramatically in the past two decades. The availability of personal computers to produce high quality print jobs ... [and] compare available [mailing] lists, has created a direct-mail environment in which the individual preferences of voters can be addressed specifically in a mass mailing. (p. 210)

These comments were written in 1996 and in the years since both computer hardware and software have advanced considerably. This means that direct mail advertising should be even easier to develop and distribute today. Heller discusses another advantage, that direct mail is less expensive than advertising on television or radio (Heller, 1987). Armstrong (1988) identifies a final potential advantage of this medium: Brochures can facilitate stealthy attacks: "Attack your opponent's record on television and he will respond in kind. Attack your opponent in the mail, and he will never even know what hit him" (p. 66).

Hollihan notes that a candidate's constituents may not live neatly in media markets: "Direct mail is especially useful in campaigns where the voting districts and television media markets do not match up" (2001, p. 102). He points to the example of the LA media market, which encompasses several counties and cities. Similarly, Napolitan (1972) explained that

> New Jersey and Delaware are difficult states in which to use television effectively. The northern end of New Jersey is a suburb of New York, the southern end a suburb of Philadelphia. To reach people in those areas you need to buy New York and Philadelphia television, expensive as hell ... . In Kentucky, for example, you have to buy time on television stations in five states – Ohio, Indiana, West Virginia, and Tennessee, as well as Kentucky – to blanket the state. (p. 75)

Television advertising rates are expensive and many candidates would have to pay to broadcast their spots to many citizens who were not constituents and so couldn't vote for the candidate. So, the medium of direct mail advertising has several important advantages in political campaigns.

Evidence indicates that these messages do reach voters. For example, in 1996 over 60% of respondents in New Hampshire reported that they had received mail from presidential candidates (Buhr, 2000). Armstrong (1988) explained that "research shows that approximately 75% of the American people open and glance at every piece of mail they receive" (p. 66), which means voters not only receive but look at these messages. Furthermore, several studies sent brochures to voters and the results indicated that voters did read these messages. Miller and Richey (1980) found that voters who received brochures had more knowledge about the candidate featured in the brochure. Pfau, Kenski, Nitz, and Sorenson (1990) found effects on voters' attitudes from the brochures they studied. Gerber and Green (2000) found that direct mail is less effective than face-to-face contract but more persuasive than telephone calls. Pfau et al. concluded that "in recent elections, direct mail has been an important channel for both incumbent survival as well as challenger success" (1990, p. 27; citing Armstrong, 1988; Heller, 1987; Reiley, 1987; Sabato, 1981). Clearly, direct mail merits scholarly attention.

The most common function of direct mail advertising is acclaims (77%), followed by attacks (23%) and defenses (0.3%). See Table 3.4. Benoit (2017) analyzed non-presidential direct mail from Ohio in 2016. Acclaims were more common than attacks. These messages focus more on policy (70%) than character (30%). Hillygus and Shields (2008) report that 70% of the presidential direct mail in 2004 was issue appeals. Benoit (2017c) found the brochures in Ohio were split about evenly between policy and character. Examples could be provided to illustrate the three functions and two topics in direct mail advertising, but hopefully those concepts are clear by now. Notice that brochures are not as negative as Armstrong (1988) suggested.

Televison Talk Shows

Television talk shows serve as another a means for politicians to reach voters. Benoit et al. (2003) observed that:

> John F. Kennedy appeared on Jack Parr's *The Tonight Show*. Clinton appeared on a number of talk shows in his 1992 campaign, including appearances in which he played the saxophone with program house bands. Clinton was also adept at using a talk show format on MTV in 1992. While there were a few appearances in 1996 (Dole appeared on *Live with Regis and Kathy Lee*) we have witnessed a tremendous explosion of such appearances in the 2000 campaign. (pp. 215–216)

Some may dismiss these venues as unimportant, but that would be a mistake. Benoit et al. (2003) explained that

> Millions of voters watch these programs. For instance, Oprah regularly has over 7 million viewers, Letterman has about 4 million viewers, and Larry King has over 1 million viewers (Fineman, 2000). Thus, these programs reach a significant number of viewers. Second, talk show programs are a source of news for many people. As noted in Chapter 7, according to the Pew Research Center for the People and the

Press, 10% of those polled reported that they gained news information from talk shows (Marks, 2000). Pfau, Cho, and Chong (2001) reported results that indicated that non-traditional campaign discourse forms, including television entertainment talk shows and television talk shows, exerted much influence on perceptions of the candidates. (p. 216)

The increase in the number of such appearances, along with the real potential for influence – which may be particularly important giving the decreasing audience for debates – means that this medium warrants scholarly attention.

We have data on candidate TV talk show appearances from 2000, 2004, and 2016. In this sample candidates acclaimed more than they attacked (69% to 24%) and devoted the smallest number of statements to defenses (8%). Candidates who appeared on talk shows, unlike most other message forms, were prone to talk more about character (56%) than policy (44%). The candidates in 2004, however, emphasized policy slightly more than character. See Table 3.7 for these data.

The research on television talk shows indicates that this medium often emphasizes personalities. Benoit et al. (2003) observed that:

> The prominence of character talk is consistent with the particular features of the talk show genre. Talk shows are a personal medium. As identified in previous studies (Haag, 1992/1993), audiences often develop pseudo-personal relationships with a talk show host. This personal ambiance likely influences the discourse of the candidates. The candidates' target audiences when they appear on these talk shows are likely less concerned with the policies of the candidates than with their personalities. Accordingly, the candidates would want to emphasize their character to these audiences: The candidates seek to portray an impression of high character value. This is consistent with research on television talk show appearances by political candidates in Europe

Table 3.7. Functions of presidential TV talk show appearances.

	Functions			Topics	
	Acclaims	Attacks	Defenses	Policy	Character
2000 Primary	896 (72%)	211 (17%)	144 (12%)	390 (35%)	**727 (65%)**
2000 General	635 (91%)	37 (5%)	31 (4%)	219 (33%)	**453 (67%)**
2004 Primary	995 (69%)	452 (31%)	10 (1%)	**736 (52%)**	691 (48%)
2004 General	847 (76%)	245 (22%)	26 (2%)	**588 (53%)**	539 (47%)
2016 Primary	486 (45%)	381 (35%)	214 (20%)	356 (41%)	**521 (59%)**
Total	3859 (69%)	1326 (24%)	426 (8%)	2289 (44%)	**2931 (56%)**

Sources: Benoit, McHale, Hansen, Pier, & McGuire, 2003; Benoit et al., 2007; Benoit & Glantz, 2020.

(Bock, 1982; Hoffmann, 1982; Holly, Kuhn, & Puschel, 1986; Lang & Lang, 1968, 1984; Weiss, 1976). (p. 226)

This suggests that television talk show appearances, like social media, are an exception to the general rule that campaign messages stress policy over character.

Presidential Campaign Posters

Candidates have employed posters to reach voters for years. Relatively little research examines this medium (see Holt, 1986; Holtz-Baha & Johansson, 2017; Johansson, 2014; Vliegenthart, 2012; or Wert, 2016). Two webpages display a variety of interesting political campaign posters (https://abcnews.go.com/Politics/OTUS/photos/presidential-campaign-posters-run-gamut-bold-bizarre-16602309/image-16602404; https://www.huffpost.com/entry/presidential-campaign-posters_n_569e635fe4b0cd99679b6001). Benoit (2018) content analyzed presidential poster from 1828 to 2012. He found that acclaims were more frequent than attacks (92% to 8%; no instances of defenses were found). These messages addressed character more than policy (80% to 20%). These data appear in Table 3.4

Comparisons Between Media

The nature of each medium, or message form, can influence the nature or content of the messages produced in that medium. Functional Theory advances several predictions about media.

Initially, notice that although every medium reported here used acclaims more than attacks, and attacks more than defenses, differences still occur between media. Acclaims vary from 63–92%, a 29% range. Attacks also vary from medium to medium with a range of 28% (8%-36%). Defenses varied between 0.1% and 9% (see Table 3.4). Overall, policy (64%) is more common than character (36%). However, the range across media is even wider: Policy varies from 20% to 83% whereas character varies frm 17% to 80%. An emphasis on character occurs in three media: television talk show appearances, candidate webpages, and campaign posters. Clearly voters receive different information from different media.

The relationship between percent of policy and year is positive and significant in four message forms: television spots, acceptances, debates, and direct mail. Radio spots also has a positive relationship between year and discussion of policy; because the *n* for radio spots is smaller (we have data on radio spots from only 7 campaigns), this relationship is only slightly smaller than the conventional criteria for a significant difference; an argument could be made that a relationship between year and percent of policy. This means that campaign messages over time tend to discuss policy in increasing amounts.

One aspect medium is the fact that a message has multiple dimensions: verbal (words spoken and printed), visual (image), and vocal (attributes such as speech rate and inflection). Pundits and journalists often indicate that the non-verbal dimension of a message is most influential. For example, a survey after one of the Nixon-Kennedy presidential debate reported that those who experienced the debate on radio (with no visuals) thought Nixon did a better job, whereas those who watched television preferred Kennedy. However, later analysis revealed that those who used the radio were more heavily Republican than TV watchers (Vancil & Pendell, 1987). So, the fact that radio listeners tended to like Nixon more, and Kennedy less, than television watchers is more likely because of the Republican makeup of the radio audience than the medium.

Another study (albeit not about campaigns) often used to show that the non-verbal dimension of messages has more influence than the verbal dimension is by Mehrabian and Ferris (1967). They reported that impression formation was influenced most by visual cues (55%), then by vocal cues (38%), and least by verbal content (7%). However, this study used neutral words (such as "maybe"), not actual messages, as the stimuli. It is surprising that as much as 7% of the impression comes from the verbal aspect when words used in this study were specifically chosen to be neutral words. Support for the importance of the non-verbal aspects of messages over verbal aspects is quite limited.

Nagel, Maurer, and Reinemann (2012) reported the result of a study of German political debates. They measured attitudes of viewers with equipment which allowed each audience member to indicate their reactions to the debate continuously by turning a dial left or right. These reactions were synchronized with analysis of the verbal (words) and non-verbal (visual and vocal) aspects of the debate. They found that viewers' impressions were "mainly influenced by verbal communication" rather than non-verbal elements (p. 833). Discussion of issues (such as foreign affairs, employment, energy, or economy) had the largest impact on candidate impressions. "In contrast to the verbal elements, visual elements had only small effects on viewers' impression .... Most vocal features [tone, pace, pitch] did not show significant effects" on impressions of candidates (p. 842). Functional Theory focuses almost exclusively on verbal elements of political election messages (this theory has recently been extended to include visual elements of presidential posters; Benoit, 2019).

Conclusion

These data show that the medium of a message can exert a significant influence on the nature of presidential campaign messages. Clear differences emerged in both function and topic across these media. Still, important similarities occur in political campaign messages across media. Most message forms have more acclaims than attacks; the least frequent function in all of these media is defenses. Most message forms address policy more than character. Nevertheless, important differences exist between these media. Acceptances and direct mail have the fewest attacks, radio spots have the most attacks, and debates use defense most frequently. Debates and direct mail advertising stress policy; television talk shows are the only medium to discuss character more than policy. It is clear that the content of political campaign messages varies by medium and that it is important to understand the nature of the various campaign message forms.

CHAPTER FOUR

The Role of Source in Campaign Discourse

Most discussions of the effects of source characteristics concern persuasiveness. Research shows that sources who are perceived by the audience to be expert and trustworthy are usually more persuasive than other sources (see, e.g., Benoit & Strathman, 2004). Accordingly, Republican voters may be more inclined to accept messages from Republican than Democratic candidates; Democratic voters may be more influenced by utterances from Democrats than Republicans (see, e.g., Winneg, Kenski, & Jamison, 2005). Bimber and Davis (2003) indicate that voters were more likely to visit the webpage of their preferred candidate than the websites of other candidates. However, the nature or identify of the source not only can affect *how an audience reacts to a message*: It can also influence *the content of messages produced* by that source. This chapter discusses three aspects of sources of political campaign messages to discover the relationship between different sources and the political campaign messages they produce: political party affiliation, surrogate sources (compared with candidates), and incumbents versus challengers. The chapter will end with a discussion of how to repair a source's damaged image.

Political Party Affiliation

Political party affiliation[1] is an important variable. Many voters are registered as, or consider themselves to be, Republicans or Democrats. Even though political party affiliation does not determine the vote choice of all voters or election outcome (see Chapter One), political party affiliation is clearly important for many voters. However, we know surprisingly little about whether or how political party affiliation influences the campaign messages produced by political candidates. Jarvis (2004; see also 2005) reported a computer content analysis of speeches from 1948 to 2000: Democrats were more likely to discuss people whereas Republicans use nouns to create coalitions and to focus more on ideals.[2,3,4,5] In this section, I will investigate the potential effects of candidates' political party affiliation on the functions and topics of political campaign discourse.

Functions of Republican and Democratic Campaign Discourse

Do candidates from different political parties emphasize different functions in their political campaign messages? West (2001), using a sample of 433 spots from 1952 to 2000, reported that Democratic television spots were more positive (50%) than Republican ads (39%). In contrast, Kaid and Johnston (2001), analyzing 1204 ads from 1952 to 1996, found that Republican ads were more positive than Democratic spots (66% to 57%). So, research on the functions of television spots from candidates representing the two major political parties is mixed. These conflicting results lead to a research question:

> S1. *Political party affiliation does not affect the function of political campaign discourse.*

Table 4.1 reports that functions of discourse by Republicans and Democrats. Overall, Democrats acclaim less (67%, 70%) and attack more (33%, 30%) than Republicans. However, this effect of political party on function is not uniform: No difference occurred in functions of TV spots or Acceptance Addresses from Democrats versus Republicans. Accordingly, the support for a contrast in functions by Democrats and Republicans is weak.

Issue Ownership and Political Party

Petrocik (1996) advanced the theory of Issue Ownership, observing that different issues are "owned" by each of the two major political parties. Over time, voters

Table 4.1. Political party and function of campaign discourse.

	Acclaims	Attacks
Acceptance Addresses		
Democrats	1479 (76%)	464 (24%)
Republicans	1306 (77%)	399 (23%)
Television Spots		
Democrats	5668 (64%)	3186 (36%)
Republicans	5097 (64%)	2816 (36%)
Debates		
Democrats	23309 (65%)	12329 (**35%**)
Republicans	**18466 (68%)**	8866 (32%)
Direct Mail		
Democrats	7924 (75%)	**2647 (25%)**
Republicans	**7839 (79%)**	2106 (21%)
Total		
Democrats	38380 (67%)	**18626 (33%)**
Republicans	**32708 (70%)**	14187 (30%)

χ^2 (df = 1) = 69.8, p < .0001. φ = .03.
Note: These data combine primary and general campaign data.
Acceptances: Benoit, Wells, Pier, & Blaney, 1999; Benoit, 2014; Benoit & Glantz, 2020.
TV Spots: Benoit, 2014a; Benoit & Glantz, 2020.
Debates: Benoit, 2014b; Benoit & Glantz, 2020.
Direct Mail: Benoit & Stein, 2005

tend to associate the Democratic and Republican parties with different sets of issues and voters tend to believe that one party or the other is better at dealing with certain issues. Every voter does not agree about which party owns a given issue; still, most voters believe one party does a better job with certain issues. The Democratic Party, for example, "owns" such issues as education, health care, and Social Security; the Republican Party, on the other hand, "owns" such issues as national defense, taxes, and foreign policy.

Petrocik explains that this reputation reflects a relationship between a party's political agenda (and record) and its supporters: The "linkage between a party's issue agenda and the social characteristics of its supporters is quite strong" (p. 828). This relationships is recursive: Groups (e.g., business, labor, minorities) tend to affiliate with a particular party because it tends to promote their interests and the party promotes those interests in order to attract and maintain these supporters. Accordingly, Petrocik observes that party ownership tends to be a "long term" phenomenon (p. 827) and "issue handling reputations emerge from ... history" (p. 828). Still, issue handling reputations are "regularly tested and reinforced." For example, when "President Bush opposed the 1991 Civil Rights Restoration Act as an inappropriate complication of business decisions, he expressed a judgment that the concerns of blacks were less weighty than those of businessmen" (p. 828). So, (1) issue handling reputations reflect a party's constituency and the behavior of elected party members and (2) these reputations are relatively stable perceptions among voters.

The key prediction of issue ownership theory concerns priming and agenda setting. Political campaign messages from Republican and Democratic candidates are likely to "emphasize issues on which they are advantaged and their opponents are less well regarded" (p. 825). If candidates can increase the salience of their own political party's issues to voters by emphasizing those issues in their campaign messages, that should give them a competitive advantage. In short, if most voters believe that Democrats do a better job dealing with health care, Democratic candidates should do better when health care is considered important by most voters. On the other hand, if most voters believe Republicans are better at handling war, Republican candidates have an edge when voters believe war is important. So, Democrats are expected to stress their own issues, such as health care, and Republicans should emphasize their own issues, such as war, to try to make these issues more important to voters.

For example, public opinion polls revealed this distribution of issue ownership in the Fall of 2002. The data reported in Table 4.2 make it clear that if voters are concerned with terrorism, Republican candidates (like President George W. Bush) start out with a 51% to 30% advantage with voters. On the other hand, if voters are thinking primarily about Social Security, Democratic candidates begin with a 50% to 33% advantage. Surely in Fall of 2003 most Republicans would prefer that voters were focused on terrorism (or crime) rather than Social Security (or health care)–and most Democrats would prefer just the opposite.

Table 4.2. Which political party do you trust to do a better job handling this issue?

	Democratic	Republican
Terrorism	30	51
Crime†	27	40
Social Security	50	33
Health care	50	35

Poll by ABC 9/23-26/02 except †Princeton Research Associates, 10/24-25/02.

Experimental research supports the prediction that owing an issue confers an advantage with voters. Ansolabehere and Iyengar (1994) created television spots for the 1992 Senate race in California. They varied whether the ads were attributed to the Republican or the Democratic candidate. Spots from Democrats had more influence on voters' perceptions of the candidates' issue positions, and a greater impact on voting preferences, when they discussed Democratic than Republican issues. Similarly, ads from Republicans had larger effects when they discussed Republican instead of Democratic issues. Abbe, Goodliffe, Herrnson, and Patterson (2003) studied the 1998 House elections. They found that "voters are more likely to support candidates who run on party-owned issues that are important to voters" and that issue agreement between candidate and voter is more important to independent than partisan voters (p. 428). Although major policy accomplishments and contentious issues also influence issue emphasis, Brasher (2003) found that issue ownership was an influence on issue emphasis in U.S. senate campaigns. Clearly, political candidates can obtain an advantage from stressing their own party's issues.

Of course it would almost certainly be unwise for candidates of either political party to discuss only their own party's issues. For example, in the 2004 campaign, Democratic candidate Kerry should not ignore the war in Iraq even though this is a Republican-owned issue. Still, a tangible benefit might have be obtained if Kerry had stressed jobs or health care more than Iraq. A candidate *might* be able to convince voters that he or she would be better able to deal with a problem owned by the other political party, but that is an uphill battle compared with persuading them that he or she can handle a problem owned by his or her party. So, the expectation is that candidates from both major political parties should discuss issues owned by both political parties, but that they should emphasize their own party's issues. Sigelman and Buell (2004) show that candidates from the two major parties do discuss the same issues frequently; of course, Issue Ownership theory does not predict no overlap in the issues discussed by candidates from different political parties, only differences in issue *emphasis*.

S3. *Democrats discuss Democratic issues more, and Republican issues less, than Republicans.*

Overall, there is a tendency for candidates from both parties to emphasize Republican-owned issues. Petrocik, Benoit, and Hansen (2003/2004) observe that the Republican Party tends to own more national issues (e.g., Republican issues like national defense are usually federal, but on Democratic issues like education there is more local money and control). Still, Democrats discuss Democratic issues more than do Republicans (47% to 34%), whereas Republicans emphasize their own issues more than Democrats (66% to 53%). Clearly, when the candidates for president discuss issues, Republicans emphasize different sets of issues than Democrats. An analysis of tweets from Clinton and Trump in 2016 confirmed this prediction (Lee & Xu, 2018). These data are reported in Table 4.3.

Table 4.3. Issue ownership in presidental campaign messages.

	Issue Mentions	
Candidate's Party	Democratic	Republican
Acceptances, 1952–2000		
Democratic	**197 (71%)**	81 (29%)
Republican	61 (39%)	**96 (61%)**
Presidential Primary TV Spots, 1952–2000		
Democratic	**1025 (65%)**	543 (35%)
Republican	860 (39%)	**1341 (61%)**
Presidential General TV Spots 1952–2000		
Democratic	**302 (73%)**	110 (27%)
Republican	175 (67%)	**86 (33%)**
Primary Debates, 1948, 1960, 1968–2000, 2016		
Democratic	**5164 (47%)**	6860 (53%)
Republican	4153 (28%)	**10703 (72%)**
General Debates. 1960, 1976–2000, 2016		
Democratic	1774 (38%)	**2850 (62%)**
Republican	1209 (32%)	**2606 (68%)**
Brochures, 1948–2004		
presiden Democratic	**1256 (64%)**	697 (36%)
Republican	1519 (50%)	**1542 (50%)**
Total		
Democratic	8118 (49%)	**8571 (51%)**
Republican	7977 (33%)	**16374 (67%)**

χ^2 (df = 1) = 1078.32, p < .0001. φ = .16.
Acceptances: Petrocik, Benoit, & Hansen, 2003–04.
Presidential Primary TV Spots: Benoit, 2014b.
Presidential General TV Spots: Petrocik, Benoit, & Hansen, 2003–04.
Presidential Primary Debates: Benoit & Hansen, 2004a; Benoit, 2018.
Presidential General Debates: Benoit & Hansen, 2004a; Benoit, 2018.
Brochures: Benoit & Stein, 2005.

Of course, candidates do not discuss only the issues of their own party. For example, in the 2000 campaign, Republican George W. Bush frequently discussed education, which is traditionally a Democratic issue. Presidential candidates will occasionally attempt to "poach" an issue from the other party in order to help build a winning coalition of voters. This practice may be useful for attracting Independent voters or potential vote defectors. However, it does have some risks. First, if many voters believe that the Democratic party is best-suited for handling problems of education, Bush could have been (inadvertently) giving them a reason to vote against him each time he mentioned education. Furthermore, Bush may have increased the importance of education (an agenda-setting effect) by emphasizing this issue. If more voters believed the Democratic candidate would best handle education, this could have exacerbated the problem.

A second risk to poaching an issue from the other party is that attempting to coopt too many of the other party's issues could alienate the candidate's base of support. For example, if Democrat Al Gore embraced across-the-board tax cuts, limits on abortion, allowing businesses to exploit the environment, and cuts in education, he could have lost the support of many Democrats while only attracting a few Republican voters. Still, when Bush stressed education that could have helped him appeal to independent and undecided voters as well as to those Democrats who might have been willing to defect. The fact that his wife, Laura Bush, had worked in a public school may have helped him on this issue.

Character in Republican and Democratic Messages

Benoit and McHale (2003) conducted a grounded theory analysis (carefully examining TV spots to discover recurrent features) of presidential television spots, using the method of constant comparison to develop a typology of personal qualities discussed in campaign ads. They concluded that the most commonly discussed character traits were sincerity, empathy, morality, and drive. Governor Michael Dukakis illustrated how a television commercial can discuss sincerity when he attacked Vice President George Bush for Bush's negative advertising in 1988: "Never seen anything like it in 25 years of public life, George Bush's negative television ads. Distorting my record: Full of lies and he knows it." Distortion and lies do not indicate sincerity. A television advertisement for Governor Jimmy Carter told voters in 1976 that he would be "a president who feels your pain and who shares your dreams." This illustrates the quality of empathy. In his 1956 re-election campaign, a television spot for President Dwight Eisenhower proclaimed that "President Eisenhower has brought integrity ... back to the White House." This excerpt illustrates the personal quality of morality. Finally, at times candidates stress their drive. In 1960, for example, a television spot for Senator John F. Kennedy told viewers that he was a "determined person." Determination indicates his drive.

Once these categories were developed they were applied deductively to campaign texts using computer content analysis to see if there are differences in the kinds of personal traits discussed by Republicans and Democrats. Table 4.4 summarizes the data on this question. In all three message forms, Republicans used a more words related to sincerity (e.g., deceit, dishonest, distort, honest, lies, truthful) and morality (e.g., crooked, decency, fair, honor, principled, sordid). than Democrats. A moral tone, reflected in sincerity and morality, is consistent with the Republican Party's ideology (e.g., opposing abortion). So, the candidates from the two major parties at times differ in their emphasis on the personal qualities of the candidates, but this effect is not as consistent as party differences on policy (Issue Ownership).

So, it is clear that the political party affiliation of the source of presidential campaign messages exerts an influence on the nature of campaign discourse. The party of the source can influence topic (Democrats discuss policy more and character less than Republicans) and the relative emphasis if issues owned by the two parties. It also may have a smaller influence on the character traits discussed in these messages.

Table 4.4. Forms of character and political party.

	Sincerity	Empathy	Morality	Drive
Acceptance Addresses				
Democrats	209	**215**	333	307
Republicans	**264**	173	344	277
General TV Spots				
Democrats	260	**246**	440	311
Republicans	**323**	201	495	408
General Debates				
Democrats	421	339	768	**560**
Republicans	457	350	791	404
Total				
Democrats	890	585	1541	1178
Republicans	**1044**	**724**	**1630**	**1089**

Note: bold in total indicates greater frequency in all three message forms. Benoit & McHale, 2003, 2004.

Surrogate Sources

Early in our nation's history presidential candidates did not themselves engage in campaigning (Hollihan, 2001). Today, however, presidential campaigns always feature messages from the candidate. Voters want to know their elected officials, so they understandably would be interested to hear what the candidates have to say. However, at times other sources besides the candidate speak in campaign messages. Data from two different kinds of campaign messages permit us to explore the effects of surrogate sources on political campaign messages: convention speeches (acceptances, keynotes) and television spots. It is common knowledge that many voters report that they dislike mud-slinging (Merritt, 1984; Stewart, 1975). If surrogates make most of the attacks, voters' disgust at attacks could be directed toward the surrogate rather than (or more than) at the candidate. This means that use of surrogates to attack could damage the opponent while protecting the candidate from voter backlash. Accordingly, Functional Theory predicts that attacks will be more common in messages from surrogates than in messages from the candidates themselves.

> *Messages from candidates use more acclaims, and fewer attacks, than messages from other sources.*

Two important speeches at political party nominating conventions are Acceptances Addresses, given by the candidates, and Keynote Speeches, given by other politicians. If surrogates attack more than candidates, we would expect to find more attacks in Keynotes than Acceptances. Table 4.5 reveals that convention speeches given by candidates in their Acceptance Addresses used more acclaims (76% to 50%) and fewer attacks (24% to 50%) than convention speeches given by other politicians in Keynote Speeches. The percentage of attacks was twice as large in Keynotes as in Acceptances. So, data from these two kinds of party nominating convention speeches support for this prediction.

Content analysis of presidential television spots (Benoit, 1999) divided utterances into those which were made by candidates (the rare statements by Vice Presidential candidates and from the candidates' spouses were considered to be candidate utterances) and those which were made by others (e.g., anonymous announcers, citizens, other politicians, or other notables such as actors). If surrogates attack more than candidates, we would expect the percentage of attacks in television spots to be higher when others are speaking rather than the candidate. Table 4.5 indicates that in presidential TV spots candidates acclaim more than

Table 4.5. George Bush in 1992. Functions and source of campaign messages.

	Acclaims	Attacks
Speeches		
Acceptances, 1952–1996	1804 (76%)	578 (24%)
Keynotes, 1960–1996	474 (50%)	463 (50%)
Speaker in Presidential TV Spots, 1952–1996		
Candidate	879 (69%)	386 (31%)
Other	1867 (61%)	1214 (39%)
Presidential Debates		
Presidential	6023 (61%)	3919 (39%)
Vice Presidential	3134 (57%)	2412 (43%)
TV Spots: Candidate vs. Groups, 2004, 2016 (primary + general)		
Candidate	1745 (57%)	1290 (37%)
Groups	810 (38%)	1339 (62%)
TV Spots: Candidate vs. Party, 2000		
Candidate	221 (74%)	79 (26%)
Party	107 (41%)	157 (59%)
Tweets, Governor, Senate, House 2016		
Tweets	2298 (72%)	904 (28%)
Retweets	895 (60%)	605 (40%)
Total		
Candidate	12970 (66%)	6635 (34%)
Other	7287 (54%)	6190 (46%)

$\chi^2 \, (df = 1) = 491.51, p < .0001. \varphi = .12$.
Acceptances: Benoit, Wells, Pier, & Blaney, 1999; Keynotes: Benoit, Blaney, & Pier, 2000
Speaker in TV Spots: Benoit, 1999
Debates: Benoit, 2014b; Benoit & Glantz, 2020
TV Spots vs. Party: Benoit, McHale, Hansen, Pier, & McGuire (2003)
Candidate vs. Group: Benoit et al., 2007; Benoit & Glantz, 2020
Twitter (tweets vs. retweets): Stein & Benoit, 2021

other sources (69%, 61%) and attack less (31%, 39%). These differences are significant, confirming the prediction.

Furthermore, content analysis has compared the frequency of attacks in the seven vice presidential debates with the percentage of attacks in the presidential debates held in the same years. Vice presidential candidates acclaim less (57% to

61%) and attack more (43% to 39%) than their running mates. Although vice presidential candidates are part of the ticket, it should be obvious that the candidate at the top of the ticket is the primary candidate, so vice presidential candidates can be considered in some sense a surrogate source, and as we would expect, they attack more frequently than presidential candidates.

Television spots are created and broadcast by candidates and groups (Political Action Committees or other groups). Table 4.5 shows that ads by candidates acclaim more (57% to 41%) and attacked less (37% to 62%) than spots from groups. In recent years the political parties, embodied in the Republican National Committee (RNC) and the Democratic National Committee (DNC), as well as in state party committees, have produced and broadcast television spots in political campaigns. Finally, in gubernatorial, senate, and house tweets from 2016, retweets had more acclaims (72% to 60%) and fewer attacks (28% to 40%) than retweets (Stein & Benoit, 2021).

Table 4.5 reports that candidates acclaimed more (66% to 34%) and attacked less (34% to 46%) than political parties. Notice that messages from candidates and others both acclaim more than they attack. Candidates, however, acclaim even more than others and candidates attack even less than others.

As noted above, many voters eschew mud-slinging or attacks. This feeling could lead candidates and their advisors to try to "shield" candidates from potential backlash from voters by relegating most attacks to party-sponsored ads. If this is the motivation behind more attacks from party- than candidate-sponsored spots, I suspect it is misguided. It seems unlikely that most voters pay attention to the sponsor of an advertisement. If a spot attacks George W. Bush, for instance, viewers will probably take it for granted that this advertisement was from Al Gore. In fact, it is unclear that the Democratic National Committee or the Republican National Committee would run an ad if they did not have at least tacit approval from the candidate. Still, the data show that messages from surrogate sources attack more, and acclaim less, than messages from the candidates themselves. It is possible that voters may realize PAC ads are not from the candidates.

A change in the laws regulating political advertising could play a role here. In 2004, candidates must appear in their ads and say, "I'm George Bush [or John Kerry] and I approve of this message." Some voters might ignore this line; others might assume that candidates have collaborated (or conspired) with non-candidate groups and deserve blame for mud-slinging. Still, it is possible this line could help limit the backlash against the candidates from attacks in non-candidate spots. The nature of the source of campaign messages, again, influences the content of those messages.

Incumbents vs. Challengers

The question of incumbency in presidential campaigns can be complex. At times the elected president runs for re-election, such as Dwight Eisenhower in 1956, Richard Nixon in 1972, Jimmy Carter in 1980, Ronald Reagan in 1984, George Bush in 1992, Bill Clinton in 1996, George W. Bush in 2004, Barack Obama in 2012, and Donald Trump in 2020. In other elections the Vice President seeks the Oval Office (e.g., Richard Nixon in 1960, Hubert Humphrey in 1968, George Bush in 1988, Al Gore in 2000). Three candidates ran for president without having served either as president or vice president: Adlai Stevenson (1952), John McCain (2008), and Hillary Clinton (2016). Between 1952 and 2016, challenger candidates in presidential elections won nine elections and eight incumbent party candidates won. However, two incumbents (President Johnson, President Bush) had not been elected president when they first ran for the Oval Office (President Johnson assumed the presidency after President Kennedy was assassinated; President Bush was serving as Vice President when he first ran for the presidency). If we look only at those candidates who were elected to the Oval Office and sought a second term, six won and three lost.

Petrocik (2004) offers data that at all levels of office incumbents win 98% of primary campaigns and 94% of general elections over the last 50 years. The Center for Responsive Politics (2017) looked as 27 campaigns for the US Senate and US House from 1964 through 2016. The average rate of incumbents who were re-elected to the Senate was 82%; for members of the House the rate was 93%. Incumbency can be an important advantage, but especially for offices other than the president.

Salamore and Salamore (1985) indicate that the most important advantages for incumbents are recognition, ability to raise campaign funds, and the ability to begin campaigning early. The Center for Responsive Politics (2017) reported that House incumbent candidates raised seven times as much money as challengers; Senate incumbents raised 11 times as much as challengers. Incumbents are also likely to receive more attention from the press than challengers (see, e.g., Trent & Trent, 1974, 1995; Trent & Friedenberg, 1991, 2000). It seems very likely that the incumbent party candidate will be better known than the challenger party candidate, particularly if the incumbent party candidate is an incumbent president running for re-election. If challengers are less well-known, the beliefs about and attitudes toward a candidate are probably easier to change for challengers than incumbents. This means that campaign messages should have more influence on knowledge and perceptions for challengers than incumbents, particularly in early stages of the campaign. Benoit and Hansen (2004) investigated the effects of watching presidential debates on issue knowledge in 1976–1984 and 1996–2000. They found no increase in issue knowledge for candidates who were serving as president during the campaign (Ford in 1976, Carter in 1980, Reagan in 1984, Clinton in 1996). On the other hand, voters did learn about all of the challengers but one (Carter in 1976). They also learned about the incumbent party candidate who had been vice president but not president (Gore in 2000). Voters know less about challengers and thus are likely to learn more about them than incumbents.

The nomination for challenging party is always contested, but one advantage many incumbents have is that they usually do not have to fight for their party's nomination. For example, Reagan in 1984, Clinton in 1996, and Bush in 2004 were not contested when they sought their party's nomination for a second term in office. In the 2020 primaries, the GOP in several states cancelled Republican primaries (Reints, 2019). President Trump did not need to face primary challenges. Absence of challengers means that incumbents are not subjected to attacks from others in their own party. For example, in 1980 Senator Ted Kennedy challenged President Jimmy Carter for the Democratic nomination. One of Kennedy's ads sharply criticized his fellow Democrat: "This man has misled the American public into the worst economic crisis since the Depression. He's broken promises and cost New York a billion dollars a year. In his latest foreign policy blunder he betrayed Israel at the UN." Similarly, in 1992 Pat Buchanan challenged President Bush for the Republican nomination. His ads also attacked the president, beginning with Bush's dramatic promise in 1988 that he would not raise taxes (which Bush broke): "Bush promised. Bush: Read my lips, no new taxes. Bush promised to cut spending, but our national debt has bone up 1.1 trillion dollars. Bush promised us jobs, but our unemployment has tripled. Now Bush is promising to fix the recession. Can we afford four more years of broken promises?" Incumbents have a substantial advantage when they are not challenged in the primary and subjected to attacks such as these.

The fact that incumbents are rarely challenged in the primary also means that they can spend more time undermining their anticipated general election opponent. For example, in 21 of Republican Bob Dole's 1996 primary ads, 2 attacked President Bill Clinton and 11 attacked other Republicans. Bill Clinton in 1996 did not have any Democratic opponents to criticize, so he could focus his primary attacks on Dole, the Republican front-runner.

Another advantage for the incumbent party candidate is the fact that the challenger's party nominating convention is always held first. The two major party candidates receive the same amount of money (assuming they accept federal funds) for the general election campaign. However, they cannot spend this money until they formally accept their party's nomination. Furthermore, they are not allowed to spend any other funds (e.g., money left over from the primary). This meant, for example, that in 2004 challenger John Kerry had to stretch his federal funds for a month longer than incumbent George Bush. Bush could continue to spend his primary money during the month between the Democratic and Republican conventions, so he had more money left for the final part of the general election campaign than Kerry.

Furthermore, only the incumbent candidate has a record in the office sought. As we will see, incumbents and challengers use this information quite differently in their campaign messages. In this section I will first contrast the messages produced by Incumbents and Challengers and then discuss Strong and Weak Incumbents ("strong" incumbents are defined here as those who were elected to the presidency and are seeking re-election to a second term in office).

Messages from Incumbents and Challengers

Functional Theory predicts differences in the discourse of incumbent-party and challenger-party candidates. These differences tend to stem from the essential difference in situation: Incumbents have a record in the office sought; challengers do not. Of course, challengers have other kinds of records. Some challengers (Kennedy 1960, Goldwater 1964, McGovern 1972, Dole 1996, and Kerry 2004; McCain in 2008) had experience in the Senate. Two had been vice president (Nixon 1968 and Mondale 1984; note that in 1988 Bush was a vice president when he first ran for president, so he was never a challenger). Other challengers (Carter 1976, Reagan 1980, Dukakis 1988, Clinton 1992, Bush 2000, and Romney 2012) had been governors. For example, Ronald Reagan touted his record as Governor:

> This is a man whose time has come. A strong leader with a proven record. In 1966, answering the call of his party, Ronald Reagan was elected Governor of California–next to President, the biggest job in the nation. What the new Governor inherited was a state of crisis. California was faced with a $194 million deficit, and was spending a million dollars a day more than it was taking in. The state was on the brink of bankruptcy. Governor Reagan became the greatest tax reformer in the state's history. When Governor Reagan left office, the $194 million deficit had been transformed into a $550 million surplus. The *San Francisco Chronicle* said, Governor Reagan has saved the state from bankruptcy. The time is now for strong leadership. Reagan for President. (Reagan, "Record," 1980)

This messages emphasized Reagan's success at turning his state's budget deficit into a surplus (and it suggests he is a strong leader). All of these candidates called on their experience to some extent. Still, none of these forms of experience (senator, governor, business) quite matches the experience gained from actually serving as president.

What is interesting about having a record in office is that in an important sense it is asymmetrical. A president's record is so vast – terms are four years long and the federal government has fingers in a myriad of pies, domestic and foreign – that there are inevitably both successes and failures to be found in the incumbent's record. The incumbent can use his own record as a resource for *acclaims*, dwelling on the successes. For example, in 1976, President Ford found bright spots in the record:

> He came to the office of the president in troubled times. He began an open administration. Now, quietly and firmly, he is leading us out of the worst recession in years. Rather than loose promises, he has made the hard decisions. Rather than frantic spending he has had the courage to say no. The worst is over. Over 2 million more Americans are working than at the bottom of the recession. Inflation is cut almost in half. President Ford is your President. Keep him. (Ford, "Accomplishments," 1976)

This advertisement stressed an increase in jobs and a decrease in inflation (it also touted Ford's qualities of openness and courage and offered an excuse, "troubled times," for problems). Similarly, Nixon in 1960 ran on the Eisenhower-Nixon record when he first sought the presidency. He argued that America's economy was growing:

> The fact is that Americans are earning more, investing more, saving more, living better than ever before. More Americans than ever before are bringing home the weekly paycheck. 68 million people are employed today. Now this is growth. The kind that ensures our strength at home, and it exceeds the economic growth in Russia today. Ours is a growth based on paying our bills, too. Not a system of reckless borrowing that will burden our children tomorrow. This is the kind of economic growth we must continue to have, in order to continue to help us keep the peace. (Nixon, "Truth Growth," 1960)

More income, investment, and saving; greater employment and growth. Note that like Ford ("Keep him") Nixon ends with a plea not to change horses in the middle of the stream: "the kind of economic growth we must continue to have." Donald Trump, who contested the Republican nomination in 2016, was a businessman and media figure. In 2020 his campaign argued that he deserved re-election because he strengthened the economy in his first term.

The challenger, in contrast, can use other parts of the incumbent's record as resources for *attacks*, focusing on the failures. Ford's opponent, Jimmy Carter, did not see the economy in the same light in 1976 as did Ford:

The Republicans say 7.9% unemployment is acceptable. They've said it so long that people began to believe it. Well 7.9% unemployment is not acceptable. It is not to be tolerated. 7.9% unemployment is what you arrive at when incompetent leaders follow outdated, unjust, wasteful, economic policies. I'm Jimmy Carter. Together we can change this. (Carter, "Unacceptable," 1976)

7.9% is high unemployment and the advertisement employed this poor record to attack the Ford's leadership ability ("incompetent leaders"). Similarly, in 1960 Vice President Richard Nixon campaigned in part on the Eisenhower/Nixon record of 1952–1960. His opponent, Senator John Kennedy, challenged the assumption that Nixon deserved any credit for the Eisenhower record. Ironically, President Eisenhower himself provided evidence to support the Democrat's attack at one of his press conferences. One of Kennedy's television spot began with the reporter's question:

Reporter:	"I just wondered if you could give us an example of a major idea of his [Nixon's] that you had adopted in that role, as the, as the decider and final–"
Eisenhower [after pause]:	"If you give me a week, I might think of one. I don't remember." [Laughter] (Kennedy, "Ike's Press Conference," 1960)

Kennedy's message exploits the difference between the president and the vice president: Does Vice President Nixon deserve any of the credit for the administration's successes? Even Nixon's boss, President Eisenhower, does not think so. The key point is to see that the incumbent's record is a source of acclaims by the incumbent and of attacks by the challenger. This ad also shows that Vice Presidents, to varying degrees, run on their record as Vice President.

In 2016, Trump dwelled on problems facing America in the general election (a practice he also followed in the Republican primary). Hillary Clinton was not an incumbent, having never been president or vice president, but she belonged to the same party as President Obama and served as Secretary of State under Obama. Thus, when Trump lamented problems in America, these statements implicitly attacked his opponent. In his nomination acceptance speech, Trump declared that:

Homicides last year increased by 17 percent in America's fifty largest cities. That's the largest increase in 25 years. In our nation's capital, killings have risen by 50 percent. They are up nearly 60 percent in nearby Baltimore. In the President's hometown of Chicago more than 2,000 people have been the victims of shootings this year alone. And almost 4,000 have been killed in the Chicago area since he took office. The number of police officers killed in the line of duty has risen by almost 50 percent compared to this point last year. Nearly 180,000 illegal immigrants with criminal

THE ROLE OF SOURCE IN CAMPAIGN DISCOURSE | 131

records, ordered deported from our country, are tonight roaming free to threaten peaceful citizens. The number of new illegal immigrant families who have crossed the border so far this year already exceeds the entire total from 2015. They are being released by the tens of thousands into our communities with no regard for the impact on public safety or resources. (Trump, Acceptance Address, July 21, 2015)

These complaints, if accepted by his audience, could make voters want to change which party sat in the Oval Office. At times he made criticism of his Democratic opponent explicit: "Decades of lies, cover-ups and scandal have finally caught up with Hillary Clinton" (Trump, "Unfit," 2016). Candidates from the party that is not in power often use attacks.

Functional Theory makes five predictions about incumbents and challengers:

Incumbents acclaim more, and attack less, than challengers.

Donald Trump, who contested the Republican nomination in 2016, was a businessman and media figure. In 2020 his campaign argued that he deserved re-election because he strengthened the economy in his first term. These different approaches illustrates the contrast between challengers or incumbents. Kaid and Johnston (2001), in their study of 1204 presidential television spots (1952–1996) also found that incumbent ads were more positive than spots from challengers (63% to 61%) and that challengers had more negative ads than incumbents (39% to 37%). These differences, however, were not statistically significant (this result could be attributable to their use of a peculiar coding unit: They code the "dominant" approach of the ad rather than coding each theme separately). Note that Functional Theory does not state that incumbents *must* acclaim more, and attack less, than challengers (this caveat applies to remaining predictions as well).

Incumbents defend more than challengers.

Table 4.6 displays data from five different message forms: Acceptance Addresses, television spots, debates, and direct mail.[6] Overall, incumbents acclaim more than challengers (68% to 54%); challengers attack more than incumbents (43% to 28%; defenses also are reported in this table). Research on vice presidential debates (Benoit & Airne, 2005) supports this prediction. Incumbent party vice presidential candidates acclaimed more (63% to 53%) and attacked less (35% to 46%) than challengers.

As noted above, incumbents tend to be better known than challengers. This is particularly true of those incumbent party candidates who were elected president and sought a second term in office (Eisenhower in 1956, Nixon in 1972, Carter in 1980, Reagan in 1984, Bush in 1992, Clinton in 1996, Bush in 2004, Obama

Table 4.6. Functions of discourse from incumbents versus challengers.

	Acclaims	Attacks	Defenses
Acceptance Addresses			
Incumbents	**1667 (81%)**	358 (17%)	21 (1%)
Challengers	1215 (67%)	**605 (33%)**	4 (0.2%)
Television Spots			
Incumbents	**2366 (57%)**	1693 (41%)	115 (3%)
Challengers	1989 (48%)	**2068 (49%)**	130 (3%)
Debates			
Incumbents	**2746 (62%)**	1250 (28%)	463 (10%)
Challengers	2558 (55%)	**1665 (36%)**	396 (9%)
Direct Mail			
Incumbents	**4039 (77%)**	1213 (23%)	15 (0.3%)
Challengers	3997 (54%)	**3393 (46%)**	33 (0.5%)
Governor, Senate, House Tweets			
Incumbents	**652 (78%)**	185 (22%)	2 (0.2%)
Challengers	818 (53%)	721 **(57%)**	6 (0.4%)
Total			
Incumbents	**11470 (68%)**	4699 (28%)	616 (4%)
Challengers	10577 (54%)	**8452 (43%)**	569 (3%)

Acclaims vs. Attacks (Defenses excluded) χ^2 (df = 1) = 880.52, p < .0001. φ = .16.
Acceptance Addresses: Benoit, 2014a; Benoit & Glantz, 2020
Television Spots: Benoit, 2014b; Benoit & Glantz, 2020
Debates: Benoit, 2014c; Benoit & Glantz, 2020
Direct Mail: Benoit & Stein, 2005
Gubernatorial, Senate, and House Tweets: Stein & Benoit, 2021

in 2012, and Trump in 2020). Similarly, the two presidents who came to office in mid-term (Johnson, Ford) were probably better known than their opponents at the time. However, even when a Vice President runs for office (Nixon in 1960, Humphrey in 1968, Bush in 1988, Gore in 2000) they may be somewhat better known than their opponents. This may encourage challengers, who are as a group less well-known than their opponents, to stress character more than incumbents.

As Chapter Two explained, the Functional approach also divides policy utterances into statements addressing past deeds, future plans, and general goals. The incumbent's record – in both acclaims about successes by the incumbent and attacks about failures by the challenger – would be represented in statements about past deeds. Brasher (2003), in a study of U.S. senate campaigns, reported that "major legislation passed by Congress does influence the campaign ... Significant accomplishments provide an opportunity to claim credit or attribute blame and are used as campaign themes by the candidates" (p. 464). Of course, both candidates discuss the challengers record in other offices at times, but more attention is devoted by *both* candidates to the incumbent's record in the White House. Thus, Functional Theory predicts:

> *Incumbents acclaim more on past deeds than challengers; challengers attack more on past deeds than incumbents.*

Overall, 70% of incumbents' past deeds were used to acclaim; in sharp contrast, challengers acclaimed in but 23% of their past deeds. On the other hand, challengers attacked far more on past deeds than incumbents (77% to 30%). See Table 4.7 for these data.

So, challengers have a clear tendency to focus on problems (attacking past deeds) than incumbents. The obvious question for challengers is, what would you do about these problems if you are elected? Challengers have an incentive, therefore, to present suggestions for correcting these problems (in other words, acclaiming future plans). Indeed, each future plan implicitly criticizes the incumbent, even if a future plan is not explicitly connected to a problem (an attack on a past deed). Incumbents can try to make things even better than they are now (acclaiming a future plan), but each future plan proposed by an incumbent is essentially an admission that something has not gone as well as hoped. This leads Functional Theory to predict:

> *Incumbents attack more on future plans than challengers; challengers acclaim more on future plans than incumbents.*

The data on this prediction, from acceptances, general television spots, and general debates, can be found in Table 4.7. Overall, incumbents attack more on future plans than do challengers (41%, 26%). Conversely, challengers acclaim more on future plans than incumbents (74%, 59%). So, challengers have a distinct tendency to acclaim more, and attack less, than incumbents on future plans.

Political Scandal and Image Repair

Scandal can tarnish a candidate's reputation with voters (Shaw, 1999a, 1999b). The reputation, image, or credibility of a candidate is a very important resource. As noted above, credibility can have an important effect on the persuasiveness of a

Table 4.7. Functions of past deeds and future plans for incumbents versus challengers.

	Past Deeds		Future Plans	
	Acclaims	Attacks	Acclaims	Attacks
Acceptance Addresses				
Incumbents	376 (76%)	121 (24%)	112 (74%)	40 (26%)
Challengers	54 (14%)	337 (86%)	71 (88%)	10 (12%)
TV Spots				
Incumbents	582 (55%)	480 (45%)	197 (38%)	328 (62%)
Challengers	219 (18%)	1007 (82%)	241 (61%)	152 (39%)
Debates				
Incumbents	976 (71%)	404 (29%)	402 (61%)	259 (39%)
Challengers	261 (17%)	1295 (83%)	493 (73%)	184 (27%)
Direct Mail				
Incumbents	1916 (76%)	609 (24%)	281 (79%)	74 (21%)
Challengers	637 (32%)	1371 (68%)	466 (82%)	102 (18%)
Gubernatorial, Senate, House Tweets				
Incumbents	164 (48%)	180 (52%)	64 (85%)	11 (15%)
Challengers	17 (9%)	163 (91%)	24 (36%)	42 (64%)
Total				
Incumbents	4014 (69%)	1794 (31%)	1056 (60%)	712 (40%)
Challengers	1188 (22%)	4173 (78%)	1295 (73%)	490 (27%)

Past Deeds: χ^2 (df = 1) = 2469.79, $p < .0001$. $\varphi = .47$. Future Plans: χ^2 (df = 1) = 65.22, $p < .0001$. $\varphi = .14$.
Acceptance Addresses: Benoit, 2014a; Benoit & Glantz, 2020
Television Spots: Benoit, 2014b; Benoit & Glantz, 2020
Debates: Benoit, 2014c; Benoit & Glantz, 2020
Direct Mail: Benoit & Stein, 2005
Tweets: Stein & Benoit, 2021

source (Benoit & Strathman, 2004). Candidates' whose reputations have been tarnished by scandal can expect to be less persuasive, at least for some voters. However, a candidate's image is also important because character is one of the two bases (along with policy) that voters can use to evaluate a candidate. Public opinion poll data presented in Table 2.2 reveals that most voters say policy is the most important determinant of their vote for president. Still, in recent campaigns as much as 34% of the electorate indicate that character is the most important determinant of their vote. And, of course, character may well matter to some of those who think policy is the most important consideration. Not surprisingly, some candidates have attempted to make their opponent's character, or lack thereof, an important issue in the campaign.

Richard Nixon faced charges of having a slush fund as Vice President. President Eisenhower considered dropping him from the ticket in the 1956 campaign, but Nixon salvaged the situation with his "Checkers" speech (Rosenfield, 1968). Gary Hart dropped out of the 1988 Democratic primary because of his relationship with Donna Rice. In 1992, Bill Clinton's character was repeatedly attacked (Blaney & Benoit, 2001). In the 2000 presidential campaign, stories that George W. Bush had been arrested for driving under the influence emerged near the end of the campaign. Gary Condit lost his seat because of allegations that he had not cooperated with the investigation into Chandra Levy's disappearance (Len-Rios & Benoit, 2004). Just before the California gubernatorial recall vote in 2003, stories about Arnold Schwarzenegger's allegedly improper behavior toward women appeared in the news (Nagourney, 2003). In 2004, Jack Ryan dropped out of the race for a U.S. Senate seat from Illinois when it was revealed that he took his wife actress Jeri Ryan to sex clubs (Dewar, 2004). President Bush's campaign in 2004, for example, repeatedly hammered Senator Kerry for being a flip-flopper.

When allegations about a political candidate's character surface in a presidential campaign surface, he or she may wish to respond to those charges in an attempt to defuse them. Responses to character attacks are a form of defense. Thus far, I have said relatively little about defense in large part because it is the least common function. However, when the attacks involve scandals, defense may assume an importance beyond its frequency. Furthermore, defenses are more common, and arguably more important, in political election debates than in other message forms.

The theory of Image Restoration Discourse offers 14 strategies for repairing a damaged image (e.g., Benoit, 1995, 2004; 2015). Table 4.8 lays out the five general strategies (denial, evade responsibility, reduce offensiveness, corrective action, mortification); the first three general strategies have two or more variants. Everyone who faces accusations or suspicions of misbehavior has the same 14 options (Benoit, 1997). However, that does not mean that all of these options are equally effective. Research on image repair has primarily employed the case study method. Intensive analysis of key instances of image restoration has sought to develop principles for effective use of these strategies.

When politicians are innocent, of course, they should deny wrong-doing to try to clear their name. Although President Bill Clinton ultimately admitted to having an improper relationship with Monica Lewinsky, he steadfastly maintained his denial that he suborned perjury (Blaney & Benoit, 2001). A denial is simple and, if

Table 4.8. Image restoration options.

Strategy	Definition	Example
Denial		
Simple Denial	accused did not commit offense	Clinton did not have sex with "that woman"
Shift Blame	another committed the offense	Bush: Congress made me raise taxes
Evade Responsibility		
Provocation	another provoked my behavior	U.S. attacked al Queda because of 9/11
Defeasibility	lacked power to avoid offense	Ford entered office with bad economy
Accident	offense was a mishap	Air Force bombed civilians by mistake
Good Intentions	accuser meant well	U.S. joined NAFTA to help American exports/jobs
Reduce Offensiveness		
Bolstering*	note accused's good qualities	I created jobs
Minimization	offense is not very serious	Bush (1992): economy is not in recession
Differentiation	other, similar offenses are more serious	Reducing increases in Medicare benefits is not as bad as a cut
Transcendence	act justified by more important values	Clinton: protecting my family justified lying
Attack Accuser	accuser should not be believed; if accuser is victim, deserved the harm	Clinton: Ken Starr is prying into my private life
Compensation	accused paid victim for damage	government will pay those whose property is needed for highways
*Corrective Action**	accused will fix and/or prevent recurrence of harm	Reagan: I will prevent future arms sales (like sales to Iran)
Mortification	accused apologizes and asks forgiveness	Clinton: I have sinned (with Monica Lewinsky)

*Bolstering and Corrective Action are basically the same as acclaims.

accepted by the audience, should redeem the politician's image. On the other hand, politicians who are guilty of wrong-doing should confess (apologize, use mortification) immediately and offer corrective action. However, human nature means that we hate to admit we were wrong and politicians often try to deny wrong-doing even when they have committed an offensive act (e.g., Nixon in Watergate [Benoit, 1982], Reagan on the Iran-Contra affair [Benoit, Gullifor, & Panici, 1991], Clinton and his affair with Monica Lewinsky [Blaney & Benoit, 2001]). Notice that in these cases, politicians committed an offense and then they compounded their troubles by doing something else wrong; lying as they deny the offensive act. A false denial means they now have committed two offenses rather than one.

Being guilty of wrong-doing does not necessarily disqualify one from public office or guarantee a loss in an election. The examples mentioned above–accusations against Clinton in 1992, George W. Bush in 2000, and Arnold Schwartzenegger in 2003–did not keep them from winning. Gary Hart, on the other hand, did not overcome his scandal. Accusations of scandal against a politician's character can be serious and they should be aware of their options.

Conclusion

These analyses reveal that the source of political campaign messages exerts influence on the nature or content of the messages they produce. Effects on the functions of campaign messages are inconsistent. Petrocik's theory of Issue Ownership correctly predicts that when policy is discussed, candidates are more likely to emphasize their own party's issues than do their opponents. Turning to character, Republicans tend to discuss sincerity and morality more, and drive and empathy less, than Democrats.

Candidates tend to use more acclaims and fewer attacks than surrogate speakers at the nominating convention. Candidates' TV spots use candidates to acclaim more than other sources. Other sources attack more than candidates in these ads. Finally, TV spots sponsored by political paries and groups are much more negative than spots sponsored by the candidates. The source clearly influences the nature of the discourse produced in political campaigns.

The messages employed by incumbent and challengers also vary. Incumbents acclaim more and attack less than challengers. Incumbents also acclaim more on and attack less on past deeds than challengers. Challengers, in contrast, tend to acclaim more and attack less on future plans than incumbents.

Candidate character is one of the two bases for making a vote choice and a candidate's credibility influences the persuasiveness of his or her campaign messages. Threats to image arise frequently in campaigns precisely because they are competitive; that is, in all contested elections an opponent has a vested interest in decreasing the other candidate's preferability. The news media may also dig up and release potentially damaging information. When threats to image arise, candidates may decide they need to respond with defenses. The theory of Image Restoration Discourse explains the options that are available to political candidates who need to dispel damage to their reputations.

Notes

1. Although occasionally a third party candidate will gain prominence (e.g., H. Ross Perot of the Reform party in 1992 and 1996; Ralph Nader of the Green Party in 2000), and potentially tip the balance (e.g., Nader may have drained enough votes from Al Gore in Florida to alter the outcome of the election), in recent years only the Republican and Democratic parties have fielded candidates who have produced enough discourse to permit meaningful comparisons among candidates representing the various other political parties. Accordingly, although acknowledging the existence of candidates representing other parties, this analysis will focus exclusively on Republican and Democratic candidates. Benoit (1999) analyzed television spots from third party candidates.
2. Only one of Jarvis's (2004) findings is directly comparable to Functional analysis, that Republicans discuss ideals more than Democrats. Here is the use of ideals in general presidential campaign discourse:

	Democrats	Republicans
Acceptance Addresses	387	373
TV Spots	189	194
Debates	245	259
Direct Mail	203	349

Only in direct mail advertising is the difference in use of ideals significant (and in the predicted direction).
3. Table 5.1 in Kaid and Johnston (2001) is mislabeled; that table reverses "image" (character) and "issue" (policy).
4. It is possible that these results were influenced by the discrepancy in samples (data do not exist on keynotes in the 1950's and the Republicans did not designate a Keynote speech in 2000, so three more campaigns are included in the Acceptance data. Accordingly, I calculated a χ^2 using only data from the same years for which we have data from Keynotes, and the results did not change.
5. Incumbency is different in congressional elections from presidential races: Races that do not feature a sitting incumbent are considered "open-seat." Unlike the president, members of the

Senate and House do not have running mates (there is nothing like a "Vice-Senator"). When vice-presidents runs for election, they usually emphasize the record in office. For example, in 1960, Vice President Richard Nixon sought to succeed President Dwight Eisenhower. On civil rights, a Nixon television spot observed that "Now the record shows there's been more progress in civil rights in the past eight years than in the preceding eighty years, because this administration has insisted on making progress." Clearly, he was trying to run as an incumbent, as a part of the Eisenhower-Nixon administration. The challengers in such elections also attacked the record under the vice-president. For example, a spot for President Ford in 1976 criticized his challenger, Jimmy Carter, for his record as Governor of Georgia:

What Jimmy Carter did as Governor, he'll do as President. His ads say that he will do the same as President that he did as Governor of Georgia. During his one term as Governor, government spending increased by 58%. Government employees went up 25%. And the state of GA went over 20% deeper into debt. Don't let Jimmy Carter give us more big government. Keep President Ford.

Similar attacks on Ronald Reagan's record as California governor (1980), Michael Dukakis's record as governor of Massachusetts (1992), and Bill Clinton's record as Arkansas's governor can be found in the campaign messages of the incumbents they challenged.

6 Incumbency is most pertinent to the general campaign.

CHAPTER FIVE

The Role of Context in Political Campaign Discourse

This chapter will discuss the influence of context on political campaign discourse. First, the context will be discussed as campaign phase (primary versus general). Next, I will discuss the relatively recent phenomenon of restricting active campaigning in the general campaign to battleground states. Finally, I will consider the influence of four other contextual factors on candidate messages will be discussed.

Campaign Phase: Primary versus General

It is common knowledge that presidential campaigns have primary phases and general phases, separated by the parties' nomination conventions (scholars have also recognized a "pre-primary" phase called "surfacing," see, e.g., Trent, 1978). Smith (2015) identifies "five indices of the emerging candidate's viability... endorsements, national opinion polls, fund-raising, press coverage, and Iowa polls" (p. 24). These factors generally influence perceptions of a presidential candidate's viability. However, in 2016 Donald Trump did not stress fund-raising during the surfacing phase. In fact, Rappeport (2016) reported that "Trump regularly boasts that he is self-funding his presidential bid." Instead, he relied primarily on press coverage of his controversial statements and tweets to demonstrate his viability. A key moment in the primary phase of a presidential campaign is the Announcement Speech (see, e.g., Benoit & Glantz, 2013, 2020; Benoit, Henson, Whalen, & Pier, 2008; Neville-Shepard, 2014), wherein the candidate officially declares that he or she is seeking his or her party's nomination for president. Candidates usually form an "exploratory" committee and so they can start raising campaign funds.

Blumenthal (1980) coined the phrase "permanent campaign" to recognize that some candidates continually campaign for office. Aspiring presidential candidates visit the states holding early primaries or caucuses and work to secure endorsements long before the Iowa caucuses or the New Hampshire primary occur. Candidates for other offices also feel the need to campaign before the election season – particularly members of the House of Representatives, who must stand for re-election every other year. Elected presidents begin running for their second term in office immediately upon entering the Oval Office (presidents enjoying their second term in office work on creating a positive "legacy").

The primary phase of the presidential campaign has also been unjustly neglected by political scholars. A focus on the general election campaign makes sense, just as the greatest emphasis in sports is accorded to the championship (e.g., the Superbowl in football, the World Series in baseball, the World Cup in football [soccer for Americans]). Presidential primaries are an important way for party members to learn about their potential leaders and then select the candidate who will represent their party in the Fall. Furthermore, primary campaigns are significant because they are an opportunity for party members to participate in democracy and exert influence on the direction their party will take. Davis (1997) observed that "in no other Western country do so many people take part in the party nominating process" (p. 2).

The primary campaign phase deserves our attention for several reasons. First, in recent history, it has been essential for a presidential candidate to secure the nomination of the Republican or Democratic Party in order to win the White House. Various candidates – including George Wallace, John Anderson, Ross Perot, and Ralph Nader – have discovered the truth of this assertion. Davis argued that "the presidential nominating process narrows the alternatives from a theoretical potential candidate pool of ... millions ... to only two candidates, one Republican and one Democrat, with a realistic chance of winning the White House" (p. 1). So, winning the primary campaign and securing the Democratic or Republican party nomination for president is a necessary (although not a sufficient) condition for becoming president.

Second, the primary campaign has become increasingly important in recent years. Bartels (1988) summarized changes in the nomination process:

The new system is dominated by candidates and by the news media; the old system was dominated by professional party politicians. The central decision-making mechanism in the new system is mass voting; the central mechanism in the old system was face-to-face bargaining. The locus of choice in the new system is the primary ballot box; the locus of choice in the old system was the convention backroom. (p. 13; see also Pious, 2006)

Because party bosses controlled the nomination, support of primary voters was a means to an end rather than an end in itself. Candidates did not run in primaries in order to win a majority of the delegates to the nominating conventions; they ran to demonstrate their *ability to garner votes*. For example, John F. Kennedy's West Virginia primary campaign was important "because it convinced powerful party leaders ... that Kennedy [a Catholic] could win Protestant votes" (Bartels, 1988, p. 15). Levine noted that in the past "presidential hopefuls generally did not even need to campaign in primaries, which were relatively few in number" (1995, p. 56). As recently as 1968, Hubert Humphrey became his party's nominee without campaigning in a single primary (Levine, 1995). In earlier years, the contests over who should be the party's nominee were often divisive–and they were broadcast over the national television. The Democratic National Convention in 1968, complete with televised riots, is a notorious example of a bitterly disputed convention that may have damaged the Democratic party and contributed to a win by Republican Richard Nixon. To avoid contentious conventions and to decrease perceptions that party leaders rather than rank and file party members determined the nomination, both parties increased their use of primaries and caucuses to select their nominees (Davis, 1997; Kendall, 2000). In 1968, there were only 16 Republican and 17 Democratic primaries (Crotty & Jackson, 1985). In 2000, primaries or caucuses were held in all states and the District of Columbia (Federal Election Commission, 2000).

Moreover, some years feature vulnerable incumbents, such as Ford in 1976, Carter in 1980, or Bush in 1992. It is distinctly possible that someone other than Jimmy Carter could have defeated Gerald Ford in 1976, that another Republican besides Ronald Reagan could have unseated Carter four years later, or that Bill Clinton was not the only Democrat who could have ousted George Bush in 1992. However, because these three candidates won their parties' nominations, they were the only ones who were entitled to challenge those weak opponents. Accordingly, in a very real sense, the primary campaign may have decided who would ultimately become the president by determining who had the right to run against a vulnerable incumbent. To return to the sports metaphor used earlier, if one conference is weaker than the other, then the playoff game or games to determine the winner of the other stronger conference (semi-finals) may in a real sense determine the overall champion, because that game determines who gets to face the representative of the weaker conference.

Finally, messages in the primary campaign can influence voters. Bartels (1988) offers the following example to illustrate this point:

> At the beginning of 1976, Jimmy Carter was a relatively unknown one-term ex-governor of a medium-sized southern state. Although he had been running for president full-time for more than a year ... [a] Gallup poll indicated that fewer than 5 percent of the Democratic party rank and file considered him their first choice for the party's nomination.
>
> Five months later, Carter was quite clearly about to become his party's nominee .... Carter was the first choice of an absolute majority of Democrats–leading his nearest rival by a margin of almost forty percentage points–and a winner by almost twenty percentage points in trial heats against the incumbent Republican president. (p. 3)

Carter's campaign, directly via his messages and indirectly as mediated by news coverage of his campaign, clearly influenced voters and made a difference. Benoit, Hansen, and Verser (2003) found that primary debates had even larger effects on viewers than general debates.

The idea that the primary phase merits scholarly attention is important because the two phases of a political campaign–primary and general–possess substantial differences. This section will discuss each of these factors, elucidate additional principles of the Functional Theory of Political Campaign Discourse that pertain to campaign phase, and compare campaign messages to test predictions about the nature of discourse produced in these two phases.

Differences Between Primary and General Campaigns

There are six important differences between primary and general campaigns. I will discuss each of these separately in this section.

Party of Opponent

In contested primaries, when more than one candidate seeks the nomination of his or her political party, it is important to realize that those fellow party members are the immediate opponents. For example, John Kerry and George W. Bush were opponents in the 2004 general election campaign, but, in a very real sense, they were not opponents in the primary. Kerry first had to defeat his Democratic rivals in the primary: Welsey Clark, Howarad Dean, Dick Gephardt, Bob Graham, Dennis Kucinich, Joe Lieberman, Carol Moseley-Braun, and Al Sharpton.

A candidate must win his or her party's nomination first: In a 1980 primary debate in New Hampshire, Ronald Reagan discussed the "eleventh commandment," that Republicans should not attack Republicans in the primary. However, primary candidates must distinguish themselves from immediate opponents, and they must convince voters that they are preferable to those opponents, and attacks on fellow party members are a means of achieving these goals.

For example, in the 2016 primaries, none of the Republican candidates had anything good to say about Secretary Hillary Clinton. Still, Bush, Christie, Rubio, Trump, and the other candidates had to get past the other Republicans to secure the nomination and have the right to challenge Clinton in the general election. Most of the Republicans attacked each other more than attacked the presumptive Democratic nominee. When a political party's nomination is contested, the candidates' real or immediate opponents are fellow party members, rather than the presumed nominee of the other party.

The nature of one's opponent influences the nature of campaign discourse. For example, compare Bill Clinton's primary campaigns from 1992 and 1996. In his first presidential campaign, the Democratic nomination was sought by Clinton as well as by other Democrats such as Jerry Brown, Tom Harkin, and Paul Tsongas. Clinton mentioned his Democratic opponents in 10 of 40 primary spots and mentioned the presumed Republican nominee, President George Bush, in but 4 primary spots. Clinton also responded to attacks from his fellow Democrats in other spots. Here is just one example of these 1992 primary television spots, which focused on one of his Democratic opponents:

> Jerry Brown says he'll fight for we the people. Question is, which people? He says he for working families. But his tax proposal has been called a flat-out fraud. It cuts taxes for the very rich in half and raised taxes on the middle class. Jerry Brown says he'll clean up politics and limit campaign contributions. But a year ago he helped lead the fight that killed campaign reform and contribution limits in California. So the next time Jerry Brown says he's fighting for the people, ask him which people and which Jerry Brown. (Clinton, 1992 Primary, "Which")

Thus, Clinton, who needed to defeat his Democratic opponents in the primary, could do little to help his general campaign in his 1992 primary messages. He waited until after he had secured the Democratic nomination to focus on attacking his Republican opponent.

In contrast, Clinton's bid for re-election in 1996 was not contested in Democratic primaries. Thus, he could, and did, focus his primary campaign on attacking Dole (the presumptive Republican nominee) instead of other Democrats. For example, in this campaign, Clinton and Democratic National Committee

(DNC) spots run during the primary season mentioned Dole or showed his picture in 25 out of 40 television spots, such as this one:

> The Oval Office. If it were Bob Dole sitting here, he would have already cut Medicare $270 billion. Toxic polluters off the hook. No to the Brady Bill; 60,000 criminals allowed to buy handguns. Slashed education. President Clinton stood firm and defended our values. But next year, if Newt Gingrich controls Congress and his partner, Bob Dole, enters the Oval Office, there'll be nobody there to stop them. (Clinton, 1996, "Nobody")

Clearly, Clinton started his general campaign early with spots such as this one. He did not need to expend effort or money getting past a primary candidates from his own political party. As noted earlier, Buchanan challenged President Bush in 1992. At least five of Bush's primary television spots explicitly responded to Buchanan. Thus, except in the case of uncontested primaries, it is vital for candidates, as well as theorists and analysts, to focus on the candidate's immediate opponent (or opponents).

Number of Opponents

The number of candidates, and therefore the number of opponents, usually varies by campaign phase. Although there are numerous third party candidates in the general campaign, there are usually only two viable candidates in that phase. In recent years, only George Wallace in 1968 and Ross Perot in 1992 attracted substantial support: Humphrey attacked Wallace in television spots and Perot was invited to the debates in 1992. Ralph Nader ran in 2000 (and some thought he drained support away from Vice President Al Gore, giving Bush the election). When there are only two viable contenders, as is usually the case in the general campaign, there is really no choice about whom to attack: The Republican nominee attacks the Democratic nominee and vice versa.

However, contested primaries may have at least four or five serious contenders and at times far more than that participate in a given debate (and in such encounters even non-viable candidates are difficult to ignore). The October 1995 New Hampshire Republican primary debate, for example, included ten candidates: Alexander, Buchanan, Dole, Dornan, Forbes, Gramm, Keyes, Lugar, Specter, and Taylor. In 2004, the early Democratic primary debates usually included nine candidates: Howard Dean, John Edwards, Dick Gephardt, John Kerry, Dennis Kucinich, Joe Lieberman, Carol Moseley-Braun, Al Sharpton and either Bob Graham (who dropped out early) or Wesley Clark (who joined the fray afterwards). In 2020, the first Democratic presidential primary debates had so many participants that candidates were split into two groups, each group having a (separate) debate. Thus, the number of viable or visible opponents may be much larger in primary campaigns and, when there are more than two potential targets, the candidates must decide whom to attack.

Strategically, the front-runner, who has the most support and should win the nomination unless the situation changes, should receive the brunt of the attacks in primary discourse. For example, Table 5.1 reports the results of a public opinion poll reporting the distribution of support for Democratic primary candidates in 2020.

Given that attacks function to decrease the preferability of an opponent, no candidate here stands to gain very much from attacks on Yang, Booker, or Klobuchar, who were ranked last in the poll. However, if one of these three candidates could reduce Bloomberg's popularity with an attack, they might perhaps rise to a tie for fifth. Bloomberg, Yang, Booker, and Klobuchar all have a strategic reason to attack Buttigieg, because he enjoyed more support than they did. Similarly, everyone who ranked below Warren in the polls had an incentive to attack Warren because they could not win the nomination without overtaking her in the polls. Candidates who trailed Sanders possessed a strategic reason to criticize Sanders. Finally, every other candidate had a strategic reason to attack Biden because Biden would win the nomination as long as he maintained his lead. Thus, more candidates have a strategic reason to attack the front-runner than to attack anyone else, and they have no strategic reason to attack those who are below them in the polls. Haynes and Rhine, analyzing news coverage of attacks in the 1992 Democratic primaries, found that rather than trying "to eliminate their nearest ideological rivals .... candidates of all political stripes focus [attacks] on the leaders" (p. 714). On the other hand, "Frontrunners are not likely to attack on average unless attacked" (p. 715). So, evidence from news reports of the 1992

Table 5.1. Support for Democratic candidates in 2020.

Candidate	Poll Number
Joe Biden	26%
Bernie Sanders	20%
Elizabeth Warren	16%
Pete Buttigieg	8%
Michael Bloomberg	5%
Andrew Yang	3%
Cory Booker	3%
Amy Klobuchar	3%

Source: Agiesta, 2019

Table 5.2. Poll position and number of attacks received, republican primary debate 10.

	Poll Position	Attacks Against
Trump	1 (42%)	104
Cruz	2 (22%)	32
Rubio	3 (13%)	13
Kasich	4 (tie 8%)	1
Carson	4 (tie 8%)	0

Democratic primary is consistent with this prediction. This idea was also dramatically confirmed in the 2016 presidential primary debates. For example, the tenth Republican Primary debate of the 2016 election showed that the higher a candidate stood in the polls the more attacks aimed at that candidate (69% of all attacks in the debate targeted front-runner Trump).

Of course, presidential candidates may have non-strategic reasons to attack as well (perhaps they genuinely disagree on issues or genuinely dislike another candidate personally), but those kinds of attacks do not provide reasons to attack any particular candidate. Strategic considerations, however, offer a strong reason to expect front-runners to be the target of most attacks.

This raises the question of whom the front-runner should attack. In fact, in the context of a primary campaign, an attack on the other party may function almost like an acclaim. That is, when Trump attacked Clinton in 2016 *in messages intended for Republicans* many in his audience probably thought more highly of Trump because of these attacks. So, in a primary, attacks by members of one political party on candidates from the other political party may not function quite the way other attacks do, reducing the desirability of one's immediate opponent. In contrast, an attack on a fellow party member in a primary would be more likely to create a backlash than an attack on a candidate from the other party.

Target Audience

In the primary, the object is to win the most votes from fellow-party members (an exception would be McCain's appeal to non-Republicans to vote for him in "open" primaries in 2000). Each state has multiple delegates to the national nominating convention and primary votes determine how these delegates will vote (which candidate they support). This means that the principal target audience in this phase of the campaign should be members of one's own party. Of course, in an uncontested primary, as with Clinton in 1996, Bush in 2004, or Trump in 2020 (in fact, as of October 2019, five states had canceled GOP presidential primaries: Alaska, Arizona, Kansas, Nevada, and South Carolina to pre-empt attacks on the president; Reints, 2019) candidates can essentially commence the general campaign early, appealing to voters beyond those in their own political party.

In the general campaign, the party nominees can count on the support of most of their party members (Trump won the GOP nomination and the Electoral College in 2016 despite the hostility of "Never Trump" Republicans). They may wish to try to increase the likelihood that their party members will actually vote on election day; they may also attempt to keep potential vote defectors from their own party from defecting to their opponent, or try to attract potential vote defectors from the other party. But effort in the general campaign should also be directed toward winning the support of the independent and undecided voters who often cluster at the middle of the political spectrum. As established in Chapter One, no candidate can assure an election win relying only on votes from his own political party because neither political party has the support of a majority of voters. Thus, the audience which matters most in a contested primary are members of one's own political party; in the general campaign, the target audience shifts to focus more on independent or undecided voters and potential vote defectors.

This analysis explains why candidates are sometimes said to "run to the right (or left) in primaries and then to the center in the general campaign." The principal audience in these two campaign phases is quite different. In order to obtain their party's nomination, a candidate must convince the majority of *his or her party members* that he or she is preferable to members of his own political party. For Republicans, this means emphasizing issues on the right of the political spectrum; for Democrats, it means stressing issues on the left of the political spectrum. However, after the party nominees have been selected and they turn to the general campaign, they can for the most part take for granted the votes of most partisans (worrying only about potential vote defectors). But to win the general phase of the election, candidates must appeal to *other groups of voters*–undecided, independent, and potential vote defectors–voters whose concerns may be quite different from those of committed partisans. Benoit and Hansen (2001) found evidence that presidential candidates' television spots focus more on their own party's issues in the primary than the general campaign, evidence that this message adaption does occur. Thus, candidates should emphasize different issues and take positions that lie more in the middle of the political spectrum in the general than the primary campaign. In other words, the shift in target audience explains a concomitant shift in campaign discourse.

Arena

The physical location of the primary tends to shift from one state or group of states to state or group of states over time. Candidates begin the primary focusing most of their time and money on Iowa and New Hampshire. Candidates do visit other states (the next states on the primary calendar, such as South Carlina), but the focus is almost always on one or both of these two states at the beginning of the primary season. However, once Iowa and New Hampshire have held their primaries, the candidates never return to these states: They move on to the next group of primary states. In the general campaign, all of the votes are cast at the polling places on a single day (except for absentee ballots). Although presidential candidates do not campaign in every state (apart from Nixon's ill-advised pledge to visit every state in the 1960 general election campaign), states are not visited and then abandoned for the remainder of the campaign as they are in the primary. Candidates will return to key states repeatedly during the general campaign. This factor influences where messages (e.g., speeches, debates, spots) are disseminated to the public.

Some candidates may choose to bypass a primary or caucus state. In 1988 Senator Tom Harkin (from Iowa) campaigned for the Democratic nomination. He was expected to win the caucuses in his home state. This led some to discount the results in Iowa; Harkin's "home field" or "favorite son" advantage in this state meant that he ought to win more votes in Iowa than he would nationally. Why risk looking like a loser by running against Harkin in his home state? In 2000, Senator John McCain conserved his limited resources in 2000 by skipping Iowa and concentrating on New Hampshire.

Sides and Vavrek (2013) describe a fairly common primary phenomena: discovery, scrutiny, and decline. Candidates sometimes receive considerable media attention. This can occur in a variety of circumstances: when a "new" candidate enters the race or when a candidate performs well (such as in a straw poll). Such candidates often surge in the polls when voters "discover" them. As a candidate rises in the polls, the media and other competing candidates start looking for, and talking about, the surging candidate's weaknesses (scrutiny). As voters learn more about that candidate, and particularly more about that candidate's weaknesses, the candidate will frequently fall in the polls (decline).

State Influence

In general election campaign, the influence of each state is determined by the number of electoral votes at stake there. However, in the primary, the date of the election can be more important than the number of delegates to the national party convention from that state because of the disproportionate publicity given to early primaries and caucuses. This is precisely why Iowa and New Hampshire, with early dates, have a disproportionate influence in the primary campaign considering the number of voters who reside in these states.

The fact that state primary elections are spread out across the calendar means that some states hold their primaries after one candidate has already won enough delegates to win the nomination, which renders those primaries superfluous. Davis (1997) reported that in 1968, only 1 primary (New Hampshire) had been held by March 31; by that same date in 1996, 26 states had held primaries. In 2000, both Al Gore and George W. Bush wrapped up their party's nominations with the March 14 "Super Tuesday" primaries even though some primaries were not held until June. Although he had not yet won enough delegates to claim the nomination, it was clear that Kerry would win the Democratic nomination after the March 3, 2004 primaries. In 2004, the Iowa caucuses were scheduled for January 13 and the New Hampshire primary for January 27. The relative importance of states, as determined by the date of a state's primary, is an important reason why the dates of the primary campaign continually creep forward, as some states leap ahead of others to make their states more important. Patterson (2003) uses California to illustrate this point:

> Traditionally, California's primary was on the final day of the nominating calendar. Until 1976 it was often a decisive encounter .... After 1976, however, the race in *every* case was over by the time it reached California. In 1996, the state moved its primary to March 26, [but] even that position was too far back to enable delegate-rich California to exert its muscle. For 2000, the state moved its primary to the first Tuesday in March, the earliest allowable date. (p. 110)

As of June 2016, neither Hillary Clinton nor Donald Trump had formally clinched the nomination, although many observers thought they were definitely going to do so by May. This is the first time in decades that the California primary had a chance of influencing the outcome of the primary. In 2016 Donald Trump had to wait for the vote at the Republican National Convention in Cleveland to be certain he was the nominee. Joe Biden clinched the Democratic nomination in early April of 2020. So, the primary calendar continually creeps forward because the date of a state's primary or caucus influences the state's importance.

The 2004 Democratic primary campaign boasted of some dubious "firsts." The earliest presidential primary debate on record was held on April 9, 2003, in Washington DC. Howard Dean aired what is probably the earliest primary television spot ever on June 17, 2003. The Iowa caucuses moved from January 24, 2000 to January 19, 2004 and the New Hampshire primary jumped from February 1 in 2000 to January 27 in 2004. In fact, most primaries in 2004 were held earlier than in 2000 (a few states have Democratic and Republican primaries or caucuses on different days; I only considered Democratic primary dates). 39 states moved the date of their primaries up by an average of almost three weeks (19.4 days). On the other hand, 11 primaries were moved back in 2000, but most by only a few days. One move that merits comment is Missouri's primary, which was moved from March 7 to February 3. This move was probably intended to give Missouri Democrat Richard Gephardt's campaign a boost from an early win. However, a poor showing in neighboring Iowa's caucuses convinced Gephardt to drop out of the race before Missouri's primary was held.

The primary season is becoming longer as the years pass (see Patterson, 2003, p. 101). It is risky for candidates to let others get in the game first:

> Even an odds-on-favorite has no choice but to start early and run hard. In 1980, Ronald Reagan discovered the risks of the waiting game. He had a four-to-one lead for the Republican nomination in national polls and decided not to participate in a televised debate in Iowa. Hawkeye State voters did not take kindly to the snub. After his loss there, Reagan's 30-point lead in New Hampshire polls shrank almost to nothing. (p. 103)

So, once one candidate starts actively campaigning, there is an important incentive for others to begin campaigning too. This means better organized and well-financed candidates have an advantage: the ability to sustain their campaigns for the longer periods of time demanded by today's extended primary season. Norrander (2000) observed that "Since 1984, the candidate who has raised the most money in advance of the opening contests has won every nominating race" (p. 2). Although this streak ended in 2004 (Dean raised the most money early in the primaries), there can be no doubt that money is an important factor in primary campaigns.

Second, the primaries are moving from being spread throughout the primary season to bunching together at the beginning of the primary season, a phenomenon known as "front-loading" (Mayer & Busch, 2004). The date of New Hampshire's "first in the nation" primary (the Iowa *caucuses* have preceded it in recent years) was March 11 in 1952. In 2004, it was January 27. Figure 5.1 shows that the date of the New Hampshire primary moved forward four times: 1976, 1988, 2000, and 2004.

Primaries and caucuses are bunching together at the beginning of the primary season. Hagen and Mayer (2000) report that in 1952, only 13% of Democratic delegates to the Democratic Nominating Convention and 17% of Republican delegates to the Republican Nominating Convention had been selected by the end of the fourth week of the primary. By 1996, 44% of Democratic and 51% of Republican delegates had been selected after four weeks. The role of dates for

Figure 5.1. New Hampshire primary dates: 1952–2016.

	January	February	March
2016		9	
2012	10		
2008	8		
2004		27	
2000		8	
1996		20	
1992		18	
1988		16	
1984			28
1980			26
1976			24
1972			7
1968			12
1964			10
1960			8
1956			13
1952			11

primary elections has moved the primary season earlier and front-loaded delegate selection. Front-loading means that the primary calendar does not simply shift earlier but primaries and caucuses bunch together at the beginning.

Front-loading is undesirable for several reasons. As noted earlier, candidates must be able to sustain their campaigns for a longer period of time. Furthermore, after the Iowa caucuses and the New Hampshire primaries, other races follow at a fast and furious (front-loaded) pace, requiring enough money to campaign in several states simultaneously. In 2020, the first four caucuses/primaries were spread apart: Iowa (February 3), New Hampshire (February 11), Nevada (February 22), and South Carolina (February 29). After this gradual start, elections ramped up quickly and then slowed down:

March 3: AL, AR, CA, CO, ME, MA, MN NC, OK, TN TX, UT, VT, VA
March 10: ID, MI, MS, MO, ND, WA
March 17: FL, IL
April 4: AL
April 7: WI
April 17: WY

April 28: OH
May 2: KS
May 12: NE
May 19: OR
May 22 HI

A candidate with little funds and organization has no chance of reaching the voters in so many states. Mayer and Busch (2004) argue that front-loading "greatly accelerates the voters' decision process and thus makes the whole system less deliberate, less flexible, and more chaotic" (p. 56).

Furthermore, Patterson (2003) argues that front-loading has hurt turnout in primary elections, which has dropped "from nearly 30% to 17% since the 1970s … Since the advent of front-loading turnout has been half again as high in contested primaries as in those held after the races were decided" (p. 111). Front-loading makes it difficult for candidates and voters alike.

Voter Knowledge

Voters know less about the candidates in the primary phase than the general campaign. This is true for two reasons. First, many of the primary contenders are simply not particularly well-known. In 2020, voters knew virtually nothing about Donald Trump's political views (note he identified as a Democrat from 2001 to 2009). They knew little about such candidates as Cory Booker, Pete Buttigieg, Tom Steyer, Jay Inslee, or or Kirsten Gillibrand. So, voters have relatively little knowledge of the presidential candidates in the primary.

Second, the two candidates who become their parties' nominees are better known to voters in the general campaign than they were in the primary. For example, because of tweets, spots, debates, other messages, and news coverage of the primary campaign, voters in 2004 knew more about Donald Trump in September, during the general campaign, than they did in February, during the primary. The need to introduce the candidates – who are less well-known in the primary – encourages an emphasis on character in that phase of the campaign.

Primary and General Campaign Messages

Based on this analysis of the nature of the presidential primary campaign, Functional Theory makes six predictions about primary campaign discourse.

> P1. *Acclaims are more common, and attacks are less common, in primary than general campaign messages.*

There are three reasons to expect fewer attacks in the primary than the general phase of the campaign. First, there are fewer policy differences between members of the same political party (compared with general election opponents from the other party) which means there are fewer opportunities to attack primary opponents. Second, the eventual nominee will want to have the support of the other candidates in the general election. That is, in 2020 Biden wanted Sanders, Warren, Buttigieg, Booker and the other Democratic primary candidates to support him in the general campaign, just as they would have wanted Biden's support if they had won the Democratic nomination. A desire to have the support of one's primary opponents may be a reason to moderate attacks in the primary; there is no similar reason to hold back in the general campaign. Perhaps more importantly, a third reason to moderate attacks in the primary is the desire to win over the support of those citizens who preferred one of your primary opponents. Will Sanders' supporters get behind Biden? Thus, Functional Theory predicts that acclaims should be more common, and attacks less common, in the primary than the general campaign.

Research supports this prediction. Chapter Two reported that overall, acclaims are more frequent than attacks in presidential campaign messages (Table 2.1). Table 5.3 breaks down the functions of television spots, debates, and direct mail brochures in primary and general campaigns. Acclaims comprised 72% of utterances in primary campaigns but only 63% of the remarks in general campaigns. On the other hand, attacks accounted for 34% of comments in the general campaign but only 26% in the primaries.

West's (2001) study of 433 "prominent" ads from 1996 to 2000 reported that the percentage of attack ads was virtually identical in the primary (56%) and general (55%) phases of the presidential campaign. However, as discussed in Chapter Three, his sample was not random (nor does "prominent" equal "most influential") but is biased toward attack ads.

P2. *Character is more common, and policy less common, in primary than general campaign messages.*

There are two reasons to expect character to be discussed more frequently, and policy less often, in the primary than the general campaign. As suggested earlier, candidates are less well-known in the primary phase, which means they need to introduce themselves to the voters. Second, as noted above, there are fewer policy differences between candidates who belong to the same party. This means fewer opportunities to attack on policy – because it would be silly, of course, for one

Table 5.3. Functions and topics of primary vs. general campaign messages.

	Functions			Topics	
	Acclaims	Attacks	Defenses	Policy	Character
TV Spots					
Primary	6646 (72%)	2481 (27%)	62 (0.1%)	5040 (55%)	4613 (61%)
General	4076 (53%)	3478 (46%)	89 (1%)	4613 (61%)	2936 (39%)
Debates					
Primary	30710 (65%)	14337 (30%)	2332 (5%)	27350 (69%)	12104 (31%)
General	5304 (55%)	3545 (37%)	859 (9%)	6320 (72%)	2490 (28%)
Direct Mail					
Primary	7776 (85%)	1361 (15%)	7 (0.1%)	5660 (62%)	3424 (38%)
General	8036 (70%)	3393 (30%)	48 (0.4%)	8742 (76%)	2687 (24%)
Presidential Social Media					
Primary	4755 (73%)	1685 (26%)	57 (1%)	2639 (41%)	3867 (59%)
General	2968 (52%)	2687 (47%)	56 (1%)	2637 (47%)	3008 (53%)
Total					
Primary	49887 (69%)	19864 (28%)	2458 (3%)	40689 (63%)	24008 (37%)
General	20384 (59%)	13103 (38%)	1052 (3%)	22312 (67%)	11121 (33%)

Functions (Acclaims vs. Attacks): χ^2 ($df = 1$) = 1180.66, $p < .0001$, $\varphi = .11$. Topics: χ^2 ($df = 2$) = 141.78, $p < .0001$, $\varphi = .04$.
Primary, General TV Spots: Benoit, 2014a; Benoit & Glantz, 2020.
Primary, General Debates: Benoit, 2014b; Benoit & Glantz, 2020.
Primary, General Brochures: Benoit & Stein, 2005.
Primary Social Media: Benoit & Glantz, 2020.
General Social Media: Shen & Benoit, 2016; Benoit & Glantz, 2020.

candidate to attack an opponent who advocated the same policy as the attacker – and fewer places to acclaim distinctiveness on policy.

Chapter Two reported that overall policy is more frequently discussed than character in presidential campaign messages (Table 2.3). Table 5.3 also breaks out four key campaign media for which we have longitudinal data: television spots, debates, and direct mail advertising from both phases of the campaign. Policy was even more frequently discussed in these general (72%) than primary (64%) campaign messages. In contrast, character was more often addressed in primary (36%) than general (28%) discourse. Frequency of topic is significantly different in these two campaign phases overall and in each specific message form. These results are consistent with those reported by Geer (1998), who reported more issue ads in the general than the primary campaign (50% to 42%) and more personal quality ads in the primary than the general campaign (38% to 21%).

Not surprisingly, the candidates who run in the general campaign tend to have a record of governmental experience: Party nominees' resumes include Vice Presidents (Nixon, Humphrey, Bush, Gore), Senators (Kennedy, Goldwater, McGovern, Dole, Obama), and Governors (Stephenson, Carter, Reagan, Dukakis, Clinton, Bush; Trump, who had no experience in elective office, was an exception). Eisenhower (a general), who ran and won in 1952 and 1956, was an exception. Obviously, candidates who ran for a second term in office (e.g., Nixon in 1972, Carter in 1980, Reagan in 1984, Bush in 1992, Clinton in 1996, Bush in 2004 and Obama in 2012) have experience as president. Although many primary candidates have similar governmental experience, a disproportionate number of those who ran in primary campaigns had little or no experience in elective office (e.g., Gary Bauer, Pat Buchanan, Wesley Clark, Elizabeth Dole, Steve Forbes, Jesse Jackson, Alan Keyes). This means that as a group, the candidates who participate in primary campaigns are less likely to have a record in office than candidates in the general campaign. This should mean that there will be fewer past deeds to acclaim or to attack in primary than general campaigns. As argued in Chapter Two, general goals are easier to propose than future plans. Hence, I expect there will be relatively less discussion of past deeds and more of general goals in the primary campaign phase.

P3. *Candidates will discuss past deeds less, and general goals more, in primary than general campaigns.*

Overall, there is a significant difference in use of these forms by campaign phase. As predicted, past deeds are employed less frequently in primary campaign messages (36%) than in general messages (49%). On the other hand, general goals occur more often in the primary (50%) than the general (35%) campaign phase. Significant differences occurred in each of the three campaign message forms (debates, television spots, direct mail brochures) with a moderate effect size. Campaign phase does influence use of past deeds and general goals.

P4. *More attacks in the primary target candidates who are members of the attacker's own party than candidates of the other party.*

As discussed earlier, one's immediate opponents in the primary are members of one's own party. Thus, attacks–designed to reduce the desirability of one's opponents–should be primarily aimed at fellow party-members.

Evidence that bears on this prediction can be drawn from several studies. First, our study of 25 presidential primary debates from 1948 to 2000 (Benoit et al. 2002) found that 1082 attacks were directed toward candidates from the attacker's own party, whereas 693 attacks were aimed at candidates from the other party (some attacks were also directed toward the establishment). Second, re-analysis of the primary television spots from 1952 to 1996 in Benoit (1999) revealed that 62% of attacks were directed toward other members of the attacker's party and 28% targeted the opposing party (10% attacked the establishment). Third, research on the 1996 primary campaign found that (in addition to television spots and debates, as just noted) more attacks were directed toward own than other party candidates in talk radio appearances (55% to 35%) and in debates (58% to 25%). Finally, our study of the 2000 primary campaign (Benoit, McHale, Hansen, Pier, & McGuire, 2003) found that candidates attacked their own party more than the other party in television spots, radio spots, and television talk shows; only in primary web pages were there more attacks on the other party than on one's own party (and, again, primary debates support this prediction as shown by Benoit et al. 2002). Thus, there is strong support for this prediction from multiple campaigns and multiple message forms.

A clear exception to this pattern occurred in the 2004 Democratic primary President Bush declared in 2000 (and again in 2004) that he was a uniter rather than a divider. However, he did not succeed at uniting the country behind him in the presidential campaign, although he did succeed in uniting his Democrat opponents. They directed more of their attacks toward Republican President George W. Bush than at each other. For example, Al Sharpton observed in the California primary debate that although he had disagreements with both Kerry and Edwards, "on their worst day, they are better than George Bush" (2/26/04). It will be interesting to watch the target of attack in future primary campaigns.

P5. *More attacks target the front-runner than other candidates.*

As discussed above, one may have ideological or other reasons to attack any candidate. However, there are strategic reasons to expect that more attacks will be directed toward the candidate who is leading in tracking polls.

More support for this prediction can be found in our study of presidential primary debates (Benoit et al., 2002). We found that the front-runners were the recipient of an average of 16.2 attacks in a primary debate. Other candidates (non-front-runners) received an average of 5.7 attacks. Furthermore, there is a significant positive correlation between rank in public opinion poll and frequency of attack. The higher a candidate's standing in the polls, the more likely that candidate is to be attacked in a primary debate.

> P6. *The front-runner attacks candidates from the opposing party more than other candidates.*

The front-runner has less strategic reason to attack members of his or her own political party. Thus, we expect that when candidates from the other party are attacked, those attacks will come most often from the front-runner.

Our study of presidential primary debates (Benoit et al., 2002) found that front-runners directed 51% of their attacks toward candidates from the *other* party and 49% to their own party, whereas other candidates directed 63% of attacks to their *own* party and only 37% of their attacks at the other party. A *chi-square* calculated on target of attack by front-runners and other candidates was significant ($\chi^2[df=1]=21.74$, $p<.0001$, $V=.12$). Thus, front-runners are apparently more likely to look ahead to the general campaign, compared with other candidates, directing more attacks to candidates representing the other political party than do non-front-runners.

> P7. *Candidates stress their own party's issues more (and the other party's issues less) in the primary than in the general campaign.*

Chapter Four introduced Petrocik's (1996) theory of Issue Ownership, which holds that the two major political parties "own" (or are generally viewed as better-suited for dealing with) different policy issues. Recall that the Democratic Party "owns" such issues as education, health care, and jobs/labor, whereas the Republican Party "owns" such issues as national defense, taxes, and illegal drugs. However, it is possible that emphasis on party-owned issues would vary between the primary and general campaign phases. If the main audience in the primary campaign consists of voters from the candidates' own political party, we would expect Democratic candidates to stress Democratic issues more than Republican issues, and vice versa.

Summary

I have identified seven differences between primary and general campaigns: opponent's party, number of opponents, target audience, state influence, and voter knowledge. Seven predictions concerning campaign phase are derived from these differences: primary messages have fewer attacks, stress character more, rely less on past deeds but more on general goals, attack members of one's own party–usually the front runner, who tends to attack the other party–and emphasize the issues of the candidate's party. Where these predictions have been tested I have indicated support that is available. The evidence clearly shows that campaign messages developed for the primary phase of the campaign differ significantly from general campaign messages. Campaign phase clearly influences campaign message production.

Nominating Conventions

The role of nominating conventions has changed radically in the last 40 years. In the past, conventions at times contained controversy over who would be the nominee or what would be the nominee's platform. Patterson (2003) explained that

> In the heyday of the televised convention–the 1950s through the 1970s–the average American household watched two to twenty hours of coverage. Voters learned more about the candidates and issues during the conventions than at any other single period in the campaign. (p. 119)

However, as noted above, the divisive Democratic National Convention of 1968 marked the change from conventions as an event which selected the nominee to one which celebrated the nominee. Now the identity of the nominees of both political parties are known well in advance of the convention. In 2004, it became clear that Senator John Kerry would be the nominee in early March, but he did not accept his party's nomination until July 29. Conventions are tightly scripted to put the best face possible on the party generally and the nominee particularly. Disagreement is discouraged and who gets to speak, for how long, and at what time (who will be on prime-time television) is carefully controlled.

These changes have been accompanied by less time on the major television networks and less time spent by voters watching the conventions. Patterson (2003) explained that "In 1976, each of the major networks ... broadcast 25 hours of coverage of each convention. In 1984, that average had fallen to 12 hours. It was a mere 5 hours in 2000" (p. 119). Taylor and Jensen (2004) reported that broadcast network news limited its coverage of the Democratic National Convention to "three hours per network this week" (p. A13). Patterson explained that the number of people who watch the conventions has also declined sharply: "Even as late as 1976, 28% of American households ... had their TV sets on and tuned to the convention. By 1988, convention ratings had slipped to 19%. In 2000, only 13% of TV households were tuned in" (p. 118). Cobb and Roth (2004) reported that "10% fewer viewers overall say the opening night of the convention this year than in 2000, even with the gains by PBS and the cable channels" (p. A11). So, less time from the conventions are broadcast by the major television networks (cable channels did provide more coverage) and fewer people are watching them.

Still, these events are worth studying. The nominee's acceptance address is "the most anticipated part of today's convention, and the most favorably received" (Patterson, 2003, p. 120). Patterson (2003) explained that "Many Americans ... picked their candidate during the 2000 conventions. The number who said they had not yet decided on a candidate fell from 55% to 41%, the sharpest drop of the campaign" (p. 120). It also is likely that the campaigns energize the faithful, who are then more likely to vote in November and talk up the candidate with friends, family, and co-workers.

From 1952 through 2004, the speeches of the candidates accepting their nomination are mostly positive: 77% acclaims, 23% attacks, and 1% defenses. Keynotes from 1960 to 2000, delivered not by the candidate, but by surrogates (see Chapter Four) are more negative in tone: 50% acclaims, 49% attacks, and 1% defenses. These two convention speeches provide essential the same emphasis on policy (acceptances: 55%; keynotes: 54%) as on character (acceptances: 45%; keynotes: 46%).

Campaigning in Battleground States

Once the party nominees reach the general election phase, a different contextual factor arises: battleground states. In the 2000 presidential election, Governor George W. Bush and Vice President Al Gore limited their general election campaigns to a list of "battleground" states. These are states in which public opinion polls indicate that both candidate has a chance of winning in the general election. Ultimately, the president is decided by the Electoral College delegate count rather than the popular vote–and, indeed, in 2000 Bush won the Electoral College vote and the presidency while Gore won the popular vote by about a half a million votes (Duchneskie & Seplow, 2000; for a discussion of the outcome of this election, including the recount in Florida, see *36 Days*, 2001). In all states but two (Nebraska and Maine) the winner of the popular vote in a state receives all of the Electoral College votes for that state. So, winning a state by a landslide gets a candidate no closer to the White House than winning by a few percentage points (or even a single vote). Similarly, a loser who gets close – say, 49% of the popular vote to the winner's 51% – will receive no more electoral votes than a loser who polls only 1% on election day (that is, both losers receive no Electoral College votes). Thus, it is a waste of time and money to campaign in either a state one is sure to win or in a state one is certain to lose. It is more effective to concentrate one's resources in states that might tip the balance – battleground states.

In 2000, the candidates actively contested 23 battleground states: Arkansas, California, Delaware, Florida, Georgia, Illinois, Iowa, Kentucky, Louisiana, Maine, Maryland, Michigan, Missouri, Nevada, New Hampshire, New Mexico, North Carolina, Ohio, Oregon, Pennsylvania, Tennessee, Washington, West Virginia, and Wisconsin. In 2004, the number of battleground states had narrowed to 18 (and as the campaign progressed, some states such as Missouri dropped out of this list as one candidate appeared to gain an insurmountable lead): Arizona, Arkansas, Delaware, Florida, Iowa, Maine, Missouri, Minnesota, Missouri, New Mexico, New Hampshire, Nevada, Ohio, Oregon, Pennsylvania, Washington, West Virginia, and Wisconsin. So, the candidates limited their paid advertising and campaign appearances to these swing states.

Research suggests that concentrating the campaign in a limited number of states does make a difference. First, recall from Chapter One that Shaw (1999a) reported that candidate TV spots and campaign appearances influence state vote totals. This suggests that the strategy of limiting the campaign to battleground states makes sense. Second, Benoit, Hansen, and Holbert (2004) found that the levels of accurate issue knowledge were higher in battleground states in 2000 than in non-battleground states (see also Patterson, 2003). Between February and the end of March 2004, a 34% shift in presidential preference occurred in battleground states from Kerry to Bush. However, in non-battleground states, where ads were not broadcast, Bush obtained only a 6% shift in his favor (Page, 2004, p. 4A). On the other hand, Winneg, Kenski, and Jamieson (2005) report that those in battleground states were more likely to believe statements in ads that were considered false by FactCheck.org. Thus, the campaigns in battleground states appear capable of informing – and misinforming – voters as well as shifting candidate preferences.

Other Contextual Factors

Some research has examined other contextual factors in addition to campaign phase and incumbency status. First, research has examined the relationship between the state of the economy (inflation and unemployment) and presidential campaign discourse. Benoit (2003c) found that the number of terms in general election televison spots which concerned inflation (e.g., CPI, inflation, inflationary, prices) was positively related to the rate of inflation (mean consumer price index from January to June). In other words, when inflation was high, presidential candidates discussed inflation more in their TV spots than when it was low.

Similarly, use of terms related to unemployment (e.g., jobs, jobless, employed, unemployment) in general television spots was directly related to the joblessness rate (mean unemployment from January to June). So, the more who were unemployed, the more the presidential candidates discussed this issue in their general campaign television advertisements. Note that the method employed here compared the rates of inflation and unemployment *before the campaign* (January-June) with the use of terms related to this campaign in the general election. This suggests that one contextual factor which presidential candidates respond to is the state of the economy. Chapter One discussed the importance of the state of the economy in presidential elections; these data show how this variable is manifest in presidential campaign messages.

Second, some candidates do a better job responding to the concerns of voters. Hansen and Benoit (2002) correlated the issues (e.g., budget deficit, unemployment, poverty) discussed by presidential candidates in their general election television spots with public opinion poll data on the relative importance of issues to voters. From 1952 to 2000, Democrats and challengers were more likely to devote the more attention to the issues that were most important to voters than Republican or challengers. Although the difference was not statistically significant, the association between importance of an issue to voters and discussion of that issue by winners was larger than for losers in 9 of 13 campaigns. This suggests that some candidates may adapt the topics emphases of their messages to voters' concerns. Of course, candidates also need to take into consideration the issues owned by their political party (Chapter Four) in deciding which issues to emphasize in their messages.

Hansen and Benoit (2002) also reported that the issues emphasized by the Republican and Democratic candidate correlated in 5 of the 13 presidential elections they examined. Four of these cases were easy to explain, because in those races the issues addressed in both candidates' spots correlated to the issues that were important to the public. However, in 1988, the issues addressed by vice president Bush and governor Dukakis in their TV spots correlated with each other but *not* with the issues that were important to the public. This suggests that the candidates may respond to one another. They suggest that "once a candidate raises an issue, his opponent feels compelled to devote time to that issue" (p. 293). Thus, candidates probably react to one another's campaigns as they develop their messages (and, indeed, the very idea of a defense shows that candidates at times react to one another's issues).

A final contextual factor that influences presidential campaign messages is their position in the race. Benoit (1999) found that, analyzing television spots from 1952 to 1996, the candidates who attacked the most were those who trailed their opponents throughout the general election campaign (51% attacks). Candidates who were in close races (i.e., the lead switched from one candidate to another during the campaign) used the fewest attacks (32% attacks). Similarly, Sigelman and Buell (2003) reported that from 1960 to 2000, statements from presidential and vice-presidential candidates quoted in the *New York Times* attacked the most when those candidates trailed (68%). Statements from candidates in close races attacked in 54% of statements (note that Chapter Seven will document the fact that news coverage is consistently more negative than candidate messages, which could explain why the levels of attack were higher in the second study, of quotations in the *New York Times*, are higher than in the first study, of candidate television spots). So, it appears that candidates who are trailing in a campaign are more likely to attack. As Sigelman and Buell (2003) explain, "if one side is running far behind, it should be expected to go on the attack in order to give itself a chance, however slight, of catching up." In contrast, "side that enjoys a clear lead presumably has little incentive to attack" (p. 521). So, state of the economy, issues important to voters, messages from one's opponent, and the candidate's position in the polls can influence the content of political campaign messages.

Conclusion

This chapter has examined context variables in political campaigns. Campaign messages from presidential candidates differ in the primary and general campaign phases. Primary messages have more acclaims and fewer attacks than general messages. Character is discussed more, and policy less, in primary than general messages. Primary messages attack candidates from one's own party more than the other party. The front-runner attracts the most attacks and is also most likely to attack candidates of the other political party.

The research examined in this chapter also identified four other factors which appear to influence the content of political campaign messages: the state of the economy, the issues most important to voters, the topics of one's opponent's messages, and the candidate's position in the race. Surely other contextual factors could be investigated as well.

These findings support the theory of the Genesis of Rhetorical Action (Benoit, 1994, 2000a), which argues that one factor which influences the production (or invention) of persuasive discourse is the context in which those messages arise. The context of a presidential campaign can be operationalized in may ways; clearly context influences the discourse produced by presidential candidates.

CHAPTER SIX

Non-Presidential, Non-U.S. Campaign Discourse

Most research on political campaigns has focused on U.S. presidential elections. However, some studies have investigated non-presidential discourse in the United States as well as campaign discourse in other countries. Both kinds of campaigns will be investigated in this chapter. Predictions developed in Chapter Two will be tested where data are available.

U.S. Non-Presidential Campaign Discourse

A disproportionate amount of the research investigating U.S. elections focuses on the presidential election: As the highest elective office in the most powerful nation, this emphasis is understandable. However, presidential elections involve only a single office and occur only once every four years. Some non-presidential elections occur every two years (e.g., elections for every U.S. house of representatives seat are held every two years; although a given U.S. senate term is six years, some senate races occur every two years). Obviously, there are thousands of non-presidential offices contested regularly (435 U.S. representatives, 100 U.S. Senators, 50 governors, and a myriad of other offices in every state of the union). Non-presidential campaigns may not have the glamour of the race for the White House but they are important because there are far more non-presidential than presidential campaigns. Recall from Chapter One that Lawless (2012) observed that the U.S. has campaigns for almost 520,000 elective offices.

Candidates invest considerable time, effort, and money in their campaigns. Both candidates and their campaign advisors are convinced that television spots are key in winning elections (Jenkins, 1997; Sinclair, 1995). Kahn and Kenney (1999) observe that "television advertisements, compared to newspaper advertisements, are considered significantly more effective in swaying voters's opinions and are used much more frequently during statewide and national campaigns" (p. 34; citing Abramowitz & Segal, 1992; Goldenberg & Traugott, 1984; Jacobson, 1987; Luntz, 1988). Herrnson (2004) reported that "registered voters reported seeing an average of about eight ads per day during the last week of the campaign" (p. 214). Analysis of NES data pertaining to US Senate races from 1988 to 1992 reveals that "campaigns matter" (Kahn & Kenney, 1999, p. 203). Specifically, they report that

> As races become more intense, people's exposure to and contact with the candidates increases, as does recognition and recall of the candidates' names …. [C]itizens can learn the themes disseminated by the candidates when the race is competitive and the candidates' messages are presented repeatedly by the candidates and the news media. Peoples' ability to identify issues and the candidates specific themes are significantly affected by the campaign setting …. When issue information is prevalent in closely contested races, citizens respond by offering issues as a reason for liking *and* disliking the candidates (p. 204, emphasis original)

This mirrors the argument advanced in Chapter One that presidential campaign messages (from both candidates and the news) are capable of informing voters. It is also consistent with evidence presented in Chapter Four concerning the effects of presidential campaign messages on voters.

Furthermore, Brazeal and Benoit argue that candidate messages may be more important for offices below the presidential level because "media coverage of campaigns for legislative offices is sporadic at best, which means that voters receive much of their information about lower-level candidates from political advertising" (p. 437). Kahn and Kenney (1999) investigated the effects of campaign intensity, a variable with three elements: candidate spending, closeness of the race (last public opinion poll before the election), and amount of newspaper coverage. They report that "the impact of issues on feeling-thermometer scores [a global measure of candidate evaluation] more than triples from low-intensity to high-intensity campaigns" (p. 218). This means that non-presidential campaigns, and the messages employed in them, merit scholarly attention.

As with presidential discourse, content analysis of non-presidential campaign messages focuses mainly on investigations of television spots. Research on the functions of non-presidential television spots suggests that attacks are generally common. As with studies of presidential ads, much of this work utilizes the entire spot as the coding unit. Pfau, Parrott, and Lindquist (1992) summarize research on senate (1984) and congressional (1986) advertising which indicates that about one-half of these spots were negative. Payne and Baukus (1988) reported that about one-third of 101 Republican Senate spots in 1984 were attack ads. Similarly, research found that 43% of congressional ads from 1984 to 1994 were negative (Hale, Fox, & Farmer, 1996). Adding a third category, Goldstein, Krasno, Bradford, and Seltz (2001) found that 27% of 1998 House and Senate spots were attack ads and 20% were contrast ads. Vavrek (2001) reported that 64% of 1998 congressional ads were positive, 16% negative, and 20% were contrast ads (with both positive and negative elements). Thus, negative ads appear to be quite common, comprising roughly half of the spots.

Some scholars used other coding units besides the entire ad (themes or mentions). Benze and Declercq (1985), investigating ads in 29 states for male and female candidates for congress (1980–1983) found that negative ideas were mentioned in just under half the spots (47% for men, 44% for women). Bystrom and Miller (1999) reported that women Senate and gubernatorial candidates in 1996 attacked in 54% of their spots, whereas men attacked in only 26% of their spots. Kahn and Kenney's (1999) analysis of 594 ads from 161 Senate candidates (1988–1992) indicated that 41% of all spots in the sample contained criticisms of the opponent. Johnston and White (1994), investigating 39 television spots for five female senate candidates in 1986, found that only 20% of their sample spots contained attacks. Lau and Pomper (2004), analyzing Senate campaigns from 1988 to 2002, found that negative campaigning ranged from 27.8% to 39.7%, with a mean of 33.7% attacks. Again, attacks are a substantial component but rarely constitute over half of the themes in spots.

The topic of non-presidential advertisements has also been studied in previous research. Johnston and White's (1994) study of female Senate candidates in 1986 reported that 54% of ads focused on issues and 45% focused on image. Joslyn (1980), analyzing 62 senate spots, found that 77% of those spots mentioned issues and 40% discussed the candidate's personal qualities. Kern (1989) found that 43% of congressional spots from 1984 addressed policy. Kahn and Kenney (1999), who analyzed senate ads in 1988–1992, indicated that issues were the focus of 36% of ads and were mentioned in 80% of the ads. Similarly, Benze and Declercq (1985) found that men and women mentioned issues in 68% of spots (men mentioned image in 90% of their spots, whereas women mentioned image in 82% of ads). West's (1994) study of primary and general U.S. senate ads in California during the 1992 elections found that domestic policy was 78% of primary and 47% of general ads whereas the personal qualities of the candidates comprised 17% of primary and 33% of general ads. Vavreck (2001) reported that 30% of ads emphasized candidate traits and 52% focused on issues (the remaining ads did not have a single dominant focus). Cooper and Knotts' 2004 study of ads from eight 2000 gubernatorial races found that positive ads (50%) were more common than negative ads (28%; 22% were contrast ads). Data from Cooper and Knotts (2004), who investigated gubernatorial ads in 2000, are consistent: Policy (59%) was a more common topic than personal qualities (10%; and 31% both policy and character). This research indicates that both policy (issue) and character (image) are commonly discussed in ads; most studies suggest that policy is more common (Benze & Declerq, 1985, indicate that image is more common than issue in ads for women).

Several studies investigate U.S. non-presidential television spots (although not every data set provides data on every hypothesis: e.g., Brazeal [2002] did not analyze spots into forms of policy and character; Airne and Benoit's [in press] sample did not include any party-sponsored spots for governors or local races; Pier [2002] did not identify whether any of the spots in her sample were sponsored by political parties). Less research has content analyzed other kinds of messages than TV spots from non-presidential candidates.

Functions and Topics of Non-Presidential Campaign Messages

Functional Theory predicts that political candidates will acclaim more than they attack and that they will attack more often than they defend. Acclaims have no draw-backs (although this does not mean they are necessarily persuasive), attacks risk a backlash from those who dislike mudslinging, and defenses have three potential drawbacks (one must identify an attack to refute it, which could inform or remind voters of a potential weakness; refuting an attack usually takes a candidate off-message; defenses make a candidate look defensive, reactive rather than proactive). The data summarized in Table 6.1 shows that acclaims are always the most common function, comprising from 51% to 98% of themes in these messages. Overall, 70% of utterances are acclaims. For example, Dan Williams acclaimed in this spot utterance in 1998: "Where does Dan Williams stand? Strengthen public schools. Reform HMOs. Stop the sale of public lands." These goals would probably appear desirable to many voters. Attacks are the second most frequent function of these messages in these media. Attacks vary from 8% to 48% and overall account for 27% of utterances in these messates. This is less than half the frequency of acclaims, which is 69%. For instance, an ad for Dennis Moore in 1998 attacked his opponent: "Vince Snowbarger sides with big insurance companies and voted against allowing doctors to discuss all treatment options with their patients.

Table 6.1. Functions and topics of U.S. non-presidential campaign messages.

	Functions			Topics	
	Acclaims	Attacks	Defenses	Policy	Character
1974–1998 Governor Spots	**1444 (72%)**	544 (27%)	16 (0.8%)	**1308 (66%)**	666 (34%)
1980–2004 Congressional Spots	**3481 (69%)**	747 (38%)	28 (0.5%)	**2572 (51%)**	2477 (49%)
1998 MO Spots	**207 (67%)**	99 (31%)	6 (2%)	**203 (66%)**	103 (34%)
2000 Senate Spots	**1003 (71%)**	441 (29%)	7 (0.5%)	**872 (62%)**	542 (38%)
2000 House Spots	**361 (62%)**	215 (37%)	4 (0.7%)	**315 (55%)**	262 (45%)
2000 Governor Spots	**313 (76%)**	94 (23%)	4 (1%)	**262 (69%)**	119 (31%)
2000 Local Spots	**186 (69%)**	82 (30%)	3 (1%)	**146 (54%)**	122 (46%)
2004 Governor Spots	**985 (70%)**	496 (29%)	14 (1%)	**720 (52%)**	671 (48%)
2004 Senate Spots	**1973 (70%)**	823 (29%)	24 (1%)	**1526 (55%)**	1270 (45%)
2004 House Spots	**1891 (75%)**	624 (25%)	46 (1%)	**1243 (49%)**	1276 (51%)
2008 Senate Spots	**632 (59%)**	431 (40%)	15 (1%)	**724 (69%)**	328 (31%)
2008 Governor Spots	**610 (68%)**	272 (31%)	9 (1%)	**534 (61%)**	347 (39%)
1998 MO Direct Mail	**322 (92%)**	28 (8%)	0	**233 (67%)**	117 (33%)
2016 Direct Mail OH	**519 (83%)**	108 (17%)	0	302 (48%)	**325 (52%)**
1998 MO Newspaper Ads	**154 (83%)**	31 (17%)	1 (0.5%)	**106 (57%)**	79 (43%)
1998 MO Webpages	**237 (98%)**	5 (2%)	0	75 (31%)	**167 (69%)**
2002–2004 Governor, Senate, House Primary Debates	**699 (71%)**	211 (22%)	68 (7%)	**531 (60%)**	349 (40%)
1994–2004 Governor Debates	**3007 (68%)**	1309 (30%)	94 (2%)	**3166 (73%)**	1150 (27%)
1998–2006 Senate Debates	**2370 (56%)**	1275 (30%)	593 (14%)	**2537 (70%)**	1064 (30%)
2005–07 Mayoral Debates	**1285 (75%)**	326 (19%)	113 (7%)	**1132 (70%)**	479 (30%)
2016 Governor Tweets	**2000 (73%)**	673 (25%)	13 (0.5%)	**1409 (53%)**	1264 (47%)

Continued

Table 6.1. *Continued*

	Functions			Topics	
	Acclaims	Attacks	Defenses	Policy	Character
2016 Senate Tweets	579 (69%)	259 (31%)	0	245 (29%)	593 (71%)
2016 House Tweets	614 (51%)	577 (48%)	5 (0.4%)	497 (42%)	684 (52%)
Total	24872 (70%)	9670 (27%)	1063 (3%)	20659 (59%)	14454 (41%)

Functions: χ^2 (df = 2) = 24492.34, p < .0001. Topics: χ^2 (df = 1) = 1096.52, p < .0001.

1974–1998 Governor: Pier, 2002.
1980–2004 Congressional: Brazeal & Benoit, 2006.
1998 Missouri: Benoit, 2000.
2000 Senate, House, Governor, Local: Airne & Benoit 2005.
2004 Governor, Senate, House Spots: Benoit & Airne, 2009.
2008 Senate, Governor Spots: Benoit, Delbert, Sudbrock, & Vogt, 2010.
2016 Direct Mail OH: Benoit, 2017.
2016 Governor, Senate, and House Tweets: Benoit & Stein, in press.
2005–2007 Mayoral Debates: Benoit, Henson, & Maltos, 2007.
2002–2004 Governor, Senate, House Primary Debates: Benoit & Henson, 2006.
1994–2006 Senate & Governor Debates: Benoit, Brazeal, & Airne, 2007f.

Snowbarger even voted to let HMOs off the hook when they make serious medical mistakes." These three allegations would likely appear undesirable to many voters, making this utterance function as an attack. The least common function in these messages is defense (3%), ranges from 0 to 14%. In 2000, Anne Northup responded to an attack from her opponent: "Jordan falsely accuses Northup of voting for a pay raise. The *Courier* says the charge is false–Northup voted to block the pay raise." This statement clearly denies the accusation, defending Northup. This sample ranges from 1974 to 2016 and includes TV spots, direct mail advertising, newspaper ads, candidate webpages, debates, and tweets.

Functional Theory also predicts that policy utterances will be more common than character remarks. Table 6.1 reports that overall, 59% of the themes in these messages concern policy and 41% address character. Most message forms conform to this prediction, but Ohio direct mail (2016), Missouri candidate webpages (1998), and Senate and House tweets (2016) emphasized character. For example, Rick White ran an advertisement in 1998 that explained "We've balanced the budget, reduced taxes." Governmental budget and taxes concern policy. On the other hand, an ad for Tom Campbell in 2000 told viewers that "His willingness to listen–unmatched." This utterance is an example of a theme discussing character. Benoit (2000) argues that political webpages from 1998 – the dawn of such media – looked like VITA put up on the web – scant attacks and an emphasis on the candidate's character. As campaign webpages became more sophisticated, their content shifted.

Functions of General Goals and Ideals in Non-Presidential Messages

Functional Theory predicted that general goals will more often be used as the basis for acclaims than for attacks. Three of these non-presidential data sets analyzed forms of policy. According to Table 6.2, acclaims account for 88% of the statements

Table 6.2. Functions of general goals and ideals in U.S. non-presidential campaign messages.

	General Goals		Ideals	
	Acclaims	Attacks	Acclaims	Attacks
1974–1998 Governor Spots	403	40	35	4
1980–2004 Congressional Spots	554	58	187	45
1998 MO Spots	70	2	54	49
2004 Senate Spots	604	97	261	51
2004 House Spots	497	43	96	3
2004 Governor Spots	284	29	123	7
2008 Senate Spots	90	153	–	–
2008 Governor Spots	96	34	–	–
1998 MO Direct Mail	87	5	112	5
2016 Direct Mail OH	197	12	31	3
1998 MO Newspaper Ads	41	0	78	1
1998 MO Webpages	35	1	165	2
2002–2004 Governor, Senate, House Primary Debates	208	13	105	6
1994–2004 Governor Debates	1267	187	102	9
1998–2006 Senate Debates	1294	220	179	47
2005–07 Mayoral Debates	611	20	70	6
2016 Governor Tweets	819	49	65	5
2016 Senate Tweets	118	23	62	5
2016 House Tweets	184	26	67	15
Total	7459 (90%)	874 (10%)	1792 (70%)	758 (30%)

General Goals: χ^2 (df = 1) = 5202.1, p < .0001. Ideals: χ^2 (df = 1) = 418.45, p < .0001.
1974–1998 Governor Spots: Brazeal, 2002.
1980–2004 Congressional: Brazeal & Benoit, 2006.
1998 Missouri: Benoit, 2000.
2004 Governor, Senate, House Spots: Benoit & Airne, 2009.
2008 Senate, Governor Spots: Benoit, Delbert, Sudbrock, & Vogt, 2010.
2016 Direct Mail OH: Benoit, 2017.
2002–2004 Governor, Senate, House Primary Debates: Benoit & Henson, 2006.
1994–2004 Governor Debates: Benoit, Brazeal, & Airne, 2007.
1998–2006 Senate Debates: Benoit, Brazeal, & Airne, 2007.
2005–2007 Mayoral Debates: Benoit, Henson, & Maltos, 2007.
2016 Governor, Senate, and House Tweets: Benoit & Stein, in press.

using general goals whereas attacks comprise only 12% of these utterances, a significant difference. Thus, general goals were used over seven times as often to acclaim as to attack. For example, a spot in 1998 acclaimed these goals: "Fighting for tax breaks for the middle class, not the rich, and new tougher sentences for drug dealers. Dan Akaka." Tom Harkin in 1986 attacked his opponent's goal for abortion: "Lightfoot wants the government, not women, to make the decision." This relationship holds true in each of the three samples which coded for the forms of policy.

A related prediction held that like general goals, ideals would most often support acclaims rather than attacks. Table 6.2 indicates that this prediction also is supported in these non-presidential television spots. Ideals were the basis of acclaims over six times as often as they were used to attack: This form of character supports acclaims 69% of the time and attacks 31% of the time. In 1996, for example, a commercial for John D. Rockefeller explained that "In West Virginia, we respect our elders. That's a value I'm working to defend." This is an example of an acclaim of an ideal (value, principle, or right). Maryanne Connelly ran an advertisement in 2000 attacking her opponent: "In Central New Jersey basic rights of women are under attack. Mike Ferguson ran an organization to end our right to choose." This illustrates a rare attack on ideals. This relationship—more acclaims than attacks on ideals—appears in all three message forms. So, the three general predictions from Functional Theory receive consistent support in non-presidential campaign messages.

Forms of Personal Qualities in Non-Presidential TV Spots

Benoit and McHale (2003) developed a list of traits discussed when candidates discuss personal qualities. Table 6.3 reports that empathy is the most common trait discussed in congressional TV spots (33%), followed by morality (24%), drive (22%), and sincerity (21%; Benoit & McHale, 2004).

Table 6.3. Forms of personal qualities in congressional TV spots. 1984–2000.

	Congressional TV Spots
Empathy	102 (33%)
Morality	76 (24%)
Drive	68 (22%)
Sincerity	66 (21%)

Benoit & McHale (2004)

Issue Ownership in Non-Presidential Campaign Messages

Petrocik's (1986) issue ownership provided the basis for the hypothesis that that Democratic candidates will discuss Democratic issues more, and Republican issues less, than Republicans. Candidates have an incentive to stress the issues on which most voters believe that candidate's party is better at solving. Although not specifically testing Issue Ownership theory, Kahn and Kenney (1999) report data relevant to this prediction. They content analyzed 594 US Senate ads (364 Republican, 230 Democratic) from 1988 to 1992. Republicans discussed the

Table 6.4. Issue ownership in non-presidential campaign messages.

	Message content	
Candidate's party	Democratic issues	Republican issues
Governor 1974–1998, 2002		
Democrats	**1100 (62%)**	683 (38%)
Republicans	576 (41%)	**813 (59%)**
1980–2000 Senate and House Spots		
Democratic	**729 (72%)**	285 (28%)
Republican	382 (44%)	**489 (56%)**
2002 Governor Spots		
Democratic	**903 (75%)**	295 (25%)
Republican	550 (54%)	**463 (46%)**
2002 Senate Spots		
Democratic	**275 (50%)**	279 (50%)
Republican	261 (45%)	**316 (55%)**
2002 House Spots		
Democratic	**270 (68%)**	127 (32%)
Republican	164 (46%)	**289 (56%)**
2000–2004 Governor and Senate Debates		
Democratic	**1414 (54%)**	1189 (46%)
Republican	1251 (48%)	**1332 (52%)**
Total		
Democratic	**4691 (62%)**	2858 (38%)
Republican	3184 (46%)	**3702 (54%)**

$\chi^2 (df = 2) = 367.3, p < .0001, \varphi = .16$.

1980–2000 House and Senate Spots: Brazeal & Benoit, 2009
2002 Governor, House, and Senate Spots: Benoit & Airne, 2005
2000, 2002, 2004 Governor and Senate Debates: Benoit, Airne, & Brazeal, 2011.

economy – which included taxes and the budget, Republican issues – in 34% of spots whereas Democrats took up this topic in 19% of ads. Democrats addressed social issues – which included health, education, and the environment, Democratic issues – in 28% of their ads, compared with 14% for Republicans. Thus, their data also support the theory of issue ownership with non-presidential television spots. We have data on this question from five samples of non-presidential television spots as well as from non-presidential debates. Table 6.4 reports data that confirm that Democrats discuss Democratic issues more (62% to 38%) and Republican issues less (46% to 54%) than Republicans.

Function of Non-Presidential Television Spots by Sponsor

Functional Theory predicts that messages from candidates are likely to use more acclaims and fewer attacks than messages from other (surrogate) sources. Two samples of spots, US Senate ads from 2000 and US House ads from 2000 (Airne & Benoit, 2005), contrasted ads sponsored by candidates with those sponsored by political parties (Table 6.5). Overall, candidates acclaimed in 76% of their messages, whereas party-sponsored ads acclaimed in 24% of remarks; spots sponsored by political parties attacked more than ads from candidates (75% to 24%). Spots from surrogate sources attacked more and acclaimed less than commercials sponsored by candidates. The idea here is that candidates probably think that they may avoid the potential backlash from voters who dislike mudslinging by letting other sources make most of the attacks.

Table 6.5. Functions of non-presidential TV spots by sponsor.

	Acclaims	Attacks
US Senate 2000		
Candidate	**927 (78%)**	255 (21%)
Party	76 (32%)	**256 (67%)**
US House 2000		
Candidate	**318 (70%)**	135 (29%)
Party	23 (30%)	**54 (70%)**
Total		
Candidate	**1245 (76%)**	390 (24%)
Party	99 (24%)	**310 (75%)**

χ^2 (df = 1) = 391.97, p < .0001, φ = .44.

Airne & Benoit, 2005.

Incumbency and Non-Presidential Campaign Messages

Functional Theory expects that incumbents will acclaim more, and attack less, than challengers. Kahn and Kenney (1999) offer data that show that challengers

Table 6.6. Functions of U.S. non-presidential campaign messages by incumbency.

	Acclaims	Attacks
Governor 1974–2000		
Incumbent	**368 (81%)**	89 (19%)
Challenger	253 (60%)	**170 (40%)**
US Congress 1980–2000		
Incumbent	**1121 (76%)**	354 (24%)
Challenger	825 (57%)	**633 (43%)**
US Senate 2000		
Incumbent	**296 (71%)**	123 (29%)
Challenger	275 (69%)	**123 (31%)**
US House 2000		
Incumbent	**112 (64%)**	63 (36%)
Challenger	65 (50%)	**65 (50%)**
Senate Debates 2000–2004		
Incumbent	**884 (76%)**	286 (24%)
Challenger	771 (57%)	**584 (43%)**
Gubernatorial Debates 2000–2004		
Incumbent	**820 (70%)**	348 (30%)
Challenger	672 (59%)	**466 (41%)**
Mayoral Debates		
Incumbent	**318 (92%)**	28 (8%)
Challenger	334 (72%)	**123 (26%)**
Total		
Incumbent	**2832 (69%)**	1291 (31%)
Challenger	1945 (58%)	**2164 (42%)**

χ^2 (df = 1) = 385.26, p < .0001, φ = 22.
1974–1998 Governor: Pier, 2002.
1980–2004 Congressional: Brazeal & Benoit, 2006.
1998 Missouri: Benoit, 2000.
2000 Senate, House, Governor, Local: Airne & Benoit 2005.
2004 Governor, Senate, House: Benoit & Airne, 2009.
2008 Senate, Governor Spots: Benoit, Delbert, Sudbrock, & Vogt, 2010.
2016 Direct Mail OH: Benoit, 2017.
2018 Governor, Senate, and House Tweets: Benoit & Stein, in press.
2000–2004 Senate and Governor Debates: Benoit, Airne, & Brazeal, 2011
2005–2007 Mayoral Debates: Benoit, Henson, & Maltos, 2007.

Table 6.7. Use of past deeds and future plans of U.S. non-presidential campaign messages by incumbency.

	Past deeds		Future plans	
	Acclaims	Attacks	Acclaims	Attacks
Governor 1974–2000				
Incumbent	168 (90%)	18 (10%)	10 (40%)	15 (60%)
Challenger	23 (21%)	88 (79%)	16 (100%)	0
US Congress 1980–2004				
Incumbent	370 (73%)	139 (27%)	120 (66%)	63 (34%)
Challenger	180 (34%)	351 (66%)	119 (79%)	31 (21%)
Governor, Senate, House 2004				
Incumbent	284 (72%)	110 (28%)	22 (88%)	3 (12%)
Challenger	87 (32%)	189 (68%)	5 (100%)	0
Senate Debates 2000–2004				
Incumbent	206 (69%)	91 (31%)	11 (41%)	16 (59%)
Challenger	125 (30%)	285 (70%)	20 (54%)	17 (46%)
Gubernatorial Debates 2000–2004				
Incumbent	403 (75%)	131 (25%)	18 (75%)	6 (25%)
Challenger	84 (21%)	311 (78%)	28 (97%)	1 (3%)
Mayoral Debates 2005–2007				
Incumbent	106 (94%)	7 (6%)	13 (76%)	4 (24%)
Challenger	24 (28%)	63 (72%)	48 (84%)	9 (16%)
Total				
Incumbent	1537 (76%)	496 (24%)	194 (64%)	107 (36%)
Challenger	523 (29%)	1287 (71%)	236 (80%)	58 (20%)

Past Deeds: χ^2 ($df = 1$) = 839.93, $p < .0001$, $\varphi = .47$. Future Plans: χ^2 ($df = 1$) = 18.57, $p < .0001$, $\varphi = .18$.
1974–1998 Governor: Pier, 2002.
1980–2004 Congressional: Brazeal & Benoit, 2006.
2004 Governor, Senate, House: Benoit & Airne, 2009.
2008 Senate, Governor Spots: Benoit, Delbert, Sudbrock, & Vogt, 2010.
2016 Direct Mail OH: Benoit, 2017.
2018 Governor, Senate, and House Tweets: Benoit & Stein, in press.
2000–2004 Senate and Governor Debates: Benoit, Airne, & Brazeal, 2011
2005–2007 Mayoral Debates: Benoit, Henson, & Maltos, 2007.

are significantly more likely than incumbents to criticize their opponent's policy agendas and to criticize their opponent's issue positions. Similarly, Lau and Pomper's (2004) analysis of Senate campaigns found that "negative campaigning

Table 6.8. Functions of U.S. non-presidential campaign messages by campaign phase.

	Acclaims	Attacks
Governor, House, Senate TV Spots 2004		
Primary	**2601 (74%)**	920 (26%)
General	2137 (70%)	**898 (30%)**
2008 Governor TV Spots		
Primary	**214 (71%)**	88 (29%)
General	384 (68%)	**177 (32%)**
2008 Senate TV Spots		
Primary	**209 (66%)**	107 (34%)
General	423 (57%)	**318 (43%)**
Governor, Senate, House Debates		
Primary	**699 (77%)**	211 (23%)
General	5377 (68%)	**2584 (32%)**
Total		
Primary	**3723 (74%)**	1326 (26%)
General	8321 (68%)	**3977 (32%)**

χ^2 (df = 1) = 62.26, p < .0001, φ = 06.

2004 Governor, Senate, House: Benoit & Airne, 2009.
2008 Senate, Governor Spots: Benoit, Delbert, Sudbrock, & Vogt, 2010.
2002–2004 Governor, Senate, House Primary Debates: Benoit & Henson, 2006.
1994–2006 Governor, Senate Debates: Benoit, Brazeal, & Airne, 2008.

was more likely if the candidate was a challenger or in an open seat contest" (p. 33). Table 6.6 indicates that overall, this was the case: Incumbents acclaimed more (69% to 58%) and attacked less (31% to 41%) than challengers.

Functional Theory predicts that incumbents are more likely to acclaim on past deeds (their record in office) whereas challengers tend to use past deeds to attack (criticizing the incumbent's record). Table 6.7 shows that overall, incumbents use past deeds to acclaim more than challengers (76%, 24%) whereas challengers use past deeds to attack more than incumbents (71%, 24%). In most cases, only the incumbent candidate has a record in the office sought; this record is a potential source of acclaims (by the candidate of successes) and of attacks (by the opponent of failures). Kahn and Kenney (1999) found that challengers are significantly more likely than incumbents to blame their opponents for unfavorable policy outcomes. This result is similar to the prediction that challengers are more likely than incumbents to attack on past deeds, and offers additional support for this prediction.

Functional Theory also holds that future plans will be used differently according to incumbency status: Incumbents are more likely to attack on future plans, whereas challengers are more likely to acclaim future plans. Table 6.7 reports that both incumbents and challengers tend to acclaim more than they attack on future plans. However, challengers acclaim more (80% to 64%) and attack less (20% to 26%) than incumbents. Each instance of future plans has the potential to imply a weakness in the incumbent's term in office. Thus, challengers have an incentive to acclaim more on future plans than incumbents. This stress on acclaims on future plans by challengers provides opportunities for the incumbent to attack.

Functional Theory predicts that messages from the primary phase of the campaign acclaim more, and attack less, than discourse in the general campaign phase. Table 6.8 reports data consistent with this prediction: primary messages acclaim more (74% to 68%) and attack less (26% to 32%) than general campaign messages. Candidates have an incentive to attack less in the primary than the general election because they hope other (unsuccessful) primary candidates and their supporters will support them in the general election if they win the nomination. Furthermore, candidates in the primary belong to the same political party and have fewer differences than opponents in the general election.

So, examination of non-presidential U.S. campaign messages shows both consistency and differences across level of office. A number or predictions developed for presidential campaign discourse were upheld for non-presidential messages: acclaims are the most common function and defenses the least; there are more acclaims and fewer attacks on general goals and ideals; candidates acclaim more and attack less than surrogate sources, incumbents acclaim more and attack less thna challengers; incumbents acclaim more and attack less on past deeds than challengers; challengers acclaim more and attack less on future plans than incumbents; more and acclaims less than incumbents; issue ownership theory was upheld; and messages from the primary acclaim more and attack less than general campaign messages.

Non-U.S. Campaign Discourse

This section will examine research on campaign messages – TV spots and debates – in non-U.S. countries. Both functions and topics will be discussed.

Table 6.9. Functions and topics of non-U.S. debates.

	Functions			Topics	
	Acclaims	Attacks	Defenses	Policy	Character
1984, 1988, 1992, 1996, 1999 Israel	165 (50%)	124 (38%)	38 (12%)	222 (77%)	67 (23%)
1988 France	353 (59%)	219 (37%)	25 (4%)	498 (87%)	74 (13%)
1995 France	363 (64%)	167 (29%)	41 (7%)	483 (91%)	47 (8%)
1997 South Korea	485 (54%)	323 (36%)	91 (10%)	666 (82%)	142 (18%)
2002 South Korea	559 (56%)	345 (35%)	89 (9%)	777 (86%)	127 (14%)
2004 Taiwan	320 (49%)	303 (46%)	35 (5%)	372 (60%)	251 (40%)
2004 Ukraine	256 (43%)	290 (48%)	52 (9%)	333 (61%)	213 (39%)
2006 Canada	882 (69%)	323 (25%)	65 (5%)	715 (59%)	490 (41%)
2007 Australia	161 (49%)	141 (43%)	28 (9%)	201 (67%)	101 (33%)
2007 France	226 (53%)	143 (33%)	59 (14%)	316 (84%)	62 (16%)
2008 Spain	591 (46%)	627 (49%)	59 (4%)	923 (76%)	296 (24%)
2010 Australia	181 (65%)	93 (33%)	5 (2%)	205 (75%)	69 (25%)
2010 Northern Ireland	84 (52%)	47 (29%)	31 (19%)	75 (57%)	56 (43%)
2010 Scotland	123 (40%)	152 (49%)	36 (12%)	213 (81%)	49 (19%)
2010 Wales	187 (5s6%)	129 (41%)	18 (5%)	270 (85%)	46 (15%)
2010 UK	1000 (60%)	604 (36%)	75 (4%)	1259 (78%)	345 (22%)
2011 Canada	293 (46%)	284 (45%)	54 (9%)	407 (70%)	170 (30%)
2012 Finland	120 (64%)	17 (9%)	51 (27%)	145 (74%)	51 (26%)
2012 France	163 (40%)	167 (41%)	81 (20%)	277 (84%)	54 (16%)
2012 London Mayor	145 (53%)	108 (40%)	19 (7%)	196 (77%)	57 (23%)
2013 Australia MP	67 (60%)	38 (34%)	7 (6%)	71 (68%)	34 (32%)
2013 Australia PM	157 (64%)	68 (28%)	22 (9%)	183 (81%)	42 (19%)
Total	6881 (55%)	4712 (37%)	981 (8%)	8807 (76%)	2843 (24%)

Functions (acclaims vs. attacks): χ^2 (df = 1) = 405.44, p < .0001. Topics: χ^2 (df = 1) = 3120.86, p < .0001.

1984, 1988, 1992, 1996, 1999 Israel: Benoit & Sheafer, 2006.
1988 France: Choi & Benoit, 2009.
1995 France: Choi & Benoit, 2009.
1997 South Korea: Choi & Benoit, 2009.
2002 South Korea: Choi & Benoit, 2009
2004 Taiwan: Benoit, Wen, & Yu, 2007.
2004 Ukraine: Benoit & Klyukovski, 2006.
2006 Canada: Benoit & Henson, 2007.
2007 Australia: Benoit & Henson, 2007.
2007 France: Choi & Benoit. 2013.

Continued

Table 6.9. *Continued*

2008 Spain: Gerrero & Benoit, 2009.
2010 Australia PM: Benoit & Benoit-Bryan, 2014.
2010 Northern Ireland, Scotland, Wales: Benoit & Benoit-Bryan, 2014.
2010 UK: Benoit & Benoit-Bryan, 2013.
2011 Canada: Benoit 2011.
2012 Finland: Paatelainen, Croucher, & Benoit, 2016.
2012 France: Choi & Benoit, 2013.
2012 London Mayoral Benoit, 2016.
2013 Australia MP, PM: Benoit & Benoit-Bryan, 2015.

Non-U.S. Debates

Political leader's debates (prime minister, president, chancellor) have become more common around the world. Some differences arise in elections conducted in other countries. Several countries have multi-party systems (the U.S. technically has more than two political parties, but only the Democrats and Republicans have had a hope of winning the presidency in recent history). In Korea, the president may not run for re-election; furthermore, Korea does not have a Vice President (in the U.S. a sitting Vice President often runs as the incumbent candidate). Table 6.9 reports analyses of debates in a variety of countries. As predicted by Functional Theory, acclaims constituted 55% of the utterances in these messages, attacks comprised 37% of statements, and 8% of comments were defenses. In only three cases (debates in the Ukraine in 2004, debates in Scotland in 2010, and debates in France in 2012) did acclaims outnumber attacks. These events addressed policy more than character (76% to 24%) and this order occurred in every country examined.

As with American presidential and non-presidential debates, more comments about general goals were acclaims than attacks and more statements about ideal were acclaims than attacks. See Table 6.10 for these data. Functional Theory argues that it is easier to praise goals (such as creating jobs or reducing crime) than to attack them; this is true for ideals as well.

Forms of Personal Qualities in Non-U.S. Debates

As mentioned earlier, Benoit and McHale (2003) developed a list of traits discussed when candidates talk about personal qualities. The data reported in Table 6.11 show that morality is the most common trait discussed in non-U.S. debates (43%), followed by drive (23%); sincerity and empathy (17%) were discussed less often (see also Benoit & McHale, 2004).

Table 6.10. Functions of general goals and ideals in non-U.S. debates.

	General Goals		Ideals	
	Acclaims	Attacks	Acclaims	Attacks
1984, 1988, 1992, 1996, 1999 Israel	22	8	0	2
1988 France	132	24	1	0
1995 France	194	48	2	0
1997 South Korea	171	27	25	1
2002 South Korea	264	54	43	0
2004 Taiwan	95	21	23	12
2004 Ukraine	93	7	28	4
2006 Canada	379	27	207	18
2007 Australia	72	17	5	0
2007 France	74	6	2	1
2008 Spain	257	106	34	26
2010 Australia	109	24	5	0
2010 Northern Ireland	43	4	6	1
2010 Scotland	46	15	12	1
2010 Wales	63	8	6	2
2010 UK	53	9	10	0
2011 Canada	173	60	30	7
2012 Finland	94	13	8	3
2012 France	25	4	12	1
2012 London Mayor	75	6	0	3
2013 Australia MP	28	14	6	0
2013 Australia PM	53	9	10	0
Total	2515 (83%)	511 (17%)	475 (17%)	82 (15%)

General Goals: χ^2 (df = 1) = 1325.84, p < .0001. Ideals: χ^2 (df = 1) = 275.88, p < .0001.
1984, 1988, 1992, 1996, 1999 Israel: Benoit & Sheafer, 2006
1988 France: Choi & Benoit, 2009
1995 France: Choi & Benoit, 2009
1997 South Korea: Choi & Benoit, 2009
2002 South Korea: Choi & Benoit, 2009
2004 Taiwan: Benoit, Wen, & Yu, 2007
2004 Ukraine: Benoit & Klyukovski, 2006
2006 Canada: Benoit & Henson, 2007
2007 Australia: Benoit & Henson, 2007
2007 France: Choi & Benoit. 2013
2008 Spain: Gerrero & Benoit, 2009
2010 Australia PM: Benoit & Benoit-Bryan, 2014a

Continued

Table 6.10. *Continued*

2010 Northern Ireland, Scotland, Wales: Benoit & Benoit-Bryan, 2014b
2010 UK: Benoit & Benoit-Bryan, 2013
2011 Canada: Benoit, 2011
2012 Finland: Paatelainen, Croucher, & Benoit, 2016
2012 France: Choi & Benoit, 2013
2012 London Mayoral Benoit, 2016
2013 Australia MP, PM: Benoit & Benoit-Bryan, 2015

Table 6.11. Forms of personal qualities in non-U.S. leaders' debates.

	Australia 2007	Australia 2010	Canada 2006	Canada 2011	UK 2010	Total
Morality	127 (44%)	68 (36%)	199 (36%)	173 (40%)	470 (48%)	1037 (43%)
Drive	68 (23%)	57 (30%)	111 (20%)	128 (30%)	204 (21%)	568 (23%)
Sincerity	47 (17%)	40 (21%)	113 (21%)	53 (12%)	166 (17%)	419 (17%)
Empathy	48 (17%)	25 (13%)	123 (23%)	74 (17%)	144 (15%)	414 (17%)

Benoit (2013)

Table 6.12. Functions and topics of non U.S. TV spots.

	Table for Functions			Topics	
	Acclaims	Attacks	Defenses	Policy	Character
France 1988	75%	25%	–	100%	0
Germany 1992	68%	32%	–	31%	69%
Germany 1994	–	–	–	69%	31%
Italy 1992	85%	15%	–	71%	29%
Britain 1992, 1997	69%	31%	–	88%	12%
Israel 1992	58%	42%	–	50%	50%
Korea 1963–1992	67%	33%	–	65%	35%
Poland 1995	93%	7%	–	66%	34%
Turkey 1995	89%	11%	–	33%	67%
Greece 1996	71%	29%	–	42%	58%
Russia 1996	72%	28%	–	58%	42%
Taiwan 1996	81%	19%	–	–	–
Subtotal	75%	25%	–	–	–
Taiwan 2000	63%	35%	3%	32%	68%
Korea 2002	72%	27%	1%	50%	50%
Mexico 2006–2012	72%	27%	1%	38%	62%

Chang (2000); Cruz & Benoit, 2021; Kaid (1999); Kaid and Holtz-Bacha (1995); Lee and Benoit (2004); Tak, Kaid, and Lee (1997); Wen, Benoit, and Wu (2004).

Non-U.S. TV Spots

Countries around the world use television advertising in elections. Kaid and Holtz-Bacha (1995) report the results of studies of the effects of political advertisements in three countries (Italy, 1992; France, 1988, Germany, 1990). They found significant changes (not always favorable to the candidate) in candidates' images, after exposure to television spots, for three of the eight candidates involved. This shows that political advertising can affect perceptions of candidates in other countries besides the U.S.

Analyses of the content of non-U.S. TV spots rarely uses Functional Theory, so defenses are not counted and forms of policy and character (e.g., past deeds, future plans, ideals) are not studied (Benoit, Wen, & Yu, 2007 and Lee & Benoit, 2004 do use Functional Theory). Several studies have investigated the functions and topics of television spots for presidents and prime ministers of other countries. Functional Theory predicts that acclaims will be more common than attacks. The percentage of positive ads ranges from 58% (Israel, 1992) to 93% (Poland, 1995). The mean percentage of positive ads (all studies but Wen, Benoit, & Yu, 2004, Lee & Benoit, 2004, and Cruz & Benoit, 2021, used the entire spot as the coding unit) was 72%; attacking ads were 27% of the sample. See Table 6.12. The two studies which coded for defenses confirmed that attacks were more frequent than defenses.

This theory also predicted that policy will be a more frequent topic of campaign messages than character. Overall, Table 6.12 indicates that 59% of the ads addressed policy and 41% concern character. However, ads were divided evenly between the two topics in Israel and Korea (2002) and in five cases (Germany, Greece, Russia, Taiwan, Mexico) character was discussed more often than policy. This means the predicted relationship obtained in 8 of the 15 samples, so this relationship is not consistent.

Another prediction indicated that incumbents will be more likely to acclaim than attack on past deeds. Consistent with this prediction, Kaid and Holtz-Bacha (1995) report that in four of five countries (France, German, Italy, Israel, but not Britain), more ads by incumbent candidates emphasized their own accomplishments than attacked record of the opponent. In contrast, in four of five countries (Germany, Italy Britain, Israel, but not France), more challenger spots attacked the opponent's record than emphasized their own accomplishments. This result is consistent with expectations from Functional Theory.

Conclusion

It is clear that, especially given the argument that far more non-Presidential races (and more non-U.S. presidential races) occur than U.S. presidential races, research on campaigns for these offices is important. The evidence presented here suggests that there are some constants in political campaigns across level of office and even across country and culture. Acclaims are more common than attacks, and defenses least common, in the non-presidential ads discussed here. This distribution of functions was also observed in non-U.S. races. Topical differences (more emphasis on policy than character) characterizes the non-presidential spots examined here. Although there are exceptions in other countries, discussion of policy overall is more common in non-U.S. ads than character. Similarly, general goals and ideals are used more often to acclaim than attack in non-presidential campaign messages.

Ads sponsored by political parties are more negative at the non-presidential level than those from candidates, as is the case at the presidential level. Issue ownership theory (Petrocik, 1996) applies well to non-presidential discourse. These differences attributable to the source of campaign messages appear to transcend level of office.

Incumbents acclaim less than challengers, who in turn attack more than incumbents. Unlike challengers, incumbents use past deeds to acclaim more than to attack. Challengers tend to use future plans to acclaim more than incumbents. Again, these differences are consistent with the effects of incumbency status on presidential messages.

There are some differences between U.S. presidential campaign messages and other political campaign messages. The effects of political party affiliation on functions and topics of non-presidential campaign messages appears less consistent than for presidential spots. Although the polls I could discover indicated that more voters reported that policy was the most important influence on their vote for congress, there was no difference in outcome by topic (unlike at the presidential level). I also noted that differences in the political system (e.g., incumbency should be less powerful in Korea because presidents may not run for re-election and there are no vice presidents). Clearly, non-presidential campaign messages share important similarities with presidential messages, yet some differences can be found.

CHAPTER SEVEN

News Coverage of Political Campaigns

Obviously, the news media devote many stories to political campaigns. As the diagram in Chapter One on information flow in campaigns shows, many people learn about the candidates from the news. Schudson (1995) explains that

> When the media offer the public an item of news, they confer upon it public legitimacy. They bring it into a common public forum where it can be discussed by a general audience. They not only distribute the report of an event or announcement to a large population, they amplify it. (p. 19)

Clearly, news coverage of political campaigns merits scholarly attention. Many important questions can be asked about this coverage (for a recent treatment of news coverage of political campaigns, see Gulati, Just, & Crigler, 2004). How much do voters learn from the news? Does the news accurately reflect the content of candidate messages? Is there a bias toward one political party? What topics do the media feature in their stories? I will take up each of these questions in this chapter.

Voter Learning from News

How much voters learn about presidential candidates from the news is a more complicated question than it might seem. Shaw (2001) identified three important variables for understanding the effects of campaign media: outlets, access, and receptivity. The number and variety of outlets has increased, particularly in recent years. In the past, newspapers and direct mail were supplemented first by radio and then by television. More recently, cable television and satellite television increased the number of outlets (e.g., news on CNN, HNN, MSNBC, Fox News). The Internet can be considered a quantum change; not only have the number of outlets increased, but ordinary citizens and small, poorly funded interest groups can disseminate messages over the Internet (although they must attract web users to their webpages to obtain an audience for their messages). Clearly, the number of news outlets has changed dramatically. More news information, in a larger variety of media outlets, is available today than ever before.

The argument that mass communication has become "balkanized," or split into many smaller audiences, is important to mention here. At the height of broadcast television in the late 1960s, most of the public watched ABC, CBS, or NBC, and these networks offered very similar content. However, technological advances permitted new sources of information to emerge: cable television, satellite television, the Internet and social media. As new information sources emerge they often offer unique (niche) content, particularly given the fact that the FCC repealed the Fairness Doctrine. For example, when Fox News joined CNN as a news network, it offered a different (conservative) perspective on the news (Benoit & Billings, 2020). Media balkanization means that many "niche" networks (and webpages, and Twitter accounts, and Facebook pages) emerged. Although these information sources reach fewer people, these smaller audiences tend to be relatively similar in interests. Niche audiences can make it easier for candidates to target specific groups of voters.

An important factor that has gone relatively unnoticed is the elimination of the "Fairness Doctrine." The Federal Communication Commission had promulgated this rule in 1949, requiring that broadcast stations present contrasting views on controversial issues. However, in 1987 the FCC repealed this regulation, a decision that was upheld in court (Gill, 2016). The consequences of this action were seen quickly, as Rush Limbaugh's radio program became syndicated in 1988. Tucker (2017) explained that in the absence of the Fairness Doctrine, "talk-radio stations across the country soon began to run right-wing agitprop from dawn to dusk, flooding the public airwaves with shameless demonization of Democrats and progressives." This rule change also liberates liberal programming. There can be no doubt that the content of network news has changed drastically. It is clear, for example, that Fox News and CNN cover different topics and offer contrasting perspectives when they do cover the same topic. Broadcasters were then free to offer a single (slanted) perspective on current events without even appearing to provide balanced coverage of controversial topics. Today webpages, Twitter feeds, and Facebook pages have no legal reason to present every side of an issue (some may offer more than one side to a topic, but they do not *have* to do so). This change enabled a wide range of content options (media "menus") for people to choose from and consume. More people have different political information today than in the past. Some overlap (common information) still occurs, but voters tend to have different kinds of information today.

It is important to keep in mind that an increasing number of outlets may not mean that any given citizen watches, reads, or hears more news than before; older media are used less as some citizens switch from using an older medium to a newer one. For example, someone who used to read the newspaper may now watch CNN instead, or at least spend less time reading newspapers. Another person might watch less television news as they begin to use online news sources more frequently. More information is available from more sources, but that does not necessarily mean the electorate overall is better informed. Furthermore, keep in mind that these new sources have different emphases, but they often repeat much the same basic information available elsewhere (Haney, Dillon, & White, 1995).

A survey in 2000 by the Pew Research Center found changing patterns in news use: "Traditional news outlets are feeling the impact of two distinct and powerful trends. Internet news has not only arrived, it is attracting key segments of the national audience. At the same time, growing numbers of Americans are losing the news habit." The number who regularly watch evening network news has dropped to 30%; 46% report that they regularly read newspapers. The number who regularly use on-line news (CNN, FoxNews, CNBC, MSNBC) ranged from 11–15% (Pew, 2000a). Use of the various media is changing in recent years.

Access to media is another key factor in understanding influence. Ansolabehere, Behr, and Iyengar (1993) report before 1950, most Americans used newspapers for news. Television has since then become the dominant conveyor of news. Today, the typical newspaper has a circulation of about 25,000. Three important national newspapers–the *New York Times*, *Los Angeles Times*, and *Washington Post*–reach about 3 million people. The three largest news magazines (*Time*, *Newsweek*, and *US News & World Report*) reach about 10 million readers. A national network news program in contrast, attracts about 20 million viewers (Ansolabehere, Behr, & Iyengar, 1993, p. 41). However, because there are many local news programs broadcast by a given station, local television news programs in the aggregate have an even larger audience (p. 48). Again, access or viewership is an important consideration in understanding the news resources available to voters.

When new technologies are introduced, it takes time for citizens to obtain access. Technology is expensive when first introduced and technical difficulties may also impede media access. The Internet is a good recent example; clearly, cost has been decreasing as user-friendliness has increased and as a result, access to this medium has increased rapidly. A Harris poll indicated that two-thirds of Americans had Internet access in 2003 (Taylor, 2003).

The third variable in evaluating media effects is receptivity, the question of how effectively a medium conveys knowledge or influences attitudes. Differences exist both within media (e.g., the information available in the *New York Times* and the *New York Post* overlap but are not identical; the same could be said of network and cable news) and between media. For example, radio has audio but no visual element; television has audio and video; newspapers have words, graphics, and still pictures but no audio; on the other hand, it is easy to re-read a print story or return to it after an interruption than a television story.

Benoit and Hansen (2004a) report data from the NES about reported use of various media to learn about the presidential campaign. Overall, people report that 69% use newspapers, 35% read magazines, 44% listen to radio, 80% watch television, 71% watch debate, and 72% discuss the campaign with friends and family. However, they also found that over time (1952–2000), significantly fewer people report that they learn about the presidential campaign from newspapers, radio, and debates. There was no significant change in reported use of magazines or television over time. The only medium which showed an increase in reported use was political discussion.

Although this is useful information, it is important to realize that it has two limitations. First, this kind of question–"Where do you learn about the presidential campaign?"–only asks *whether* they learned from these media, not *what* or *how much* they learned. The answer to this kind of question should be the same – "Yes, I learned about the presidential campaign from ____ [this medium]" – for, say, newspapers and television news, even if the respondent learned one piece of information from newspapers and dozens of things from television.

Second, this question, "Where do you learn about the presidential campaign," is a self-report measure, asking voters to tell where they think they learn about political information. Self-report questions have two important limitations (Benoit & Benoit, 1986). First, the respondent must actually know the answer to the question; if not, he or she is likely to reply with a guess. It seems very unlikely that most people keep track of where they learn about the presidential race. Surely people do *not* keep track of where they learn information as in this hypothetical example:

> So, the Republican candidate wants to create business enterprise zones. I learned this fact from the newspaper article I'm now reading, so that means so far I've learned 10

pieces of information from newspapers, 6 from television news, 14 from discussions with friends, co-workers, and family, and 4 from television spots.

Instead of reporting where they actually obtained information, voters are almost certainly telling where they *think* they learned it. Their guesses could be correct, but on the other hand, they might guess wrong. As this chapter reveals, much news coverage concerns horse-race instead of questions about issues or leadership. People may be unaware of this fact. Similarly, they may not know that candidate messages, including televison spots, discuss policy more than character (as reported in Table 2.3). Citizens might tend to assume that the news provides more information than it actually supplies. If so, they might overestimate their learning from some media, like the news, and underestimate their learning from other media, like television spots.

Better evidence about where voters learn about candidates' issue positions and character can be obtained from analyses which measure each voter's actual knowledge and relates that information to their media use. This approach still relies on self-report data, but there are two key differences. First, the questions asked in these kinds of analyses are different: "How often do you watch television news?" "Did you watch a presidential debate?" Arguably the answers to these questions require less guesswork than "Did you *learn about the presidential campaign* from television news (or from a debate)? Second, these studies measure the voters' actual campaign knowledge (e.g., which candidate favors gun control) and reported media use is statistically related to their actual knowledge levels.

Patterson and McClure (1976) studied the 1972 presidential campaign. Their research on voters found that "Regular viewing of network news had no influence on how much these people learned" (p. 49). On the other hand, "newspaper readers became much better informed of the same election issues during the 1972 campaign (p. 51). Keep in mind that more people report watching television news than reading newspapers; however, to be an effective information source people must not only use in (read it or watch it) but *actually learn from it*.

Hofstetter also investigated network television coverage of the 1972 general presidential campaign; he did not look for statements about horse race coverage. He reported that stories about issues (41%) were more common than stories about candidates (30%) or political parties (8%).

Hansen (2004) conducted an extensive review of the literature on the question of whether the news media fosters issue knowledge during presidential campaigns. He found that only 17 of 34 studies on newspaper use found a significant effect on learning – and the more recent studies were less likely to find effects than earlier research. Research on television indicated that only 11 of 33 studies found that watching television news created issue knowledge. Hansen then used NES data from 1960 to 2000 to analyze the impact of various sources of information on issue knowledge. Newspaper use was associated with higher levels of knowledge in each of these eleven campaigns; television news use was related to issue learning in 8 of 11 campaigns. Both his review of the research and his new study indicate that newspaper use is more likely to create knowledge than television news use, but both are capable of informing the electorate.

Amount of Campaign News Coverage

It is important to realize that the news is selective in its reporting of information to voters. The news performs a "gatekeeping" function as Hollihan (2001) explains: "journalists and editors decide what stories will be covered" in the news (p. 75). Several factors limit the amount of information available in the news about political campaigns. First, the presidential campaign is but one topic in the news among many (e.g., sports, entertainment, business). Graber (1989) explained that "election news competes for audience with many other types of stories; this accounts, in part, for its limited impact" (p. 207). Unfortunately for voters, the trend in recent years has been for the news to devote less time to covering the presidential campaign than in the past.

One of the earliest programs of research investigating news coverage of campaign was initiated by Guido Stempel in 1960. He investigated presidential campaign stories in 15 newspapers. He discovered that the number of newspaper stories about the presidential candidates steadily decreased over time. In 1960, 101,402 stories were published in these 15 papers (Stempel, 1961). The total number of campaign articles dropped in 1964 to 97,351 (Stempel, 1965). A bigger drop occurred in the next campaign, when only 87,806 stories covered the 1968 presidential campaign (Stempel, 1969). He replicated his study in 1980 (after one newspaper had gone out of business), finding that only 64,007 articles concerned the presidential campaign (Stempel & Windhauser, 1984). Another, more recent study found that coverage of the 1996 presidential campaign "in major newspapers dropped by over 40%" compared with 1992 (Jamieson, Waldman, & Devitt, 1998, p. 323). It is obvious that the amount of newspaper coverage of the presidential campaign has diminished substantially over time.

Other research investigates campaign coverage in television news, but the story is the same: The number of stories reporting on the presidential campaign is also dwindling. Steele and Barnhurst (1996) discovered that between 1968 and 1988, the number of political news stories decreased 20%. Exacerbating this trend,

Hallin (1992) found that in the same time period the average *length* of a typical political news story decreased by about 20%. Farnsworth and Lichter (2003) show that network news coverage of presidential campaigns has declined over time. In 1988, 589 stories of 1116 minutes discussed the presidential campaign. By 2000, 462 stories of 805 minutes covered it (p. 44). Jamieson, Waldman, and Devitt (1998) reported that the final two months of the 1996 presidential campaign "network coverage of the presidential election declined by 55 percent from 1992" (p. 323; see also Lichter, Noyes, & Kaid, 1999). There simply is less opportunity for the news to educate voters because the volume of campaign news stories in newspapers and on television is decreasing.

One comparison which may drive home the fact that the news offers less campaign information than we tend to assume comes when we compare the number of minutes of campaign news stories with the number of minutes of candidate television advertisements broadcast. Studies by Patterson and McClure (1976) and Kern (1989) investigated the amount of time television advertisements and campaign news were broadcast in the 1972 and 1984 presidential campaigns respectively. Recording news and advertisements during the campaign, both studies found that about four times as many minutes of presidential spots as minutes of news coverage of the presidential campaign were aired. Therefore, one limitation on the ability of the news to inform and influence voters is the fact that Americans are exposed to far fewer minutes of news coverage of campaigns than candidate messages. The recent development of restricting campaigns to "battleground" states means that voters in those states are exposed to even more minutes of advertising than campaign news stories.

Finally, some research has addressed the question of "who speaks" in campaign news coverage. Benoit, Stein, and Hansen (2004) analyzed *New York Times*' campaign stories from 1952 to 2000. They found 44% of the statements in these stories were unattributed (i.e., the reporter was the source), 35% were from candidates, 16% from candidates' supporters, and 5% of sources were others. Hallin (1992) reported that when candidates were quoted in a television news story, the quotation last an average of 43 seconds in 1968. By 1988, it had dropped to 9 seconds. Lichter, Noyes, and Kaid (1999) found that candidate quotations averaged 8.2 seconds in 1996. Steele and Barnhurst (1996), found that over the same time period, journalists talked more frequently as time passed. Consistent with this picture, Patterson (2003) reported that in 2000, "the two candidates received only 12% of the election coverage. Anchors and correspondents took up three-fourths of the time, with the rest allocated to other sources, including voters, experts, and group leaders" (p. 63). There are fewer and shorter stories and we hear far more from reporters and anchors in recent years than from the candidates themselves in the news.

Bias in Campaign News Coverage

In the next two sections of this chapter I will discuss two related topics. The first is *bias*, which investigates whether the news coverage favors one candidate or party over another. In the next section, I will look at the question of *accuracy*, which concerns the extent to which the coverage correctly reflects the content of candidate messages.

A very early study of campaign news coverage analyzed stories in eight newspapers from 1952 (Klein & Maccoby, 1954). They selected four newspapers which had endorsed Eisenhower and four which had endorsed Stevenson. They found that both sets of newspapers had more stories about Eisenhower than Stevenson, not surprising given the fact that General Eisenhower was considered to be a war hero (if not *the* war hero) at the time. They did report that as the campaign progressed, the number of Stevenson stories increased.

Stempel conducted a number of stories investigating the presence of ideological bias in newspaper campaign coverage. In 1961, the Democratic candidate had a slight advantage: 50.2% of the stories concerned Senator John Kennedy, whereas 49.8% were mainly about Vice President Richard Nixon (Stempel, 1961). In 1964, President Lyndon Johnson, held a 52% to 48% advantage over Senator Barry Goldwater (Stempel, 1965). Vice President Hubert Humphrey led the way in 1968, with 41% of stories; Richard Nixon garnered 37% of the press and third party candidate former Governor George Wallace accounted for 22% of the newspaper stories (Stempel, 1969). Skipping to 1980, Governor Ronald Reagan was the primary subject of 45% of stories; President Jimmy Carter was the subject of 42% of articles and independent candidate John Anderson received 12% of stories (Stempel & Windhauser, 1984). Stovall (1982) reported that in 1980, horse race stories (campaign events, polls, debates) accounted for 86% of stories; issues comprised 14% of newspaper stories. Stovall (1988), using a sample of 49 daily papers, reported that in 1984 50.6% of stories concerned President Reagan and 49.4% were about former Vice President Walter Mondale. In 1988, Vice President George Bush was the subject of 51% of stories and Governor Michael Dukakis was the topic of 49% of stories (Stempel & Windhauser, 1989). These studies indicate that the coverage is roughly, but not exactly, balanced. In three years one party's candidate received the most press and twice the other party's candidate was the subject of most stories. The difference between the two leading candidates is never more than four percentage points.

Evarts and Stempel (1974) examined news coverage of the 1972 presidential campaign but looked beyond newspapers. They classified sentences as favorable to Democrats or Republicans. The three broadcast television networks combined devoted 55% of favorable statements to Democrats and 44% to Republicans. Combining data from six newspapers (*Louisville Courier-Journal, New York Times, Christian Science Monitor, Washington Post, Chicago Tribune,* and *Los Angeles Times*) yielded virtually the same results: 56% of statements were favorable to Democrats and 44% to Republicans. Analysis of three major news magazines (*Newsweek, Time,* and *US News & World Report*), in contrast, found that more evaluative statements favored Republicans (55%) than Democrats (45%). Here we again see biases, but this bias is not consistent across medium: Television news and newspapers were more favorable to Democrats but news magazines were more favorable to Republicans.

Meadow (1973), analyzing three newspaper and the three network news programs, reported that newspapers (58.3–63.2%) published more favorable stories about Senator George McGovern in 1972 than President Nixon (as a candidate; 36.8–41.7%). Television news showed the same trend; more stories favorable to McGovern (58.2–64%) than Nixon (36–41.8%). This study suggests a larger differential in 1972 than in other years. Kenney and Simpson (1993) compared the number of stories about the presidential race in 1988 in two Washington newspapers. They found balanced coverage in the *Washington Post* but a bias toward the Republican party in the *Washington Times*.

Watts, Domke, Shah, and Fan (1999) investigated the alleged liberal bias of the news in the 1988, 1992, and 1996 presidential elections. Analyzing a mixture of newspapers and network news, they suggested that perceptions of a liberal bias may be more related to *criticisms* of the media than *content* of the media.

Having illustrated the kind of findings in research on media bias with these studies, I will not examine every individual study. This is not necessary because a meta-analysis has used statistical procedures to combine the results from various studies in this area. D'Alessio and Allen (2000) first examined gate-keeping bias, in which bias emerges in the selection of stories for publication or broadcast. Overall, no significant bias was found, although they cautioned that only five studies investigated this potential form of bias.

Second, they examined coverage bias, the amount of coverage devoted to a candidate or party (e.g., Stempel, 1965). No significant overall bias was found after combining 17 studies of column inches, 19 studies of the number of stories, or 8 studies of the number of photographs published in newspapers. No significant overall bias occurred when 10 studies of length of television stories were combined or 18 investigations of the number of television stories. Eight studies of news magazines (e.g., *Time*) also revealed no significant overall coverage bias.

The third type of bias they investigated was tone of coverage (e.g., Evarts & Stempel, 1974), which they label statement bias. The observed bias was very small in 16 studies of newspaper tone, 19 studies of favorability in television stories, and 8 studies of news magazine tone. D'Alessio and Allen (2000), as one might expect from the two studies reviewed earlier, conclude that there is bias in newspaper coverage of campaigns, but not a bias which favors one party overall:

> This is not to say that every reporter and every newspaper is unbiased. Quite the opposite: A wide variety of data (Shoemaker & Reese, 1991; White, 1950; Millspaugh, 1949) indicates that specific newspapers or specific reporters and editors can show substantial (and substantive) ideological bias .... What the results of this meta-analysis do say is that on the whole, across all newspapers and all reporters, there is only negligible, if any, net bias in the coverage of presidential campaigns. (p. 148)

They also concluded that bias in television and news magazines was quite small.

> Analyzes of coverage bias and statement bias in TV network news coverage of presidential campaigns reveal a very small, and not completely consistent, liberal (or at least pro-Democratic) bias. There was a slight pro-Republican coverage bias and an even slighter pro-Republican statement bias [in news magazines]. (p. 149)

So, the news coverage of political campaigns reveals the existence of some bias toward one party or the other in particular campaigns or particular news outlets or media. However, overall there is no consistent bias toward either party. It is important to realize that such bias exists in some media. No voter can read every paper and watch every network. This means that many individual voters are exposed to biased news coverage of political campaigns. The Media Tenor report (2004), analyzing network television coverage of the 2004 presidential campaign from September 1 through October 14, concluded that "representation of the U.S. economy on the whole on network evening news and Fox's Special Report with Brit Hume could not be more different ... While the networks covered the economy in a dire tone, Fox News drew a rather optimistic picture." The report concluded that "voters' decision on election day might depend on which news channels they have been watching before going to the polls." Indeed, many voters probably decide which paper to read or which network to watch because a given medium leans in the same direction as the voter. So, there are biases in individual outlets, which could have effects on the voters who use these outlets, but there is no overall liberal (or conservative) bias in news coverage.

Accuracy of Campaign News Coverage

Another question that can be asked of campaign news coverage is whether it accurately reflects the content of the candidate messages it reports. Returning to the diagram in Chapter One, this question concerns media filtering of candidate messages, from path 2 to path 3 (messages from candidates that are passed on to voters by the news). We have data which compares the content of three kinds of candidate messages with the content of news coverage of those messages. We selected messages which occurred on particular dates and which were likely to attract the attention of the press. In each of these studies, we located newspaper stories about these particular campaign messages and employed the same procedures to content analyze the stories. This allowed us to compare the campaign messages with the news coverage of those messages, to determine whether the news accurately represented the content of these messages. Jamieson, Waldman, and Devitt (1998) reported that "as in previous years, in 1996 broadcast news overreported attacks in candidates and speeches. But unlike previous years, it also overreported attacks in candidate advertising" (p. 325). They also argued that network news tends to leave out evidence candidates offer from their claims: "While 95% of Clinton's and Dole's claims were backed by evidence, only 40% of those reported by commercial networks included proof" (p. 327).

Primary Debates

Benoit, Hansen, and Stein (2004) investigated newspaper coverage of three presidential primary debates from each campaign from 1980 through 2004 (they studied four debates, two Democratic and two Republican, from 1988, and six, three from each party, in 2000). They located five articles about each debate. Newspaper articles systematically over-represent attacks and under-represent acclaims. Newspaper stories discussed attacks in 52% of statements about the debates; attacks comprised only 30% of the statements made by candidates. In contrast, acclaims constituted 66% of the comments in debates, but newspaper stories discussed acclaims in only 43% of remarks in the article. These differences were statistically significant with a relatively large effect size ($V=.21$) and this pattern emerged in each one of the seven campaigns studied (see Reber & Benoit, 2001, who found the same pattern using two different primary debates from the 2000 campaign).

If voters think that campaigns are negative, one possible explanation is the news coverage accentuates the negative. This emphasis is not surprising because attacks are points of conflict, and conflict is interesting. Attacks can reveal differences between candidates which means attacks can be useful to voters. However, acclaims are also useful too, and voters who learn about primary debates from reading about them in newspapers do not get the entire story.

Benoit, Hansen, and Stein (2004) also investigated the topics of newspaper coverage of primary debates. Overall, both debates and newspapers emphasized policy, but policy was discussed even more frequently in debates (65%) than in stories (60%). On the other hand, newspaper reports emphasized character (40%) more than the candidates (35%). This effect was significant but with a smaller effect size (V=.05). The effect was also not consistent over time. Three campaigns (1980, 1984, 1996) saw a greater emphasis of character in newspapers than in debates. However, one campaign (1996) saw the reverse (more emphasis on policy in newspapers than in debates) and the two most recent campaigns saw no significant difference in topic of newspaper stories and debates. Therefore, there is some tendency for the news to emphasize character more, and policy less, than debates.

Patterson (1994) observed that "The news is not a mirror held up to society. It is a selective rendition of events" (p. 60). Benoit, Hansen, and Stein (2004) also investigated the degree of gate-keeping in these stories. They calculated that the average story on a political primary debate reports 7% of the statements in the debate (the range is 4–15%). Reporters decided which statements readers should know about. Thus, as we might expect, newspaper stories are highly selective, reporting an average of 7% of the candidates' statements. Stories consistently over-report attacks and under-report acclaims. More often than not, the topics of the debates are not accurately represented in stories, with newspaper stories more often stressing character more and policy less than debates, but this effect is less consistent.

General Debates

Studying only stories broadcast or published after the debates, Patterson (1980) reported that the media dwelt on the horse race when reporting the 1976 debates (network news 50%, newspapers 53%, news magazines, 46%). Substantive matters, including policy and character, accounted for about one-third of the stories (network news, 34%, newspapers, 33%, news magazines, 35%). However, this does not reveal whether the substantive coverage was accurate.

Although they did not content analyze the debates themselves, Lemert, Elliot, Bernstein, Rosenberg, and Nestvold (1991) content analyzed ABC and CBS stories on presidential debates. They found that discussion of issues and the candidates' record decreased over time (1976: 40%; 1980: 22.3%; 1984: 12.5%; 1988: 13.8%)

while discussions of tactics increased (1976: 12.7%; 1980: 15.3%; 1984: 20.4%; 1988: 25.9%). Discussions of debate performance were substantial parts of television news, ranging from 44.5% (1976) to 61.9% (1984). These analyses indicate that tactics and performance are emphasized in television stories about the debates, but again, we do not have benchmark (the content of the debates themselves) for comparison.

Miller and MacKuen examined news coverage of the 1976 presidential debates. They found that debates discussed competence (4.1%) and personality (5.1%) less than newspapers (competence: 16.3%; personality: 12.2%) and television (competence: 18.5%; personality: 20.4%). In contrast, the debates focused on issues such as domestic and foreign policy and previous record (70.1%), more so than newspapers (61.1%) or television news (46.3%). Sears and Chaffee (1979) summarized the findings of several studies of the 1976 debates:

> The heavy issue focus of the debates was largely ignored, however, in the subsequent coverage by television, radio, newspapers, and magazines. All studies agreed that there was less than 40% issue content in the post-debate coverage; this means less than half the issue focus of the debates themselves ... . Instead of their overt content, news reports of the debates were preoccupied with "who won" and generally with the competitive, horse-race aspect. (p. 229)

Thus, news coverage of the 1976 debates, across media, focused substantially less on issues or policy than the debates themselves.

Benoit, Stein, and Hansen (2004) also investigated newspaper coverage of general debates from 1980 to 2000 using the same procedures (locating five newspaper stories on each debate, content analyzing the debates for function and topic, and comparing news coverage with the debates). Once again they found that newspapers dwell on the negative. Newspaper articles reported attacks 50% of the time whereas the candidates attacked in only 31% of their debate utterances. Candidates acclaimed in 61% of their statements, but acclaims constituted only 41% of newspaper stories. These differences were significant, occurred in each of the six campaign studied, and had a relatively large effect size ($V=.19$).

Benoit, Stein, and Hansen (2004b) found that newspaper articles on debates focused on character more (31% to 26%) and policy less (69% to 74%) than the debates. This effect was significant, but as with primary debates, it was not consistent and the effect size was small. in fact, the difference in topics was significant in only two campaigns (1992, 1996).

Newspaper stories about general debates also performed a substantial gatekeeping function. The average story reported almost 11% of the statements made in debates (the range was 3.2–30.3%). So, again we see that newspaper stories emphasize attacks, de-emphasize acclaims, and occasionally stress character more than policy.

Benoit and Currie (2001) also investigated newspaper coverage of the 1996 and 2000 general presidential debates, with similar findings. However, they also tried to study television coverage of debate. The problem with television news is that general campaign debates always are broadcast *after* the national evening news is over. The television stories leading up to debates cannot, of course, report on what was said in the debates. They do make predictions and discuss whether third party candidates (such as Ross Perot in 1992 and 1996, Ralph Nader in 2000) will be allowed to debate. However, because television stories after the debates are broadcast the next evening, they rarely report what happened in debates. By this time the debates are nearly a day old. Coverage may focus on a dramatic event (e.g., Lloyd Bentsen telling Dan Quayle that "He is no Jack Kennedy") or supposedly "telling" events (e.g., President George Bush looking at his watch in 1992). However, most often stories after the debates have occurred have moved on to reactions to the debates rather than coverage of what was said in them. This means television news is not the ideal place to learn what candidates told voters in debates.

Campaign Speeches

Benoit, Stein, and Hansen (2004a) also investigated newspaper coverage of nomination convention acceptance addresses by the Democratic and Republican candidates. The found no overall differences in functions or topics between newspaper stories and acceptance addresses. They found differences in emphasis in some campaigns. Interestingly, when differences arose newspaper articles sometimes discussed attacks *less* and policy *more* than did the speeches. Furthermore, this study shows that newspaper stories do not always emphasize the same ideas (they do not always over-represent attacks or character).

Analysis of particular campaign events has established that we cannot assume that newspaper articles about a campaign event will necessarily be report campaign messages accurately. Particularly in debates, there is a clear tendency for stories to accentuate the negative and, at times, newspaper articles will focus on character more and policy less than the candidates themselves. Buchanan (2004), discussing research from the Center for Media and Public Affairs, noted that "In 1996 the candidates offered three positive or self-promoting remarks for each criticism of a rival (74% positive). But the critical remarks made up a majority (52%) of the candidate quotes that make the evening news" (p. 13). As Farnsworth and Lichter (2003) concluded from their study of television news coverage, "the unmediated campaign–be it through speeches, web pages, talk show content, or even political advertising–is far more substantial, far more issue based, and far ness negative in orientation than the campaign described in network news accounts" (p. 191). News coverage of election campaigns can be superficial.

Television Spots

West (2001) analyzed news coverage of presidential television advertisements. Examining the *New York Times* (1952–2000), the *Washington Post* (1972–2000), and the CBS *Evening News* (1972–2000), he found that overall slightly more stories concerned primary (52%) than general ads (48%), although the *New York Times* bucked this trend. He indicated that 55% of the stories about ads had a negative tone. Given the fact that Table 3.3 reports that attacks constitute 34% of the themes in primary and general ads combined, news coverage of ads is more negative than the ads. Looking more closely at CBS news coverage, West found that 65% of the stories concerned campaign strategy, 25% policy, and 10% personal qualities of the candidates. Once again the evidence indicates that news coverage of specific campaign messages – primary debates, general debates, acceptance addresses, primary and general television spots – is more negative than the messages themselves.

Schudson (1995) noted that the high level of negativity in news coverage occurs in part because the "news tends to emphasize conflict, dissension, and battle" (p. 9). The high levels of negativity in the news (higher than the negativity of candidates) could have deleterious effects on democracy. Buchanan (2004) observed that "The net effect [of over-representing negative candidate remarks in the news] was to exaggerate the extent of the candidates' actual reliance on attack and to make the campaign seem more negative that it really was" (p. 13). Just, Crigler, and Buhr (1999) observed that:

> If candidates spend most of their time attacking each other, journalists should not be blamed for reporting that they do. On the other hand, if reporters distort the candidates' messages, they may heighten the cynicism or negativity of the campaign. (p. 35)

Ansolabehere and Iyengar (1995) have argued that attacks in political advertising reduce voter turnout (Ansolabehere & Iyengar, 1995; Ansolabehere, Iyengar, & Simon, 1999; Ansolabehere, Iyengar, Simon, & Valentino, 1994). However, as Finkel and Geer (1998) point out, one of Ansolabehere and Iyengar's analyses used content analysis of *news stories* about the campaign (rather than content analysis of *television advertising*) to determine the level of attack in a campaign. In other words, this study actually demonstrated that negative tone in *newspaper coverage* of the campaign reduced voter turn-out. The negative tone of news coverage of campaign messages like debates, which the research reviewed here reveals is much more negative than the messages from the candidates, could be detrimental to voter turnout.

Finally, it should be noted that the various news media may not be equally effective in conveying information to voters. Bennett (2005) reported that "viewers of FOX news were more than twice as likely as viewers of the *News Hour* on PBS to have the basic facts wrong about such key issues as connections between Iraq and terrorism" (p. 216). We must keep in mind that there are at least two different explanations for this finding (and either or both could be true for some viewers): FOX news may misinform its viewers more than the *News Hour* and/or those who choose to watch the *News Hour* instead of FOX may be better informed generally. Still, these results should provide a caution about assuming that all news media are equally informative.

Nature of Campaign News Coverage

An important question about news coverage of political campaigns is what topics are explored in stories and articles. This is important because research has shown that the amount of coverage received by candidates, the tone of the coverage, and the amount of horse race coverage focusing on a candidate can influence voters' perceptions of candidates (Ross, 1992). Farnsworth and Lichter (1999) argue that horse-race coverage had more influence on candidate popularity than other topics (character, substance).

One of the earliest studies of campaign news coverage investigated the 1952 contest. Klein and Maccoby (1954) found that 60% of stories concerned policy or issues, 16% candidates' personal qualities (character) and 5% was about scandals.[1] In the 1968 campaign, McCombs and Shaw reported that 63% of news coverage of the presidential campaign in television, newspapers, and news magazines concerned the horse race and 37% addressed issues. Graber (1971) reported that more stories in 1968 discussed personal qualities (66%) than issues (34%). Using a somewhat different method (counting mentions instead of stories), Graber (1976) found the same result in 1972: more mentions of candidate personal qualities (20,362) than of issues (11,187).

Patterson and McClure (1976) analyzed the content of network television coverage of the 1972 presidential campaign. They found that campaign activity, including polls, accounted for 72% of coverage. Issues were 20% and character/leadership comprised 8% of news coverage. Patterson (1980) investigated news coverage of the 1976 presidential campaign on network news, in three newspapers, and in two news magazines. He found that game coverage predominated (networks, 58%, newspapers, 55%, news magazines, 54%). Substantive coverage, focusing on policy and character, made up less than one-third of the stories (networks, 29%, newspapers, 30%, news magazines, 31%).

Newspaper coverage of the 1968 and 1976 presidential campaigns was investigated by Russonello and Wolf (1979). The largest category of articles was horse race (56% in 1968, 47% in 1976). The candidates' personal qualities (1968: 17%, 1976: 25%) and issues (1968: 22%; 1976: 21%) received about half as much attention in the newspapers.

Robinson and Sheehan (1983) analyzed news coverage of the 1980 campaign from January through October, concluding that:

> At every level, in every phase, during each and every month, CBS and UPI allocated more news space to competition between the candidates than to any other aspects of the campaign .... "Horse race" permeates almost everything the press does in covering elections and candidates ... about five of every six campaign stories made some meaningful reference to the competition, but, by comparison, well over half of the same stories made no mention of issues. (p. 148)

They concluded that, combining both the primary and the general campaign (January through October), CBS and UPI devoted 65% of their coverage to the horse race, 26% to issues, and 10% to candidates (p. 149).

Stempel and Windhauser (1991) reported on the content of newspaper coverage of the 1984 and 1988 presidential campaigns. In 1984, issues were 39% of stories, followed by campaign events (35%), candidate character (21%), and horse race (5%). In 1988, issues dropped to 22%, campaign events were 34%, character 27% and horse race (7%). Buchanan (1991) content analyzed news coverage of the 1988 general election campaign, examining newspapers, news magazines, and television coverage. He reported that 65% of stories concerned the horse race, 18% policy, and 17% character. Mantler and Whiteman (1995) reported that in 1992, issues accounted for 49.5% of newspaper coverage, followed by horse race at 41.4% and character at 9.1%.

Kahn (1995) analyzed newspaper coverage from 1983 to 1988 of senate and gubernatorial races. However, she also reported information on the nature of presidential campaign coverage in 1984 and 1988. Horse race accounted for 55% of paragraphs, issues were 27%, and personality traits were 18%.

Lichter and Noyes (1988) contrasted the topics of campaign news stories and speeches by the candidates in the 1992 presidential campaign. News coverage devoted 53% of newspaper and television campaign stories to the horse race. Issues and the candidates' records accounted for 24% of the stories and character and ability comprised 10% of stories. In sharp contrast, the candidates' speeches focused on issues (77%) more than horse race (14%) or character (4%).

Coverage of campaigns from 1988 to 1996 was investigated by Jamieson, Waldman, and Devitt (1998). Their concept of "strategic coverage" is essentially horse race coverage (winning and losing, sports and war metaphors, focus on people, emphasis on candidate style, and use of polls). In 1988 broadcast news devoted 64% of coverage to strategy, 50% in 1992, and 47% in 1996.

Just, Crigler, and Buhr (1999) found that many campaign stories in 1992 referred to policy (70% in papers, 49% in network television and 38% on local television). Horse race was also very common, accounting for 39% of newspaper stories, 43% of network television news, and 47% of local news). Character comprised 34% of newspaper coverage, 24% of network television, and roughly 15% of local news (the exact percentage for character in local news was not provided). Farnsworth and Lichter (2003) reported that horse race coverage increased from 58% of network television stories in 1988 to 71% in 2000 (p. 51); substantive matters – policy and character – varied between 32% and 40% (these sum to more than 100% because a story could stress horse race and substance). The Annenberg Public Policy Center analyzed national network news coverage of the 2000 campaign. About three-quarters of the stories concerned the horse race, whereas only a quarter focused on issues (Alliance for Better Campaigns, 2000).

The Lear Study analyzed local television coverage of the 2004 presidential campaign. Kaplan, Goldstein, and Hale (2005) investigated the local evening news coverage on 44 stations in 11 markets. They found that 55% of the broadcasts included a story about the presidential campaign. A typical half-hour news program included just over 2 minutes of stories about the presidential campaign. As a point of comparison, advertising accounted for almost 9 minutes and sports and weather over 6 minutes of programming. Campaign stories tended to emphasize campaign strategy and horse race coverage (44%) more than issues (32%).

Campaign coverage in five newspapers from 1888 to 1988 (in 20-year increments) was investigated by Sigelman and Bullock (1991). They found that candidate traits had remained relatively steady at about 10% of coverage. Policy issues accounted for about 25% coverage, with a small decrease starting in 1948. Campaign events accounted for about 40% of stories and this should a slight drop over time. One of the main conclusions was documenting "the meteoric rise of the horse race theme during the television era" (p. 21).

Another longitudinal study investigated *New York Times'* coverage of the presidential campaign from 1952 to 2000 (Benoit, Stein, & Hansen, 2004). Over this time period, horse race coverage was most common (40%), followed by discussions of candidate character (31%), policy (25%), voters (4%), scandal (0.2%), and election information (0.1%). They further analyzed the nature of horse race coverage. Most common were themes about strategy (34%), followed by campaign events (24%), polls (22%), predictions (13%), endorsements (13%), vote choice (2%), fund raising (1%), and spending (0.3%).

Rudd and Fish (1989) investigated the *depth* of television news issue coverage in the 1984 presidential campaign. They found that barely half of stories in which issues were mentioned actually identified at least one candidate's position on the issues. They concluded that:

> campaign issue coverage provided by television news is frequently superficial. While commercial television news, in particular, frequently puts its coverage in a confrontational frame, and presidents the image of candidates challenging one another on the issues, it often fails to identify the issue positions of either candidate – much less provide any explanation for those issue positions. (p. 201)

Thus, we should not assume that the fact that a news story mentions an issue means that voters can make an informed choice between competing candidates on the basis of that issue.

To illustrate the content of news coverage, consider television reporting on a discrete and important campaign event: presidential debates. Kaid, McKinney, and Tedesco (2000) list the topics covered in network television coverage of the presidential debates in 1996. Most of the stories were aired before the debates and discussed such topics as whether Ross Perot would participate in the debates. After the first debate, the news discussed campaign strategy on all three broadcast networks. ABC and NBC reported citizen responses to the debate. NBC interviewed one of Clinton's college debate opponents. CBS ran a story checking claims made in the debates but no story focused simply on *reporting* what the candidates said in the debate. Following the second debate, all three networks broadcast stories on campaign strategy. If you missed the debate and hoped to find out what the candidates said in the debate by watching the television news, you were out of luck. At times the news media does provides useful information about the candidates; however, it would be a mistake to simply assume that the news informs voters about the issues or the content of important campaign events in a campaign.

The news also has a tendency to focus on scandals. Farnsworth and Lichter (2003) noted that network news coverage "tilts heavily toward scandal coverage, which like horse race can also crowd out coverage of policy matters" (p. 12). Scandal may be titillating and voters may need to know about candidates' foibles. However, coverage of issues tends to be slighted.

Why do the media concentrate on horse race and scandal rather than on substantive issues? Graber (1989) explains that a survey of newspaper and television editors found that the three most important factors in choosing whether to air or print a story are conflict, proximity, and timeliness; "Conspicuously absent from their choice criteria was the story's overall significance" (p. 86). Furthermore, Patterson explains that "Policy problems lack the novelty that the journalist seeks. ... The first time that a candidate takes a position on a key issue, the press is almost certain to report it. Further statements on the same issue become progressively less newsworthy, unless a new wrinkle is added" (1994, p. 61). In the 2000 campaign, for example, the first time Bush proposed a plan for younger workers to invest Social Security funds in the stock market, that was news. However, later discussions of proposed changes to Social Security were simply not as newsworthy as the initial announcement, even if they contained more specific details about Bush's plans. Stimson (1999) explained that "Journalists pursue 'news' as a criterion of relevance. Change is news. Stability isn't" (p. xxiii). Where the candidates are campaigning today, who is leading the latest poll, and similar horse race comments are new everyday; the candidates' policy positions, particularly when they stay "on message," are not new – or news. Finally, reporting polls data in particular may foster the impression that reporters are objective (Traugott, 1985), not themselves favoring one candidate over another.

This research is rich, examining different of media over many campaigns. However, this variety difficult to summarize because of the differences in approaches. Some research distinguishes between policy (issues or substance) and character (or candidate personal qualities) but other studies combine these concepts into one category, substance. Some studies separate polls from campaign events but other research combines these into a single horse race category. Table 7.1 summarizes studies of general campaign news coverage. The most common news story addressed horse race. This category accounted for 39–86% of campaign stories, a mean of 54%. Policy stories ranged from 14–70% (32%) and character topics varied from 0–34% (21%). 14 of the 20 studies which distinguished between these two topics found that policy was more common than character. So, the research demonstrates clearly that news coverage in newspapers, on television, and in news magazines, devotes more time and space to the horse race than to policy or character.

News coverage also displays a tendency to emphasize candidate character over policy. Bennett (2005) explains two factors which encourage an emphasis on personalities rather than policy. First,

Table 7.1. Literature on general campaign news coverage.

	Campaign	HR/game/ Medium	events	Policy/issues/ substance	character
Klein and Maccoby (1954)	1952	NP		60%	16%
McCombs and Shaw (1972)	1968	TV, NP, Mag	63%	37%	
Russonello and Wolf (1979)	1968	NP	56%	22%	17%
Graber (1971)	1968	NP		34%	66%
Graber (1976)	1972	NP		35%	65%
Patterson and McClure (1976)	1972	TV	72%	20%	8%
Hofstetter (1976)	1972	TV		41%	30%
Patterson (1980)	1976	TV	58%	29%*	
Patterson (1980)	1976	NP	55%	30%*	
Patterson (1980)	1976	Mag	54%	31%*	
Russonello and Wolf (1979)	1976	NP	47%	21%	25%
Robinson and Sheehan (1983)	1980	CBS+UPI	65%	26%	10%
Stovall (1982)	1980	NP	86%	14%	
Kahn (1995)	1984, 1988	NP	55%	27%	18%
Stempel and Windhauser (1991)	1984	NP	5% HR 35% event	39%	21%
Stempel and Windhauser (1991)	1988	NP	7% HR 34% event	22%	27%
Buchanan	1988	NP, TV, Mag	65%	18%	17%
Lichter and Noyes (1995)	1992	NP+TV	53%	24%	10%
Jamieson et al. (1998)	1988	TV	64%		
Jamieson et al. (1998)	1992	TV	50%		
Jamieson et al. (1998)	1996	TV	47%		
Mantler and Whiteman (1995)	1992	NP	41%	50%	9%
Just, Crigler, and Buhr (1999)	1992	NP	39%	70%	34%
Just, Crigler, and Buhr (1999)	1992	TV	43%	49%	24%

Continued

Table 7.1. *Continued*

	Campaign	HR/game/ Medium	events	Policy/issues/ substance	character
Just, Crigler, and Buhr (1999)	1992	local TV	47%	38%	15%
Buchanan (2004)	1992	NP+TV	30%	31%	7%
Farnsworth and Lichter (2003)	1988	TV	58%	39%	
Farnsworth and Lichter (2003)	1992	TV	58%	32%	
Farnsworth and Lichter (2003)	1996	TV	48%	37%	
Buchanan (2004)	1996	TV	48%	37%	1%
Farnsworth and Lichter (2003)	2000	TV	71%	40%	
Annenberg (2005)	2000	TV	75%	25%	
Lear Center (2005)	2004	local TV	44%	32%	
Sigelman and Bullock (1991)	1888–1988	NP	40%	25%	10%
Mean			54%	32%	21%

NP = newspaper, TV = network television news, Mag = news magazine.
*Numbers combine policy and character; for mean, one-half assigned to each category.

> Personalization ... is the overwhelming tendency to downplay the big social, economic, or political picture in favor of the human trials, tragedies, and triumphs that sit on the surface of events. For example, instead of focusing on power and process, the media concentrate on the people engaged in political combat over the issues. The reasons for this ... [include] the journalist's fear that probing analysis will turn off audiences to the relative ease of telling the human interest side of the story as opposed to explaining deeper causes and effects. (p. 40)

So, personalization should encourage journalists to emphasize the horse race (competition between the candidates), including campaign strategy, and character or personality over policy. Bennett also identifies dramatization as a problem. This reflects a tendency for the news to use "the reporting form of stories or narrative" rather than analytical essays, polemics, or scientific reports. "News dramas emphasize ... personalities" (p. 41). Both personalization and dramatization help explain why the news tends to emphasize the topics which occur so frequently in political campaign coverage.

What is the result of this trend toward fewer and shorter campaign news stories, and stories that focus more on horse race and less on the issues? Bartels (1988) observed that "in covering a presidential campaign, the media tells us more about who is winning and losing than they do about who is fit to be president" (p. 32). Similarly, Farnsworth, and Lichter (2003) reported that "Polls have repeatedly shown that voters have a very good idea which candidate is likely to win the presidency, but voters are less able to demonstrate their knowledge of issue stands" (p. 53). Lichter and Noyes (1995) reported that "voter knowledge does not increase from exposure to day-to-day TV coverage, and increases modestly with day-to-day newspaper reading. Voters do learn from TV coverage of live campaign events, such as convention speeches and debates" (p. 101). The emphasis on the horse race in news coverage means that voters do know the candidates' poll numbers. Thus, the news media, because the amount of coverage steadily decreases over time while the emphasis shifts from issues and candidate qualifications to the horse race, is less useful to voters than many assume. Unfortunately, some journalists believe horse race coverage saves the campaign from being "a mighty dry and colorless affair" (Floyd, 2004, p. 1B). It is unfortunate that some reporters apparently believe issues are boring and that they are incapable of writing about issues in any way that makes them interesting.

I do want to mention that one study investigated coverage of the major party nominating conventions on network news, in newspapers, and in news magazines. Patterson (1980) found that in 1976 horse race or game coverage constituted between 54–58% of the convention stories whereas substance (policy and character) was between 29–31% of coverage. Again, horse race dominates news coverage of presidential campaigns.

News Coverage of Presidential Primary Campaigns

Fewer studies have investigated primary than general campaign coverage, but the results are consistent. Patterson (1980) investigated the 1976 presidential primaries, looking at network news, three newspapers, and *Time* and *Newsweek*. He reported that the game (horse race; winning, losing, polls, events) accounted for almost two-thirds of the coverage in all three media. Substance (including policy and candidate character) comprise about one-quarter of the stories. Graber (1988) found in the 1976 presidential election that news coverage "during the primaries concentrated very heavily on fleeting campaign activities and vote tallies in state contests, slighting a discussion of the policy stands taken by the candidates" (p. 79). Robinson and Sheehan's study of the 1980 presidential campaign found an emphasis on horse race coverage in the primary as well as the general campaign phase. Brady (1989) analyzed UPI coverage of the 1984 presidential primary campaign. Only 16% of the lines in these stories concerned the candidates' policy positions and 23% the candidate's character and leadership ability. 21% discussed potential success of the candidates, 9% their supporters, 20% campaign events, and 11% attacks on opponents. Lichter, Amundson, and Noyes (1988) examined television coverage of the primary in 1988: 50% horse race, 29 campaign issues (similar to character), and 20% policy. Farnsworth and Lichter (2003) found that network television news coverage of horse race in the primary campaign increased from 49% in 1988 to 78% in 2000 (p. 59).

A close look into the nature of horse race coverage was provided by King (1990), who analyzed sentences in *USA Today* and the *New York Times* coverage of the 1988 presidential primaries. She reported that the horse race dominated both papers' coverage (88.8% for *USA Today*, 73.7% for *New York Times*). Campaign issues (e.g., controversies, and gaffes) were the second most common topic at (7.5% and 11.2%). Policy issues (2.1%, 7.5%) and the candidates personal qualities (1.6%, 7.5%) were less common topics. It appears that the papers differed in emphasis, with *USA Today* focusing most on the horse race and the *New York Times* devoting more coverage to issues and candidates' character.

Another study of the 1988 primaries focused only on horse race coverage in two newspapers and the three broadcast networks. Using the theme as the unit of analysis, Johnson (1993) reported that polls accounted for 23% of newspaper and 29% of television coverage; expectations 22% and 20%, momentum 18%, 15%, outcome/delegates 16%, organization/finances 14%, 7%, and endorsements 8%, 13%, in these two news media. This study did not attempt to quantify the discussion of policy issues or character in these stories.

Wasserman (1999) investigated factors influencing the amount of coverage received by a candidate in the primary campaign during the 1988 Super Tuesday primary. Content analysis of 16 state newspapers revealed that the amount of money spent by a candidate in a state and the number of visits to that state was positively related to newspaper coverage of that candidates. Candidates who were ranked higher in preference polls received more coverage than those trailing in the polls. "Favorite son" candidates (those who were from the state in which the election was held, and the newspapers were based, received a disproportionate share of coverage. Finally, Wasserman also reported that the size of the newspaper's news staff influenced the number of stories published.

Kendall (2005) used participant observation to obtain insights into New Hampshire presidential primaries from 1988 to 2004. She noted that "Although journalists' self-reports did not describe their work in the horse race frame, lead stories on two networks ... framed the campaign as a horse race" (p. 165). Benoit et al. (2005) analyzed news coverage of the 2004 Democratic primary in local and national newspapers and on national television. Horse race statements predominated (65%), followed by comments about the candidates' character (22%) and policy (13%). Looking just at horse race comments, the five most common forms of coverage were strategy comments (38%), polls (20%), campaign events (9%), electability (7%), and endorsements (7%).

Table 7.2 summarizes the research on primary campaigns. Again, horse race was the most common topic, accounting for 49–81% of the coverage (61%). Most studies found that horse race was more common than substance (policy: 22%; character: 17%). It appears that the emphasis on horse race may be even greater in the primary than the general phase of the campaign, perhaps because there are usually more candidates in the primary campaign and journalists use polls to discriminate between those contenders. Only four studies looked at character separately. Three of those studies found the emphasis on character was greater than on policy (and in the remaining study policy and character were equally common).

Furthermore, the presidential primary campaign, as we saw in Chapter Five, is different from the general campaign in several key ways. Here, the main difference

Table 7.2. Nature of primary campaign news coverage.

		Medium	HR, events, game	Policy, issues, substance	Character
Patterson (1980)	1976	TV	64%	24%*	
Patterson (1980)	1976	NP	62%	26%*	
Patterson (1980)	1976	news mag	62%	24%*	
Brady (1989)	1984	NP (UPI)	50%	16%	23%
Lichter, Amundson, and Noyes (1988)	1988	TV	50%	20%	29%
King (1990)	1988	NP	81%	5%	5%
Farnsworth and Lichter (2003)	1988	TV	49%	16%	
Farnsworth and Lichter (2003)	1992	TV	55%	72%	
Farnsworth and Lichter (2003)	1996	TV	56%	44%	
Farnsworth and Lichter (2003)	2000	TV	78%	22%	
Benoit et al. (2005)	2004	NP + TV	65%	13%	22%
Mean			61%	22%	17%

NP = newspaper, TV = network television news.
*Numbers combine policy and character; for mean, one-half assigned to each category.

is that American citizens vote over a period of weeks or months rather than all on the same day, as in the general campaign. This is important for two reasons. First, "momentum" (and expectations) are important in the primary phase of the campaign.[2] Second, the news devotes a disproportionate amount of primary campaign coverage to early primaries.

The notion of "momentum" arises from the fact that, unlike the general election, in which all voters cast votes on the same day, primary elections are spread out through a month or more. Candidates who start out strong, winning or showing well in early primaries, may falter later when more delegates are at stake. Other candidates may start out slower but then begin to do better as the primary season unfolds. The latter group of candidates are said to have gained momentum. The idea of momentum is, of course, encouraged by the media's obsession with horse race coverage.

Arguably, the fixation of news coverage on horse race, and a desire on the part of reporters to *create* interest in a particular primary campaign, can at times have pernicious effects on the election process. For example, Dover (1994) discussed media coverage of the Democratic primary election in New Hampshire in 1972:

> Many news reporters initially had not believed that a contest actually existed in New Hampshire since they considered Muskie a certain winner .... [T]elevision news media did not want the Democratic party to go without a contest of sorts. Without one readily available, political reporters helped to create one .... [S]everal reporters eventually persuaded him [Muskie] to admit that he needed half of the total vote cast in order to claim victory.
>
> Muskie ... received more votes than any of this four rivals, but he ... garnered approximately 48% of the vote, while McGovern finished in second place with about 37%. Television news media soon described Muskie's first place finish as a setback and McGovern's performance, objectively a loss, as a victory because it was better than expected. (p. 55)

Anyone in a multi-candidate field who receives 48% of the vote should be considered a winner. A candidate who received 37% of the vote in that contest must be considered a serious contender, but characterizing McGovern's performance as a victory, in my opinion, seriously misrepresents this outcome. Similarly, Baker (1993) explained that in 1992 Paul Tsongas won the New Hampshire primary by eight percentage points, but the media story was that Bill Clinton beat expectations and was "The Comeback Kid."

Of course, the candidates too play the expectations game. Candidates often downplay their own support because exceeding expectations—even expectations that are deliberately set low—can appear more successful that failing to meet expectations. In 1968, President Lyndon Johnson sought another term in office. However, Senator Eugene McCarthy contested the Democratic nomination. At first, the Johnson campaign attempted to create the expectation that McCarthy was not a serious candidate; that position became untenable as McCarthy's support became evident.

> During the 1968 primary, supporters of Lyndon Johnson attempted to reduce the status of the McCarthy challenge by talking down the expectation for his final vote tally. Once it became clear that McCarthy would outperform these expectations, Johnson supporters reversed the strategy and raised their expectations in the hope that reporters would accept the new inflated levels as realistic benchmarks. (Palmer, 1997, p. 105)

This strategy (or these two strategies) did not work, as Brady explained (1989): "McCarthy's success [in New Hampshire] led to Johnson's withdrawal from the presidential race" (p. 90). So, media can dwell on expectations and at times candidates feed this emphasis in an attempt to encourage the interpretation that puts them in the best light.

When the news focuses on momentum or expectations, that detracts from helping voters learn about the candidates' character and their issue positions. Lichter and Noyes (1995) argued that "increasing numbers [of voters] cast their votes not with an eye toward each candidate's relative merits, but with a strategic sense of each candidate's viability" (p. 8; see also Abramson, Aldrich, Paolino, & Rohde, 1992). However, one similar concept that may be important to voters is *electability*: How likely is it that a primary candidate will be able to defeat the nominee from the other major political party in the Fall general election campaign? Exit polls from the 2004 Democratic primary indicated that the most important factor was the ability of the candidates to defeat President George W. Bush (Associated Press, 2004).

News coverage of the primary campaign is driven by the timing of the primary. Graber (1989) reported that "Iowa and New Hampshire, with less than three percent of the U.S. population, received almost one-third of the total media coverage during the 1984 primaries" (p. 224; see Adams, 1987]. Robinson (1980) analyzed 616 television and print stories on the 1976 presidential campaign. 250 stories (41%) concerned New Hampshire (34% of print stories, 54% of television stories). New York's primary, involving forty times more voters and happening only one week later, was the subject of only 71 stories (12%). Clearly, coverage favors earlier primaries out of proportion of their importance as indicated by number of voters.

Robinson and Lichter (1991), studying the 1988 Democratic primary, and Benoit (2004), studying the 2000 Democratic and Republican primaries, found a significant relationship between the date of a state's primary election (or caucus) and the amount of news coverage: the earlier the primary, the more the coverage (but cf. Adams, 1987, who studied the 1984 primaries). Adams (1987) found a relationship between the importance of a state's primary election (measured by number of delegates from the state) and the number of stories about that state. However, Benoit found no relationship in 2000 between delegates and stories. Benoit did find that the primaries which were tighter races (measured by subtracting the percentage of votes won by the second place candidate from the percentage of votes won by the winner) received more stories. So, although the results are not always consistent from year to year, it appears that the date of the primary influences news coverage, the closeness of the race influences coverage, and the importance of the state's primary may influence coverage.

Patterson's study of the 1976 presidential primary investigated coverage on network news, in three newspapers, and in *Time* and *Newsweek* for the 13 weeks of the primary season. He found that the number of stories about a candidate was directly related to the candidates' order of finish in a primary. In each medium, the winner was the subject of the most stories (by a huge margin, almost 60% of stories), the second-place finisher received about 20% of stories, third-place 15%, and fourth-place was the subject of about 7% of stories. Stories focus on the horse race and, in particularly, on primary winners.

It should be obvious that when voters lack information about some candidates, their decision-making is disadvantaged. Graber (1989) noted that "television commercials often provide the only chance to gain information about the many candidates who are ignored by the media" in primary or non-presidential campaigns (p. 196). Sometimes the media pick the wrong candidates to cover. Napolitan (1972) explained that in the 1968 Democratic primary, "Kennedy and McCarthy were getting all the press; Humphrey was getting the delegates" and won the nomination (p. 24). Once again, the news *may* provide voters with useful information about the candidates, but it would be a mistake to assume the news *will* provide what voters need. Thus, we cannot expect news coverage of the primary campaign to do a good job of helping voters select the best candidate for office.

Hofstetter and Moore (1982) examined network news coverage of the 1972 and 1976 Democratic presidential primaries. They argued that the candidates' popularity appears to be influenced more by winning important primaries than by the sheer amount of news coverage devoted to them. On the other hand, the news media's emphasis on horse race assures that most voters know something about the campaign: "people knew more about winners and losers in primaries than they knew about anything else" (Robinson & Chauncey, 1985, p. 61). Again, the media's emphasis on the horse race means many voters know more about the popularity of candidates than their policy positions or the kind of person or leader they are.

News Coverage of Non-Presidential Campaigns

Although most scholarship has focused on news coverage of the presidential campaign, some work has looked at coverage of other political races. Graber (1989) explained that news coverage varies by race: "The role of the media varies substantially, depending upon the particular office being contested, and the news appeal of a campaign" (p. 194). Stempel (1994) notes that "coverage of presidential campaigns ... is far more intensive than that of state and local campaigns" (p. 40). Kahn and Kenney (1999) identify several factors that influence the amount of newspaper coverage: the competitiveness of the race (as one would expect, more hotly contested races [closer] receive more coverage), whether the newspaper has endorsed a candidate (coverage tends to favor endorsed candidates), and other campaigns (presidential and gubernatorial races tend to reduce senatorial coverage). Kahn (1995), who analyzed newspaper coverage of 24 senate and 21 gubernatorial races from 1983 to 1988, reports more and longer stories about gubernatorial than senate races. She also reported that non-presidential races have less horse race coverage (president: 55%; senate: 25%; gubernatorial: 15%), less personality coverage (president: 18%; senate: 10%; gubernatorial: 13%), but more issue coverage (president: 27%; senate: 65%; gubernatorial: 72%) than presidential races.

Kelley (1958), who analyzed six local newspapers in two congressional districts, found relatively little coverage of congressional races in Michigan in 1956: "The average paper published fewer column inches about both local congressional candidates in the entire six week period studied than it published on sports in a single, typical, week day issue" (p. 448). He also reported that character stories were "five times as frequent" as policy stories (p. 448).

News coverage of the 1966 California gubernatorial race between Reagan and Brown in two papers (one pro-Democratic: Sacramento *Bee*; one Republican: Oakland *Tribune*). Becker and Fuchs (1967) reported that the stories in the Democratic *Bee* favored the Brown (70.5% favorable to Brown, 19.5% favorable to Reagan) whereas the stories published by the Republican *Tribune* was favorable to Reagan (53.8% favorable to Reagan, 46.2% favorable to Reagan).

Ostroff and Sandell (1984) examined television campaign coverage in 1982, examining six television stations in two cities. They found that less than 4% of news concerned campaigns; a average of slightly more than 30 seconds of campaign news per station per day. Most coverage, an average of 21 minutes per station, concerned the governor's race. Next, with about 8 minutes per station, was news about the senate campaign. Other races (attorney general, auditor, treasurer, secretary of state, supreme court justice) received less than 2 minutes of coverage per station.

Vermeer (1987) analyzed coverage in 33 local (small town or rural) newspapers in Iowa, Kansas, and Nebraska during the 1984 elections. Only 475 stories "mentioned the local congressional candidates" (p. 81) in the period of September 1 to November 6. The average varied from 10 stories per paper in one state to 20 stories per paper in another. More stories mentioned the incumbent than the challenger (380 to 280; some mentioned both candidates).

Kahn and Kenney (1999) investigated newspaper coverage of U.S. Senate races from 1988 to 1992. They report that "on average, about 154 paragraphs about issues are published during a Senate campaign, with incumbents averaging 190 paragraphs, open candidates about 175, and challengers about 109" (p. 117). Character is discussed less than issues, with "about 54 paragraphs" about "the personal characteristics of candidates" (p. 117). Kahn and Kenney found that "The discussion of horse race in the newspapers is not as prevalent as trait or issue information.... Only about 40 paragraphs are published about the candidates' viability, on the average" (p. 117). They attribute this "to the fact that public opinion pools of statewide races are less common than surveys of presidential contests" (p. 124). Apparently issue coverage, and stories about character, are more common than horse race in these Senate campaigns.

Tidmarch, Hyman, and Sorkin (1984) investigated newspaper stories from 1982 about three kinds of non-presidential offices. They report a difference in the amount of issue coverage by office. The mean percentage of stories that mentioned issues was 48.3% for house races, 50.1% for senate races, and 60.1% for gubernatorial races. Unfortunately, the study did not report the extent of horse race or character coverage.

Graber (1989) reported the results of a study of newspaper coverage of the 1983 mayoral race in Chicago. Averaging the results from three newspapers studied, stories about the campaign comprised 47% of primary and 42% of general campaign coverage. Policies constituted 24% of primary and 21% of general campaign stories. The qualities of the candidates accounted for 15% of primary and 17% of general campaign coverage. This suggests that newspaper coverage of local races also focuses on horse race or campaign event coverage. West's (1994) study of *LA Times* coverage of the 1992 U.S. Senate campaign in California found that "news coverage of the primaries tended to emphasize the campaign while ads focused on questions of domestic policy" (p. 1058). In the general campaign, 35%

of stories emphasized the campaign, 29% were on candidate qualities and 18% concerned domestic affairs. Horse race coverage was very common.

Kahn's (1995) study of senate and gubernatorial races (1983–1988) also examined the content of newspaper stories. Most coverage addressed issues (65% on senate races; 72% on gubernatorial contests). Horse race was the second most common topic (senate: 25%; governor: 15%). The least common topic in these stories was personality or character (senate: 10%; gubernatorial: 13%). So, issues were discussed more frequently than the horse race or character.

An investigation of 49 U.S. Senate races from 1988 to 1992 was reported by Simon (2002). Examining the newspaper in each state with the largest circulation, he reported that horse race was the most common topic at 52%. This was followed by issue coverage (29%) followed by character coverage (16%).

Serini, Powers, and Johnson (1998) analyzed newspaper coverage of the 1994 Illinois Democratic gubernatorial primary: 169 stories (54%) concerned horse race and 143 policy issues (46%). They provided breakdowns which give an idea of the emphasis in horse race coverage. Campaign strategy was 30%, polls and projections constituted 28%, endorsements 15%, and finances/funding 12%, campaign debates, 9%, campaign events 7%, attacks on the incumbent, 4%, and other topics comprised 4% of the horse race stories. Again, it appears that horse race coverage tends to dominate the news.

The Lear Center (2003) analyzed 7 weeks of the top rated half-hour evening news broadcasts in 2002 on 122 stations in the top 50 U.S. media markets. They found that 56% of these programs contained no election stories. The average campaign story was 86 seconds in length. These stories were most likely to discuss campaign strategy (38%), issues (24%), horse race (9%), character (6%), and ad watch stories (3%) were less common. I would group these together into three categories: 47% campaign stories (strategy, horse race), 30% issue or character (issue, character), and 3% ad watch. Coverage of gubernatorial races (38%) was more frequently than stories about U.S. Senate (20%), U.S. House (7%), or local races (7%).

Television spots aired much more often than campaign stories (3.6 ads for each story) in these newscasts. More news programs featured at least one ad (82%) than featured at least one campaign story (44%); more programs included at least three spots (49%) than programs with at least three news stories (7%). There were 10,066 broadcasts, 33% with issue, candidate, or ad watch stories (2462). This translates to 58.8 hours of campaign news stories that could help inform voters about the candidates and issues. On those programs 26860 ads were broadcast. Assuming these were 30 seconds long, this equals 223.8 hours of campaign ads, almost four times as much air time devoted to ads as to stories about candidates and issues. Although he did not supply data on absolute levels, Patterson (2003) indicated that news coverage of non-presidential campaigns dropped 40% between 1994 and 2002.

A Lear Center study of news coverage of the 2004 campaign was reported by Kaplan, Goldstein, and Hale (2005). Analyzing the evening news coverage of 44 local affiliates in 11 markets during the general election campaign, they found that just 8% of broadcasts contained a story about a local candidate race (as noted above, 55% of broadcasts included a story about the presidential campaign). Stories emphasized campaign strategy and horse race more than issues.

A study by Tidmarch, Hyman, and Sorkin (1984) analyzed stories about senate and gubernatorial races in 12 newspapers during the 1982 campaign. They concluded that

> The national policy agenda, while visible, is a demonstrably smaller presence in gubernatorial campaigns coverage than in House and Senate coverage. Some issues chiefly in the realm of state power (education, crime, public works) make up a proportionally greater share of the gubernatorial [than the House or Senate] news agenda. (p. 1239).

So, the nature of issues emphasized in campaign news coverage varies by the office sought.

Similarly, Atkeson and Partin (2001) contrasted newspaper coverage for U.S. Senate and gubernatorial races during 1986 in four states. They expected that coverage of senate races would be more likely to stress redistributive and international issues, whereas coverage of gubernatorial campaigns would focus more on developmental policies. They found that newspaper stories on governors races stressed education, the economy, the environment, and transportation more than stories about Senate campaigns. On the other hand, coverage of Senate races was more likely than coverage of gubernatorial campaigns to discuss agriculture, policies for children and the elderly, and foreign policy (stories on both kinds of races discussed crime and drugs). They also indicate that coverage of governors races was more likely to discuss the candidates' records and competence than stories on Senate campaigns. So, the responsibilities of the office can influence the topics of election news coverage.

Finally, Sinclair (1982) content analyzed coverage of the British elections of 1979 in four British "prestige" newspapers. He found that issues accounted for 34% of the coverage, horse race comprised 34%, and personal qualities of the candidates comprised 13%. He also divided horse race coverage into four categories. Campaign activity was the most common topic of horse race coverage at 43%, and polls (16%), mood of country (14%), and campaign strategy (13%) occurred in roughly similar proportions.

These studies are summarized in Table 7.3. We see more variance in this research than in presidential news coverage. Horse race accounted for 36% of stories and issues constituted 41% of news articles. Stories about character addressed character 26% of the time.

Why does the press emphasize these topics? It is important for news to be interesting to attract and maintain the interest of readers. The horse race, by definition, is about competition. This can add suspense (unless the horse race indicates one candidate will be a runaway winner, of course) and interest to stories. Patterson (1994) explains that "Reporters are drawn irresistibly to controversy" (p. 136). Strategic coverage may be so common because of the area of expertise of for most

Table 7.3. Nature of non-presidential campaign news coverage.

	Campaign	Medium	Horse Race	Issues	Character
Kelley (1958)	1956 MI congressional	NP		17%	83%
Tidmarch, Hyman, and Sorkin (1984)	1982 house	NP		48%	
Tidmarch, Hyman, and Sorkin (1984)	1982 senate	NP		50%	
Tidmarch, Hyman, and Sorkin (1984)	1982 governor	NP		62%	
Graber (1989)	1983 mayoral	NP	45%	23%	22%
Kahn and Kenney (1999)	1988–92 US Senate	NP	16%	62%	22%
Kahn (1995)	1983–88 senate	NP	25%	65%	10%
Kahn (1995)	1983–88 gubernatorial	NP	15%	72%	13%
Simon (2002)	1988–92 senate	NP	52%	29%	16%
West (1994)	1992 senate	NP	32%	18%	29%
Serini, Powers, and Johnson (1998)	1994 primary, gubernatorial	NP	54%	46%	
Lear Center (2003)	2002 various	local TV news	47%	30%	
Lear Center (2005)	2004 various	local TV news	44%	32%	
Sinclair (1982)	1979 Britain	NP	34%	34%	13%
Mean			61%	13%	22%

NP=newspaper.

campaign reporters: "The prevalence of strategic coverage can be partly explained by the fact that most political reporters, particularly those who cover campaigns, are greater experts in politics than they are in policy" (Jamieson & Waldman, 2003, p. 168). Similarly, Schudson (1995) explained that an emphasis on strategy in news coverage occurs because "Political reporters tend to be politics-wonks rather than policy-wonks, absorbed in 'inside baseball' analysis rather than fascinated by the question of how government should run the country" (p. 10). It makes sense for reporters to stress what they know most about. An additional factor is that reporters may believe that horse race journalism is more interesting than policy journalism. Discussing horse race coverage, Marcus, Newman, and MacKuen (2000) explained that "Journalists have discovered that a narrative form that emphasizes winners and losers, heroes and villains, attracts an audience" (p. 137). So, an emphasis on horse race journalism may ensue from the areas of expertise of reporters and perceptions about what topics will interest readers or viewers.

An emphasis on attacks in news coverage, a negative tone, may also be thought to attract an audience because conflict is interesting. Furthermore, the notion that the press is a watchdog, increasing since the Vietnam War and Watergate, may have encouraged the press to be more cynical. Patterson (1994) explained that:

> The rules of reporting changed with Vietnam and Watergate, when the deceptions perpetrated by the Johnson and Nixon administrations convinced reporters that they had let the nation down by taking political leaders at their word. Two presidents had lied; therefore no politician was to be trusted. (p. 19)

This "watchdog" mentality may also encourage an emphasis on negative tone. Reporters may be able to create the impression of impartiality if they criticize all candidates indiscriminately. So, the need to create interest, reporters' expertise, and distrust fostered by earlier presidential misbehavior combine to encourage both strategic (horse race) and negative coverage.

This may explain horse race coverage emphasis and a comparatively negative tone in election coverage. But why does news coverage emphasize character more, and policy less, than the candidates in their messages? Clarke and Evans (1983), who surveyed 82 reporters who covered U.S. House of Representative races in 1978 (and content analyzed the newspaper stories in these papers), may shed some light on this question:

> Candidates are above all recognized for speaking out on particular policy positions …. Strikingly, issue-related topics recede when reporters turn to analyzing the strengths and weaknesses that they think will determine the election …. On the whole, candidates do not dwell on these [personal] characteristics in their appeals to voters.

Yet journalists believe that they are important factors in determining the outcome of a congressional race. (pp. 39–42)

So, candidates focus more on issues than personal characteristics in their appeals to voters (campaign messages). However, journalists believe that personal characteristics are more important to the election outcome. This may explain why journalists have a tendency to emphasize character more than the candidates themselves in campaign coverage.

Finally, there may be differences in campaign news coverage across medium. Sandell (1994) explained that "Above all, television is a visual medium.... The audience is attracted to action, to movement, which naturally favors coverage of events rather than issues" (p. 51). This may encourage television news to focus more on campaign events, and less on issues, than other media.

Other Effects of News Coverage

In response to the rise of the "limited effects" model discussed in Chapter One, mass communication scholars began investigating the possibility that the mass media have other effects besides instilling knowledge or changing attitudes. Three important effects of mass communication have been identified: agenda-setting, framing, and priming (for a useful review, see Scheufele, 2000).

Agenda-Setting

The press, or the mass media, does more than inform readers and viewers about current events. Lazarsfeld and Merton (1948) recognized the power of the mass media to "confer status on public issues, persons, organization, and social movements" (p. 101). Cohen (1963) succinctly expressed the basic idea of agenda-setting when he wrote that the press "may not be successful much of the time in telling people what to think, but it is stunningly successful in telling its readers what to think about" (p. 13). In other words, the mass media may not be able to tell people what to think about unemployment (who is responsible; what should be done about it), but they can tell people that unemployment is something they should be thinking about (is an important issue). McCombs and Shaw coined the phrase "agenda-setting" with the first published study of this phenomenon (1972). They found a positive correlation between the number of mentions of an issue topic (such as foreign policy) in news articles, editorials, and broadcast news stories and the perceived importance of that issue for a group of undecided voters. The mass media may not have told them *what to think* about foreign policy (may not have changed their attitudes), but the media did tell them *that they should be thinking* about foreign policy (which issues were most important).

Translating this idea into the context of presidential elections, the limited effects model may have declared that the mass media will not tell voters which candidate to support (in this example, which candidate's foreign policy proposals are best), but the mass media can tell voters that foreign policy should be an important factor in their presidential vote choice. For example, in 1992 President George Bush was widely respected for his conduct as commander-in-chief during Operation Desert Storm. However, many citizens had questions about the state of the economy. Surely the president enjoyed a considerably greater advantage in the 1992 presidential campaign among those voters who thought *national defense* was most important than among those who believed the *economy* was the most important issue. If the news alters the relative importance of foreign policy and the economy via agenda-setting, that could change the number of voters who supported President Bush.

Recently scholarship has extended the basic idea of agenda-setting, which factors influence *voters'* attitudes about the relative importance of issues, to the related question of which factors influence the *media's* agenda. Furthermore, agenda-setting research has begun to investigate the question of whether media *can*, after all, influence attitudes (what to think) as well as issue importance (what to think about). A number of works investigate the nature of the agenda-setting effect (see, e.g., Dearing & Rogers, 1996; McCombs, Shaw, & Weaver, 1997; Protess & McCombs, 1991; Shaw & McCombs, 1977; Wanta, 1997). McCombs explained that

> Observations have found agenda-setting effects all across the United States in a variety of small towns and large cities. These effects have also been found abroad in cities as diverse as Tokyo, Japan and Pamplona, Spain, and in countries as different as Argentina and Germany. Altogether, there are now more than 400 empirical studies of agenda-setting, many ... conducted during political campaigns, others monitoring public opinions in non-election periods. There is considerable diversity in the public issues that have been examined ..., encompassing the economy, civil rights, drugs, the environment, crime, a variety of foreign policy questions, and dozens of other public issues. Agenda-setting is a robust and widespread effect of mass communication. (p. 37)

McCombs also noted that several studies also examined the "real world" to see whether, for example, news emphasized crime, and people believed crime was more important, because of a crime wave. However, the agenda-setting effect has been documented where "there was no correlation at all between the trends in news coverage of major issues and the reality of those issues" (p. 26). So, the increased salience of an issue from news coverage stems from the message (communication), not from changes in the real world. See also Weaver, McCombs, and Shaw (2004) for another recent overview of this theory.

Priming

Priming concerns the relative salience (or cognitive accessibility) of certain information or topics. For example, when people are asked about an intentionally ambiguous symbol (somewhat like the one displayed below), those who were "primed" to look for *numbers* "saw" the number "thirteen," but those who were expecting to see *letters* "saw" the letter "B."

13

Priming concerns a voter's expectations, which can influence whether they attend to this information and how what he or she learns is perceived, construed, or interpreted. Priming is not specifically concerned with the relative importance of issues, but rather with which information and ideas are most salient or cognitively accessible to voters. Scheufele (2000) explained that "political issues that are most salient or accessible in a person's memory will most strongly influence perceptions of political actors and figures" (p. 300). When campaign messages discuss an issue, that issue becomes more of a "top of the head" concern than when the issue is ignored in a campaign.

Note that issue importance (agenda-setting) and issue accessibility (priming) are similar concepts but they are not identical. For example, consider a relatively young, single, well-educated business executive who considers education the most important issue. Because this voter is single (no children) and because he or she in business (neither a student nor a teacher), he or she may not think about education very often even though education is considered very important. Social Security, on the other hand, may be less important to that voter (because he or she is far from retirement age). If the campaign (the news and/or candidates) begins to discuss Social Security rather than education, that could increase the salience of Social Security ("prime" it). It is possible that this voter would still consider education to be the most important issue, but because Social Security had been discussed recently, Social Security might be more accessible in this executive's memory. It is possible for an issue to be primed and accessible without being considered highly important.

Framing

The concept of framing works from the assumption that meaning is influenced by a person's point of view (or the context used to interpret something). Thinking about a person or event from one perspective or context may well give rise to a different evaluation than considering it from another perspective. To return to the example of President Bush and Desert Storm, voters' evaluations of Bush might have differed according to whether they were thinking of him as "commander-in-chief" or as "head of the American government." The former frame should make his military successes seem more relevant; the latter frame might make his (apparent) economic failures appear more relevant. Bush could also be framed in other ways, like "a candidate for reelection to the presidency." The "candidate" frame might encourage some people to wonder whether he is doing things merely to get re-elected (Presidents seeking re-election are often thought, for example, to authorize spending in locations that might win votes). Influencing the frame (or context or perspective) used to understand and evaluate a person or event can therefore shape our attitudes toward that person or event.

In his 1996 nomination acceptance address Senator Bob Dole made an off-hand reference to a bridge to the past: "Let me be the bridge to an America that only the unknowing call myth. Let me be the bridge to a time of tranquility, faith, and confidence in action" (1996, p. 675). Note that Dole never actually used the phrase "bridge to the past" in his speech.

The Democratic Convention occurred later because a Democratic inhabited the White House. President Bill Clinton titled his acceptance address "A Bridge to the Future" and "explicitly juxtaposed his idea of a bridge to the future with Dole's offer to be a bridge to the past" (Benoit, 2001, p. 75). The idea of Dole being a "bridge to the future" was woven throughout Clinton's speech. These two metaphors offer different perspectives for framing (understanding) Clinton and Dole. One is oriented to the future, one to the past. Presumably, one is more "in step" now and in the future (the one who is elected president, obviously, will serve in the future). This contrast may have reminded voters of the fact that Dole was older than Clinton (and then they may have drawn inferences about how vigorous the candidates were).

Although we do not have evidence of how voters reacted to this frame, evidence suggests that the news media were affected by Clinton's attempt to frame his opponent:

> A Lexis/Nexis search of major newspapers for "Dole" and "Acceptance" during the two weeks after his Acceptance Address retrieved 213 hits. Significantly, not one of these essays characterized his speech or his political agenda as a "bridge to the past."

Only one article even used the phrase, and it was quoting Peter Knight, manager of the Clinton/Gore campaign. In sharp contrast, of the 75 articles featuring "Dole" and "Acceptance" during the two weeks after *Clinton's* Acceptance Address, 18 adopted Clinton's rendering of Dole's utterance: "a bridge to the past." For example, an editorial in the *Atlanta Journal and Constitution* somewhat erroneously reported that "The GOP presidential nominee proclaimed himself a bridge to the past, focusing attention on concerns about his age." (Benoit, 2001, p. 80)

Clinton's campaign message altered how Dole was discussed in the press by framing Dole as a "bridge to the past." Of course, Dole opened himself up to this frame, but the press did not adopt this frame to understand Dole's message until *after* Clinton's speech.

Thus, after the "limited effects" model gained ascendency, media scholars searched for less direct effects from mass media generally and political campaigns specifically. Three particularly important ideas are agenda-setting, priming, and framing. Notice that even if we believe media can have powerful effects (there are limits to mass media, but the "limited effects" model overstates those limits), these three other potentially important effects can still occur.

Functional Analyses of Campaign News Coverage

Research conducted from the Functional perspective has examined news coverage of political campaigns. This work looked for acclaims and attacks as well as policy and character. It also examined newspaper texts for statements about the horse race. One advantage of this work is the fact that the procedures employed were adopted from Functional Theory. This means that studies of news coverage and candidate messages – acclaims, attacks, policy and character – are directly comparable. Research has investigated news coverage of a variety of campaigns: American presidential primary coverage (Benoit, Hemmer, & Stein, 2010), American presidential general campaign coverage (Benoit, Hansen, & Stein, 2005); news coverage of governor, senate, and mayoral campaigns (Benoit, Furgerson, Siefert, & Sargardia, 2013); and news coverage of campaigns in Australia, Canada, and the United Kingdom (Benoit, Compton, & Phillips, 2013).

Table 7.4 shows that overall, statements about the horse race were more common (51%) than statements about character (27%) or policy (22%). The only exception occurred in mayoral campaign news coverage, where the horse race accounted for 32% of statements (second most common topic). It is also clear from this table that news coverage discussed policy more than character except in Australia.

Table 7.4. Newspaper coverage of political campaigns.

	Horse Race	Character	Policy
American Presidential Primary	3231 (70%)	799 (17%)	590 (13%)
American Presidential General	1332 (41%)	1041 (32%)	851 (26%)
Total	4563 (58%)	1849 (24%)	1441 (18%)
2010 Senate	807 (52%)	425 (27%)	331 (21%)
2020 Governor	658 (36%)	601 (33%)	546 (30%)
2009–2011 Mayor	592 (32%)	735 (41%)	483 (27%)
Total	2057 (40%)	1761 (34%)	1360 (26%)
2010 Australia	1217 (61%)	306 (15%)	482 (24%)
2010 Canada	516 (50%)	329 (32%)	184 (18%)
2011 U.K.	602 (40%)	584 (39%)	317 (21%)
Total	2335 (51%)	1219 (27%)	983 (22%)
Grand Total	8955 (51%)	4829 (27%)	3784 (22%)

χ^2 (df = 2) = 2533.23, p < .0001.
American General Presidential Campaigns, 1952–2000: Benoit, Stein, & Hansen, 2005.
American Presidential Primary Campaigns, 1952–2004: Benoit, Hemmer, & Stein, 2010.
American Non-Presidential Campaigns, 2009–2011: Benoit, Furgerson, Seifert, Sargardia, 2013.
Non-U.S. Leaders Debates, 2010–2011: Benoit, Compton, & Phillips, 2013.

This work compared news coverage with candidate messages. It contrasted American presidential primary campaigns with primary TV spots, debates, and direct mail advertising. It compared coverage of American general election campaigns with presidential TV spots, debates, and brochures. Senate campaign coverage is compared with Senate television advertisements and debates. The same is true for coverage of governor's campaigns. We do not have Functional data for mayoral campaigns, so news coverage of these campaigns is compared with the content of mayoral debates. News coverage of campaigns for prime minister in Australia, Canada, and the United Kingdom is compared with prime ministers' debates from these countries. Overall, the news reported acclaims less (46% to 71%) and attacks more (54% to 29%) than the candidates used these functions in their messages. The relationship – that attacks were reported more frequently than they occurred – occurred in every message form. Notice that American general election presidential campaign coverage reports acclaims more often than attacks – but it emphasizes acclaims less, and attacks more, than candidates.

Table 7.5. Functions and topics of news coverage versus news.

	Functions		Topic	
	Acclaim/Positive	Attack/Negative	Policy	Character
Presidential Primary				
News Coverage 1952–2004	1230 (56%)	960 (44%)	590 (42%)	799 (58%)
TV Spots 1952–2004	3501 (71%)	1451 (29%)	3061 (54%)	2614 (46%)
Debates 1960, 1968, 1972, 1980–2004	9984 (65%)	5446 (35%)	13248 (69%)	5966 (31%)
Brochures 1952–2004	7776 (85%)	1361 (15%)	6020 (62%)	3636 (38%)
Presidential General				
News Coverage 1952–2000	803 (41%)	1177 (59%)	851 (45%)	1041 (55%)
TV Spots 1952–2000	3072 (61%)	1998 (39%)	3102 (61%)	1968 (39%)
Debates 1960, 1976–2000	3952 (75%)	1295 (25%)	3852 (75%)	1295 (25%)
Brochures 1952–2000	8742 (76%)	2587 (24%)	8742 (76%)	2687 (24%)
Senate				
News Coverage	341 (42%)	474 (58%)	331 (44%)	425 (56%)
TV Spots	S3939 (67%)	1945 (33%)	3286 (56%)	2583 (44%)
Debates	2370 (65%)	1275 (35%)	2537 (70%)	1064 (30%)
Governor				
News Coverage	658 (56%)	526 (44%)	546 (48%)	601 (52%)
TV Spots	3392 (71%)	1364 (29%)	2839 (60%)	1921 (40%)
Debates	3007 (70%)	1309 (30%)	3166 (73%)	1150 (27%)
Mayor				
News Coverage	541 (54%)	461 (46%)	483 (40%)	735 (60%)
Debates	1285 (80%)	326 (20%)	1132 (70%)	479 (30%)
Australia				
News Coverage	352 (34%)	687 (66%)	482 (61%)	306 (39%)
Debates	181 (66%)	93 (34%)	205 (75%)	69 (25%)
Canada				
News Coverage	166 (41%)	238 (59%)	184 (36%)	329 (64%)
Debates	293 (51%)	284 (49%)	407 (70%)	170 (30%)
U.K.				
News Coverage	387 (40%)	573 (60%)	317 (35%)	584 (65%)
Debates	1000 (62%)	604 (38%)	1259 (78%)	345 (22%)

Continued

Table 7.5. *Continued*

	Functions		Topic	
	Acclaim/Positive	Attack/Negative	Policy	Character
Total News	4328 (46%)	5096 (54%)	3784 (44%)	4820 (56%)
Total Candidate Messages	52494 (71%)	21338 (29%)	52586 (67%)	25947 (33%)

Functions: χ^2 (df = 1) = 244.1, p < .0001, φ = 17. Topics: χ^2 (df = 1) = 1792.89, p < .0001, φ = 4.

American General Presidential Campaigns, 1952–2000: Benoit, Stein, & Hansen, 2005.
American Primary and General TV Spots: Benoit, 2014c.
American Primary and General Debates: Benoit, 2014b.
American Primary and General Brochures: Benoit & Stein, 2005.
American Presidential Primary Campaigns, 1952–2004: Benoit, Hemmer, & Stein, 2010.
American Non-Presidential Campaigns, 2009–2011: Benoit, Furgerson, Seifert, Sargardia, 2013.
Non-U.S. Leaders Debates, 2010–2011: Benoit, Compton, & Phillips, 2013.
US Non-Presidential TV Spots: Airne & Benoit, 2005; Benoit & Airne, 2009; Benoit, Delbert, Sudbrock, & Vogt, 2010; Brazeal & Benoit, 2001; Pier, 2002.
US Debates: Benoit, Brazeal, & Airne, 2007; Benoit, Henson, & Maltos, 2007.
Non-U.S. Debates: Benoit, 2011; Benoit & Benoit-Bryan, 2012, 2013.

Table 7.6. Source of statement in news coverage of political campaigns.

	Reporter	Candidate	Supporter	Other
American Presidential General	1502 (44%)	1171 (35%)	551 (16%)	159 (5%)
American Presidential Primary	2719 (55%)	1204 (25%)	557 (11%)	425 (9%)
Total American Presidential	4221 (51%)	2375 (29%)	1108 (13%)	584 (7%)
2010 Senate	853 (55%)	506 (32%)	79 (5%)	126 (8%)
2020 Governor	903 (49%)	702 (38%)	41 (2%)	197 (11%)
2009–2011 Mayor	1259 (57%)	1630 (31%)	181 (3%)	453 (9%)
Total Non-Presidential	3006 (43%)	2838 (41%)	301 (4%)	776 (11%)
2010 Australia	957 (74%)	197 (15%)	89 (7%)	52 (4%)
2010 Canada	603 (64%)	244 (26%)	30 (3%)	68 (7%)
2011 U.K.	868 (66%)	377 (27%)	125 (9%)	44 (3%)
Total Non-U.S.	2428 (66%)	818 (22%)	244 (7%)	164 (4%)
Grand Total	9655 (52%)	6031 (32%)	1653 (9%)	1524 (8%)

χ^2 (df = 3) = 9617.51, p < .0001.

American General Presidential Campaigns, 1952–2000: Benoit, Stein, & Hansen, 2005.
American Presidential Primary Campaigns, 1952–2004: Benoit, Hemmer, & Stein, 2010.
American Non-Presidential Campaigns, 2009–2011: Benoit, Furgerson, Seifert, and Sargardia, 2013.
Non-U.S. Leaders Debates, 2010–2011: Benoit, Compton, & Phillips, 2013.

This research also contrasted the topics of campaign coverage with candidate messages for presidential primary campaigns, general campaigns, senate campaigns, gubernatorial campaigns, mayoral campaigns, and prime minister campaigns for Australia, Canada, and the U.K. Table 7.5 also reports that news coverage discusses policy less (44% to 67%) and character more (56% to 33%) than the candidates' messages. Again, this relationship occurs in every data set. Note that in Australia, policy was discussed more than character in the news, but still the news stressed policy less than the candidates themselves.

Studies of news coverage of election campaigns also investigates the source of statements in these messages. Most commonly, reporters wrote without identifying a source (52%). Candidates were the source of 32% of news statements. The candidates' supporters (9%) and others (8%) made up the sources of remaining statements. See Table 7.6.

Conclusion

News coverage matters, because many citizens do not actively follow the campaign and it supplements the information available to those who do pay attention to the campaign. However, this chapter shows that the news, particularly in recent campaigns, focuses more on the horse race than on substantive concerns (policy, character). This stress on the horse means that citizens are less informed about issues and character, although they do know who is most popular. Patterson (2003) observed that political campaign coverage has become more negative over time: "Political coverage started to become more negative in the 1960s and by the 1980s attack journalism was firmly in place" (p. 65). Steele and Barnhurst (quoted in Patterson, 2003, p. 71) explained that "a study of 1988 election coverage found that television journalists spent three-fourths of their time 'evaluating what was right, good, or desirable' and only one-fourth providing factual information" to voters. Ranney (1983) argued further that televised political news has

> altered the culture significantly, by intensifying ordinary American's traditional low opinion of politics and politicians, by exacerbating the decline in their trust and confidence in government and its institutions, and by helping to make them even less inclined to vote than they used to be. (pp. 86–87)

Repeated accusations of "fake news" has further undermined trust in the media. The evidence suggests that news coverage of political campaigns suffers from several problems. Research informed by Functional Theory has reinforced the emphasis on the horse race. It has also established that news coverage is more negative than the candidates' own messages and the news stressed character more (and policy less) than candidates in their messages. Finally news coverage is mainly voiced by reporters (52%) rather than the candidates themselves (32%).

Notes

1. Several of the studies discussed in this section included an "other" category, which I do not report. I also at times converted the data reported in the original studies (e.g., if separate figures were reported for ABC, CBS, and NBC, I combined the data into a single variable to represent network television news). Buchanan (1991) combined candidate character (including competence) with candidate issue positions (and discussions of issues not tied to candidates were coded separately). Separating character from issue coverage was difficult because breakdowns of candidate character and candidate issue positions only reported part of the sample (those on which two of three coders agreed). I also excluded other categories when calculating percentages for Buchanan.
2. Candidates who are "gaining" or "rising" (doing better in later than earlier primaries) are said to have momentum. Although leading polls and winning primaries is almost always the optimum position, it is better to be gaining momentum than losing steam.

CHAPTER EIGHT

Voters: Campaign Messages and Election Outcome

Citizens, as the ultimate audience for campaign messages and the ones' whose votes decide the outcome of the election, can be considered the most important element of campaign persuasion (candidates, context, news media [and other non-candidate sources], messages, audience). The candidate who wins the votes of most voters (at least, in sufficient states to win the electoral college in the presidential election) will become president. This chapter will begin by examining the relationship between campaign messages (and the information available in them, particularly policy and character) and voters. It will discuss three key influences on voters: policy, character, and party/ideology. I want to note that character is not as important in vote choice as many believe: King (2002) summarized the results of several studies of the role of character in 51 elections held in 6 countries, noting that the "almost universal belief that leaders' and candidates' personalities are almost invariably hugely important in determining the outcomes of elections is simply wrong" (p. 216). Character is an element in vote choice, but it is not all important. This chapter will adopt the voter's perspective to explain how voting decisions are made. It will discuss the role of emotions in elections and address public opinion polls, an important means of understanding voters and their attitudes.

Three Influences on Vote Choice

I propose a model of voting behavior in which policy preferences, candidate character, and political party play key roles (recall Campbell, Gurin, & Miller, 1954, from Chapter One). Of course, we must keep in mind that other variables, such as ethnicity, gender, education, or occupation can also influence voting behavior.

The first assumption in my approach to understanding voter behavior is that not all citizens vote in the same way.

1. The relative influence of policy preferences, candidate character evaluations, and political party identification (or ideology)[1] in vote choice varies from voter to voter.

I take this assumption into account by positing that the three potential influences on vote choice can have different weights for different voters. For example, some citizens may decide entirely on the basis of character, which would give weights of zero to policy and party ID. On the other hand, voters who decide solely on the basis of ideology or the political party of the candidate will have weights of zero for policy and character. Other voters may use a combination of these factors, such as considering both policy and character. Note that I do not assume that the vote decision is necessarily a conscious process, with voters making lists of pros and cons. The information to which voters are exposed during the campaign probably gradually shapes their knowledge and attitudes. Some voters may reflect on the choices facing them and "realize" their attitudes lead to a particular vote choice rather than make a conscious decision.

Second, the relative importance of these three factors can vary over time (within a campaign and across campaigns).

2. The relative importance of policy, character and party (or ideology) can vary for a particular voter during a campaign.

I believe that some voters use political party affiliation as a short-cut, such that their vote choice is guided by their political party affiliation *until* they obtain information about the candidates that they consider pertinent, at which point the information starts to supplant political party affiliation as an influence on vote choice. If a voter knows little or nothing about a candidate's policy or character, he or she may have not other option than to base the vote choice on political party affiliation. However, after he or she acquires information that seems pertinent, that voter tends to rely more on policy (or character, or both) than on political party to make a vote choice. Holbert, Benoit, and McKinney (2002) reported that before watching a debate, ideology and party ID were the two most important factors in differentiating Bush supporters from Gore supporters. However, after watching the debate – which provided viewers with information about the candidates' policy positions – the two most important discriminators were Bush's and Gore's positions on the issues. This provides support for the idea that party affiliation (and ideology) can serve as a shortcut, a basis for citizens to express a vote preference *before* they learn about the candidates. The study also suggests that the basis for their vote choice changed as they gained information about the candidates.

A voter's choices in the voting booth can be characterized as "straight-ticket" or "split-ticking" voting. In the former case, a citizen votes only for candidates of his or her political party. In the latter case, a person votes for a least one candidate from different political parties. Straight-ticket voting has varied over time. Looking just at candidates for President and Senate, in 1920 98% of votes were straight-ticket (voting for a president and a senator of the sampe political party; Phillips, 2016). In 1972, 1984, and 1988 straight ticket dropped to a low of 49%. However, in 2016, 100% of citizens voted for a Senator and a President of the same party. Split ticket voting is a mirror image straight ticket voting (low in 1920; high in 1972, 1984, and 1988; and a low of 0 in 2016). In an era when split-ticket voting is high, with many swing voters, such voters can be a very important audience for election messages. On the other hand, when split-ticket voting is low (as it is currently), candidates may spend more time, money, and effort on getting out the base. Today's high level of straight-ticket voting is a manifestation of the high level of polarization in America discussed in Chapter One. President Trump faced several threats to his popularity and re-election hopes in 2020 including over 100,000 deaths from Covid-19 (the CDC puts US deaths from this pandemic at 116,862 on June 17, 2020) and seething protests over the killing of George Floyd.

Another way to win an election besides activating one's base and trying to persuade swing voters – one that is reprehensible in my opinion – is to suppress the votes of citizens who support one's opponent. Given the smaller numbers of swing voters, this approach is particularly relevant today. Waldman argued that "Voter suppression is at the very heart of Republican electoral strategy" (2020). He explained some of the strategies to suppress votes: "You pass voter ID laws, because you know poor people and minorities are going to be less likely to have approved IDs. Then you limit early voting and start closing polling places. Then when Election Day comes, you deploy your 'ballot security' troops" who challenge some voters (2020). President Trump lamented the fact that if Democratic voting reforms were adopted "You'd never have a Republican elected in this country again"

(Levine, 2020). Republicans claim their efforts are designed to thwart vote fraud. However, the Brennan Center for Justice reported that:

> Politicians at all levels of government have repeatedly, and falsely, claimed the 2016 and 2018 elections were marred by millions of people voting illegally. However, extensive research reveals that fraud is very rare, voter impersonation is virtually nonexistent, and many instances of alleged fraud are, in fact, mistakes by voters or administrators ….
>
> The Brennan Center's seminal report *The Truth About Voter Fraud* conclusively demonstrated that most allegations of fraud turn out to be baseless and that most of the few remaining allegations reveal irregularities and other forms of election misconduct. Numerous other studies, including one commissioned by the Trump administration, have reached the same conclusion. (2020)

Political party affiliation is a complex factor influencing citizens' vote choices.

3. Policy and character can have complex influence on vote choice.

Policy and character are both relatively complex variables. First, there are many potential policy issues, such as fighting pandemics, education, employment, environment, foreign policy, gun control, health care, immigration, Social Security, and taxation. Some voters might be "single-issue" voters, which means that their vote choice is determined by only one policy question. For example, depending on which issue is most important, such a citizen could vote for the candidate who favors or opposes gun control, who will best protect the environment, or who will do the better job of providing for senior citizens. The research in Chapter One suggests that the economy can be an important influence on vote choice, but even there some dispute exists among scholars about the relative influence of particular aspects of the economy, such as income, GNP, inflation, or unemployment on voting. Presumably, the single-issue voter compares the candidates – their records and/or their campaign promises – on that one issue and votes for the candidate who appears to offer the best prospects on that issue.

Other voters might base their vote choice on several issues. This is obviously more complex because it involves more than one issue and one candidate might not be preferred to the opposition on all of the issues that matter to a given voter. For example, in 2000 George W. Bush advocated private school vouchers and allowing people to invest part of their Social Security funds in the stock market. How should a citizen vote who believes that these are the two most important issues but agrees with the first proposal but not the second? Agenda-setting (e.g. McCombs, 2004; McCombs & Shaw, 1972) seems particularly relevant here, because those multi-issue voters might prefer one candidate over another depending upon which issues appear most salient to them at the time. That is, if this hypothetical voter believed that private school vouchers was more important than Social Security, he or she might prefer Bush, but *not* if the voter thought Social Security was more important. This idea of issue importance could explain some of President George Bush's popularity shifts in 1991 and 1992. When Operation Desert Storm was in full-swing and this issue was highly salient, Bush's popularity was quite high. However, as that foreign policy success faded into the past and economic concerns became more important to many voters, his popularity waned and he lost his re-election bid to Bill Clinton.

When a voter privileges issues, that makes retrospective and prospective voting important considerations. For some voters, the evidence reviewed earlier (e.g., Fair, 1978; Kramer, 1977) demonstrated that a strong economy benefits incumbents whereas a weak economy benefits challengers. Although Key (1966) reiterated the thesis of limited effects (e.g., Lazarsfeld, Berelson, & Gaudet, 1948), he added to it the idea that voters can be influenced by their perceptions of the incumbent party's record in office:

> The hullabaloo of a presidential campaign so commands our attention that we ascribe to campaigns great power to sway the multitude. Campaigning does change votes and it does bestir people to vote. Yet other influences doubtless outweigh the campaign in the determination of the vote. As voters mark their ballots they may have in their minds impressions of the last TV political spectacular of the campaign, but, more important, they have in their minds recollections of their experiences of the past four years. These memories may be happy ones or they may be memories of dissatisfaction with what government has done or has left undone. (p. 9)

Key recognized that voters can make retrospective assessments of how the incumbent party has performed and suggested that this information can influence their vote. However, he draws a false dichotomy between campaigning and the economy – campaigns often *discuss* the economy, informing voters about how it is doing.

Downs' (1957) Economic Theory of Democracy begins by assuming that citizens vote for the party they believe will maximize rewards and minimize costs. This appears to be a largely prospective decision: The voter "makes his [sic] decision by comparing future performances he expects from the competing parties" (p. 39). However, Downs recognized that information acquisition is costly (in time, effort, and sometimes even in monetary terms). He observed that people obtain "free political information" from political parties, television, interest groups, private discussion, and entertainment sources, and noted that information arises "in the course of making production or consumption decisions" (pp. 222–223; cf. Popkin, 1994).

Fiorina (1981) argued that voters used retrospective assessments of governmental outcomes to decide their vote choice in a presidential election. Citizens have some reason to distrust politicians, so they may discount their campaign promises. Citizens may not be able to resolve debates over political issues, particularly when both sides are supported by experts. However, Fiorina argued that voters

> typically have one comparatively hard bit of data: They know what life has been like during the incumbent's administration. They need *not* know the precise economic or foreign policies of the incumbent administration in order to see or feel the *results* of those policies. (p. 5; emphasis original)

Thus, many voters focus on past *results* (their perception of how is the economy doing, or the state of foreign affairs) rather than on the details of public policy. Drawing on Downs' notion that obtaining information can be costly to voters, Fiorina explains that obtaining information to support retrospective assessments of presidential (or political party) performance does not require excessive cost:

> The retrospective voter need not spend his life watching "Meet the Press" and reading the *New York Times*. He can look at the evening news and observe the coffins being unloaded from Air Force transports, the increasing price of a basket of groceries between this month and last, and the police arresting demonstrators of one stripe or another. (p 10)

Thus, citizens can learn about foreign conflicts, inflation, or social unrest from the news. Finally, Fiorina attempts to synthesize fundamental ideas proposed by Key and Downs:

> Like Key, we should view the mass public as concerned with the ends of government policy [results] more than with the means (except when the two are equated ...). But like Downs we should view the voter as looking ahead and choosing between alternative futures. Past trends are not ignored, to be sure; they are incorporated into future projections .... Good past performance, which creates favorable future expectations, is a helpful thing for an incumbent candidate to have. But there is still an opponent who may succeed in stimulating even more favorable future expectations. And he may win. (p. 198)

Therefore, Fiorina argues that voters do reflect on the performance of the incumbent party, using it as an index of how that party might perform if returned to office. However, voters do not completely ignore the challenger; they also consider the likely outcomes if that party wins the election.

Here the theory of Issue Ownership (Petrocik, 1996), which was discussed in Chapter Four, can come into play. Petrocik argues that over time political parties have developed reputations among voters for domains of policy expertise. Most voters tend to believe that the Republican Party is better able to handle issues (problems) of, for example, national defense and foreign policy. The Democratic Party, on the other hand, is generally thought to be better at dealing with such issues or problems as health care, unemployment, and the environment. Thus, Fiorina argues that voters who are unemployed might well

> turn against the incumbent administration – *but only if that administration is Republican* (e.g., in 1972 and 1976). When the incumbent administration is Democratic, those experiencing unemployment have an increased tendency to vote Democratic (e.g., in 1964). (p. 41, italics added)

Thus, *retrospective* evaluations of the incumbent political party performance, when used as the basis for *prospective* judgments, can be tempered by perceptions of which political party is better equipped (or more likely) to solve the current problems. Clearly, issue voting can be a complex phenomenon.

Character is another complicated factor. Functional theory distinguishes between multiple aspects of character, including personal qualities (character traits like honesty and compassion) and leadership ability (or experience in office). Some voters likely prefer the candidate who appears to be most honest or moral (or better on some other character trait that is important to those voters). Leadership ability or effectiveness in office is another dimension of character. A voter could be faced with a situation in which one candidate appeared to support policies more in line with that voters' preferences but another candidate seemed likely to be more effective in implementing public policy when in office. Popkin (1994; see Bruner & Korchin, 1946) relates the story of Boston Mayor James Curley who was re-elected while he was serving time in prison: "None of the candidates with more desirable issue positions and better reputations appeared capable of controlling government and getting things done" (p. 62). Thus, it is possible that at some times, or for some voters, leadership ability or competence could outweigh other character factors and issues. So, just as the case with policy, the influence of character on vote choice can be a complex process.

As indicated earlier, the idea that these three factors play a role in voting is not new. Campbell, Gurin, and Miller (1954) argued that three factors influence voters: ideology, issues (which I call policy), and character. Twenty-five years later, Markus and Converse (1979) and Page and Jones (1979) proposed similar models, simplified in Figure 1.4. Page and Jones (1979), whose model allows for reciprocal influences among variables, concluded that policy and character were more important influences on overall candidate evaluation and then on vote choice than political party (with policy being somewhat more important than character). Markus and Converse (1979) presented data that personal qualities were more important than policy or party identification (both of which were about equally important).

Some evidence suggests that policy is more important than character. Public opinion poll data from each election from 1976 to 2000 indicated that more voters reported that policy was the most important determinant of their vote for president, rather than character (Benoit, 2003b). Analysis of the content of presidential campaign messages reveals that winners emphasize policy more, and character less, than losers (Benoit, 2003b). Furthermore, Kirkpatrick, Lyons, and Fitzgerald (1975) conclude that an increase in the importance of candidate image over time does not necessarily mean that personality has become more important because domestic and foreign policy has become linked more with candidate images and less with party image over time.

Regardless of which factor is *most* important (and I would argue that the relative importance of these factors varies from voter to voter and generally from election to election), the claim that these three factors – policy, candidate character, and political party or ideology – all have the potential to influence voter choice seems reasonable. However, the most important question for our purposes is the role of campaign messages in this process.

I propose a model in which these three factors – policy, character, and ideology – work together to influence the voters' image or overall impression of the candidate. After all, inside the voting booth, citizens vote for *candidates* rather than policies. Zakahi and Hacker (1995) explain that

> Candidate images are cognitive representations of candidates that are held by voters. These representations result from the processing of messages from other candidates,

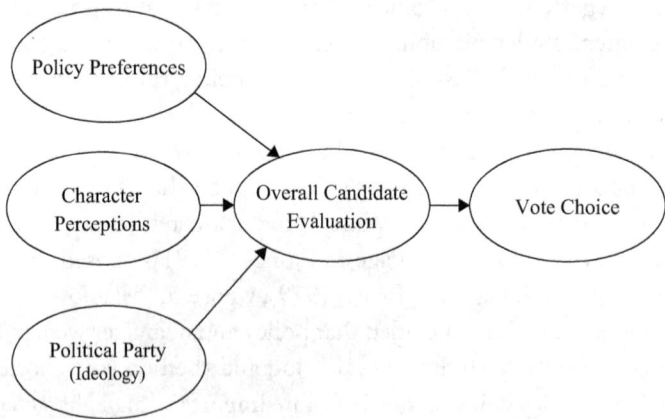

Figure 8.1. Influences on Vote Choice

voters, journalists, and other sources of political information (Trent & Friedenberg, 1991; Denton & Woodward, 1990; Nimmo & Savage, 1976). (p. 68)

So, candidate images are impressions or perceptions of the candidates held by voters. These perceptions are formed from and influenced by messages from candidates, the news, and other sources, including discussions among voters.

Candidate images can be divided into two main segments or portions, as Hollihan (2001) explains:

> First is the political image. This might include the candidate's identification with a particular party, discernable ideological commitments, positions on issues, and linkages to other known political figures and/or interest groups. Second is the personal image. Candidates possess a set of traits and characteristics, such as age, intellectual abilities, speaking style, and so on. (p. 64)

In short, a candidate's image can be viewed as having a policy and a character component. Information about political party affiliation and ideology is useful insofar as each political party is associated with a set of issues, as Petrocik's (1996) issue ownership theory explains. In short, knowing that President George W. Bush is a Republican, or Senator John Kerry is a Democrat, allows voters to draw inferences about the probable consequences of their behavior (policy choices) if elected. Of course, candidate's "positions on the issues" can reinforce these assumptions or, occasionally, tell voters that a candidate is taking a different position from his or her political party as a whole. Second, a candidate's overall image is shaped by voters' perceptions of character traits and leadership ability (competence). Thus, the statement that voters develop an "image" of the candidates and that they cast votes on the basis of that image should *not* be taken to mean that voters decide on the basis of *character*, ignoring *policy*. The voters perceptions of both character and policy combine to create an overall image of the candidate.

Although I argue below that policy is very important, it is important to keep in mind that the election is a choice between candidates. Sniderman (2000) reported that Norman Jacobson observed that "we do not have our choice of choices; we have to choose from the alternatives on offer" (p. 74). For example, in 1996 President Clinton proposed targeted tax cuts while Senator Dole promised a 15% across-the-board tax cut. Voters who wanted a 20% (or 11%) across-the-board tax cut were out of luck, because that was not a choice. Similarly, people who thought targeted tax cuts were better, but who wanted a *different set of specific tax cuts from those advocated by Clinton* could not vote for a different set of tax cuts. Voters in 1996 could not vote for no tax cuts. The only choice voters could make was Clinton or Dole (or Ross Perot or another minor party candidate). Thus, ultimately voters are choosing a person (and the general set of policy proposals articulated by that candidate). Again, this does not mean policy is unimportant; policy is a component of candidate image, and arguably it is a very important component for many voters.

Acclaims, attacks, and defenses help those voters who decide their vote completely or in part by policy and/or character. The effects of these functions tend to accumulate over time as a voter encounters more messages. Acclaims tend to make the candidate appear better, attacks are prone to make the target look worse, and defenses have a tendency to undermine attacks. These three functions work together as an informal version of cost-benefit analysis: If persuasive to a voter, acclaims tend to increase a candidate's benefits, attacks are likely to increase the target's costs, and defenses work to reduce costs. Calling this a version of cost-benefit analysis is not meant to imply that voters carefully quantify costs or benefits and then apply mathematical operations (adding or averaging) to determine vote choice.

How Voters Decide Their Vote Choice

I want to focus next on the question of how *voters* process campaign messages, develop attitudes, and make vote choices. Once a voter has information about the candidates and their policies – and have formed attitudes toward each – how do they decide how to vote (as suggested earlier, I do not assume that every voters makes a conscious vote choice; some may gradually come to have attitudes which indicate a vote preference)? This question is much easier to ask than to answer because different voters decide in different ways. In general, a citizen's voting decision making process is determined by two factors: (1) which factor or factors (policy, character, and/or party affiliation or ideology) is most important to that voter and (2) what information or attitudes the voter possesses about the most important element or elements.

For example, suppose Jane is a single issue (policy) voter who only really cares about gun control. When making a vote choice, Jane should reflect on what information and attitudes she has about the candidates' positions on gun control. Jane should vote for the candidate whom Jane believes will have appropriate gun control policies. Note that it does not matter whether she favors more or less gun control; she should vote for the candidate whose gun control policies are closest (in Jane's perceptions) to her own preferred gun control position. Jamal, on the other hand, believes that honesty is the most important element in choosing a president. When he casts a vote, Jamal should choose the candidate he believes is more honest. Bob votes only for Democratic candidates. His vote choice will be determined by his knowledge of the candidates' political party affiliation. Bob will vote for the candidate who is affiliated with the Democratic Party and it seems likely that if he is a strong partisan he will surely know the identify of the Democratic candidate.

Of course, some voters do not vote based on a single element or issue. Sally believes that education and jobs are the most important issues. She can be expected to vote for the candidate whom she believes is most likely to improve education and create jobs. George thinks that tax policy (lower taxes, in particular) and morality are the most important factors in his presidential vote choice. So, he will reflect on which candidate is most likely to reduce taxes and who is (in George's opinion) most moral. Of course, as indicated earlier, these decisions are more complex because, for example, it is possible that the candidate who is likely to reduce taxes is less moral than the opponent (or, in Sally's case, the candidate whom she believes is most likely to help education is not the candidate most likely to create jobs). Still, these voters should make a vote choice based on the element or elements most important to each one and their knowledge and attitudes about the candidates on these elements.

However, as observed earlier, many citizens have relatively low interest in politics and do not actively seek out information about the candidates and their issue positions. Popkin (1994) explained that many "voters do not have much incentive to gather information about politics solely in order to improve their voting choice" (p. 13). Research has consistently found that many voters lack basic information about government affairs. Delli Carpini and Keeter (1996) reviewed over 2,000 public opinion poll questions asked from 1940 to 1994 that measured various forms of political knowledge. "Only 13% of the more than 2,000 political questions could be answered correctly by 75% or more of those asked, and only 41% could be answered correctly by more than half" (p. 101). Of course, the topics of the questions included varied widely (e.g., name a UN agency, define "monetary policy") and some are arguably not information required to cast an informed vote. Nevertheless, it is clear that many Americans have unfortunately low levels of political knowledge. For example, in the 1992 presidential campaign between President George Bush and Governor Bill Clinton:

> 86% of a random sample of likely voters knew that Bush's family dog was named Millie ... but only 15% knew that both candidates favored the death penalty and only 5% knew that both had proposed cuts in the capital gains tax. (Delli Carpini & Keeter, 1996, p. 63)

Delli Carpini and Keeter do qualify their claim, noting that "political knowledge levels ... are high enough among some segments of the population, and on some topics, to foster optimism about democratic possibilities" (p. 269). Some citizens are well-informed, particularly on certain topics salient to them, but still voters in America have less political knowledge than they might. Wattenberg (1998), however, explains that the task facing American voters is particularly difficult:

> Electoral politics is inordinately more complicated and time consuming for the average citizen in the United States than for those in almost any other democratic country in the world. First of all, Americans are expected to vote for a plethora of political offices including president, senator, representative, governor, state senator, state representative, mayor, city council member, school board members, sherrif, drain commissioner, and a host of others depending on the locality. Second, American voters are asked to exercise their franchise unusually often. While the typical European voter may be called upon to case two or three ballots in a four year period, many Americans are faced with a dosen or more separate elections in the span of four years. (pp.13–14)

It should come as no wonder that many Americans are not as well-informed on all of the candidates in all of these races as one might hope. When citizens do lack the knowledge they do need to make a vote choice, what can they do?

Voters in this situation can use information shortcuts, sometimes labeled heuristics, to make vote choices. Popkin (1994), citing Down's book *An Economic Theory of Democracy*, mentioned earlier, noted that voters rely on information shortcuts when they have limited information. Similarly, Sniderman, Brody, and Tetlock (1991) explain that "Citizens frequently can compensate for their limited information about politics by taking advantage of judgmental heuristics. Heuristics are judgmental shortcuts, efficient ways to organize and simplify political choices" (p. 19). In fact, Delli Carpini and Keeter (1996) explain that "we all use shortcuts in making political decisions; no one ever has all the relevant information" (p. 52).

There are many possible decision short-cuts available to voters: Which one a voter uses depends on what information and attitudes that voter has (relevant to the element or elements that matter most to that person). For example, a voter who wants to see a reduction in taxes but who did not know the candidates' positions on taxation could use political party affiliation as an shortcut. That voter could reason that, in general, Republicans are more likely than Democrats to support lower taxes. In essence, a short cut can be considered an *educated guess*. It is possible that a specific Republican candidate might not support lower taxes or that a particular Democrat might be in favor of lower taxes. So, a voter who uses political party affiliation as a short-cut for knowledge of a candidate's tax policy might guess incorrectly in some cases. However, if he or she wants to vote for the candidate who is most likely to reduce taxes, and if that voter does not know for certain the tax proposals of these candidates, making a choice based on political party affiliation allows him or her to cast a vote (and he or she probably might make a reasonable choice).

Voters can rely on other shortcuts, such as endorsements. A person who considers labor issues paramount – and, again, one who does not know the candidates' positions on labor issues – might reasonably choose to vote for the candidate endorsed by the AFL-CIO. Similarly, voters who care about education might choose the candidate who is endorse by the National Education Association. It is possible that some voters who cared about education might have selected Governor Bush in 2000 because they knew his wife had been a teacher, and made an educated guess based on this information that he would be likely to try to improve education. One could vote for a candidate because of his or her ethnicity or gender. *Any information (or attitude) that seems relevant to the voter* can be used as the basis for a decision shortcut, or an educated guess.

Popkin (1994) discusses several possible sources of information used to make voting decisions: information from friends and co-workers, media, candidate endorsers, and the candidates, as well as information about the incumbent party's performance in office. He also lists several possible shortcuts: candidate demographics, behavior of the candidates in the campaign, inferences from the candidates' private morality to their public policy, inferences based on party reputation (issue ownership), the candidates' performance in other elected offices (e.g., as governor), and inferences from the current state of affairs (retrospective voting).

Keep in mind that shortcuts are not used when voters have the information they need to make a choice between the candidates. Only voters who lack what we might call direct information (e.g., knowledge of the candidates' stands on taxes, education, or jobs; or perceptions about the candidates' character traits) need to resort to shortcuts or educated guesses. Voters who want to participate and lack the information that seems most relevant can still vote using shortcuts. It is possible that they might make some mistakes (accidentally choosing the wrong candidate because in *this* race the Democrat is more likely to lower taxes more), but the point here is explaining how voters choose their candidates rather than evaluating the quality of that choice.

This means that voters who are better informed are less likely to use information shortcuts. However, it also suggests that shortcuts might be more common in some stages of the campaign than others. For example, there are more candidates, who are generally less well-known, in the primary than the general election stage (Chapter Five). So, short-cuts are likely to be used more frequently in the primary than the general phase of the election. Similarly, voters may rely more on shortcuts when they reflect on challengers rather than incumbents, because the latter are typically better known. Particular kinds of information shortcuts, such as endorsements, might play a larger role in the primaries when many voters have less information, and fewer attitudes, about the candidates. Similarly, the news focuses more on national than local election campaigns. So, use of shortcuts may be more common when voting for local than national candidates.

It is also possible that this analysis sheds some light on the apparent prevalence of retrospective voting. In order to engage in prospective voting – which candidate is likely to do a better job if elected – a citizen needs to have information about *both* candidates, an idea of the likely outcomes of both candidates' policy proposals. However, retrospective voting does not require that a voter has knowledge of the challenger: If I believe things are going well, I will vote for the incumbent candidate (or incumbent party); if I think things are going poorly, I will vote against the incumbent. Of course, people are likely to know more about the incumbent than about the challenger, and they probably know (or believe they know) more about the state of the nation than about the outcomes of implementing the incumbent's and the challenger's policy proposals. So, Sniderman, Glaser, and Griffin (1991) explain that poorly informed voters, who probably know little about the challenger, are more likely to vote as a referendum on the incumbent. Thus, lack of knowledge in some voters may hinder retrospective voting.

Information Processing

How do voters process the information in the messages they consume? Fans who watched a game between two football teams "saw" different fouls (Hastorf & Cantril, 1954). Their perceptions of reality were influenced by their attitudes. *All in the Family* was a sitcom in the 1970s which portrayed Archie Bunker as a white bigot. The audience for this show did not react uniformly to the message it portrayed: Some disliked Archie Bunker as a bigot whereas others liked him and his attitudes. Vidmar and Rokeach (1974) speculated that "prejudiced and unprejudiced personas ascribe different meanings" to the show: "Nonprejudiced viewers and minority group viewers may perceive and enjoy the show as satire, whereas prejudiced viewers may perceive and enjoy the show ... [for] 'telling it like it is'" (p. 37). Different viewers "saw" the show and its lead character is conflicting ways – their reactions influenced by their attitudes. The same phenomenon occurs in politics. Jarman (2005) studied reactions to the second general election presidential debate in 2004. Those who watched this debate reacted more favorably to comments from the candidate of their own party than to comments by candidates of the opposing party (see also Warner, McKinney, Bramlett, Jennings, & Funk, 2020). Similarly, voters who watched the first presidential debate in 1996 evaluated arguments supporting their attitudes as stronger than arguments against their attitudes. Post debate attitudes were even more polarized than pre-debate attitudes (Munro et al., 2002; see also Lord, Ross, & Lepper, 1979). Different people can react to the same message in different ways, "seeing" different things. Imagine what could happen when different people (such as Democrats and Republicans) use *different information sources* and thereby obtain *different information*.

Furthermore, voters do not simply accept the information they acquire; different people *process that information differently*. Lodge and Taber (2013) developed a systematic approach to understanding how voters process the information encountered in messages. Their book is titled *The Rationalizing Voter* and it is an approach to Motivated Political Reasoning (or Motivated Skepticism). People possess "partisan goals, which motivate them to apply their reasoning powers in defense of a prior, specific conclusion" or their existing attitudes or ideology (p. 150; see also Kruglanski & Webster, 1996). Fishbein and Azjen (2010) argue that beliefs (loosely speaking, "facts,") and values (preferences) are the building blocks of attitudes. Some writers discuss "cognitions" and "feelings/affect" which are quite similar to the concepts of beliefs and values.

Lodge and Taber (2005) argued for the "hot cognition" thesis: "Affect is primary in our theory because it arises first in the stream of processing, is unintentional, and is difficult to control" (p. 20). Knobloch-Westerwick (2015) explained that "Someone encountering a spider, cockroach, or rat may find himself or herself having moved away several steps before even becoming fully mentally aware of the animal. Likewise, sensing enormous heat makes us pull our hands back before we totally realize the meaning of the sensation" (p. 20). Some reactions occur before conscious thought. Lodge and Taber also explain that "when an individual is exposed to a communication, the concepts in the message – whether consciously attended to or not – begin to activate the attendant concepts in *long-term memory*. Once a concept is activated, its activation spreads to all of its related concepts" (1996; see also Collins & Loftus, 1975). The "spreading effect" means that ideas in a message (names, images) call to mind related ideas. So, when an idea or person (e.g., Donald Trump, Hillary Clinton, immigration) occurs in a message, other concepts (our beliefs, values, and attitudes) which are connected to that stimulus in long term memory are immediately activated. For example, when some Republicans hear the name "Obama" (or see an image of Barack Obama), this stimulus could immediately activate or bring to mind such concepts as African-American, Obamacare, President, born in Kenya, or assault weapons ban. These concepts are likely to have negative affect toward Obama for these people in the GOP. The trigger "Obama" could evoke some of the same ideas in Democrats (probably not "born in Kenya"), but Democrats are likely to have positive affect or feelings toward these ideas. Most Republicans and most Democrats disagree about whether "ObamaCare" (The Affordable Care Act) is a good or bad policy; this means they have different affect about this idea. Just as with Obama, a Republican who encounters a message with the name "Donald Trump" (or his image) could have ideas such as these triggered: businessman, Trump Tower, "The Apprentice," real estate mogul, or President. Some of ideas might be activated in Democrats, with the possible addition other ideas such as "married three times" or "multiple bankruptsies." So, as soon as a voter identifies the topic of a message, before he or she begins processing the ideas, arguments, and evidence in a message, recognition of people, images, or ideas in a message immediately activates cognitions in long term memory (the spreading effect) and these ideas influence subsequent message processing. Please notice that I am NOT claiming that all Republicans have negative feelings toward African-Americans or Barack Obama. Nor do I believe that every Democrat has negative feelings about "The Apprentice" or "married three times." I do argue that most Democrats and Republicans are likely to have different sets of beliefs and feelings triggered by these stimuli.

The activation of related cognitions can be triggered by images (say, of an candidate or a gun), or by words (such as "Mitch McConnell," "Nancy Pelosi," "gun control," or "immigrant"), or by sounds (such as upbeat or ominous music or sound effects). Before we can even begin to consider the arguments and evidence in the message, our feelings, ideas, emotions related to that initial trigger are activated and influence our subsequent thoughts (the primary of affect). Research has shown that voters view their preferred candidate more favorably than they view their dispreferred candidate. Jarman (2005), for example, examined reactions to the second general election presidential debate in 2004. These viewers reacted more favorably to comments from the candidate of their own party than to comments by candidates of the opposing party. In other words, people interpret a message differently according to their attitudes.

After the initial stimulus from a message primes our affect, we begin thinking about a message's ideas (arguments and evidence) and biased processing ensues. Taber, Cann, and Kucsova (2009; see also Kraft, Lodge, & Taber, 2015; Lord, Ross, & Lepper, 1979; Taber & Lodge, 2006) conclude that there is "strong and consistent evidence of an *attitude congruence bias*, a *disconfirmation bias*, and a resultant *attitude polarization*" (p. 153; emphasis original). A congruence bias means that arguments which support a person's prior attitudes are perceived to be more powerful than arguments for the other side. So, for example, liberals have a tendency to see arguments for gun control as stronger than arguments opposing gun control. In the same way conservatives are prone to think that arguments against gun control are more powerful than arguments against such policies.

On the other hand, a disconfirmation bias means that people have a tendency to counter-argue evidence for the other side; existing attitudes can become strengthened in the face of contradictory evidence. When exposed to arguments that contravene their own attitudes people are likely to discount, diminish, or reject those arguments. For instance, if a person who opposes legalizing marijuana for recreational use encounters a pro-legalization messages, that person may think about their conviction that pot is a gateway drug. This means that voters have a demonstrated tendency to (1) view ideas that support their own views as strong and (2) view ideas that contradict their own views as weak. Kraft, Lodge, and Taber (2015) reported that many studies show that partisans "systematically denigrate, deprecate, and counterargue evidence that is contrary to their political views but accept uncritically the supportive evidence" (pp. 121–122). Presumable as a result, research found that people recalled more positive than negative information about the preferred candidate as well as more negative than positive information about the opponent (Meffert, Chung, Joiner, Waks, & Garst, 2006). This analysis of the primacy of affect and the subsequent processing of message content does not mean conversion (attitude change) is impossible. It does mean that reinforcement of existing attitudes is more likely given the way humans process stimuli and how they store and access information.

These two information processing biases do not always color our thinking. Lodge and Taber (2000, pp. 184–185) explain that bias in cognitive processing of is most likely to occur when:

one's attitudes are challenged (Kunda, 1987; Stevens & Fiske, 1995)

an affective judgment is called for (Fazio, 1995)

one's attitude is strong (Abeson, 1987; Krosnick & Petty, 1995)

the consequences of being wrong are weak (Tetlock, 1985)

the judgmental task is complex (Eagly & Chaiken, 1993)

"objective" evidence is not readily available or the evidence is ambiguous (Tversky & Kahneman, 1974)

disconfirming evidence is not highlighted (Klayman & Ha, 1987)

counterarguments come easily to mind (Lord, Ross, & Lepper, 1979)

one is distracted or under time pressure (Petty & Cacioppo, 1986a).

Some of the circumstances identified here occur commonly in political communication: for example, challenge to attitudes, affective judgments, strong attitudes, counterarguments come easily to mind (see also the discussion of fake news and coordinated political defenses below).

It is important to realize that motivated reasoning is not limited to one party or ideology. both Democrats/Liberals and Republicans/Conservatives use biased processing. This phenomenon is not limited to any group of voters. It seems likely, though, that any differences in use of motivated reasoning are not driven by party or ideology but by strength of partisan loyalty or ideology. Higher partisan loyalty to either political party (or stronger ideological commitment) may well incline a voter to greater use of biased processing. The accusations of "Fake News," though, and the consequences for voters, is largely limited to Republican/Conservative voters. In 2018, for example Axelrod reported that public opinion poll data show that 48% of Republicans believe that the news media is "the enemy of the American people." Only 12% of Democrats agreed.

The disconfirmation bias has been augmented in contemporary political discourse by a systematic attempt to vilify groups of information sources, reducing their credibility and influence. President Trump has repeatedly attacked the news media for reporting "fake news." For example, in a press conference held in February of 2017, about a month after he took office, the President offered several assertions about the news:

> Russia … was all fake news …. It's all fake news. It's all fake news.
>
> Russia is fake news, Russia – this is fake news put out by the media.
>
> The news is fake because so much of the news is fake.
>
> The reporting is fake.
>
> Very fake news now.
>
> Reince [Priebus] is working so hard just putting out fires that are fake fires. They're fake. They're not true.
>
> But I want to just tell you, the false reporting by the media, by you people – the false, horrible, fake reporting makes it much harder to make a deal with Russia.

The President repeatedly advanced the claim that the media present "fake news." Stelter (2018) reported that "between January 20, 2017 [Trump's inauguration] and today [1/17/18] Trump has used the work 'Fake' at least 404 times in tweets and public appearances." Many other Republicans echo his attacks – and his defenses – in an apparently co-ordinated effort. Research has shown that repetition of ideas (such as "fake news" or "witch hunt") can reinforce beliefs and values and the resulting attitudes (see, e.g., McCullough & Ostrom, 1974).

President Trump took this line of attack on news media even further, declaring the fake news to be "the enemy of the people."

> On February 17, 2017, President of the United States Donald Trump declared on Twitter that The New York Times, NBC News, ABC, CBS, and CNN were "fake news" and the "enemy of the people." Trump repeated the assertion on February 24 at the Conservative Political Action Conference, saying, "A few days ago I called the fake news the enemy of the people and they are. They are the enemy of the people." At a June 25, 2018 rally in South Carolina, Trump singled out journalists as "fake newsers" and again called them "the enemy of the people." (Enemy of the people, 2019)

So, if a conservative voter accidentally happens upon a message from a liberal source, that voter may very well reject the information from that source as false (this works as part of the disconfirmation bias). Of course, Democratic voters may reject information form conservative sources, but the Republicans generally, and President Trump specifically, have consistently harped on the claim of fake news and attacked news as the enemy of the people. I believe our forefathers, who considered the news to be the informal fourth branch of government, would have been horrified by this attack.

This analysis could be seen as hostile to Republicans generally and President Trump in particular. This is not my purpose. Other politicians have criticized the news media. For example Vice President Spiro Agnew complained about the liberal news media. He charged that they were elite, privileged, and "intellectually dishonest" (Holden, 2019). Canderone and Thompson (2019) reported that "Democrats and progressives expressed some frustration with the media in 2016, claiming that journalists neglected Senator Bernie Sanders early on and that they were obsessed with Hillary Clinton's emails." Nevertheless, no previous U.S. president has attacked the news media as systematically and vehemently as President Trump. This activity has important implications for how voters process information they obtain from the media.

The Cognitive Response Model and Information Processing

Social psychologists noticed that attitude change occurs when we think about a message and/or its topic. An early approach to message-related thinking was called the Cognitive Response Model (Greenwald, 1968; Perloff & Brock, 1980). This approach to persuasion argues that attitude change (including reinforcement) is not caused directly by messages: We are persuaded by our thoughts about a the message. So, persuasive messages create attitude change by encouraging the audience to have favorable thoughts about the message and its topic. Attitude change is related to (1) the number of thoughts an audience member has about a message and (2) the valence of those thoughts (whether those thoughts are primarily or exclusively favorable to the message or unfavorable to the message). All or mostly favorable thoughts mean persuasion is likely; all or mostly negative thoughts mean persuasion is unlikely (and a boomerang effect is possible). A large body of research supports the Cognitive Response Model (see, e.g., Eagly & Chaiken, 1993).

Two "Routes" to Persuasion

Petty and Cacioppo's (1981; 1986a, 1986b) developed the Elaboration Likelihood Model (ELM), the most influential cognitive response theory (see also the Heuristic/Systemic Model of Persuasion, Chaiken, 1980). "Elaboration" refers to the amount of processing (thinking) an audience member does while seeing or hearing a message. Petty and Cacioppo (1986a, 1986b) explain that there are two "routes" to persuasion ("routes" is an unfortunate metaphor because it may imply that they are mutually exclusive – one travels either one route or another between two places – but processing exists on a continuum). The central route to persuasion involves thoughtful consideration of the arguments (ideas, content) in a message (high elaboration likelihood). Central processing requires that an audience member has both the *motivation* and the *ability* to think about the message and its topic. When a person engages in central processing, the most important factor in persuasion is the strength or the quality of the arguments in the message.

The peripheral route to persuasion (low elaboration likelihood) occurs when the receiver does not think carefully about the ideas and arguments in a message. Instead, the audience member decides whether to agree with the message based on other cues, including whether the source of the message is perceived to be credible (an expert on the topic) or attractive, the number of arguments in a message, or the length of message. Peripheral processing happens when the listener lacks the ability or motivation (or both) to engage in careful thought about the message and/or the message topic.

The ELM predicts that attitudes which are changed through the central route to persuasion will have different effects from attitudes changed through the peripheral route. Petty and Cacioppo (1986a) explain that "Attitude changes that result mostly from processing issue-relevant arguments (central route) will show greater temporal persistence, greater prediction of behavior, and greater resistance to counterpersuasion than attitude changes that result mostly from peripheral cues" (p. 21). These three effects (longer lasting, greater influence on behavior, and greater resistance to opposing messages) are important outcomes, particularly in political campaign communication.

Motivation and Involvement

Involvement refers to the importance of the topic of a persuasive message to the audience. When a listener cares about a topic, is interested in a topic, or believes that a topic is relevant, he or she is involved in the topic. This means the listener is willing to exert the cognitive effort necessary to think about a message, its arguments, and/or its topic (Petty & Cacioppo, 1979). On the other hand, when a topic seems irrelevant or unimportant to us, we are uninvolved and less likely to spend the effort to think about a message on that topic. A person who cares about the immigration (or employment, or national security) is likely to think carefully about a message on this topic. Another person, for whom these topics are not a high priority, will be less involved in those topics and is likely to produce fewer thoughts about the same messages.

Ability

Motivation is not enough to assure that central processing will occur: Receivers must also have the ability to think about the message. Several factors influence a person's ability to process a message. If the audience is distracted, tired, under the influence of drugs or alcohol, or ill, it will be more difficult for them to think carefully about a message. Research has shown that listeners who are distracted as they listen to or watch a message produce fewer thoughts about the message than those who are not distracted (Osterhouse & Brock, 1970; Petty, Wells, & Brock, 1976). Other factors can also influence the receiver's ability to process a message. Messages that are more difficult to understand are likely to produce fewer thoughts. Message repetition can increase the audience's ability to process a message, although too much repetition could make a message boring, which could reduce that message elaboration (Cacioppo & Petty, 1985). If the listener knows little about a topic or if a message is difficult to understand (using unfamiliar terms, confusing, spoken too fast, or spoken with a thick accent), ability is impaired and central processing is unlikely. Elaboration likelihood is low in these cases regardless of how important the topic is to the audience. It is important to acknowledge that the two variables of motivation and ability are not dichotomous variables (i.e., either high or low).

Rather, cognitive processing of a message is best understood as a continuum that ranges from peripheral (few thoughts) to central (many thoughts).

Favorable and Unfavorable Thoughts

The kind of thoughts (favorable or unfavorable to the message) an audience member has when processing a messages is another important variable. Thinking thoughts that are favorable to a message is likely to result in attitude change; thinking thoughts unfavorable thoughts to a message is not likely to cause attitude change (and could result in a boomerang effect, changing attitudes in the direction opposed to the message). So, a successful persuader encourages the audience to think favorable thoughts (and lots of them). One factor that influences the valence or kind of thoughts receivers have is argument quality or strength. Strong arguments are more persuasive than weak ones (Benoit, 1987; Cacioppo, Petty, & Morris, 1983; Petty, Cacioppo, & Goldman, 1981) because strong arguments create more favorable thoughts, and fewer unfavorable thoughts, than weak arguments (Benoit, 1987; Petty & Cacioppo, 1984).

Peripheral Cues

Research has shown that messages with more arguments create more attitude change than those with fewer arguments (Calder, Insko, & Yandell, 1974; Chaiken, 1980; Petty & Cacioppo, 1984). However, argument quantity, unlike argument quality, is a peripheral cue. Argument quantity serves as a "short-cut" enabling a person to decide how to react to a message without thinking deeply about it. When receivers realize that a message has a large number of arguments, they have a tendency to accept that message. Similarly, when receivers perceive the source of a message to be physically attractive, they may can attractiveness as a another peripheral cue, accepting the message without thinking carefully about it (Petty & Cacioppo, 1981). When listeners believe that several sources endorse a message position (rather than a single source) they may be more likely to accept that message. Harkins and Petty (1981) found that more arguments and more sources each generate more favorable cognitive responses and more attitude change than messages with fewer arguments and sources. As noted above, the ELM predicts that attitude change that results from central processing has three differences from persuasion that arises from peripheral processing, but peripheral processing can create attitude change.

The two kinds of bias discussed earlier – attitude congruence bias and disconfirmation bias – are compatible with the cognitive response model. People who are less interested (less involved) in politics are less likely to engage in central processing, relying on peripheral cues. In contrast, those who are more interested in politics are more likely to engage in central processing (assuming no important limitations of their ability to process a message). When an involved audience member perceives that a message agrees with his or her current attitude, he or she is likely to produce thoughts that agree with that message (favorable thoughts), which tend to reinforce that attitude (congruence bias). In contrast, when an involved person perceives that a message disagrees with his or her existing attitudes, that person is likely to produce thoughts that are unfavorable to the message (disconfirmation bias); such thoughts reduce the likelihood that the message will change the receiver's attitudes.

Emotions and Politics

Scholars have been working to understand the role of affect (emotions) in political judgment. Affect is the "engine of behavior – the motivating, directing, prioritizing function of the brain" (Neuman, Marcus, Crigler, & MacKuen, 2007, p. 15). The concept of affect is similar to Fishbein and Ajzen's (2010) idea of a value (which is coupled with a belief to create an attitude). A belief is a commonly known as a "fact," something true or false or at least potentially verifiable. A value is a judgment of worth. For example, if I have a belief that candidate Smith is a Republican but I do not have a corresponding value (either that Republicans are good or that Republicans are bad) this belief cannot influence my attitudes or behavior. However, if I accept the value that Republicans are good, then my belief that Smith is a Republican inclines me to donate to Smith, or tell my friends how good Smith is, or vote for Smith on election day. If I hold a value that Republicans are bad, my attitudes and behavior toward Smith will be completely different. Without a value to accompany a belief, no motivation drives my behavior. Notice that some people hold their values with such fervor that they believe they are facts, but this is not the case.

Marcus, Neuman, and MacKuen (2000) propose the Theory of Affective Intelligence, which argues

> that emotions arise from the structure of the brain, and that two different systems are at work. The first, the dispositional system, operates on routine information, disposing of it without much effort, and generating emotional responses on an "enthusiasm" dimension. The second, the surveillance system, becomes aroused when the environment changes from the expected to the unexpected (read "dangerous") the surveillance system heightens awareness and prepares us to respond by elevating "anxiety" levels.

This process is not driven by cognitive processing of the environment but by an emotional response to an unexpected stimulus. The result is that in this aroused state learning is enhanced, since one needs to understand the nature of whatever threat has been encountered. (Redlawsk, 2006, pp. 4–5)

The disposition system is "primarily responsible for managing reliance on habits, previously learned strategies." Reliance on the dispositional system is the default mode: We process messages and react to situations using our habits and routines. In contrast, the surveillance system "is primarily responsible for identifying novel and threatening circumstances, precisely the sort of circumstance in which reliance on habit would be ill-advised, and for initiating a shift to reasoned consideration" (Marcus, Neuman, & MacKuen, 2000, p. 46). A potential threat jars us out of our habitual routines, evoking a heightened state of surveillance. We pay closer attention to this potential threat and think more deeply about how we ought to respond.

Affective Intelligence Theory argues that two moods are especially relevant to these two systems: Enthusiasm works well with the disposition system; anxiety invokes the surveillance system. Marcus, Neuman, and MacKuen (2000) turn to Watson (Watson, Clark, & Tellegen, 1988) to flesh out these two moods We could quibble about the list (e.g., how does scared differ from afraid) but these are a good starting point for understanding moods and emotions in politics. See Table 8.1.

Brader (2006) lists seven key emotions, several of which are ideas from this table: fear (scared, afraid), enthusiasm (enthusiastic), anger (upset), pride (proud),

Table 8.1. Positive and negative moods.

Positive moods	Negative moods
enthusiastic	scared
interested	afraid
determined	upset
excited	distressed
inspired	jittery
alert	nervous
active	ashamed
strong	guilty
proud	irritable
attentive	hostile

Note: The moods in each row are not meant to be related, so enthusiasm is not the opposite of fear. Marcus, Neuman, and MacKuen (2000), drawing on Watson, Clark, and Tellegen (1988)

compassion, sadness, and amusement. It is not clear we must agree on a single list with an exhaustive and mutually exclusive list of emotions.

Brader (2006) content analyzed 1595 TV spots from 1999 and 2000 (see also Kern, 1989). Brader's sample included primary and general ads, ads from candidates, parties, and interest groups, and from a variety of offices (president, governor, U.S. and senators, U.S. and state representatives, mayor, and state supreme court justices). This is an impressive sample of advertisements. It would be interesting to replicate this study using advertisements (and perhaps other messages, such as Tweets) from 2020.

These two categories are not mutually exclusive; an emotion which is dominant in an ad is also counted as present in that ad. These results reveal how often various emotional appeals are employed in political advertising. It may seem odd that appeals to enthusiasm are so much more common than fear appeals, but these are the data available on this question.

Table 8.1 and Brader's list give us a clear idea of the potential emotions in politics. Brader relates these concepts to campaigning, arguing that election messages can evoke emotions or moods in viewers: "Enthusiasm appeals motivate viewers to get involved and act on existing loyalties, while fear appeals provoke viewers to seek out new information and reconsider their choices" (p. 13). He goes on to explain that "enthusiasm-evoking appeals only make sense with a [TV spot] script that has a generally positive message, whereas fear-evoking appeals are plausible only with a generally negative message" (p. 80). This work starts with the way the brain operates, identifies two modes of thought (dispositional, surveillance) and two moods (enthusiasm, anxiety) that are compatible with these

Table 8.2. Frequency of emotional appeals in political advertising.

Emotion	Present	Dominant
Fear	41%	8%
Anger	46%	11%
Fear and Anger (equally)	16%	7%
Enthusiasm	73%	40%
Pride	54%	3%
Enthusiasm and Pride (equally)	18%	12
Compassion	21%	2%
Sadness	9%	1%
Amusement	9%	3%

Brader (2006).

mental systems. Finally, appeals to enthusiasm are most compatible with positive messages (acclaims); appeals to anxiety are most compatible with negative messages (attacks).

Fragmentation of the Mass Audience

Whether voters rely on direct knowledge of the candidates' policy positions and character, or on shortcuts, they must get the information they use to make their vote choices from somewhere. Remember from Chapter One what Ralph Nader said about reaching voters: Ralph Nader, who ran unsuccessfully for president in 2000 as the Green Party nominee, explained that "You cannot reach in direct personal communication even one percent of the eligible voters. In essence you don't run for president directly; you ask the media to run you for president or, if you have the money, you can pay the media for exposure" (p. 155). Figure 3.1 depicts the movement of information in messages from candidates and other sources to voters.

In the past, many messages have attracted extremely large audiences. For instance, the Commission on Presidential Debates (2019) reports that the first Nixon-Kennedy debate on September 26, 1960 drew 66.4 million viewers, which was 36.7% of the U.S. population. President Nixon's resignation speech in 1974 had 128 million viewers. But now far fewer media events attract such a large proportion of the public. The most watched primary debate in history, the first Republican debate in 2016, was viewed by only 24 million people (Stelter, 2015). This represented about 7% of the populace at the time. Mark (2019) reported that about 13 million people watched the first day of the public Trump impeachment hearings. Former FBI Director James Comey's Senate testimony and Supreme Court nominee Brett Kavanaugh's Senate appearance were each watched by about 20 million people – about 6% of the population. So, the huge audiences of the past (especially when considered as a percent of the potential audience) are much less common today than they were in the past. Audience sizes have dropped because viewing options have proliferated. The decreasing size of audiences for content sources (and concomitant increase in the number of diverse audiences) cannot help but dilute the potential influence of content sources. "Content sources" can be operationalized at various levels of abstraction, to include news media generally, particular networks, or individual broadcasts. Similarly this phrase encompasses social media generally, more specific social media (such as Twitter and Facebook), and particular Twitter feeds or Facebook pages. Content sources can include newspapers generally or specific newspapers. These sources all offer some form of content or message to an audience.

For years people were limited to three viewing options – ABC, NBC, CBS – and perhaps a fuzzy PBS station. At that time there were no VCR's or DVD players, no Internet, no satellite or cable tv. For example, when the Nixon-Kennedy debates occurred in 1960, if your television was turned on while a debate was in progress you had no choice but to watch the debate. These important political events appeared on all networks; no other options existed on television. Because the content was mostly constant across networks (in fact, for a time, presidential debates had only one camera feed for all networks). As time progressed, technology introduced other options for attracting viewers' attention such as VHS (and Betamax) and DVR recording. Cable TV brought audiences dozens and then hundreds of channels. Satellite TV provided further options for viewers. The Internet exploded with a a huge number of other choices for viewers. The Internet also made social media possible.

This means that, unlike in 1960, today people who are uninterested in politics had many other viewing options if they did not wish to watch debates. Technological advances increased the number of content sources and reduced the size of audience for campaign (and other) messages. As technology advanced the heyday of broadcast television ended and the mass audience began to fragment into hundreds and then thousands of smaller audiences, a trend that has increased exponentially in recent years. Using different sources means people have different information.

Audiences can be split in many different ways, with each possible grouping splitting the potential audience into smaller slices. One could divide audiences by a variety of variables, such as age, socioeconomic status, gender orientation, ethnicity, or education level. People in these subgroups (e.g., folk in different age strata) consume different groups of messages and so acquire different pools of information. Some overlap in information between these groups is likely, but each group uses a different constellation of media (the word "constellation" is adopted from Campbell & Jamieson [1978], who use it in their definition of genres of rhetoric). I want to focus here on ideological divisions in audiences.

When a new content source emerges – e.g., when ABC, CBS, and NBC were joined by Fox News – the developers must decide what content to offer on their media. One could try to duplicate existing content (ABC, CBS, NBC) or offer niche content. Most new outlets chose the latter strategy, developing content that is new and different from existing media. This is why we have such diverse networks as The CW, Court TV, WVC, the Weather Channel, Fresh Great Outdoors, Telemundo, History Channel, God TV, Rev'n, Comedy Central, and Family Channel (and many more). So, proliferation of media has a tendency to create heterogeneous content sources. As new content sources arise with focused (niche) programming, audience members can self-select into relatively small audience groups. These new audiences are often homogeneous within and heterogeneous without (members of a niche audience have interests in common with other members of that audience but different from members of other groups).

Today, voters can choose between an incredible array of content sources, many with different content. Statista (2016) reports network viewers between December 29, 2014 through November 29, 2016. The six most frequently watched networks are listed below. The Census Bureau (2016) reported that as of July 1, 2015, the U.S. population was 321,418,820. Using these figures, here are the percentage of people who view these networks:

CBS 9,419,000 2.9%
NBC 7,757,000 2.4%
ABC 6,894,000 2.1%
Fox 5,198,000 1.6%
CNN 672,000 0.21%
MSNBC 576,000 0.18%
Total 9.5

This leaves over 90% of the public who do not use these network choices. In contrast, during the mid-1970s "the three-network share of audience hovered around 90%" (Lowry, 1997; see also Prior, 2007). Network television use has been declining as other options opened up and the "mass" in "mass communication" continued to shrink.

The rise of social media played an important role in fragmenting viewing audience. We only have such much time in a day and when we begin to use a new content source, we have to cut back or eliminate our use of other sources. Two prominent social media are Facebook and Twitter. In 2018, Facebook enjoyed 205 million monthly active Facebook users in the United States. In the United States alone 68 million people used Twitter at least monthly in 2019; worldwide 330 million people use Twitter monthly (Statista, 2019). These are obviously huge potential audiences. However, these people do not all follow the same Twitter feeds or the same Facebook pages. No Twitter feed attracts all 205 million Twitter users, just as no network or TV show is watched by all television viewers. Some people do have huge followings on social media. For example, Portuguese soccer player Cristiano Ronaldo was the most-liked person on Facebook in 2019, with over 120 million followers ("List of most-liked," 2019). The most followed Twitter account at the time belonged to singer Katy Perry (about 107 million followers;

Statista, 2019). Messages from these two people – and others – are clear examples of mass communication. Nevertheless, overall Facebook pages have an average of 155 friends (Knapton, 2016); Twitter feeds have an average of 208 followers (Beevolve, 2017). These an extremely tiny portion of the 205 monthly Facebook users or the 68 million monthly Twitter users. Neither 155 nor 208 should be considered mass audiences. Furthermore, these are *averages*, so many Twitter and Facebook users have even smaller audiences. The universe of Facebook and Twitter users are splintered into many, many audiences, some large audiences but most small. Some of social media messages should be considered mass communication because they attract large numbers of users but many do not actually qualify as mass media.

These fractured audiences are not random (or representative) subgroups of the general public but have distinct characteristics. To return to an earlier illustration there is probably relatively little overlap in the audiences for the History Channel, QVC, Fresh Great Outdoors, and The CW. For example, examining viewers of the first six Democratic and first six Republican primary debates in 2016, Nielsen (2016) reported that "about 30.2 million viewers watched only the Democratic debates while roughly 29.2 million viewers only viewed the Republican debates. Additionally, 37.8 million viewers watched both debates." This means that viewers of these presidential primary debates can be meaningfully divided into three groups: 30 million Democratic debate viewers, 29 million Republican debate viewers, and 38 million others who watched both – so these campaign messages have already split the electorate into three groups, two of which received completely different messages from the candidates (Democratic primary debates, Republican primary debates), once group who watched debates from both political parties, and those who watched none of these debates. As each of these groups of voters used various combinations of other media (different broadcast news, different webpages, different Twitter feeds or Facebook pages) in addition to these primary debates, the initial audiences became further fragmented into smaller and smaller audiences, each of which consumed a different group of content sources and learned different information about the candidates.

An important factor in play here is the elimination of the "Fairness Doctrine." The Federal Communication Commission (FCC) had promulgated this rule in 1949, requiring that broadcast stations present contrasting views on controversial issues. However, in 1987 the FCC repealed this regulation, a decision that was upheld in court (Gill, 2016). The consequences of this action were seen quickly, as Rush Limbaugh's radio program became syndicated in 1988. Tucker (2017) argued that in the absence of the Fairness Doctrine, "talk-radio stations across the country soon began to run right-wing agitprop from dawn to dusk, flooding the public airwaves with shameless demonization of Democrats and progressives." Broadcast stations no longer had to cover both sides of controversial issues. This rule change also allowed liberal programming to stop covering both sides of issues. The content of network news has changed drastically. It is clear, for example, that Fox News and CNN cover different stories/topics and offer contrasting perspectives when they do discuss the same topic. Broadcasters are free to offer a single (slanted) perspective on current events without even appearing to provide balanced coverage of controversial topics. Networks, webpages, Twitter feeds, Facebook pages, and other content sources are under no compulsion to present every side of an issue (some may choose to offer more than one side to a issue, but they do not *have* to do so and many content sources joyfully present their own personal point of view). This change enabled a wide range of content options (media menus) for people to choose from and consume. A consequence of the splintering of the mass audience and the rise of nice media is that these changes have altered substantially the knowledge base available to voters.

The once "mass" media have become Balkanized into a myriad of media with smaller audiences by the emergence of alternative media and FCC rule changes. The word "Balkanization" is an instructive metaphor for changes in mass media audiences. *Wikipedia* notes that this term began as "is a geopolitical term for the process of fragmentation or division of a region or state into smaller regions or states that are often hostile or uncooperative with one another" ("Balkanization," 2019). This term aptly describes the current state of media: Audiences are splinted into smaller fragments, some of which are hostile to one another by design (think of CNN or MSNBC versus FOX).

Holbert and Benoit (2009) articulated "Media Connectedness Theory" which argues that a person's choice of which information sources to consume is not random. They contrasted media with different information orientations (one-sided versus two-sided) and developed the "Complementary Axiom" (p. 310). This axiom predicts that people who use a media outlet with a specific information orientation (one-sided or two-sided) are likely, in subsequent media consumption, to use other media with a similar orientation. They found that "Pre-debate conservative political talk radio served as a statistically significant predictor of post-debate FOX cable TV news exposure … and pre-debate FOX cable TV news exposure served as a statistically significant predictor of post-debate conservative political talk radio" (p. 318; they also found that use of two-sided information sources are likely to be followed by additional use of other two-sided information sources). So, fragmented audiences who tend to use ideologically-slanted (one-sided) information sources are prone to use other, similarly biased, sources.

Williams and Delli Carpini observed that "At the height of the Age of Broadcast News each of the three dominant networks broadcast similar programming designed to attract the largest audience possible" (2011, p. 78). However, recent media changes – particularly the Internet and social media – have actually fragmented audiences into smaller and smaller groups as new media developed niche content to attract particular audiences. The audience for the three major networks in the 1970s, the apex of mass audiences (particularly in terms of percentage of total population), splintered apart as many smaller groups of people watched different messages in a variety of media. Consider the differences, for example, in the content of CNN and Fox News. Or consider the recent nationwide protests over the killing of George Floyd.

> "The president seems to think that dominating black people, dominating peaceful protesters, is law and order," CNN's Anderson Cooper said. "It's not. He calls them thugs. Who's the thug here?" At the same time on Fox News Channel, Tucker Carlson said that Trump provided "a powerful symbolic gesture, a declaration that our country, our national symbols, our oldest institutions, will not be desecrated and defeatedd by nihilistic destruction." (Bauder, 2020)

Television visuals echoed this contrast: On the left side, President Donald Trump talking about restoring law and order. On the right, a tear-gassed young woman vomiting in a Washington street" (Bauder, 2020). It is clear that what information you have, what you "know," depends not on what is the case in the world (both of these images are "true": Donald Trump did hold up a bible and a young woman did throw up in Washington, DC) but your understanding of events depends on which information sources you use. Hardly anyone was actually present in Washington to see these events; we had to rely on what others (reporters, tweets, blogs, Facebook pages, and so forth) told us about them. And many sources (most? virtually all?) have a perspective and only show us part of what happened.

Similarly, *The Washington Post* reported in June of 2020 that viewers' acceptance of falsehoods was related to their media diet:

> Three serious research efforts have put numerical weight — yes, data-driven evidence — behind what many suspected all along: Americans who relied on Fox News, or similar right-wing sources, were duped as the coronavirus began its deadly spread. Dangerously duped. Those who relied on mainstream sources — the network evening newscasts or national newspapers that President Trump constantly blasts as "fake news" — got an accurate assessment of the pandemic's risks. Those were the news consumers who were more likely to respond accordingly, protecting themselves and others against the disease that has now killed more than 123,000 in the United States with no end in sight. Those who relied on Fox or, say, radio personality Rush

Limbaugh, came to believe that vitamin C was a possible remedy, that the Chinese government created the virus in a lab, and that government health agencies were exaggerating the dangers in the hopes of damaging Trump politically. (Goddard, 2020; see also Jamieson, & Albarracin, 2020)

It is clear that the consequences of different and biased information (or misinformation) in various information sources are dire, with over 123,000 American dead of Covid19 in June of 2020. Our attitudes are determined by what information we have, and what information we have is determined by where we get our information.

Divergence between audiences of the left and right of the political spectrum goes far beyond which messages to consume, which information they acquire. Mutz explained that "Selectivity can take place at several junctures with respect to mass media, including *exposure* to a particular source of news, *attention* to what the source says, and biased *interpretation* when processing the content of political news" (2006, p. 225). Meffert et al. observed that a "bias toward the preferred candidate was present at all stages of information processing," reading, message processing, evaluation, and recall (2016, p. 44). This bias is inherent as content sources become so specialized that people often switch from general outlets (such as ABC, CBS, or NBC) when a source with niche content is available that is congruent with their attitudes.

So, different groups of voters attend to different constellations of content sources Some content overlaps between different sources but a great deal of the information to which voters are exposed is different. When voters rely on different sources of information (e.g., opposing candidates who stress different groups of issues, different news media with contrasting content, or social media accounts with different information), their attitudes and behavior diverge.

Finally, I want to argue that the polarization of the electorate (discussed in Chapter One) and the fragmentation of the mass media and of audiences are intertwined in a recursive process. As information sources fragment, audiences become more polarized. As people become more polarized, they are likely to select more partisan information sources. Consuming partisan information sources produces more polarized audiences. And so on.

Public Opinion Polls

Public opinion polls are an attempt to understand the knowledge, attitudes, and voting intentions of voters. Modern political campaigns rely heavily on polls (as well as on focus groups) if they have the funds to conduct them; Luntz (1988) called polls "indispensable" (p. 15) over twenty years ago and their importance has only increased in the meantime. Use of polls by candidates makes good sense because voters are the ultimate audience for their campaigns; only by understanding the target audience can candidates hone and more precisely target their campaign messages. Although these internal campaign polls are extremely important, people outside the campaign which conducted them usually do not learn about the results.

The news media makes heavy use of public opinion polls. In 2004, for example, between May and November, over 1350 public opinion polls asked whether voters were likely to vote for Bush or Kerry in individual states; obviously, there were many other polls with national samples (Electoral Vote Predictor, 2004b). Traugott and Lavrakas (2004) explain that polls reported in the news can have important effects during a political campaign:

> Poll results have an impact on the vitality and viability of candidates, affecting who can raise money, organize a field staff, and secure volunteers. News coverage containing poll results has an impact on assessments that citizens make of candidates and how, and even if, they decide to vote. And polls have an effect on how campaigns are covered, as reporters, editors, and producers use their information to make decisions about who to cover and how to frame the coverage. (pp. xii-xiii)

This section is designed to help understand polls and the data provided to the public from them. One basic fact to keep in mind is that today many pollsters collect and release public opinion poll data. However, they do not all use the same procedures. This is one reason polls differ. It is possible that some polls are biased and that they vary in quality (see, e.g., Bishop, 2005). The Electoral Vote Predictor webpage analyzed the final predictions for several polls. The Rasmussen poll, for example, was correct in every state predicted; Zogby was correct 91% of the time, Gallup 80%, and Strategic Vision made correct predictions only 64% of the time (Electoral Vote Predictor, 2004a). Although I would not say that the final predictions made for the 2004 presidential race are the best or only way to evaluate the quality of a poll, it seems clear that some poll results will differ simply because some pollsters use better procedures than others. I want to discuss several other factors that are important in understanding what public opinion poll data mean.

Public opinion polls typically employ sampling. This means that rather than ask *all* voters a question (or even all voters in a single state), polls only survey a relatively small portion, or *sample*, of the target population. Sampling is a practical necessity for several reasons. With a voting age population of about 257 million in 2020, for example (Federal Register, 2021), no pollster could survey all U.S. voters in a poll. However, sampling theory shows that it is possible to obtain *reasonably* accurate estimates of a large population from a small sample. Of course, the sample must be representative of the larger population in order to give a reasonably accurate picture of the population. The fact that public opinion polls measure a sample rather than the entire population is important for a variety of reasons.

First, all samples have sampling error. During presidential elections, the sample size of polls often questions roughly 1,000–2,000 respondents. Because the sample is only a small portion of the entire population, if two samples were taken at the same time, there is a chance that the two samples will have different results. Sample A might show that 54% of the people plan to vote for President Bush and 46% for Senator Kerry. Sample B might show that the voters are split 50/50 between Bush and Kerry. Typically, sampling error for a survey of about 1,000 voters is about +/- 3–4%. This means that most of the time (usually, pollsters strive for 95% of the time), the *actual population value* is within 3 (or 4) percentage points of the value found in the *sample*. So, speaking more precisely, the poll of sample A means that (there is a 95% chance) that between 50% and 58% of the voters (54% +/- 4%) in the entire population support Bush and that between 42% and 50% support Kerry (46% +/- 4%). Two polls conducted at the same time (54/46 and 50/50) *appear* to be different but they are not really inconsistent when properly interpreted, when sampling error is taken into account. News stories are doing a better job reporting and interpreting polls with the margin of error, but some stories still do not make this important point clear. It is vital to keep in mind the sampling error when trying to understand a poll.

A second important consideration related to sampling is the question of which population is being studied by the pollster. Some polls are only interested in the opinions of certain groups (e.g., Hispanics, women, the elderly) and their opinions could be quite different from those in the general population. We must know the nature of the target population in order to properly interpret poll data from a sample of that population. Furthermore, some groups are more likely to vote than others. Wattenberg (2002) explained that "Those who are not very interested in politics, not very partisan, not very well educated, and not very old" are less likely to vote (pp. 80–81). In a very real sense the only voters whose opinion matters are those who actually vote on election day. Some groups of voters are more likely to vote than others (e.g., those who are older are more likely to vote than younger citizens). So, a random sample of *citizens* may not represent the *true population of interest*, those who vote on election day. When some polls report a poll of *citizens*, others report a poll of *registered voters*, and still other polls report data from *likely voters*, their results may vary because they are not trying to sample the same target population. Of course, locating the last group, those people who will actually vote on election day, is guesswork. One must understand the population being sampled to understand the results of a poll. Knowing who will cast votes in 2020 will be especially difficult with events such as the killing of George Floyd that could substantially influence turn-out.

A third important implication of sampling arises from the fact that public opinion is not static. It does not often shift wildly, but shifts in attitudes and opinions do occur over time. The entire point of political campaigns is an attempt to move public opinion in the direction of one candidate. Two polls can offer different results because they sampled different time periods. A poll of the same people in August might find different results than a poll in November because some of those people changed their minds. In a real sense, the population is different in these two cases: the *public in August* is not exactly the same as the *public in November*. It is also important to realize some polls are collected for a short period of time (1–3 days) whereas others are "in the field" over a longer time, sometimes as long as two weeks or more. Even if public opinion does not change to a huge degree, it is possible that it can shift during the course of a longer poll. In 2004, Gallup polls (Newport & Moore, 2004) indicated that "Bush gained significantly ... after the GOP convention, an improved positioning he held onto until the first debate in Miami. At that point, Kerry immediately moved back to parity with Bush." Polls conducted a few days apart should have different results when public opinion shifts.

A key to sampling is obtaining a sample that accurately represents the population being studied. The usual method (and the best approach in sampling theory) is to use a random sample, which is likely to avoid bias by over-representing one part of the population (e.g., Republicans, Democrats, or undecided voters). Most pollsters use telephone surveys. However, Morin (2004) explained that "cell phones, caller ID, and increasingly elaborate call screening technologies make it harder than ever to reach a random sample of Americans" (p. C1). If the people who are not being included in polls have different opinions from those who have other telephones, the sample will not accurately reflect the entire population. For example, Nevius (2004) discussed young voters: "We know they exist, but their beliefs are a mystery (Pollsters can't reach them on their cell phones)" (p. B1). If some groups of voters in the population are not adequately represented in polls (included in the sample), that is a source of inaccuracy in polls. One kind of political poll is the "exit poll" conducted as voters leave polling locations. Problems can arise in exit polls because those who agree to stop and answer questions may not be a random sample of those who voted.

Public opinion polls have other limitations that are not related to sampling. As indicated in Chapter One, many voters wait until near the end of the campaign to make a vote choice. However, pollsters do not like "I haven't made up my mind" as an answer and they usually pressure respondents to at least report which way they "lean." This means when a poll reports that 48% of voters support a candidate, some of those 48% have not made up their minds. Some of the 48% is firm support that is unlikely to change on election day, but not all of it.

Another concern is that pollsters ask different questions and some are easier to answer than others. One of the most common question asks voters, "If the election were held today, would you vote for candidate A or candidate B?" Another question frequently asked is "What is the most important issue [or most important problem] in America today?" Voters can probably do a reasonable good job answering these questions. However, other polls – especially exit polls – ask voters "Why did you vote as you did?" As suggested earlier, the vote decision may emerge gradually as information encountered during the campaign creates or changes knowledge and attitudes. Attitude change is not necessary a conscious process; we may not even realize that our attitudes have changed after exposure to a persuasive message. Zimbardo and Leippe (1991) explained that

> influence often occurs at a level below our conscious awareness. Influence tactics [persuasive messages] may have a predictable effect on how someone thinks, feels, or acts yet the person is not aware of how those tactics affected his or her state of mind or behavior. (p. 245)

Even if we are aware that a message changed our attitudes (or vote choice), we may not know what it was in the message that had this effect. As we have seen, even 30 second television commercials can discuss several topics and include multiple images. Who knows for certain which part or parts of a message made a difference? Zimbardo and Leippe (1991) state that

> It is not the thinking but the *products* of thought that appear in the mind and direct behavior. Because we have no conscious access to how the mind acts on stimuli [messages] and integrates them, we typically cannot accurately report how particular stimuli affected" us. (pp. 254–255)

So, it is not clear to me that voters know what caused them to vote as they did. In short, voters know the answers to some questions better than others and the fact that they are willing to provide an answer to one question does not necessarily mean it is a correct answer rather than simply a guess.

Conclusion

This chapter began with a discussion of the three influences on vote choice: policy, character, and party identification (or ideology). These three factors vary in importance for different voters and indeed can shift in relative importance for a given voter over the course of a campaign (as he or she acquires information about one factor, that factor might increase in importance while another factor becomes less important). This chapter discusses how citizens make a vote choice. This process may be a conscious decision for some voters, but I argue that voters may reach their vote decision gradually as they acquire and integrate information throughout the campaign. When a voter has acquired information about the factor or factors (policy, character, party ID/ideology) which matters most to that voter, he or she will use that information to make a vote choice. However, when direct information is lacking, voters can also rely on information shortcuts (heuristics) to make educated guesses about how they should vote. The role of emotions in election campaigns is also discussed.

This chapter also addressed the meaning of public opinion polls, our window on voters and their knowledge and attitudes. The most important considering is that polls use a sample of a population to draw an inference about the entire population. This means that all polls have sample error and that when samples are non-random the results are likely to be inaccurate. Also, it is very important to understand which population is being sampled (e.g., all citizens, registered voters, likely voters, or particular subgroups). Finally, voters are more likely to be able to provide an accurate answer to some questions rather than others (e.g., it is not clear that voters are consciously aware of *why* they voted as they did).

Note

1   Political party identification and ideology are distinct concepts. However, Democrats tend to be liberal and Republicans as a group are likely conservative. Therefore, these two concepts – political party identification and ideology – overlap in important ways even though they are not synonymous.

CHAPTER NINE

Conclusions

The evidence reported here supports several important conclusions about the nature of political campaign communication. The first prediction was that acclaims will be more frequent than attacks in political campaign discourse. This prediction was upheld overall in U.S. presidential campaign discourse, U.S. non-presidential campaign messages, and in non-U.S. campaign discourse. Functional Theory also expects that defenses will be the least common function. This hypothesis was supported in U.S. presidential, U.S. non-presidential, and non-U.S. political campaign messages.

Functional theory explains why this very high consistency of emphasis in message function occurs: Acclaims have no drawbacks, attacks may alienate some voters who dislike mudslinging, and defenses have three drawbacks (they probably take a candidate off message; they require the candidate to identify the attack, which may remind or inform voters of a potential weakness; they make the candidate appear reactive rather than proactive). This means that the nature of the basic situation in political campaigns (a candidate's campaign for elective office) shapes the messages created in this situation.

A third general prediction held that statements discussion policy would be more common than those addressing character. This expectation was also supported in a variety of data: U.S. presidential campaigns, U.S. non-presidential messages, and non-U.S. presidential campaigns. The only consistent exceptions occurred in what might be considered more personal media: television talk show appearances, social media, and campaign posters, which might be expected to stress the candidates' character or personality over policy. Elected officials either make policy (legislators) or implement it (e.g., presidents, governors). It should come as no surprise that more citizens say that policy is the most important determinant of their vote or that politicians tend to emphasize policy over character in most of their campaign messages.

Functional Theory hypothesized that general goals and ideals would more often serve as the basis for acclaims than attacks. This prediction was supported in U.S. presidential campaign messages, U.S. non-presidential campaigns, and non-U.S. campaigns. It is far easier to agree with goals and ideals (acclaiming them) than to disagree with them (attacking them).

The theory of the genesis of rhetorical action (Benoit, 1984, 2000a) offers a systematic way to understand how persuasive messages, such as political campaign discourse, are produced. The persuader's purpose (i.e., to convince voters that he or she is preferable), the medium in which the message occurs (e.g., television spots, debates), the situation in which messages are produced (e.g., campaign phase), the nature of the persuader (e.g., candidate or other source) all influence the nature of campaign messages.

Political party affiliation influences which policy topics a political candidate is likely to emphasize. Petrocik's theory of issue ownership was supported in a variety of presidential and non-presidential campaign messages (it would be interesting to see how political parties are associated with issues in other countries). Voters have a tendency to believe that each political party is better able to deal with some issues or problems than the other party. In order to make use of these advantages candidates have a significant proclivity to discuss the issues owned by their own political party.

Furthermore, candidates are different kinds of sources from surrogates (e.g., keynote speakers, ads sponsored by the political party instead of the candidate). Surrogate sources attack more than candidates. Some voters profess to dislike mudslinging; presumably the idea is that if a surrogate voices more of the attacks, any backlash from the attacks will strike the surrogate rather than (or more than) the candidate.

Another source factor is incumbency status of the candidates. Incumbents are consistently more positive than challengers; incumbents are prone to defend more in response to those attacks. Incumbents have a record in the office sought; challengers do not. Candidates who are in both situation use past deeds in their campaign messages, but incumbents are much more likely to acclaim on past deeds (boasting of their first term accomplishments), whereas challengers are prone to attack on past deeds (criticizing their opponent's record in his first term). Furthermore, challengers tend to offer more future plans (acclaims) than incumbents, and incumbents often attack the challengers' proposals.

Another factor that influences the nature of political campaign messages is the situation or context. Primary messages have fewer attacks and more acclaims than general campaign messages. Furthermore, messages from the primary phase of the campaign and discuss character more and policy less than general campaign messages.

Thus, we have seen important similarities in the nature of political campaign messages across time, media, level of office, and even country. Nevertheless, there are consistent differences as well, differences that can be explained by medium, context, and source of political campaign messages. Up to this point the discussion has focused on messages from the candidates. However, as made clear in Chapter One, citizens also receive information from the news media. Chapter Seven investigates the nature of political campaign news coverage. Unfortunately (for those who believe that the candidates' policy positions and their character are important), the news media is obsessed with horse race coverage (i.e., campaign strategies, public opinion polls, campaign events, predictions). Research consistently supports prediction N1, that news coverage focuses on horse race coverage. These findings occur in primary campaign coverage, general campaign coverage, and non-presidential campaign stories (Tables 7.1 to 7.3). These findings on particular message forms, such as primary and general debates and acceptance addresses, show that news coverage of campaigns consistently over-represents attacks and defenses and under-represents acclaims (N2). There is some evidence of a tendency to over-emphasize character at the expense of policy (N3), but that evidence is less consistent.

This book has also discussed the ultimate target for campaign messages, voters. Apart from such decisions as whether to watch a debate, voters face two key decisions: whether to vote and, if the answer to that question is yes, for whom to vote. I have discussed how campaign messages can influence these two decisions. The evidence for a demobilization effect (negative advertising decreases turnout) is weak. However, campaigns which emphasize character more tend to experience higher levels of turnout.

Citizens make the vote choices based on three influences: policy, character, and party/ideology (the relative importance of these three factors can vary from voter to voter). Voters use information short-cuts when they lack "direct" information about the candidates' policy positions and character. Turning to campaign messages in particular, prediction O1 posited that functions are unrelated to outcome (another null hypothesis). Overall, winners tend to acclaim slightly more than losers, but this effect is neither large nor consistent (Table 6.2). A larger and more consistent relationship exists between topic and outcome, with winners emphasizing policy more and character less than losers (O2, Table 6.3). An even strong relationship exists between outcome and topic of attack (O3): Winners tend to attack more on policy, and less on character, than losers (Table 6.3). So, some relationship exists between the nature of political campaign messages and election outcome.

Obviously, much work remains to be done on understanding political campaigns. Research on non-presidential and non-U.S. political campaigns (discussed in Chapter Eight) would be particularly useful. Turn-out, particularly among younger citizens, is another important topic for future research. However, this book has systematically examined political campaign messages (particularly from presidential candidates) and is a beginning.

The 2016 presidential campaign overturned many expectations. Donald Trump, a candidate with no experience in elective office, unexpectedly won the Republican primary nomination and the Electoral College in the general election (he did not win the popular vote). He was considered to be nasty by some in part because of his habit of giving derogatory nicknames to opponents. He used social media more effectively than any presidential candidate had ever done and possibly better than any political candidate. He also spent less on television advertising than recent presidential candidates. It will be interesting to see how the 2020 general election unfolds (this campaign has become more complicated with the outbreak of the coronavirus pandemic and the controversy over the killing of Floyd George).

APPENDIX 1

Coding Procedures and Texts Studied

Four steps were used in the content analysis of these campaign messages (the Codebook used in this research can be found in Benoit, 2017). First, the candidates' statements in a message were unitized into themes, the unit of analysis. Themes are referred to throughout this text as "utterances," "comments," "statements," "remarks" or "claims." Berelson (1952) defined a theme as "an assertion about a subject" (p. 138). Similarly, Holsti (1969) stated that a theme is "a single assertion about some subject" (p. 116). In this study a theme is basically a argument (specifically, an argument$_1$, to use O'Keefe's terminology [1977]) about the candidates. Because messages tend to be enthymematic (or elliptical), themes can be as short as a phrase or as long as several sentences.

Most content analysis of political campaign messages investigates television spots and the unit of analysis in that research is usually the entire spot (e.g., Kaid & Johnston, 2001; West, 2001). Because television spots often contain a mixture of ideas, this requires a subjective judgment of the spot's "dominant theme." Another approach to content analyzing messages is to count the number of ads that "mention" issues or image. Unitizing the messages into themes, instead of coding the entire spot, adds another step but I believe it is important for two reasons.

First, it facilitates comparisons between different message forms (e.g., spots, debates, speeches). Content analysis of debates outside the Functional approach is not as common in the literature as content analysis of TV spopts, but would one consider the entire debate to be the coding unit, or the entire answer to a question (or opening statement or closing argument)? For example, in the first 2000 presidential debate, the first question was directed to Vice President Al Gore. Governor George W. Bush's rebuttal to Gore's statement:

> Well, we do come from different places. I come from West Texas. I've been a governor. A governor is the chief executive officer and learns how to set agendas. And I think you're going to find the difference reflected in our budgets.
>
> I want to take one half of the surplus and dedicate it to Social Security, one quarter of surplus for important projects. And I want to send one quarter of the surplus back to the people who pay the bills.
>
> I want everybody who pays taxes to have their tax rates cut, and that stands in contrast to my worthy opponent's plan, which will increase the size of government dramatically. His plan is three times larger than President Clinton's proposed plan eight years ago. It's a plan that will have 200 new programs, or expanded programs. It'll create 20,000 new bureaucrats. In other words, it empowers Washington, and tonight you're going to hear that my passion and my vision is to empower Americans to be able to make decisions for themselves in their own lives.

Bush begins by acclaiming his leadership ability, which is an aspect of his character, saying that he has learned how to set agendas. Then he discusses Social Security and tax cuts. He acclaims his proposals to devote half of the surplus to Social Security one-fourth for important projects and one-fourth for tax cuts. Then he attacks Gore for proposing to balloon the government and tosses in a swipe at President Bill Clinton. He ends by discussing his character, passion and vision. This statement discusses both policy – Social Security, tax cuts, size of government – and character – leadership ability, passion, vision. It both acclaims Bush's experience and his policy proposals and attacks Gore's proposals. So, coding spots and debates by themes makes comparisons easier.

Second, coding themes rather than spots (or debate statements) more accurately represents the content of these messages than coding entire spots. To illustrate this problem, consider one of Bill Clinton's television spots from 1996. Kaid and Tedesco (1999) use this spot to illustrate a negative spot:

> *America's values. The President bans deadly assault weapons*; Dole/Gingrich vote no. *The President passes family leave*; Dole/Gingrich vote no. *The President stands firm: a balanced budget, protects Medicare, disabled children*; No again. Now Dole resigns, leaves gridlock he and Gingrich created. *The President's plan: balance the budget, protect Medicare, reform welfare. Do our duty to our parents, our children. America's values* (p. 213; emphasis added).

In this text the acclaims are italicized and the attacks are set in plain type. An analysis that classifies this spot as *either* positive *or* negative clearly provides an incomplete understanding of this spot. Labeling this message as a negative spot ignores all of the acclaims that occur in it: assault weapons, family leave, balanced budget, Medicare, disabled children, welfare reform, America's values.

Contrast that spot with the next one, which also is taken from Clinton's 1996 re-election campaign:

Dole:	"I will be the president who preserves and strengthens and protects Medicare."
Dole:	"I was there, fighting the fight, voting against Medicare, one of 12, because we knew it wouldn't work."
Announcer:	Last year, Dole/Gingrich tried to cut Medicare $270 billion.
Dole:	"Give children a chance in life, give them an education."
Dole:	"We're going to eliminate the Department of Education. We don't need it in the first place. I didn't vote for it in 1979."
Announcer:	Dole tried to slash college scholarships.
Dole:	"Voting against Medicare."
Announcer:	Wrong in the past.
Dole:	"We're going to eliminate the Department of Education."
Announcer:	Wrong for our future.

Unlike the previous advertisement, the second one is completely negative. It contains no positive utterances about Clinton. Yet coding the entire spot would count these two spots the same, each as one negative spot.

Accordingly, the Functional approach analyzes and classifies *each utterance* (or theme) in a given commercial, providing a more precise picture of the *degree to which* a political spot is positive, negative, or defensive. Note that a few analyses of spots include a third option: positive, negative, and comparative or contrast ads (both positive and negative). However, many spots which include both acclaims and attacks do not balance these two functions equally (e.g., some comparative ads have 25% acclaims and 75% attacks whereas others have 90% acclaims and 10% attacks; similarly, spots that address both policy and character may not devote exactly half of the spot to each topic). Benoit and Airne (2009) analyzed non-presidential spots from the 2004 campaign. Almost half (42%) of the ads in this sample employed both acclaims and attacks; 75% discussed both policy and character. There is no question that coding entire spots is less accurate representation of content than coding themes.

Some research uses three categories to classify spots (positive, negative, comparative). This is a step forward from using only two categories (positive and

Table A.1. Sample of presidential messages.

Message Form	Campaigns	Candidates*
Primary TV Spots	1952, 1960–2016	111
Primary Debates	1948, 1960, 1968, 1972, 1980–2016	114
Primary Brochures	1948–2004	78
Acceptances	1952–2016	34
General TV Spots	1952–2016	34
General Debates	1960, 1976–2016	34
VP Debates	1976, 1984–2016	16
General Brochures	1952–2004	18

*Some candidates ran in more than one campaign.
Primary and general TV spots: Benoit (2014c), Benoit and Glantz (2020).
Primary debates: Benoit (2014b), Benoit and Glantz, (2020).
Primary and general brochures: Benoit and Stein (2004).
Acceptance addresses: Benoit (2014a).
General debate data from Benoit (2014b) and Benoit and Glantz (2020).
Vice Presidential debates: Benoit (2014b) and Benoit and Glantz (2020).

negative), but the Functional approach, which classifies each remark (theme, idea unit) as acclaiming, attacking, or defending, is clearly more accurate. As noted in Chapter Two, another advantage of using the theme as the coding unit is that it more accurately reflects the difference between ads of different lengths. A 60 second spot can contain twice as much content as a 30 second ads, but using the entire spot as a coding unit counts each equally (as one positive, one negative; or one issue, or one image spot).

The second step in the procedure codes (classifies, content analyzes) each theme's function, using these rules:

> *Acclaims* are statements by a candidate which portray that candidate in a favorable light.
>
> *Attacks* are statements which characterize the opposing candidate in an unfavorable light.
>
> *Defenses* are statements which respond to attacks, attempting to repair the candidate's own reputation.[1]

Third, coders classified the topic of each theme:

> *Policy* statements concern governmental action (past, current, or future) and problems amenable to governmental action.

Table A.2. Sample of non-presidential messages.

Message Form	Campaigns	Candidates
US Congress	1980–2004	718
US Congress MO	1998	16
Governor, Senate, House	2000	584
Governor, Senate, House	2004	188
Governor, Senate	2008	111
US Congress	2000	
Gubernatorial	2000	
Local	2000	
US Congress	1998	
Local	1998	
Gubernatorial	1974–1998	46

Gubernatorial 1974–1998 from Pier (2002).
US Congressional 1980–2004 from Brazeal (2002).
US Congressional 2000, Gubernatorial 2000, Local 2000 from Airne & Benoit
US Congress 1998 from Benoit (2000c)
Local 1998 from Benoit (2000c)
2000 Senate, House, Governor: Airne & Benoit, 2005.
2004 Governor, Senate, House Spots: Benoit & Airne, 2009.
2008 Senate, Governor Spots: Benoit, Delbert, Sudbrock, & Vogt, 2010.

Table A.3. Sample of non-U.S. campaign messages.

Message Form	Campaigns	Candidates
TV Spots		
Taiwan	2000	3
South Korea	2002	2
Debates		
Ukraine	2004	2
Israel	1984, 1988, 1992, 1996, 1999	10
Australia	2007	2
Canada	2006	4
Taiwan	2004	2
France	1988	2
France	1995	2
South Korea	1997	3
South Korea	2002	3
France	2007	2
Spain	2008	2
U.K.	2010	3
Australia	2010	2
Northern Ireland	2010	4
Scotland	2010	4
Wales	2010	4
Canada	2011	4
France	2012	2
Australia MP	2013	3
Australia PM	2013	2
London Mayor	2012	3
Finland	2012	2

South Korea TV Spots: Lee & Benoit, 2004.
Taiwan TV Spots: Wen, Benoit, & Yu, 2004.
Ukraine: Benoit & Klyukovski, 2006.
Israel: Benoit & Sheafer, 2006.
Australia 2007 Canada 2006: Benoit & Henson, 2007.
Taiwan 2004: Benoit, Wen, & Yu, 2007.
France 1988, 1995, South Korea 1997, 2002: Choi & Benoit, 2009.
Spain 2009: Herrero & Benoit, 2009.
UK 2010: Benoit & Benoit-Bryan, 2013.

Table A.3. *Continued*

Australia 2010: Benoit & Benoit-Bryan, 2014.
Canada 2011: Benoit, 2011.
France 2007, 2012: Choi & Benoit, 2013.
Northern Ireland, Scotland, Wales 2010: Benoit & Benoit-Bryan, 2014.
London Mayor 2012: Benoit, 2016
Finland 2012: Paatelainen, Croucher, Benoit, 2016.

Table A.4. Forms of policy and character.

	Policy
Past Deeds	The unemployment rate is up at six percent under this president. The budget deficits have exploded. They have ruined this economy. We are not creating new jobs or new wealth in this country. There's a health care crisis. (Carol Moseley-Braun)
Future Plans	We ought to start where Al Gore and I proposed in 2000: expand the children's health insurance program, which would have covered every child in America with health insurance by 2005, and let their parents buy into Medicaid at a cheaper rate than they can get in the private market. (Joseph Lieberman)
General Goals	I got into this race because I wanted health care for every American, I wanted a balanced budget. (Howard Dean)
Character	
Personal Qualities	When he [Dean] questions my courage, I really think that anybody who has measured the tests that I think I have performed over the last years on any number of fights in the United States Congress, as well as my service in Vietnam, that I don't need any lectures in courage from Howard Dean. (John Kerry)
Leadership Ability	I believe that [what] Americans are looking for in the next president [is] someone with executive experience. For eight years I was governor of the fourth largest state in this nation, which I think is the best preparation to be president and the American people think so too, since four of the last five presidents elected had been governors of their state before they became president. (Bob Graham)
Ideals	I believe there is a fundamental right to privacy. I do not believe the government belongs in people's bedrooms. I think that applies to both gay and lesbian couples and heterosexual couples. (John Edwards)

All excerpts were taken from the South Carolina Democratic Primary Debate, May 3, 2003

Character statements address characteristics, traits, abilities, or attributes of the candidates.

Fourth, coders identified which of the three forms of policy (past deeds, future plans, general goals) or the three forms of character (personal qualities, leadership ability, or ideals) was used in each theme. See Table A.3 for examples of acclaims and attacks on the forms of policy and character.

Coder training began with consideration of previous research employing the functional approach. Definitions and examples of each category from political campaign texts were supplied to coders. A set of coding rules explained how to apply these categories to texts (see Benoit, 2017). Coders practiced coding related texts (e.g., coders analyzing a debate practiced on a different debate). Intercoder reliability was calculated on a subset of 10% of the texts.

References

Abelson, R. (1987). Conviction. *American Psychologist, 43*, 267–275.

Abramowitz, A. I., & Segal, J. A. (1992). *Senate elections*. Ann Arbor: University of Michigan Press.

Abramowitz, A. I., & Webster, S. W. (2016). The rise of negative partisanship and the nationalization of US elections in the 21st century. *Electoral Studies, 41*, 12–22.

Abramowitz, A. I., & Webster, S. W. (2018). Negative partisanship: Why Americans dislike parties but behave like rabid partisans. *Advances in Political Psychology, 39*, 119–135.

Abramson, P. R., Aldrich, J. H., Paolino, P., & Rohde, D. W. (1992). "Sophisticated" voting in the 1988 presidential primaries. *American Political Science Review, 86*, 55–69.

Adams, W. G. (1987). As New Hampshire goes …. In G. R. Orren & N. W. Polsby (Eds.), *Media and momentum: The New Hampshire primary and nomination politics* (pp. 42–59). Chatham, NJ: Chatham House.

Agiesta, J. (2019). New poll shows Joe Biden holds lead ahead of December debate. CNN. Accessed 1/29/22: https://www.abc57.com/news/cnn-poll-joe-biden-holds-lead-heading-into-december-debate.

Airne, D., & Benoit, W. L. (2005a). Political advertising in campaign 2000. *Communication Quarterly, 53*, 473–492.

Allen, M., & Burrell, N. (2002). The negativity effect in political advertising: A meta-analysis. In J. P. Dillard & M. Pfau (Eds.), *The persuasion handbook: Developments in theory and practice* (pp. 83–96). Thousand Oaks, CA: Sage Publications.

Alliance for Better Campaigns. (2000). The calm before the chad: Networks skimped on candidate, issue coverage during campaign, study finds. *Political Standard*. Accessed 3/8/05: http://www.bettercampaigns.org/standard/display.php?StoryID=72.

Allison, B., Rojanasakul, M., Harris, B., & Sam, C. (2016, December 9). Tracking the 2016 presidential money race. *Bloomberg News*. Accessed 2/18/17: https://www.bloomberg.com/politics/graphics/2016-presidential-campaign-fundraising/

Alvarez, R. M. (1998). *Information & elections: Revised to include the 1996 presidential election*. Ann Arbor, MI: University of Michigan Press.

Amsalem, E., & Nir, L. (2019). Does interpersonal discussion increase political knowledge? A meta-analysis. *Communication Research, 46*, 1–23.

Anderson, M. (2015). More Americans are using social media to connect with politicians. *Pew Research Center*. Accessed 8/1/16: http://www.pewresearch.org/fact-tank/2015/05/19/more-americans-are-using-social-media-to-connect-with-politicians/

Anderson, N. (2004, November 2). The race for the White House: Silence of the wolves, and their ilk, in swing states; A record-setting barrage of political ads that hit a feverish pitch in the final week is all over. *Los Angeles Times*, p. A19.

Ansolabehere, S., Behr, R., & Iyengar, S. (1993). *The media game: American politics in the television age*. New York: Macmillan.

Ansolabehere, S., & Iyengar, S. (1994). Riding the wave and claiming ownership over issues: The joint effects of advertising and news coverage in campaigns. *Public Opinion Quarterly, 58*, 335–357.

Ansolabehere, S., & Iyengar, S. (1995). *Going negative: How attack ads shrink and polarize the electorate*. New York: Free Press.

Ansolabehere, S., Iyengar, S., & Simon, A. (1999). Replicating experiments using aggregate and survey data: the case of negative advertising and turnout. *American Political Science Review, 93*, 901–910.

Ansolabehere, S., Iyengar, S., Simon, A., & Valentino, N. (1994). Does attack advertising demobilize the electorate? *American Political Science Review, 87*, 829–838.

Armstrong, R. (1988). *The next hurrah: The communication revolution in American politics*. New York: Beach Tree Books.

Associated Press. (2004, February 3). Exit polls show ability to beat Bush was No. 1 quality voters sought. Accessed 1/29/22: https://www.post-gazette.com/news/politics-nation/2004/02/04/Exit-polls-show-ability-to-beat-Bush-was-No-1-quality-voters-sought/stories/200402040185.

Associated Press. (2016, November 15). Ad spending. Accessed 1/6/17: http://elections.ap.org/content/ad-spending.

Associated Press. (2020, October 19). Debate commission adopts new rules to mute mics. *PBS*. Accessed 10/26/20: https://www.pbs.org/newshour/politics/debate-commission-adopts-new-rules-to-mute-mics

Atkeson, L. R., & Partin, R. W. (2001). Candidate advertisements, media coverage, and citizen attitudes: The agendas and roles of senators and governors in a federal system. *Political Research Quarterly, 54*, 795–813.

Atkin, C. K. (1977). Effects of campaign advertising and newscasts on children. *Journalism Quarterly, 54*, 503–508.

Atkin, C., & Heald, G. (1976). Effects of political advertising. *Public Opinion Quarterly, 40*, 216–228.

Auer, J. J. (1962). The counterfeit debates. In S. Kraus (Ed.), *The great debates: Background, perspective, effects* (pp. 142–150). Bloomington: Indiana University Press.

Auter, Z. J., & Fine, J. A. (2016). Negative campaigning in the social media age: Attack advertising on Facebook. *Political Behavior, 38*, 999–1020.

Baker, R. K. (1993). Sorting out and suiting up: The presidential nomination. In G. M. Pomper (Ed.), *The election of 1992: Reports and interpretations* (pp. 39–73). Chatham, NJ: Chatham House.

Balkanization. (2019). *Wikipedia*. Accessed 11/5/19: https://en.wikipedia.org/wiki/Balkanization.

Bandwatch. (2019a). 53 incredible Facebook statistics and facts. Accessed 4/9/20: https://www.brandwatch.com/blog/facebook-statistics/

Bandwatch. (2019b). 60 incredible and interesting Twitter stats and statistics. Accessed 4/9/20: https://www.brandwatch.com/blog/twitter-stats-and-statistics/

Balz, D. (2012, July 29). 8 Questions. Dan Balz on topics that will shape the 2012 campaign in the final 100 days. Accessed 7/29/12: http://www.washingtonpost.com/wp-srv/special/politics/8-questions-final-100-days/question7/index.html.

Bartels, L. M. (1988). *Presidential primaries and the dynamics of public choice*. Princetonn NJ: Princeton University Press.

Bartels, L. M. (1993). Messages received: The political impact of media exposure. *American Political Science Review, 87*, 267–285.

Bartels, L. M. (2000). Partisanship and voting behavior, 1952–1996. *American Journal of Political Science, 44*, 35–50.

Basil, M., Schooler, C., & Reeves, B. (1991). Positive and negative political advertising: Effectiveness of ads and perceptions of candidates. In F. Biocca (Ed.), *Television and political advertising* (vol. 1, pp. 245–262). Hillsdale, NJ: Erlbaum.

Bauder, D. (2020, June 11). Trump as thug or hero? Depends on what network you watch: Is Donald Trump a thug, a modern-day dictator. *ABC News*. Accessed 6/20/20: https://abcnews.go.com/Entertainment/wireStory/trump-thug-hero-depends-network-watch-71012465

Becker, J., & Fuchs, D. A. (1967). How two major California dailies covered Reagan versus Brown. *Journalism Quarterly, 44*, 645–653.

Becker, L. B., & Doolittle, J. C. (1975). How repetition affects evaluations of and information seeking about candidates. *Journalism Quarterly, 52*, 611–617.

Beevolve. (2017). An exhaustive study of Twitter users across the world. Accessed 2/17/17: http://www.beevolve.com/twitter-statistics.

Bennett, W. L. (2005). *News: The politics of illusion* (6th ed.). New York: Pearson-Longman.

Benoit, P. J. (1997). *Telling the success story: Acclaiming and disclaiming discourse.* Albany: State University of New York Press.

Benoit, P. J., & Benoit, W. L. (2005). Criteria for evaluating political campaign webpages. *Southern Communication Journal, 70,* 230–247.

Benoit, W. L. (1982). Richard M. Nixon's rhetorical strategies in his public statements on Watergate. *Southern Speech Communication Journal, 47,* 192–211.

Benoit, W. L. (1987). Argument and credibility appeals in persuasion. *Southern Speech Communication Journal, 52,* 181–197.

Benoit, W. L. (1994). The genesis of rhetorical action. *Southern Communication Journal, 59,* 342–55.

Benoit, W. L. (1995). *Accounts, excuses, and apologies: A theory of image restoration strategies.* Albany: State University of New York Press.

Benoit, W. L. (2000c). A functional analysis of political advertising across media, 1998. *Communication Studies, 51,* 274–295.

Benoit, W. L. (2001b). The functional approach to presidential television spots: Acclaiming, attacking, defending 1952–2000. *Communication Studies, 52,* 109–126.

Benoit, W. L. (2003a). The emergence of discursive conventions in presidential advertising, 1952–2000. *Advertising & Society Review, 4(3).* Available: http://muse.jhu.edu/journals/advertising_and_society_review/v004/4.3benoit.html.

Benoit, W. L. (2003b). Presidential campaign discourse as a causal factor in election outcome. *Western Journal of Communication, 67,* 97–112.

Benoit, W. L. (2003). Topic of presidential campaign discourse and election outcome. *Western Journal of Communication, 67,* 97–112.

Benoit, W. L. (2014a). *A functional analysis of presidential television advertisements* (2nd ed.). Lanham, MD: Lexington Books.

Benoit, W. L. (2014b). *Political election debates: Informing voters about policy and character.* Lanham, MD: Lexington Books.

Benoit, W. L. (2017a). The Functional Theory of political campaign discourse. In R. E. Denton (Ed.), *Political campaign communication: Theory, method and practice* (pp. 3–32). Lanham, MD: Lexington.

Benoit, W. L. (2017b). The Functional Theory of political campaign communication. In K. Kenski & K. H. Jamieson (Ed.), *Oxford handbook of political communication* (pp. 195–204). Oxford, UK: Oxford University Press. DOI: 10.1093/oxfordhb/9780199793471.013.2

Benoit, W. L. (2017c). A Functional Analysis of 2016 direct mail advertising in Ohio. *American Behavioral Scientist, 61,* 481–492. DOI: 10.1177/0002764217693274

Benoit, W. L. (2018). Issue ownership in 2016 presidential debates. *Argumentation & Advocacy, 54,* 95–103.

Benoit, W. L. (2019). A Functional analysis of visual and verbal symbols in presidential campaign posters, 1828–2012, *Presidential Studies Quarterly, 49*. 4–22.

Benoit, W. L., & Airne, D. (2005b). Issue ownership for non-presidential television spots. *Communication Quarterly, 53*, 493–503. DOI: 10.1080/01463370500102137.

Benoit, W. L., & Airne, D. (2009). A Functional analysis of non-presidential TV spots in campaign 2004. *Human Communication, 12*, 91–117.

Benoit, W. L., Airne, D., & Brazeal, L. (2011). Determinants of issue emphasis in gubernatorial and senate debates. *Human Communication, 14*, 127–136.

Benoit, P. J., & Benoit, W. L. (1986). Consciousness: The mindlessness and verbal report controversies. *Western Journal of Speech Communication, 50*, 41–63.

Benoit, W. L., & Benoit, P. J. (2008). *Persuasive messages: Balancing influence in communication.* Oxford, UK: Blackwell. Translated into Korean, Croation.

Benoit, W. L., & Benoit-Bryan, J. M. (2013). Debates come to the UK: A Functional analysis of the 2010 British Prime Minister election debates. *Communication Quarterly, 61*, 463–478.

Benoit, W. L., & Benoit-Bryan, J. M. (2014a). A functional analysis of the 2010 Australian Prime Minister debate. *Journal of Argumentation in Context, 3*, 153–168. doi 10.1075/jaic.3.2.03ben

Benoit, W. L., & Benoit-Bryan, J. M. (2014b). A functional analysis of UK debates in Northern Ireland, Scotland, and Wales. *Western Journal of Communication, 78*, 653–667. DOI: 10.1080/10570314.2013.868032.

Benoit, W. L., & Benoit-Bryan, J. M. (2015). A functional analysis of 2013 Australian member of parliament and prime minister debates. *Studies in Media and Communication, 3*, 1–8.

Benoit, W. L., & Billings, A. (2020). *The rise and fall of mass communication.* New York: Peter Lang.

Benoit, W. L., Blaney, J. R., & Pier, P. M. (2000). Acclaiming, attacking, and defending: A functional analysis of nominating convention keynote speeches, 1960–1996. *Political Communication, 17*, 61–84.

Benoit, W. L., Bough, B., & Hansen, G. J. (2003). *The dynamic impact of presidential campaign information sources on voter issue knowledge and salience.* Unpublished paper.

Benoit, W. L., Brazeal, L. M., & Airne, D. (2007). A Functional analysis of televised U.S. Senate and gubernatorial campaign debates. *Argumentation and Advocacy, 44*, 75–89.

Benoit, W. L., & Compton, J. (2014). A Functional analysis of 2012 Republican primary TV spots. *American Behavioral Scientist, 58*, 497–509. DOI: 10.1177/0002764213506209.

Benoit, W. L., & Currie, H. (2001). Inaccuracies in media coverage of presidential debates. *Argumentation and Advocacy, 38*, 28–39.

Benoit, W. L., & Delbert, J. (2009). A functional analysis of the Lincoln-Douglas debates. *Argumentation and Advocacy, 46*, 110–115.

Benoit, W. L., Delbert, J., Sudbrock, L. A., & Vogt, C. (2010). Functional analysis of 2008 senate and gubernatorial TV spots. *Human Communication, 13*, 103–125.

Benoit, W. L., Furgerson, J., Seifert, J., & Sargardia, S. (2013). Newspaper coverage of senate, gubernatorial, and mayoral elections. *Human Communication, 16*, 215–229.

Benoit, W. L., & Glantz, M. (2015). A Functional analysis of 2012 United States general election presidential and vice presidential debates. In C. Bieber & K. Kamps (Eds.), *Die US-präsidentschaftswahl 2012* (pp. 289–306). Wiesbaden, Germany: Springer.

Benoit, W. L., & Glantz, M. (2017). *Persuasive attack on Donald Trump in the 2016 Republican primaries*. Lanham, MD: Lexington Books.

Benoit, W. L., & Glantz, M. (2020). *Presidential campaigns in the age of social media: Clinton and Trump*. New York City, NY: Peter Lang.

Benoit, W. L., Glantz, M. J., Phillips, A. L., Rill, L. A., Davis, C. B., Henson, J. R., & Sudbrock, L. A. (2011). Staying "on message": Consistency in content of presidential primary campaign messages across media. *American Behavioral Scientist, 55*, 457–468. DOI: 10.1177/0002764211398072.

Benoit, W. L., Glantz, M., & Rill, L. (2016). Campaigning on the Internet: 2008 presidential general webpages. *KOME – An International Journal of Pure Communication Inquiry, 4*, 46–58.

Benoit, W. L., Gullifor, P., & Panici, D. A. (1991). President Reagan's defensive discourse on the Iran-Contra affair. *Communication Studies, 42*, 272–294.

Benoit, W. L., & Hansen, G. J. (2002). Issue adaptation of presidential television spots and debates to primary and general audiences. *Communication Research Reports, 19*, 138–145.

Benoit, W. L., & Hansen, G. J. (2004a). The changing media environment of presidential campaigns. *Communication Research Reports, 21*, 164–173.

Benoit, W. L., & Hansen, G. J. (2004b). Issue ownership in primary and general presidential debates. *Argumentation and Advocacy, 40*, 143–154.

Benoit, W. L., & Hansen, G. J. (2004c). Presidential debate watching, issue knowledge, character evaluation, and vote choice. *Human Communication Research, 30*, 121–140.

Benoit, W. L., Hansen, G. J., & Holbert, R. L. (2004). Presidential campaigns and democracy. *Mass Communication & Society, 7*, 177–190.

Benoit, W. L., Hansen, G. J., & Stein, K. A. (2004). Newspaper coverage of presidential primary debates. *Argumentation and Advocacy, 40*, 246–258.

Benoit, W. L., Hansen, G. J., & Verser, R. M. (2003). A meta-analysis of the effects of viewing U.S. presidential debates. *Communication Monographs, 70*, 335–350.

Benoit, W. L., & Harthcock, A. (1999). Functions of the Great Debates: Acclaims, attacks, and defense in the 1960 presidential debates. *Communication Monographs, 66*, 341–357.

Benoit, W. L., Hemmer, K., & Stein, K. (2010). *New York Times'* coverage of American presidential primary campaigns, 1952–2004. *Human Communication, 13*, 259–280.

Benoit, W. L., & Henson, J. (2006). A functional analysis of non-presidential primary debates. *Speaker & Gavel, 43*, 22–31.

Benoit, W. L., & Henson, J. R. (2007). A functional analysis of the 2006 Canadian and 2007 Australian election debates. *Argumentation & Advocacy, 44*, 36–48.

Benoit, W. L., Henson, J., Davis, C., Glantz, M., Phillips, A., & Rill, L. (2013). Stumping on the Internet: 2008 presidential primary candidate campaign webpages. *Human Communication, 16*, 1–12.

Benoit, W. L., Henson, J. R., & Maltos, S. (2007). A functional analysis of mayoral debates. *Contemporary Argumentation and Debate, 28*, 20–37.

Benoit, W. L., Henson, J., Whalen, S., & Pier, P. M. (2008). "I am a candidate for president": A functional analysis of presidential announcement speeches, 1960–2004. *Speaker & Gavel, 45*, 3–18.

Benoit, W. L., & Holbert, R. L. (2010). Political communication. In C. R. Berger, M. E. Roloff, & D. R. Roskos-Ewoldsen (Eds.), *Handbook of communication science* (2nd ed., pp. 437–452). Thousand Oaks, CA: Sage.

Benoit, W. L., & Klyukovski, A. A. (2006). A Functional analysis of 2004 Ukrainian presidential debates. *Argumentation, 20*, 209–225.

Benoit, W. L., Leshner, G. M., & Chattopadhyay, S. (2007). A meta-analysis of political advertising. *Human Communication, 10*, 507–522.

Benoit, W. L., & McHale, J. P. (2003). Presidential candidates' television spots and personal qualities. *Southern Communication Journal, 68*, 319–334.

Benoit, W. L., & McHale, J. P. (2004). Presidential candidates' personal qualities: Computer content analysis. In K. Hacker (Ed.), *Presidential candidate images: Issues of theory and measurement*. Lanham, MD: Rowman & Littlefield.

Benoit, W. L., McHale, J. P., Hansen, G. J., Pier, P. M., & McGuire, J. (2003). *Campaign 2000: A functional analysis of the presidential campaign at the dawn of the new millennium*. Lanham, MD: Rowman & Littlefield.

Benoit, W. L., Pier, P. M., Brazeal, L., McHale, J. P., Klyukovski, A., & Airne, D. (2002). *The primary decision: A functional analysis of debates in presidential primaries*. Westport, CT: Praeger.

Benoit, W. L., & Rill, L. (2013). A functional analysis of 2008 general election debates. *Argumentation and Advocacy, 50*, 34–46.

Benoit, W. L., & Sheafer, T. (2006). Functional theory and political discourse: Televised debates in Israel and the United States. *Journalism & Mass Communication Quarterly, 83*, 281–297.

Benoit, W. L., & Stein, K. A. (2005). A functional analysis of presidential direct mail advertising. *Communication Studies, 56*, 203–225. DOI: 10.1080/10510970500181181.

Benoit, W. L., & Stein, K. A. (2021). A functional analysis of 2016 senate, house, and gubernatorial tweets. *American Behavioral Scientist, 65*, 432–447.

Benoit, W. L., Stein, K. A., & Hansen, G. J. (2004a). How newspapers cover presidential nomination acceptance addresses. *Newspaper Research Journal, 25*, 83–89.

Benoit, W. L., Stein, K. A., & Hansen, G. J. (2005). *New York Times'* coverage of presidential campaigns, 1952–2000. *Journalism & Mass Communication Quarterly, 82*, 356–376.

Benoit, W. L., Stein, K. A., McHale, J. P., Chattopadhyay, S., Verser, R., Price, S. (2005). *Bush versus Kerry: A functional analysis of campaign 2004*. Unpublished ms.

Benoit, W. L., & Strathman, A. (2004). Source credibility and the Elaboration Likelihood Model. In R. Gass & J. Seiter (Eds.), *Readings in persuasion, social influence, and compliance gaining* (pp. 95–111). Boston, MA: Allyn and Bacon.

Benoit, W. L., & Wells, W. T. (1996). *Candidates in conflict: Persuasive attack and defense in the 1992 presidential debates*. Tuscaloosa: University of Alabama Press.

Benoit, W. L., Wells, W. T., Pier, P. M., & Blaney, J. R. (1999). Acclaiming, attacking, and defending in nomination convention acceptance addresses, 1960–1996. *Quarterly Journal of Speech, 85*, 247–267.

Benoit, W. L., Wen, W.-C., & Yu, T. (2007). A Functional analysis of 2004 Taiwanese political debates. *Asian Journal of Communication, 17*, 24–39. DOI: 10.1080/01292980601114521.

Benze, J. G., & Declercq, E. R. (1985). Content of television political spot ads for female candidates. *Journalism Quarterly, 62*, 278–283, 288.

Berelson, B. (1952). *Content analysis for the social sciences and humanities*. Reading, MA: Addison-Wesley.

Berelson, B. R., Lazarsfeld, P. F., & McPhee, W. N. (1954). *Voting: A study of opinion formation in a presidential campaign*. Chicago, IL: University of Chicago Press.

Bimber, B., & Davis, R. (2003). *Campaigning online: The Internet in U.S. elections*. New York: Oxford University Press.

Bishop, B., & Cushing, R. G. (2008). *The big sort: Why the clustering of like-minded America is tearing us apart*. Botson, MA: Mariner Books.

Bishop, G. F. (2005). *The illusion of public opinion: Fact and artifact in American public opinion polls*. Lanham, MD: Rowman and Littlefield.

Blake, A. (2020, September 30). Trump was the interrupter-in-chief at Tuesday's debate. It wasn't close. *Washington Post*. Accessed 10/27/20: https://www.washingtonpost.com/politics/2020/09/30/trump-was-interrupter-in-chief-tuesdays-debate-it-wasnt-close/

Blue shift. *Wikipedia*. Accessed 11/7/20: https://en.wikipedia.org/wiki/Blue_shift_(politics)

Blumenthal, S. (1980). *The permanent campaign: Inside the world of elite political operatives*. Boston, MA: Beacon Press.

Bock, J. (1982). *Zur Inhalts-und Funktionsanalyse der Politikerrede. Ein Beitrag zur Verbesserung der Kommunikation zwischen Staatsburger und Politiker* [Analysis of content and function in politician's speeches. Toward a better understanding between citizens and politicians]. Frankfurt, Germany: Haag und Herrchen.

Borah, P. (2016). Political Facebook use: Campaign strategies used in 2008 and 2012 presidential elections. *Journal of Information Technology & Politics, 13*, 1–13.

Brader, T. (2006). *Campaigning for hearts and minds: How emotional appeals in ads work*. Chicago, IL: University of Chicago Press.

Brady, H. E. (1989). Is Iowa news? In P. Squire (Ed.) *The Iowa caucuses and the presidential nominating process* (pp. 89–119). Boulder, CO: Westview.

Brasher, H. (2003). Capitalizing on contention: Issue agendas in U.S. senate campaigns. *Political Communication, 20*, 453–471.

Brians, C. L., & Wattenberg, M. P. (1996). Campaign issue knowledge and salience: Comparing reception from TV commercials, TV news, and newspapers. *American Journal of Political Science, 40*, 172–193.

Bruner, J., & Korchin, S. (1946). The boss and the vote: A case study in city politics. *Public Opinion Quarterly, 10*, 1–23.

Bryant, J. (2004). Paid media advertising: Political communication from the stone age to the present. In J. A. Thurber & C. J. Nelson (Eds.), *Campaigns and elections American style* (2nd ed., pp. 90–108). Boulder, CO: Westview.

Buchanan, B. (1991). *Electing a president: The Markle Commission research on campaign '88.* Austin: University of Texas Press.

Buchanan, B. (2004). *Presidential campaign quality: Incentives and reform.* Upper Saddle River, NJ: Pearson Prentice Hall.

Buhr, T. (2000). What voters know about the candidates and how they know it: The 1996 New Hampshire Republican primary as a case study. In W. G. Mayer (Ed.), *In pursuit of the White House: How we choose our presidential nominees* (pp. 203–253). New York: Chatham House.

Burns, A., & Martin, J. (2016, March 19). Republican leaders map a strategy to derail Donald Trump. *New York Times.* Accessed 5/22/20: https://www.nytimes.com/2016/03/20/us/politics/donald-trump-republican-party.html

Bycoffe, A. (2020, February 10). Tracking every presidential candidates TV ad buys. *FiveThirtyEight.* Accessed 2/11/20: https://projects.fivethirtyeight.com/2020-campaign-ads/

Bystrom, D. G., & Miller, J. L. (1999). Gendered communication styles and strategies in campaign 1996: The videostyles of women and men candidates. In L. L. Kaid & D. G. Bystrom (Eds.), *The electronic election: Perspectives on the 1996 campaign communication* (pp. 293–302). Mahwah, NJ: Lawrence Erlbaum.

Cacioppo, J. T., & Petty, R. E. (1985). Central and peripheral routes to persuasion: The role of message repetition. In L. F. Alwitt & A. A. Mitchell (Eds.) *Psychological processes and advertising effects: Theory, research, and application* (pp. 91–111). Hillsdale, NJ: Lawrence Erlbaum.

Cacioppo, J. T., Petty, R. E., & Morris, K. (1983). Effects of need for cognition on message evaluation, recall, and persuasion. *Journal of Personality and Social Psychology, 45*, 805–818.

Calder, B. J., Insko, C. A., & Yandell, B. (1974). The relation of cognitive and memorial processes to persuasion in a simulated jury trial. *Journal of Applied Social Psychology, 4*, 62–93.

Chaiken, S. (1980). Heuristic versus systemic information processing and the use of source versus message cues in persuasion. *Journal of Personality and Social Psychology, 39*, 751–766,

Campbell, A., Converse, P. E., Miller, W. E., & Stokes, D. E. (1960). *The American voter, unabridged version.* Chicago, IL: University of Chicago Press.

Campbell, A., Gurin, G., & Miller, W. E. (1954). *The voter decides.* Evanston, IL: Row, Peterson.

Campbell, A., & Stokes, D. (1959). Partisan attitudes and the presidential vote. In E. Burdick & A. Brodbeck (Eds.), *American voting behavior* (pp. 356–357). New York: Free Press.

Campbell, J. E. (2000). *The American campaign: U.S. presidential campaigns and the national vote.* College Station, TX: Texas A&M University Press.

Campbell, J. E. (2001). When have presidential campaigns decided election outcomes? *American Politics Research, 29*, 437–460.

Campbell, K. K., & Jamieson, K. H. (1978). *Form and genre: Shaping rhetorical action*. Falls Church, VA: Speech Communication Association.

Caslon Analytics. (2003). Ketupa.net media profiles timeline. Accessed 3/2/03: http://www.ketupa.net/timeline.htm.

321,418,820 [persons under 18 years old 24.0% so Adults: 244,278,303]

Center for Responsive Politics. (2012). 2012 presidential race. *OpenSecrets.org*. Accessed 5/7/16: https://www.opensecrets.org/pres12/

Center for Responsive Politics. (2017). Election overview: Incumbent advantage. *Open Secrets*. Accessed 2/25/17: https://www.opensecrets.org/overview/incumbs.php

Chaffee, S. H. (1979). Approaches of U.S. scholars to the study of televised political debates. *Political Communication Review, 4*, 19–33.

Chang, C. (2000). Political advertising in Taiwan and the U.S.: A cross-cultural comparison of the 1996 presidential election campaigns. *Asian Journal of Communication, 10*, 1–17.

Christ, W. B., Thorson, E., & Caywood, C. (1994). Do attitudes toward political advertising affect information processing of televised political commercials? *Journal of Broadcasting & Electronic Media, 38*, 251–270.

Clarke, P., & Evans, S. H. (1983). *Covering campaigns: Journalism in congressional elections*. Stanford, CA: Stanford University Press.

Clinton, B. (1996). A bridge to the future. *Vital Speeches of the Day, 62*, 706–712.

Cobb, K., & Roth, B. (2004, July 29). 2004 Democratic Convention Boston: Fewer viewers are tuning in "Big Three"; Networks see drop-off, but PBS and cable make gains in coverage of convention. *Houston Chronicle*, p. A11.

Cohen, B. C. (1963). *The press and foreign policy*. Princeton, NJ: Princeton University Press.

Collins, A., & Loftus, E. (1975). A spreading-activation theory of semantic processing. *Psychological Review, 82*, 240–247.

Commerce Department. (2021, May 6). *Federal Register*. Accessed 1/29/22: https://www.federalregister.gov/documents/2021/05/06/2021-09422/estimates-of-the-voting-age-population-for-2020

Converse, P. E. (1964). The nature of belief systems in mass politics. In D. Apter (Ed.), *Ideology and discontent* (pp. 206–261). New York: Free Press.

Converse, P. E. (1966). The concept of a normal vote. In A. Campbell, P. E. Converse, W. E. Miller, & D. E. Stokes (Eds.), *Elections and the political order* (pp. 9–39). New York: John Wiley.

Converse, P. E. (1972). Changes in the American electorate. In A. Campbell & P. Converse (Eds.), *The human meaning of social change* (pp. 263–331). New York: John Wiley.

Converse, P. E., Miller, W. E., Rusk, J. G., & Wolfe, A. C. (1969). Continuity and change in American politics: Parties and issues in the 1968 election. *American Political Science Review, 63*, 1083–1105.

Cooper, C. A., & Knotts, H. G. (2004). Packaging the governor: Television advertising in the 2000 elections. In D. A. Shultz (Ed.), *Lights, camera, campaign! Media, politics, and political advertising* (pp. 101–120). New York: Peter Lang.

Cornfield, M. (2004). *Politics moves online: Campaigning and the Internet*. New York: Century Foundation Press.

Coyne, B. (2016, November 7). How #Election2016 was tweeted so far. *Twitter Blog*. Accessed 4/15/20: https://blog.twitter.com/official/en_us/a/2016/how-election2016-was-tweeted-so-far.html

Crotty, W., & Jackson, J. S. (1985). *Presidential primaries and nominations*. Washington, DC: Congressional Quarterly Press.

Cruz, U., & Benoit, W. L. (2021). Presidential television advertisements: Testing Functional Theory in Mexico and the United States. *American Behavioral Scientist, 65*, [online first].

Cundy, D. T. (1986). Political commercials and candidate image: The effect can be substantial. In L. L. Kaid, D. Nimmo, & K. R. Sanders (Eds.), *New perspectives on political advertising* (pp. 210–234). Carbondale: Southern Illinois Press.

D'Alessio, D., & Allen, M. (2000). Media bias in presidential elections: A meta-analysis. *Journal of Communication, 50*, 133–156.

Damore, D. E. (2002). Candidate strategy and the decision to go negative. *Political Research Quarterly, 55*, 669–685.

Davenport, D. (2017, December 13). A growing cancer on Congress: The curse of party-line voting. *Forbes*. Accessed September 14, 2018: https://www.forbes.com/sites/daviddavenport/2017/12/13/a-growing-cancer-on-congress-the-curse-of-party-line-voting/#22b69cb86139.

Davis, J. W. (1997). *U.S. presidential primaries and the caucus-convention system*. Westport, CT: Greenwood Press.

Davis, R. (1999). *The web of politics: The Internet's impact on the American political system*. New York: Oxford University Press.

a-billion-dollars-last-year–and-still-had-nearly-200-million-heading-into-2020/2020/01/03/10ba1612-2dad-11ea-bcd4-24597950008f_story.html

Dearing, J. W., & Rogers, E. M. (1996). *Agenda-setting*. Thousand Oaks, CA: Sage.

DeFleur, M. L., Davenport, L, Cronin, M., & DeFleur, M. (1992). Audience recall of news stories presented by newspaper, computer, television, and radio. *Journalism Quarterly, 69*, 1010–1022.

Delli Carpini, M. X., & Keeter, S. (1996). *What Americans know about politics and why it matters*. New Haven, CT: Yale University Press.

Denton, R. E. (1998). Communication variables and dynamics of the 1996 presidential campaign. In R. E. Denton (Ed.), *The 1996 presidential campaign: A communication perspective* (pp. 1–50). Westport, CT: Praeger.

Denton, R. E., & Woodward, G. C. (1990). *Political communication in America*, 2nd ed. New York: Praeger.

Devlin, L. P. (1977). Contrasts in presidential campaign commercials of 1972. *Central States Speech Journal, 28*, 238–249.

Devlin, L. P. (1986). An analysis of presidential television commercials, 1952–1984. In L. L. Kaid, D. Nimmo, & K. R. Sanders (Eds.), *New perspectives on political advertising* (pp. 21–54). Carbondale: Southern Illinois Press.

Devlin, L. P. (1987). Campaign commercials. In L. P. Devlin (Ed.), *Political persuasion in presidential campaigns* (pp. 208–216). New Brunswick, NJ: Transaction Books.

Devlin, L. P. (1989). Contrasts in presidential campaign commercials of 1988. *American Behavioral Scientist, 32,* 389–414

Devlin, L. P. (1993). Contrasts in presidential campaign commercials of 1992. *American Behavioral Scientist, 37,* 272–290.

Devlin, L. P. (1997). Contrasts in presidential campaign commercials of 1996. *American Behavioral Scientist, 40,* 1058–1084.

Devlin, L. P. (2001). Contrasts in presidential campaign commercials of 2004. *American Behavioral Scientist, 44,* 2388–2369.

Devlin, L. P. (2005). Contrasts in presidential campaign commercials of 2004. *American Behavioral Scientist, 49,* 279–313.

Dewar, H. (2004, June 26). Republican Ryan quits Senate race in Illinois; GOP leaders had urged candidate to step down. *Washington Post,* p. A3.

Diamond, E., & Bates, S. (1993). *The spot: The rise of political advertising on television* (3rd ed.). Cambridge, MA: MIT Press.

Dole, B. (1996). The best days are yet to come. *Vital Speeches of the Day, 62,* 674–679.

Donohue, T. R. (1973). Viewer perceptions of color and black-and-white paid political advertising. *Journalism Quarterly, 50,* 660–665.

Dover, E. D. (1994). *Presidential elections in the television age: 1960–1992.* Westport, CT: Praeger.

Downs, A. (1957). *An economic theory of democracy.* New York: Harper and Row.

Drinkard, J. (2004, February 18). Primaries show money isn't deciding factor: Kerry's rapid rise proves momentum, message crucial. *USA Today,* p. 5A.

Duchneskie, J., & Seplow, S. (2000, December 15). Gore's vote lead totals 540,435. *Philadelphia Inquirer,* p. A1.

Eagly, A., & Chaiken, S. (1993). *The psychology of attitudes.* Fort Worth, TX: Harcourt Brace Jovanovich.

Eggen, D. (2012, October 12). Direct mail still a force in campaigns. *Washington Post.* Accessed 11/16/16: https://www.washingtonpost.com/politics/decision2012/direct-mail-still-a-force-in-campaigns/2012/10/12/24f6f830-0bf9-11e2-bb5e-492c0d30bff6_story.html

Electoral Vote Predictor. (2004a). *Predicted versus actual results.* Accessed 11/15/04: http://www.electoral-vote.com/pollsters/index.html#Predicted.

Electoral Vote Predictor. (2004b). *Previous polls.* Accessed 11/15/04: http://www.electoral-vote.com/pastpolls.html.

Elmelund-Praestekaer, C. (2010). Beyond American negativity: Toward a general understanding of the determinants of negative campaigning. *European Political Science Review, 2,* 137–156.

Email. (2017a). *Wikipedia.* Accessed 2/15/17: https://en.wikipedia.org/wiki/Email.

Erikson, R. S. (1989). Economic conditions and the presidential vote. *American Political Science Review, 83*, 567–573.

Estimated cost of ads aired for 2016 U.S. presidential election, by candidate as of May, 2016 (in million U.S. dollars) (2016). *Statista*. Accessed 6/29/16: http://www.statista.com/statistics/564155/cost-estimate-of-ads-aired-2016-us-presidential-election-by-candidate/

Evarts, D., & Stempel, G. H. (1974). Coverage of the 1972 campaign by TV, news magazines, and major newspapers. *Journalism Quarterly, 51*, 645–648, 676.

Faber, R. J., & Storey, M. C. (1984). Recall of information from political advertising. *Journal of Advertising, 13*, 39–44.

Faber, R. J., Tims, A. R., & Schmitt, K. G. (1993). Negative political advertising and voting intent: The role of involvement and alternative information sources. *Journal of Advertising, 22*, 67–76.

Fair, R. C. (1978). The effect of economic events on votes for president. *Review of Economics and Statistics, 55*, 1–21.

Fair, R. C. (1982). The effect of economic events on votes for president: 1980 results. *Review of Economics and Statistics, 64*, 322–325.

Fair, R. C. (1988). The effect of economic events on votes for president: 1984 update. *Political Behavior, 10*, 168–179.

Fair, R. C. (1996a). Econometrics and presidential elections. *Journal of Economic Perspectives, 10*, 89–102.

Fair, R. C. (1996b). The effect of economic events on votes for president: 1992 update. *Political Behavior, 18*, 119–139.

Fair, R. C. (2002). *Predicting presidential elections and other things*. Stanford, CA: Stanford University Press.

Farnsworth, S. J., & Lichter, S. R. (2003). *The nightly news nightmare: Network television's coverage of U.S. presidential elections, 1988–2000*. Lanham, MD: Rowman & Littlefield.

Fazio, R. (1995) Attitudes as objective-evaluation associations: Determinants, consequences, and correlations of attitude accessibility. In R. Petty & J. Krosnick (Eds.), *Attitude strength: Antecedents and consequences* (pp. 247–282). Hillsdale, NJ: Lawrence Erlbaum Associates.

Federal Election Commission. (2000a). *Disbursements of 1999–2000 presidential campaigns through April 30, 2000*. Obtained on-line: http://www.fec.gov/finance/pdism5.htm.

Federal Election Commission. (2003). Federal elections 2000. Accessed 7/27/03: http://www.fec.gov/pubrec/fe2000/tcontents.htm

Fineman, H. (2000, October 2). The talk-show primary. *Newsweek*, 26–27.

Finkel, S. E. (1993). Reexamining the "minimal effects" model in recent presidential campaigns. *Journal of Politics, 55*, 1–21.

Finkel, S. E., & Geer, J. G. (1998). A spot check: Casting doubt on the demobilizing effect of attack advertising. *American Journal of Political Science, 42*, 573–595.

Fiorina, M. P. (1981). *Retrospective voting in American national elections.* New Haven, CT: Yale University Press.

Fishbein, M., & Ajzen, I. (2010). *Predicting and changing behavior: The reasoned action approach.* New York: Psychology Press.

Floyd, J. (2004, August 30). When horse races go too far astray. *Dallas Morning News*, p. 1B.

Freedman, P., Frantz, M., & Goldstein, K. (2004). Campaign advertising and democratic citizenship. *American Journal of Political Science, 48*, 723–741.

Gainous, J., & Wagner, K. M. (2014). *Tweeting to power: The social media revolution.* Oxford, UK: Oxford University Press.

Garramone, G. M. (1984). Voter responses to negative political ads. *Journalism Quarterly, 61*, 250–269.

Garramone, G. M. (1985). Effects of negative political advertising: The roles of sponsor and rebuttal. *Journal of Broadcasting and Electronic Media, 29*, 147–159.

Garramone, G. M., Atkin, C. K., Pinkleton, B. E., & Cole, R. T. (1990). Effects of negative political advertising on the political process. *Journal of Broadcasting and Electronic Media, 34*, 299–311.

Geer, J. G. (1998). Campaigns, party competition, and political advertising. In J. G. Geer (Ed.), *Politicians and party politics* (pp. 186–217). Baltimore, MD: Johns Hopkins University Press.

Geer, J. G. (2006). *In defense of negativity: Attack ads in presidential campaigns.* Chicago: Univeristy of Chicago Press.

Geiger, S. F., & Reeves, B. (1991). The effects of visual structure and content emphasis on the evaluation and memory for political candidates. In F. Biocca (Ed.), *Television and political advertising* (vol. 1, pp. 125–143). Hillsdale, NJ: Erlbaum.

Gerber, A. S., & Green, D. P. (2000). The effects of canvassing, telephone calls, and direct mail on voter turnout: A field experiment. *American Political Science Review, 94*, 653–663.

Gill, K. (2016, March 23). What is the Fairness Doctrine? About.com. Accessed 12/3/16: http://uspolitics.about.com/od/electionissues/a/fcc_fairness_2.htm

Glantz, M., Benoit, W. L., & Airne, D. (2013). A Functional analysis of 2012 U.S. presidential primary debates. *Argumentation and Advocacy, 49*, 275–285.

Glennon, M. J. (1993). *When no majority rules: The Electoral College and presidential succession.* Washington, DC: CQ Press.

Goddard, T. (2020, June 28). Fox News kept millions from taking virus seriously. *Political Wire.* Accessed 6/29/20: https://politicalwire.com/2020/06/28/fox-news-kept-millions-from-taking-virus-seriously/

Goldenberg, E. N., & Traugott, M. W. (1984). *Campaigning for congress.* Washington, DC: Congressional Quarterly Press.

Goldstein, K., & Freedman, P. (2002b). Lessons learned: Campaign advertising in the 2000 elections. *Political Communication, 19*, 5–28.

Goldstein, K. M., & Krasno, J. S., Bradford, L., & Seltz, D. E. (2001). Going negative: Attack advertising in the 1998 elections. In P. S. Herrnson (Ed.), *Playing hardball: Campaigning for the U.S. congress* (pp. 92–107). Upper Saddle River, NJ: Prentice-Hall.

Gottfried, J., Barthel, M., Shearer, E., & Mitchell, A. (2016, February 4). The 2016 presidential campaign – a news event that's hard to miss. *PewResearchCenter*. Accessed 1/17/17: http://www.journalism.org/2016/02/04/the-2016-presidential-campaign-a-news-event-thats-hard-to-miss/

Graber, D. A. (1971). Press coverage patterns of campaign news: The 1968 presidential race. *Journalism Quarterly, 48*, 502–512.

Graber, D. A. (1976). Effect of incumbency on coverage patterns in 1972 presidential campaign. *Journalism Quarterly, 53*, 499–508.

Graber, D. A. (1988). *Processing the news: How people tame the information tide* (2nd ed.). White Plains, NY: Longman.

Graber, D. A. (1989). *Mass media and American politics* (3rd ed.). Washington, DC: Congressional Quarterly.

Greenwald, A. G. (1968). Cognitive learning, cognitive response to persuasion, and attitude change. In A. G. Greenwald, T. C. Brock, & T. M. Ostrom (Eds.), *Psychological foundations of attitudes* (pp. 147–170). New York: Academic Press.

Gronbeck, B. E. (1978). The functions of presidential campaigning. *Communication Monographs, 45*, 268–280.

Gross, J. H., & Johnson, K. T. (2016, October 18). Twitter taunts and tirades: Negative campaigning in the age of Trump. *Political Science Now*. Accessed 2/17/17: http://www.politicalsciencenow.com/twitter-taunts-and-tirades-negative-campaigning-in-the-age-of-trump/

Gulati, G. J., Just, M. R., & Crigler, A. N. (2004). News coverage of political campaigns. In L. L. Kaid (Ed.), *Handbook of political campaign research* (pp. 237–256). Mahwah, NJ: Erlbaum.

Haag, L. (1992/93). Oprah Winfrey: The construction of intimacy in the talk show setting. *Journal of Popular Culture, 26*, 115–121.

Hacker, K. L., Zakahi, W. R., Giles, M. J., & McQuitty, S. (2000). Components of candidate images: Statistical analysis of the issue-persona dichotomy in the presidential campaign of 1996. *Communication Monographs, 67*, 227–238.

Hagen, M. G., & Mayer, W. G. (2000). The modern politics of presidential selection: How changing the rules really did change the game. In W. G. Mayer (Ed.), *In pursuit of the White House 2000: How we choose our presidential nominees* (pp. 1–55). New York: Chatham House.

Hale, J. F., Fox, J. C., & Farmer, R. (1996). Negative advertisements in U.S. Senate campaigns: The influence of campaign context. *Social Science Quarterly, 77*, 329–343.

Hallin, D. (1992). Sound bite news: Television coverage of elections, 1968–1988. *Journal of Communication, 42(2)*, 5–24.

Haney, R. D., Dillon, J., & White, H. A. (1995). The effects of news mix on primary election coverage. *Journal of Mediated Communication, 10*, 21–34.

Hansen, G. J. (2004). *The informational function of communicative sources in presidential campaigns: Effects on issue knowledge and character evaluation*. Unpublished Ph.D. dissertation, University of Missouri.

Hansen, G. J., & Benoit, W. L. (2001). The role of significant policy issues in the 2000 presidential primaries. *American Behavioral Scientist, 44*, 2082–2100.

Hansen, G. J., & Benoit, W. L. (2005). Presidential campaigning on the Web: The influence of candidate World Wide Web Sites in the 2000 general election. *Southern Communication Journal, 70,* 219–229.

Hastorf, A. H., & Cantril, H. (1954). They saw a game; a case study. *The Journal of Abnormal and Social Psychology, 49,* 129–134.

Heller, D. J. (1987). Mail, money, and Machiavelli. *Campaigns & Elections, 8,* 32–34.

Hellweg, S. A., Pfau, M., & Brydon, S. R. (1992). *Televised presidential debates: Advocacy in contemporary America.* New York: Praeger.

Henson, J. R., & Benoit, W. L. (2009). Functional Federalism in political campaign debates. *Publius: The Journal of Federalism, 39,* 696–706. DOI: 10.1093/publius/pjp018.

Herrero, J. C., & Benoit, W. L. (2009). El abuso de los ataques: un análisis funcional de los debates electorales de 2008 a la presidencia del Gobierno [The abuse of attacks: A functional analysis of the 2008 Spanish presidential debates]. *Zer, 14,* 61–81.

Herrnson, P. A. (2004). *Congressional elections: Campaigning at home and in Washington* (4th ed.). Washington, DC: CQ Press.

Hill, R. P. (1989). An exploration of voter responses to political advertisements. *Journal of Advertising, 18,* 14–22.

Hillygus, D. S., & Shields, T. G. (2008). *The persuadable voter: Wedge issues in presidential campaigns.* Princeton, NJ: Princeton University Press.

Hitchon, J. C., & Chang, C. (1995). Effects of gender schematic processing on the reception of political commercials for men and women candidates. *Communication Research, 22,* 430–458.

Hoffmann, R. (1982). Politische Fernsehinterviews [Televised political interviews]. *Reihe Medien in Forschung und Unterricht, 9,* 37–58.

Hofstetter, C. R. (1976). *Bias in the news: Network television coverage of the 1972 election campaign.* Columbus, OH: Ohio State University Press.

Hofstetter, C. R., & Moore, D. W. (1982). Television coverage of presidential primaries. *Journalism Quarterly, 59,* 651–654.

Holbert, R. L., Benoit, W. L., Hansen, G. J., & Wen, W-C. (2002). The role of communication in the formation of an issue-based citizenry. *Communication Monographs, 69,* 296–310.

Holbert, R. L, Benoit, W. L., & McKinney, M. S. (2002). *The role of debate viewing in establishing "enlightened preference" in the 2000 presidential election.* Seoul, South Korea: ICA.

Holbrook, T. M. (1996). *Do campaigns matter?* Thousand Oaks, CA: Sage.

Holden, C. (2019, November 10). Fifty years ago – Spiro Agnew and the "Des Moines" speech. Accessed 12/8/19: https://www.desmoinesregister.com/story/opinion/columnists/2019/11/10/fifty-years-ago-spiro-agnew-and-des-moines-speech/4166207002/

Hollihan, T. A. (2001). *Uncivil wars: Political campaigns in a media age.* Boston, MA: Bedford/St. Martin's.

Holly, W., Kuhn, P. & Puschel, U. (1986). *Politische Fernsehdiskussionen* [Political debates on television]. Tubingen, Germany: Niemeyer.

Holsti, O. (1969). *Content analysis in communication research*. New York: Free Press.
Holt, L. L. (1986). Campaign posters: The 1972 presidential election. *Journal of American Culture, 9*, 65–81.
Holtz-Bacha, C, & Johansson, B. (Eds.). (2017). *Election Posters around the Globe: Political Campaigning in the Public Space*. Chan, Switzerland: Springer.
Hrbkova, L., & Zagrapan, J. (2014). Slovak political debates: Functional theory in a multi-party system. *European Journal of Communication, 29*, 735–744.
Ingraham, C. (2017, April 14). Somebody just put a price tag on the 2016 election. It's a doozy. *Washington Post*. Accessed 1/4/20: https://www.washingtonpost.com/news/wonk/wp/2017/04/14/somebody-just-put-a-price-tag-on-the-2016-election-its-a-doozy/
Internet Live Stats. (2017). *InternetLiveStats*. Accessed 2/14/17: http://www.internetlivestats.com/
Isotalus, P. (2011). Analyzing presidential debates: Functional theory and Finnish political communication culture. *Nordicom Review, 32*, 31–43.
Iyengar, S., & Kinder, D. R. (1987). *News that matters: Television and American opinion*. Chicago, IL: University of Chicago Press.
Jackson, D., & Fritze, J. (2020, October 2). President Trump hospitalized at Walter Reed after testing positive for COVID-19. *USA Today*. Accessed 10/26/20: https://www.usatoday.com/story/news/politics/elections/2020/10/02/trump-heads-walter-reed-hospital-after-positive-covid-19-test/5894256002/
Jacobson, G. C. (1987). *The politics of congressional elections*. New York: Harper Collins.
James, K. E., & Hensel, P. J. (1991). Negative advertising: The malicious strain of comparative advertising. *Journal of Advertising, 20*, 53–69.
Jamieson, J. H. (1992). *Packaging the presidency: A history and criticism of presidential campaign advertising* (2nd ed.). New York: Oxford University Press.
Jamieson, J. H. (1996). *Packaging the presidency: A history and criticism of presidential campaign advertising* (3rd ed.). New York: Oxford University Press.
Jamieson, K. H., & Albarracin, D. (2020). The relation between media consumption and misinformation at the outset of the SARS-CoV-2 pandemic in the US. *Harvard Kennedy School Misinformation Review, 1*, 2–22.
Jamieson, K. H., & Birdsell, D. S. (1988). *Presidential debates: The challenge of creating an informed electorate*. New York: Oxford University Press.
Jamieson, K. H., & Waldman, P. (2001). *Electing the president 2000: The insiders' view*. Philadelphia, PA: University of Pennsylvania Press.
Jamieson, K. H., & Waldman, P. (2003). *The press effect: Politicians, journalists, and the stories that shape the political world*. Oxford, UK: Oxford University Press.
Jamieson, K. H., Waldman, P., & Devitt, J. (1998). Mapping the discourse of the 1996 US presidential general election. *Media, Culture, & Society, 20*, 323–328.
Jamieson, K. H., Waldman, P., & Sherr, S. (2000). Eliminate the negative? Categories of analysis for political advertisements. In J. A. Thurber, C. J. Nelson, & D. A. Dulio (Eds.), *Crowded*

airwaves: Campaign advertising in elections (pp. 44–64). Washington, DC: Brookings Institution.

Jarman, J. W. (2005). Political affiliation and presidential debates: A real-time analysis of the effect of the arguments used in the presidential debates. *American Behavioral Scientist, 49*, 229–242.

Jarvis, S. E. (2004). Partisan patterns in presidential campaign speeches, 1948–2000. *Communication Quarterly, 52*, 403–419.

Jaye, E. (2016, July 14). Three reasons why direct mail is growing. *Campaigns & Elections*. Accessed 11/16/16: https://www.campaignsandelections.com/campaign-insider/three-reasons-why-direct-mail-is-growing

Jenkins, K. (1997). Learning to love those expensive campaigns. *U.S. News and World Report [On-line], 122 (9)*.

Johansson, B. (2014). Negativity in the public space: Comparing a hundred years of negative campaigning on electoral posters in Sweden. In M. J. Canel & K. Voltman (Eds.), *Comparing political communication across time and Space: New studies in an emerging field* (pp. 67–81). London, UK: Palmgrave Macmillan.

Johnson, J. (2021a). *Political rhetoric, social media, and American presidential campaigns*. Lanham, MD: Lexington.

Johnson, T. J. (1993). Filling out the racing form: How the media covered the horse race in the 1988 primaries. *Journalism Quarterly, 70*, 300–310.

Johnson-Cartee, K. S., & Copeland, G. (1989). Southern voters' reactions to negative political ads in the 1986 election. *Journalism Quarterly, 66*, 888–893, 986.

Johnson-Cartee, K. S., & Copeland, G. (1997). *Manipulation of the American voter: Political campaign commercials*. Westport, CT: Praeger.

Johnston, D. D. (1989). Image and issue political information: Message content or interpretation? *Journalism Quarterly, 66*, 379–382.

Johnston, R., Manley, D., Jones, K., & Rohla, R. (2020). The geographical polarization of the American electorate: a country of increasing electoral landslides? *GeoJournal, 85*, 197–204.

Johnston, A. & White, A. B. (1994). Communication styles and female candidates: A study of the political advertising during the 1986 elections. *Journalism Quarterly, 71*, 321–329.

Jones, J. M. (2020, July 6). Trump's job approval rating steady at lower level. *Gallup*. Accessed 7/8/20: https://news.gallup.com/poll/313454/trump-job-approval-rating-steady-lower-level.aspx

Joslyn, R. A. (1980). The content of political spot ads. *Journalism Quarterly, 57*, 92–98.

Jos

Just, M., Crigler, A., & Buhr, T. (1999). Voice, substance, and cynicism in presidential campaign media. *Political Communication, 16*, 25–44.

Just, M., Crigler, A., & Wallach, L. (1990). Thirty seconds or thirty minutes: What viewers learn from spot advertisements and candidate debates. *Journal of Communication, 40*, 120–132.

Kahn, K. F. (1995). Characteristics of press coverage in senate and gubernatorial elections: Information available to voters. *Legislative Studies Quarterly, 20*, 23–35.

Kahn, K. F., & Kenney, P. F. (1999a). Do negative campaigns mobilize or suppress turnout? Clarifying the relationship between negativity and participation. *American Political Science Review, 93,* 877–889.

Kahn, K. F., & Kenney, P. J. (1999b). *The spectacle of U.S. Senate campaigns.* Princeton, NJ: Princeton University Press.

Kaid, L. L. (1997). Effects of the television spots on images of Dole and Clinton. *American Behavioral Scientist, 40,* 1085–1094.

Kaid, L. L. (1999). Comparing and contrasting the styles and effects of political advertising in European democracies. In L. L. Kaid (Ed.), *Television and politics in evolving European democracies* (pp. 219–236). Commack, NY: Nova Science.

Kaid, L. L. (2004). Political advertising. In L. L. Kaid (Ed.), *Handbook of political campaign research* (pp. 155–202). Mahwah, NJ: Erlbaum.

Kaid, L. L., & Boydson, J. (1987). An experimental study of the effectiveness of negative political advertisements. *Communication Quarterly, 35,* 193–201.

Kaid, L. L., & Davidson, D. K. (1986). Elements of videostyle: Candidate presentation through television advertising. In L. L. Kaid, D. Nimmo, & K. R. Sanders (Eds.), *New perspectives on political advertising* (pp. 184–209). Carbondale: Southern Illinois Press.

Kaid, L. L., & Holtz-Bacha, C. (1995). Political advertising across cultures. In L. L. Kaid & C. Holtz-Bacha (Eds.), *Political advertising in Western democracies* (pp. 206–227). Thousand Oaks, CA: Sage.

Kaid, L. L., & Johnston, A. (1991). Negative versus positive television advertising in U.S. presidential campaigns, 1960–1988. *Journal of Communication, 41,* 53–64.

Kaid, L. L., & Johnston, A. (2001). *Videostyle in presidential campaigns Style and content of televised political advertising.* Westport, CT: Praeger.

Kaid, L. L., Leland, C. M., & Whitney, S. (1992). The impact of televised political ads: Evoking viewer responses in the 1988 presidential campaign. *Southern Communication Journal, 57,* 285–295.

Kaid, L. L., McKinney, M., & Tedesco, J. C. (2000). *Civic dialogue in the 1996 presidential campaign: Candidate, media, and public voices.* Cresskill, NJ: Hampton Press.

Kaid, L. L., & Sanders, K. R. (1978). Political television commercials: An experimental study of type and length. *Communication Research, 5,* 57–70.

Kaid, L. L., & Tedesco, J. C. (1999). Presidential candidate presentation: Videostyle in the 1996 presidential spots. In L. L. Kaid & D. G. Bystrom (Eds.), *The electronic election: Perspectives on the 1996 campaign communication* (pp. 209–221). Mahwah, NJ: Erlbaum.

Kamber, V. (1997). *Poison politics: Are negative campaigns destroying democracy?* Cambridge, MA: Perseus.

Kane, T. (1987). The Dewey-Stassen primary debate of 1948: An examination of format for presidential debates. In J. Wenzel (Ed.), *Argument and critical practices* (pp. 249–253). Annandale, VA: Speech Communication Association.

Kaplan, M., Goldstein, K., & Hale, M. (2005, February 15). *Local news coverage of the 2004 campaigns: An analysis of nightly broadcasts in 11 markets.* Accessed 2/15/05: www.localnewsarchive.org.

Kelley, D. (1958). Press coverage of two Michigan congressional elections. *Journalism Quarterly, 35*, 447–449, 503.

Kelley, S., & Mirer, T. W. (1974). The simple act of voting. *American Political Science Review, 68*, 572–591.

Kelly, C. (2020, October 28). White House lists ending Covid-19 pandemic as an accomplishment despite cases spiking to record levels, *CNN*. Accessed 10/29/20: https://www.cnn.com/2020/10/27/politics/white-house-ending-covid-19-pandemic-accomplishment-record-cases-spike/index.html

Kendall, K. E. (2000). *Communication in the presidential primaries: Candidates and the media, 1912–2000.* Westport, CT: Praeger.

Kendall, K. E. (2005). Constructing the primary story: Embedded with the media in New Hampshire. *American Behavioral Scientist, 49*, 157–172.

Kenney, K., & Simpson, C. (1993). Was coverage of the 1988 presidential race by Washington's two major dailies biased? *Journalism Quarterly, 70*, 345–355.

Kern, M. (1989). *30 Second politics: Political advertising in the eighties.* New York: Praeger.

Key, V. O. (1966). *The responsible electorate: Rationality in presidential voting 1936–1960.* Cambridge, MA: Belknap Press of Harvard University Press.

Kiewiet, D. R., & Rivers, D. (1984). A retrospective on retrospective voting. *Political Behavior, 6*, 369–393.

King, A. (2002). Conclusions and implications. In A. King (Ed.), *Leaders' personalities and the outcomes of democratic elections* (pp. 210–221). Oxford, UK: Oxford University Press.

King, E. G. (1990). Thematic coverage of the 1988 presidential primaries: A comparison of *USA Today* and the New York *Times. Journalism Quarterly, 67*, 83–87.

Kirkpatrick, S. A., Lyons, W., & Fitzgerald, M. R. (1975). Candidates, parties, and issues in the American electorate: Two decades of change. *American Politics Quarterly, 3*, 247–283.

Klapper, J. T. (1960). *The effects of mass communication: An analysis of research on the effectiveness and limitations of mass media in influencing the opinions, values, and behavior of their audiences.* Glencoe, IL: Free Press.

Klayman, J., & Ha, Y. W. (1987). Confirmation, disconfirmation, and information in hypothesis testing. *Psychological Review, 94*, 211–228.

Klein, M. W., & Maccoby, N. (1954). Newspaper objectivity in the 1952 campaign. *Journalism Quarterly, 31*, 285–296.

Knapton, S. (2016, January 20). Facebook users have 155 friends. *Telegraph.* Accessed 2/17/17: http://www.telegraph.co.uk/news/science/science-news/12108412/Facebook-users-have-155-friends-but-would-trust-just-four-in-a-crisis.html

Knobloch-Westerwick, S. (2015). *Choice and preference in media use: Advances in selective exposure theory and research.* New York: Routledge.

Kraft, P. W., Lodge, M., & Taber, C. S. (2015). Why people "don't trust the evidence": Motivated reasoning and scientific beliefs. *Annals of the American Society of Political and Social Science, 658*, 121–133.

Kramer, G. H. (1977). Short-term fluctuations in U.S. voting behavior, 1896–1964. *American Political Science Review, 65*, 131–143.

Krosnick, J. & Petty, J. Attitude strength: An overview. In R. Petty & J. Krosnick (Eds.), *Attitude strength: Antecedents and consequenes* (pp. 1–247). Hillsdale, NJ: Lawrence Erlbaum Associates.

Kraus, S. (1996). Winners of the first 1960 televised presidential debate between Kennedy and Nixon. *Journal of Communication, 46(4)*, 78–96.

Kreig, G. (2016, December 22). It's official: Clinton swamps Trump in the popular vote. *CNN*. Accessed 6/2/18: https://www.cnn.com/2016/12/21/politics/donald-trump-hillary-clinton-popular-vote-final-count/index.html

Kruglanski, A., & Webster, D. (1996). Motivated closing of the mind: "Seizing" and "freezing." *Psychological Review, 103*, 263–283.

Lang, A. (1991). Emotion, formal features, and memory for televised political advertisements. In F. Biocca (Eds.), *Television and political advertising* (vol. 1, pp. 221–243). Hillsdale, NJ: Erlbaum.

Lang, K., & Lang, G. E. (1968). *Politics and television*. Chicago, IL: Quadrangle.

Lang, K., & Lang, G. E. (1984). *Politics and television re-viewed*. Beverly Hills, CA: Sage.

Lau, R. L., & Pomper, G. M. (2004). *Negative campaigning: An analysis of U.S. senate campaigns*. Lanham, MD: Rowman & Littlefield.

Lau, R. R., Sigelman, L., Heldman, C., & Babbitt, P. R. (1999). The effectiveness of negative political advertising: A meta-analytic assessment. *American Political Science Review, 93*, 851–876.

Lawless, J. (2012). *Becoming a candidate*. Cambridge, UK: Cambridge University Press.

Lazarsfeld, P. F., & Merton, R. K. (1948). Mass communication, popular taste, and organized social action. In L. Bryson (Ed.), *The communication of ideas: A series of addresses* (pp. 95–118). New York, NY: Harper.

Lazarsfeld, P. F., Berelson, B., & Gaudet, H. (1948). *The people's choice: How the voter makes up his mind in a presidential campaign* (2nd ed.). New York: Columbia University Press.

Lear Center. (2003). *Local TV news coverage of the 2002 general election*. Accessed 9/1/03: www.localnewsarchive.org.

Lee, J., & Xu, W. (2018). The more attacks, the more retweets: Trump's and Clinton's agenda-setting on Twitter. *Public Relations Review, 44*, 201–213.

Lieberman, D. (2004, August 18). Cable, satellite, Net grab chunk of election ad bucks. *USA Today*, p. B1.

Lemert, J. B., Elliot, W. R., Bernstein, J. M., Rosenberg, W. L., & Nestvold, K. J. (1991). *News verdicts, the debates, and presidential campaigns*. New York: Praeger.

Lenhart, A. (2015, August 6). Teens, technology, and friendships. PewResearchCenter. Accessed 2/15/17: http://www.pewinternet.org/2015/08/06/teens-technology-and-friendships/

Levine, M. A. (1995). *Presidential campaigns and elections: Issues and images in the media age*. Itasea, IL: Peacock Publishers.

Levine, S. (2020, Marcy 30). Trump says Republicans would "never" be elected again if it was easier to vote. *The Guardian*. Accessed 6/18/20: https://www.theguardian.com/us-news/2020/mar/30/trump-republican-party-voting-reform-coronavirus

Lewis-Beck, M. S., & Rice, T. W. (1984). Forecasting presidential elections: A comparison of naive models. *Political Behavior, 6*, 9–21.

Lichter, S. R., Amundson, D., & Noyes, R. (1988). *The video campaign: Network coverage of the 1988 primaries*. Lanham, MD: American Enterprise Institute.

Lichter, S. R., & Noyes, R. E. (1995). *Good intentions make bad news: Why Americans hate campaign journalism*. Lanham, MD: Rowman & Littlefield.

Lichter, S. R., Noyes, R. E., & Kaid, L. L. (1999). No news or negative news: How the networks nixed the '96 campaign. In L. L. Kaid & D. G. Bystrom (Eds.), *The electronic election: Perspectives on the 1996 campaign communication* (pp. 3–13). Mahwah, NJ: Erlbaum.

Lichterman, J. (2015, July 14). New Pew data: More Americans are getting news on Facebook and Twitter. *Nieman Lab*. Accessed 8/1/16: http://www.niemanlab.org/2015/07/new-pew-data-more-americans-are-getting-news-on-facebook-and-twitter/

Lippmann, W. (1922). *Public opinion*. New York, NY: Macmillan.

Lodge, M., & Taber, C. (2000). Three steps toward a theory of motivated political reasoning. In A. Lupia, M. D. McCubbins, & S. L. Popkin (Eds.), *Elements of reasoning: Cognition, choice, and the bounds of rationality* (pp. 183–213). Cambridge, UK: Cambridge University Press.

Lodge, M., & Taber, C. S. (2013). *The rationalizing voter*. Cambridge, UK: Cambridge University Press.

Lord, C. G., Ross, L., & Lepper, M. R. (1979). Biased assimilation and attitude polarization: The effects of prior theories on subsequently considered evidence. *Journal of Personality and Social Psychology, 37*, 2098–2109.

Lowry, B. (1997, September 2). Cable stations gather strength. *LA Times*. Accessed 12/12/16: http://articles.latimes.com/1997/sep/02/entertainment/ca-28033

Lowden, N. B., Anderson, P. A., Dozier, D. M., & Lauzen, M. M. (1994). Media use in the primary election: A secondary medium model. *Communication Research, 21*, 293–304.

Luntz, F. I. (1988). *Candidates, consultants, and campaigns: The style and substance of American electioneering*. Oxford, UK: Basil Blackwell.

Mahtesian, C. (2016, June 15). What are the swing states in 2016? *Politico*. Accessed 5/6/20: https://www.politico.com/blogs/swing-states-2016-election/2016/06/what-are-the-swing-states-in-2016-list-224327.

Maier, J., & Jansen, C. (2015). When do candidates attack in election campaigns? Exploring the determinants of negative candidate messages in German televised debates. *Party Politics, 23*, 1–11.

Mantler, G., & Whiteman, D. (1995). Attention to candidates and issues in newspaper coverage of 1992 presidential campaign. *Newspaper Research Journal, 16*, 14–28.

Marcus, G. E., Neuman, W. R., & MacKuen, M. (2000). *Affective intelligence and political judgment.* Chicago, IL: University of Chicago Press.

Mark, M. (2019, November 15). The number of Americans watching Trump's impeachment hearings on TV pales in comparison to Nixon. Accessed 11/25/19: https://www.businessinsider.com/trump-impeachment-tv-viewership-comparisons-2019-11

Marks, P. (2000, July 21). Candidates invited to a late-night debate. *New York Times*, p. A15.

Markus, G. B. (1988). The impact of personal and national economic conditions on the presidential vote: A polled cross-sectional analysis. *American Journal of Political Science, 32*, 137–154.

Markus, G. B., & Converse, P. E. (1979). A dynamic simultaneous equation model of electoral choice. *American Political Science Review, 73*, 1055–1070.

Martel, M. (1983). *Political campaign debates: Issues, strategies, and tactics.* New York: Longman.

Matera, F. R., & Salwen, M. B. (1996). Unwieldy questions? Circuitous answers? Journalists as panelists in presidential election debates. *Journal of Broadcasting & Electronic Media, 40*, 309–317.

Mayer, W. G., & Busch, A. E. (2004). *The front-loading problem in presidential nominations.* Washington, DC: Brookings Institution.

McClure, R. D., & Patterson, T. E. (1974). Television news and political advertising: The impact of exposure on voter beliefs. *Communication Research, 1*, 3–21.

McCombs, M. (2004). *Setting the agenda: The mass media and public opinion.* Cambridge, UK: Polity.

McCombs, M. E., & Shaw, D. L. (1972). The agenda setting function of the mass media. *Public Opinion Quarterly, 36*, 176–187.

McCombs, M., Shaw, D. L., & Weaver, D. (1997). *Communication and democracy: Exploring the intellectual frontiers in agenda-setting theory.* Mahwah, NJ: Lawrence Erlbaum.

McCullough, J. L., & Ostrom, T. M. (1974). Repetition of highly similar messages and attitude change. *Journal of Applied Psychology, 59*, 395–397.

McGuire, W. J. (1986). The myth of massive media impact: Savaging and salvaging. In G Comstock (Ed.), *Public communication and behavior* (pp. 173–257). Orlando, FL: Academic Press.

McHale, J. P., & Benoit, W. L. (2003). *A functional analysis of presidential campaign discourse in television talk show subgenres.* Unpublished manuscript.

McKinney, M. S., & Carlin, D. B. (2004). Political campaign debates. In L. L. Kaid (Ed.), *Handbook of political campaign research* (pp. 203–234). Mahwah, NJ: Erlbaum.

Meadow, R. G. (1973). Cross-media comparison of coverage of the 1972 presidential campaign. *Journalism Quarterly, 50*, 482–488.

Meadow, R. G., & Sigelman, L. (1982). Some effects and non-effects of campaign commercials: An experimental study. *Political Behavior, 4*, 163–175.

Meffert, M. F., Chung, S., Joiner, A. M., Waks, L., & Garst, J. (2006). The effects of negativity and motivated information processing during a political campaign. *Journal of Communication, 56*, 27–51.

Mehrabian, A., & Ferris, S. R. (1967). Inference of attitudes from nonverbal communication in two channels. *Journal of Consulting Psychology, 13*, 248–252.

Merritt, S. (1984). Negative political advertising: Some empirical findings. *Journal of Advertising, 13*, 27–38.

Miller, G A. (1956). The magic number seven plus or minus two: Some limits on our capacity to process information. *Psychological Review, 63*, 81–97.

Miller, R. E., & Richey, W. M. (1980). The effects of a campaign brochure "drop" in a county-level race for state's attorney. *Communication Yearbook, 4*, 483–495.

Millspaugh, M. (1949). Baltimore newspapers and the presidential election. *Public Opinion Quarterly, 13*, 122–123.

Monroe, K. R. (1979). Econometric analyses of electoral behavior: A critical review. *Political Behavior, 1*, 137–173.

Montellaro, Z. (2020, August 13). Trump says he opposes USPS funding in an effort to block mail-in voting. *Politico*. Accessed 8/30/20: https://www.politico.com/news/2020/08/13/trump-opposes-usps-funding-394692

Moore, D. W. (2001, September 24). Bush job approval highest in Gallup history: Widespread support for war on terrorism. *Gallup Polls*. Accessed 1/19/20: https://news.gallup.com/poll/4924/bush-job-approval-highest-gallup-history.aspx

Morin, R. (2004, October 28). Don't ask me; As fewer cooperate on polls, criticism and questions mount. *Washington Post*, p. C01.

Munro, G. D., Ditto, P. H., Lockhart, L. K., Fagerlin, A., Gready, M., & Peterson, E. (2002). Biased assimilation of sociopolitical arguments: Evaluating the 1996 U.S. presidential debate. *Journal of Basic and Applied Social Psychology, 24*, 15–26.

Nagel, F., Maurer, M., & Reinemann, C. (2012). Is there a visual dominance in political communication? How verbal, visual, and vocal communication shape viewers' impressions of political candidates. *Journal of Communication, 62*, 833–850.

Nai, A., & Walter, A. S. (2015). The war of words: The art of negative campaigning. In Nai & Walter (Eds.), *New perspectives on negative campaigning: Why attack politics matter* (pp. 3–33). Colchester, UK: ECPR.

Nielsen. (2016, March 17). Are Americans watching the Republican or Democratic debates – or both? Accessed 11/12/16: http://www.nielsen.com/us/en/insights/news/2016/are-americans-watching-the-republican-or-democratic-debates-or-both.html

Neville-Shepard, R. (2014). Presidential campaign announcements: A third-party variant. *Southern Communication Journal, 79*, 130–146.

New York Times. (2017, February 10). Presidential election results: Donald Trump wins. Accessed 2/17/17: http://www.nytimes.com/elections/results/president

Nagourney, A. (2003, October 6). The California Recall: Political memo; Schwarzenegger win could have downside for Bush. *New York Times*, p. A13.

Napolitan, J. (1972). *The election game and how to win it*. Garden City, NY: Doubleday & Company.

Newman, W. R., Marcus, G. E., Crigler, A. N., & MacKuen, M. (2007). *The affect effect: Dynamics of emotion in political thinking and behavior*. Chicago: University of Chicago Press. Nevius, C. W. (2004, October 19). Young voters discovering campaign. *San Francisco Chronicle*, p. B1.

Newhagen, J. E., & Reeves, B. (1991). Emotion and memory responses for negative political advertising: A study of television commercials used in the 1988 presidential election. In F. Biocca (Ed.), *Television and political advertising* (vol. 1, pp. 197–220). Hillsdale, NJ: Erlbaum.

Newspaper Association of America. (2002). *Daily newspaper readership trends*. Available: http://www.naa.org/marketscope/databank/tdnpr1299.htm

Nie, N. H., Verba, S., & Petrocik, J. R. (1999). *The changing American voter* (enlarged ed.). San Jose: toExcel in arrangement with Harvard University Press.

Nimmo, D. D., & Savage, R. L. (1976). *Candidates and their images*. Pacific Palisades, CA: Goodyear.

Norrander, B. (2000). *Candidate attrition during the presidential nominating system*. Paper presented at the Joan Shorenstein Center on the Press, Politics, and Public Policy Roundtable, Harvard University. Cited in Patterson, 2003, p. 228n.

Number of ads aired for 2016 U.S. presidential election, by candidate as of May, 2016. (2016). *Statista*. Accessed 6/29/16: http://www.statista.com/statistics/564053/number-of-ads-aired-2016-us-presidential-election-by-candidate/

Number of ads aired for 2016 U.S. presidential election by outside groups as of May, 2016. (2016). *Statista*. Accessed 6/29/16: http://www.statista.com/statistics/564477/number-of-ads-aired-2016-us-presidential-election-by-outside-groups/

Oppenheim, M. (2020, May 24). Biden slams Trump in new campaign ad for playing golf over Memorial Day weekend as "nearly 100,000 Americans have died." *Insider*. Accessed 1/29/22: https://www.businessinsider.com/biden-slams-trump-playing-golf-covid-19-death-toll-rises-2020-5.

Osterhouse, R. A, & Brock, T. C. (1970). Distraction increases yielding to propaganda by inhibiting counterarguing. *Journal of Personality and Social Psychology, 15*, 344–358.

Ostroff, D. H., & Sandell, K. (1984). Local station coverage of campaigns: A tale of two cities in Ohio. *Journalism Quarterly, 61*, 346–351.

Paatelainen, L., Croucher, S., & Benoit, W. L. (2016). A functional analysis of the Finnish 2012 presidential elections. *Studies in Media and Communication, 4*, 70–80.

Page, B. I. (1978). *Choices and echoes in presidential elections: Rational man and electoral democracy*. Chicago, IL: University of Chicago Press.

Page, B. I., & Jones, C. C. (1979). Reciprocal effects of policy preferences, party loyalties, and the vote. *American Political Science Review, 73*, 1071–1089.

Page, S. (2004, March 30). TV ads score big in Bush turnaround: Kerry's wide lead erased in states targeted by both. *USA Today*, p. 4A.

Palmer, N. A. (1997). *The New Hampshire primary and the American electoral process*. Westport, CT: Praeger.

Patterson, T. E. (1980). *The mass media election: How Americans choose their president*. New York: Praeger.

Patterson, T. E. (1994). *Out of order*. New York: Random House, Vintage Books.

Patterson, T. E. (2003). *The vanishing voter: Public involvement in an age of uncertainty*. New York: Random House.

Patterson, T. E., & McClure, R. D. (1973). Political advertising on television: Spot commercials in the 1972 presidential election. *Maxwell Review, 57*–69.

Patterson, T. E., & McClure, R. D. (1976). *The unseeing eye: The myth of television power in national politics*. New York: Putnam.

Payne, J. G., & Baukus, R. A. (1988). Trend analysis of the 1984 GOP senatorial spots. *Political Communication and Persuasion, 5*, 161–177.

Perloff, R. M., & Brock, T. C. (1980). "And thinking makes it so": Cognitive responses to persuasion. In M. E. Roloff & G. R. Miller (Eds.), *Persuasion: New directions in theory and research* (pp. 67–99). Beverly Hills, CA: Sage.

Peterson, D. A. M., & Djupe, P. A. (2005). When primary campaigns go negative: The determinants of campaign negativity. *Political Research Quarterly, 58*, 45–54.

Petrocik, J. R. (1996). Issue ownership in presidential elections, with a 1980 case study. *American Journal of Political Science, 40*, 825–850.

Petrocik, J. R. (2004). Hard facts: The media and elections with a look at 2000 and 2002. In J. A. Thurber & C. J. Nelson (Eds.), *Campaigns and elections American style* (2nd ed., pp. 129–147). Boulder, CO: Westview.

Petrocik, J. R., Benoit, W. L., & Hansen, G. L. (2003–2004). Issue ownership and presidential campaigning, 1952–2000. *Political Science Quarterly, 118*, 599–626.

Petty, R. E., & Cacioppo, J. T. (1979). Issue involvement can increase or decrease persuasion by enhancing message-relevant cognitive processes. *Journal of Personality and Social Psychology, 37*, 1915–1926.

Petty, R. E., & Cacioppo, J. T. (1981). *Attitudes and persuasion: Classic and contemporary approaches*. Dubuque, IA: W. C. Brown.

Petty, R. E., & Cacioppo, J. T. (1984). The effects of involvement on responses to argument quantity and quality: Central and peripheral routes to persuasion. *Journal of Personality and Social Psychology, 46*, 69–81.

Petty, R. E., & Cacioppo, J. T. (1986a). *Communication and persuasion: Central and peripheral routes to attitude change*. New York: Springer-Verlag.

Petty, R., & Cacioppo, J. (1986b). The Elaboration Likelihood Model of persuasion. In L. Berkowitz (Ed.), *Advances in experimental social psychology* (pp. 123–205). New York: Academic Press.

Petty, R. E., Cacioppo, J. T., & Goldman, R. (1981). Personal involvement as a determinant of argument-based persuasion. *Journal of Personality and Social Psychology, 41*, 847–855.

Petty, R. E., Wells, G. L., & Brock, T. C. (1976). Distraction can enhance or reduce yielding to propaganda: Thought disruption versus effort justification. *Journal of Personality and Social Psychology, 34*, 874–884.

Pew Research Center. (2016, February 3). 2016 will be the most diverse in U.S. history. Acccessed 2/17/17: http://www.pewresearch.org/fact-tank/2016/02/03/2016-electorate-will-be-the-most-diverse-in-u-s-history/

Pfau, M., & Burgoon, M. (1989). The efficacy of issue and character attack message strategies in political campaign communication. *Communication Reports, 2*, 53–61.

Pfau, M., Cho, J., & Chong, K. (2001). Communication forms in U.S. presidential campaigns: Influences on candidate perceptions and the democratic process. *Harvard International Journal of Press/Politics, 5(4)*, 88–105.

Pfau, M., & Kenski, H. C. (1990). *Attack politics: Strategy and defense.* New York: Praeger.

Pfau, M., Kenski, H. C., Nitz, M., & Sorenson, J. (1990). Efficacy of inoculation strategies in promotion resistance to political attack messages: Application to direct mail. *Communication Monographs, 57*, 25–43.

Pfau, M., Parrott, R., & Lindquist, B. (1992). An expectancy theory explanation of the effectiveness of political attack television spots: A case study. *Journal of Applied Communication Research, 20*, 235–253.

Phillips, A. (2016, November 17). Is split-ticket officially dead? *Washington Post.* Accessed 2/19/17: https://www.washingtonpost.com/news/the-fix/wp/2016/11/17/is-split-ticket-voting-officially-dead/?utm_term=.121ef51d6208

Pier, P. M. (2002). *He said, she said: A functional analysis of gender differences in political campaign messages.* Unpublished doctoral dissertation, University of Missouri.

Pious, R. M. (2006). The presidency and the nominating process: Politics and power. In M. Nelson (Ed.), *The presidency and the political system* (8th ed., pp. 195–218). Washington, DC: CQ Press.

Pomper, G. M. (1975). *Voters' choice: Varieties of American electoral behavior.* New York: Dodd, Mead, & Company.

Popkin, S. L. (1994). *The reasoning voter: Communication and persuasion in presidential campaigns* (2nd ed.). Chicago, IL: University of Chicago Press.

Popkin, S. L., Gorman, J., Smith, J., & Phillips, C. (1976). Comment: toward an investment theory of voting behavior: What have you done for me lately? *American Political Science Review, 70*, 779–805.

Prater, M. (2020). Bookmark ASAP. Accessed 4/9/20: https://blog.hubspot.com/marketing/google-search-statistics

Prior, M. (2007). *Post-broadcast democracy: How media choice increases inequality in political involvement and polarizes elections.* Cambridge, UK: Cambridge University Press.

Procter, D. E., & Schenck-Hamlin, W. J. (1996). Form and variations in negative political advertising. *Communication Research Reports, 13*, 147–156.

Protess, D., & McCombs, M. E. (Eds.). (1991) *Agenda setting: Readings on media, public opinion and policy making.* Lawrence Erlbaum.

Racine Group. (2002). White paper on televised political campaign debates. *Argumentation and Advocacy, 38*, 199–218.

Ranney, A. (1983). *Channels of power: The impact of television on American politics.* New York: Basic Books.

Rappeport, A. (2016, June 21). Donald Trump's self-funding includes payments to family and his companies. *New York Times.* Accessed 5/13/20: https://www.nytimes.com/2016/06/22/us/politics/donald-trump-self-funding-payments.html

Redlawsk, D. P. (2006). Feeling politics: New research into emotion and politics. In D. P. Redlawsk (Ed.), *Feeling politics: Emotion in political information processing* (pp. 1–10). New York: Palgrave.

Reilley, C. (1987). Direct mail on target. *Campaigns & Elections, 6*, 36–40.

Reinhold, R. (1076, October 30). Demand for clues and data spurs proliferation of polls. *New York Times.* Accessed 8/12/21: https://www.nytimes.com/1976/10/30/archives/demand-for-clues-and-data-spurs-proliferation-of-polls.html

Reints, R. (2019, October 10). Five states have already canceled GOP primaries. Here's what you should know. *Fortune.* Accessed 4/15/20: https://fortune.com/2019/10/10/trump-2020-republican-primaries-cancelled/

Robinson, M. J. (1980). Media coverage in the primary campaign of 1976. In W. Crotty (Ed.), *The party symbol: Readings on political parties* (pp. 178–191). San Francisco, CA: Freeman.

Robinson, M. J., & Lichter, S. R. (1991). "The more things change … ": Network news coverage of the 1988 presidential nomination races. In E. M. Buell & L. Sigelman (Eds.), *Nominating the president* (pp. 196–212). Knoxville, TN: University of Tennessee Press.

Roddy, B. L., & Garramone, G. M. (1988). Appeals and strategies of negative political advertising. *Journal of Broadcasting & Electronic Media, 32*, 415–427.

Sandell, K. (1994). How electronic media approach campaign coverage. In G. H. Stempel (Ed.), *The practice of political communication* (pp. 50–70). Englewood Cliffs, NJ: Prentice-Hall.

Scheufele, D. A. (2000). Agenda-setting, priming, and framing revisited: Another look at cognitive effects of political communication. *Mass Communication & Society, 3*, 297–316.

Schudson, M. (1995). *The power of news.* Cambridge, MA: Harvard University Press.

Senate Results. (2020, November 13). *CNN.* Accessed 11/13/20: https://www.cnn.com/election/2020/results/senate

Serini, S. A., Powers, A. A., & Johnson, S. (1998). Of horse race and policy issues: A study of gender in coverage of a gubernatorial election by two major metropolitan newspapers. *Journalism & Mass Communication Quarterly, 75*, 194–204.

Shaw, D. R. (1999a). The effect of TV ads and candidate appearances on statewide presidential votes, 1988–96. *American Political Science Review, 93*, 345–362.

Shaw, D. R. (1999b). A study of presidential campaign event effects from 1952 to 1992. *Journal of Politics, 61*, 387–422.

Shaw, D. R. (2001). Communicating and electing. In R. P. Hart & D. R. Shaw (Eds.), *Communicating in U.S. elections: New agendas* (pp. 1–27). Lanham, MD: Rowman & Littlefield.

Shaw, D., & McCombs, M. E. (Eds.) (1977). *The emergence of American political issues: The agenda setting function of the press.* St. Paul, MN: West.

Shea, D. M. (1996). *Campaign craft: The strategies, tactics, and art of political campaign management.* Westport, CT: Praeger.

Shearer, E. (2018, December 10). Social media outpaces print newspapers in the U.S. as a news source. *Pew Research Center.* Accessed 2/5/20: https://www.pewresearch.org/fact-tank/2018/12/10/social-media-outpaces-print-newspapers-in-the-u-s-as-a-news-source/

Shen, F. (2012). Informational/transformational appeals in political advertising: An analysis of the advertising strategies of 2010 U.S. gubernatorial campaigns. *Journal of Nonprofit & Public Sector Marketing, 24*, 43–64.

Shen, I., & Benoit, W. L. (2016). 2012 presidential campaign and social media: A functional analysis of major candidates' Facebook public pages. *Midsouth Political Science Review, 17*, 53–80.

Shepsle, K. A. (1972). The strategy of ambiguity: Uncertainty and electoral consequences. *American Political Science Review, 66*, 555–565.

Shoemaker, P. J., & Reese, S. D. (1991). *Mediating the message: Theories of influences on mass media content.* New York: Longman.

Sides, J., & Vavrek, L. (2013). *The gamble: Choice and chance in the 2012 presidential election.* Princeton, NJ: Princeton University Press.

Sigelman, L., & Buell, E. H. (2003). You take the high road and I'll take the low road? The interplay of attack strategies and tactics in presidential campaigns. *Journal of Politics, 65*, 518–531.

Sigelman, L., & Buell, E. H. (2004). Avoidance or engagement? Issue convergence in U.S. presidential campaigns, 1960–2000. *American Journal of Political Science, 48*, 650–661.

Sigelman, L., & Bullock, D. (1991). Candidates, issues, horse races, and hoopla: Presidential campaign coverage, 1988–1988. *American Politics Quarterly, 19*, 5–32.

Simon, A. F. (2002). *The winning message: Candidate behavior, campaign discourse, and democracy.* Cambridge, UK: Cambridge University Press.

Sinclair, J. R. (1995). Reforming television's role in American political campaigns: rationale for the elimination of paid political advertisements. *Communications and the Law, 17*, 65–97.

Sinclair, K. (1982). "Horserace" vs. "Substance" in coverage of elections by British prestige press. *Journalism Quarterly, 59*, 598–602.

Skaperdas, S., & Gofman, B. (1995). Modeling negative campaigning. *American Political Science Review, 89*, 49–61.

Smith, C. A. (1990). *Political communication.* San Diego, CA: Harcourt Brace Jovanovich.

Smith, C. A. (2015). *Presidential campaign communication* (2nd ed.). Malden, MA: Polity.
Sniderman, P. M. (2000). Taking sides: A fixed choice theory of political reasoning. In A. Lupia, M. D. McCubbins, & S. L. Popkin (Eds.), *Elements of reason: Cognition, choice, and the bounds of rationality* (pp. 1–20). Cambridge, UK: Cambridge University Press.
Sniderman, P. M., Brody, R. A., & Tetlock, P. E. (1991). The role of heuristics in political reasoning: A theory sketch. In P. M. Sniderman, R. A. Brody, & P. E. Tetlock, (Eds.), *Reasoning and choice: Explorations in political psychology* (pp. 14–30). Cambridge, UK: Cambridge University Press.
Sniderman, P. M., Glaser, J. M., & Griffin, R. (1991). Information and electoral choice. In P. M. Sniderman, R. A. Brady, & P. E. Tetlock (Eds.), *Reasoning and choice: Explorations in political psychology* (pp. 164–178). Cambridge, UK: Cambridge University Press.
Statista. (2017). Percentage of U.S. population with a social media profile from 2008 to 2016. Accessed 1/15/17: https://www.statista.com/statistics/273476/percentage-of-us-population-with-a-social-network-profile/
Statista. (2019a). Internet usage in the United States – Statistics & facts. Accessed 4/9/20: https://www.statista.com/topics/2237/internet-usage-in-the-united-states/
Statista. (2019b). Twitter: Number of monthly active U.S. users 2010–2019, Accessed 6/6/19: https://www.statista.com/statistics/274564/monthly-active-twitter-users-in-the-united-states/
Steele, C. A., & Barnhurst, K. G. (1996). The journalism of opinion: Network news coverage of U.S. presidential campaigns, 1968–1988. *Critical Studies in Mass Communication, 13*, 187–209.
Stein, K. A., & Benoit, W. L. (2021). A Functional Analysis of 2016 non-presidential campaign tweets. *American Behavioral Scientist, 65*, 432–447.
Stelter, B. (2015). Fox's GOP debate had record 24 million viewers. *CNN*. Accessed 6/15/16: http://money.cnn.com/2015/08/07/media/gop-debate-fox-news-ratings/
Stelter, B. (2018, January 17). Trump averages a "fake" insult every day. Really. We counted. *CNN Business*. Accessed 12/6/19: https://money.cnn.com/2018/01/17/media/president-trump-fake-news-count/index.html.
Stelzner, H. G. (1971). Humphrey and Kennedy court West Virginia, May 3, 1960. *Southern Speech Journal, 37*, 21–33.
Stempel, G. H. (1961). The prestige press covers the 1960 presidential campaign. *Journalism Quarterly, 38*, 157–163.
Stempel, G. H. (1965). The prestige press in two presidential elections. *Journalism Quarterly, 42*, 15–21.
Stempel, G. H. (1969). The prestige press meets the third party challenge. *Journalism Quarterly, 46*, 699–706.
Stempel, G. H. (1994). Print media campaign coverage. In G. H. Stempel (Ed.), *The practice of political communication* (pp. 40–49). Englewood Cliffs, NJ: Prentice Hall.
Stempel, G. H., & Windhauser, J. W. (1984). The prestige press revisited: Coverage of the 1980 presidential campaign. *Journalism Quarterly, 61*, 49–55.

Stempel, G. H., & Windhauser, J. W. (1989). Coverage by the prestige press of the 1988 presidential campaign. *Journalism Quarterly, 66*, 894–896, 919.

Stempel, G. H., & Windhauser, J. W. (1991). Newspaper coverage of the 1984 and 1988 campaigns. In G. H. Stempel & J. W. Windhauser (Eds.), *The media in the 1984 and 1988 presidential campaigns* (pp. 13–66). New York: Greenwood Press.

Stewart, C. J. (1975). Voter perception of mud-slinging in political communication. *Central States Speech Journal, 26*, 279–286.

Stevens, L., & Fiske, S. (1995). Motivation and cognition in social life: A social survival guide. *Social Cognition, 13*, 189–214.

Stimson, J. A. (1999). *Public opinion in America: Moods, cycles, and swings* (2nd ed.). Boulder, CO: Westview Press.

Stovall, J. G. (1982). Foreign policy issue coverage in the 1980 presidential campaign. *Journalism Quarterly, 59*, 531–540.

Stovall, J. G. (1988). Coverage of 1984 presidential campaign. *Journalism Quarterly, 65*, 443–449, 484.

Sullivan, J., & Sapir, E. V. (2012). Modeling negative campaign advertising: Evidence from Taiwan. *Asian Journal of Communication, 22*, 289–303.

Taber, C. S., Cann, D., & Kucsova, S. (2009). The motivated processing of political arguments. *Political Behavior, 31*, 137–155.

Taber, C. S., & Lodge, M. (2006). Motivated skepticism in the evaluation of political beliefs. *American Journal of Political Science, 50*, 755–769.

Tak, J., Kaid, L. L., & Lee, S. (1997). A cross-cultural study of political advertising in the United States and Korea. *Communication Research, 24*, 423–430.

Taylor, H. (2003, February 5). Those with Internet access continue to grow but at a slower rate. *Harris Interactive*. Accessed 7/5/03: http://www.harrisinteractive.com/harris_poll/index.asp?PID=356

Taylor, J., & Jensen, E. (2004, July 28). The Democratic National Convention: TV ratings dip sharply from 2000. *Los Angeles Times*, p. A13.

Tetlock, P. E. (1985). Accountability: A social check on the fundamental attribution error. *Social Psychology Quarterly, 48*, 227–238.

36 days: The complete chronicle of the 2000 presidential election crisis. (2001). New York: Times Books.

Thorson, E., Christ, W. G., & Caywood, C. (1991). Effects of issue-image strategies, attack and support appeals, music, and visual content in political commercials. *Journal of Broadcasting and Electronic Media, 35*, 465–486.

Tidmarch, C. M., Hyman, L. J., & Sorkin, J. E. (1984). Press issue agendas in the 1982 congressional and gubernatorial election campaigns. *Journal of Politics, 46*, 226–242.

Traugott, M. W. (1985). The media and the nominating process. In G. Grassmuck (Ed.), *Before nomination: Our primary nominating problems* (pp. 101–115). Washington, DC: American Enterprise Institute.

Traugott, M. W., & Lavrakas, P. J. (2004). *The voter's guide to election polls* (3rd ed.). Lanham, MD: Rowman & Littlefield.

Trent, J. S. (1978). Presidential surfacing: The ritualistic and crucial first act. *Communication Monographs, 45*, 281–292.

Trent, J. D., & Trent, J. S. (1974). The rhetoric of the challenger: George Stanley McGovern. *Central States Speech Journal, 25*, 11–18.

Trent, J. D., & Trent, J. S. (1995). The incumbent and his challengers: The problem of adapting to prevailing conditions. In K. E. Kendall (Ed.), *Presidential campaign discourse: Strategic communication problems* (pp. 69–92). Albany: State University of New York Press.

Trent, J. S., & Friedenberg, R. V. (1991). *Political campaign communication: Principles and practices* (2nd ed.). New York: Praeger.

Trent, J. S., & Friedenberg, R. V. (2000). *Political campaign communication: Principles and practices* (4th ed.). Westport, CT: Praeger.

Trent, J. S., Mongeau, P. A., Trent, J. D., Kendall, K. E., & Cushing, R. B. (1993). The ideal candidate. *American Behavioral Scientist, 37*, 225–239.

Trent, J. S., Short-Thompson, C., Mondeau, P. A., Nusz, A. K., & Trent, J. D. (2001). Image, media bias, and voter characteristics. *American Behavioral Scientist, 44*, 2101–2124.

Trent, J. S., Short-Thompson, C., Mongeau, P. A., Metzler, M. S., & Trent, J. D. (2005). The idealized presidential candidate: A vision over time. *American Behavioral Scientist, 49*, 130–156.

Trent, J. S., Trent, J. D., Mongeau, P. A., & Short-Thompson, C. (1997). The ideal candidate revisited. *American Behavioral Scientist, 40*, 1001–1019.

Tucker, D. R. (2017, July 31). How the repeal of the Fairness Doctrine gave us Donald Trump. *Washington Monthly*. Accessed 1/4/19: https://washingtonmonthly.com/2017/07/31/how-the-repeal-of-the-fairness-doctrine-gave-us-donald-trump/

Tversky, A., & Kahneman, D. (1974). Judgment under uncertainty: Heuristics and biases. *Science, 185*, 1124–1131.

U.S. Census Bureau. (2011, November). Congressional apportionment. Accessed 1/15/17: https://www.census.gov/prod/cen2010/briefs/c2010br-08.pdf.

U.S. Election Results 2020: Joe Biden defeats Donald Trump to win presidency. *CNN*. Accessed 11/16/20: https://www.theguardian.com/us-news/ng-interactive/2020/nov/16/us-election-results-2020-joe-biden-donald-trump-presidential-electoral-college-votes

Vancil, D. L., & Pendell, S. D. (1987). The myth of viewer-listener disagreement in the first Kennedy-Nixon debate. *Central States Speech Journal, 38*, 16–27.

Vavreck, L. (2001). The reasoning voter meets the strategic candidate: Signals and specificity in campaign advertising, 1998. *American Politics Research, 29*, 507–529.

Vermeer, J. P. (1987). Congressional campaign coverage in rural districts. In J. P. Vermeer (Ed.), *Campaigns in the news: Mass media and congressional elections* (pp. 77–89). New York: Greenwood Press.

Vidmar, N., & Rokeach, M. (1974). Archie Bunker's bigotry: A study in selective perception and exposure. *Journal of Communication, 24*, 36–47.

Vliegenthart, R. (2012). The professionalization of political communication? A longitudinal analysis of Dutch election campaign posters. *American Behavioral Scientist, 56*, 135–150.

Vogel, K. P. (2016, January 28). Record-setting 2016 spending spree reaches beyond ads. *Politico.* Accessed 11/16/16: http://www.politico.com/story/2016/01/spending-2016-campaign-218390

Voter turnout in United States presidential elections. (2022). *Wikipedia.* Accessed 2/23/22: https://en.wikipedia.org/wiki/Voter_turnout_in_United_States_presidential_elections

Wanta, W. (1997). *The public and the national agenda: How people learn about important issues.* Mahwah, NJ: Lawrence Erlbaum.

Warner, B. R., & McKinney, M. S. (2013). To unite and divide: The polarizing effect of presidential debates. *Communication Studies, 64*, 508–527.

Warner, B. R., McKinney, M. S., Bramlett, J. C., Jennings, F. J., & Funk, M. E. (2020). Reconsidering partisanship as a constraint on the persuasive effects of debates. *Communication Monographs, 87*, 137–157.

Wasserman, D. P. (1999). The local contours of campaign coverage: State newspapers and the 1988 Super Tuesday campaign. *Communication Research, 26*, 701–725.

Watson, D., Clark, L. A., & Tellegen, A. (1988). Development and validation of brief measures of positive and negative affect: The PANAS scales. *Journal of Personality and Social Psychology, 54*, 1073–1070.

Wattenberg, M. P. (1991). *The rise of candidate-centered politics: Presidential elections of the 1980s.* Cambridge, MA: Harvard University Press.

Wattenberg, M. P. (1998). *The decline of American political parties, 1952–1996.* Cambridge, MA: Harvard University Press.

Wattenberg, M. P. (2002). *Where have all the voters gone?* Cambridge, MA: Harvard University Press.

Wattenberg, M. P., & Brians, C. L. (1999). Negative campaign advertising: Demobilizer or mobilizer? *American Political Science Review, 93I*, 891–899.

Weatherford, M. S. (1978). Economic conditions and electoral outcomes: Class differences in the political response to recession. *American Journal of Political Science, 22*, 917–938.

Weaver, D., McCombs, M., & Shaw, D. L. (2004). Agenda-setting research: Issues, attributes, and influences. In L. L. Kaid (Ed.), *Handbook of political campaign research* (pp. 257–282). Mahwah, NJ: Erlbaum.

Weiss, H. J. (1976). *Wahlkampf im Fernsehen* [*Election campaigns on television*]. Berlin, Germany: Spiess.

Wen, W.-C. (2014). Facebook political communication in Taiwan: 1.0/2.0 messages and election/post-election messages. *Chinese Journal of Communication, 7*, 19–39.

Wen, W.-C., Benoit, W. L., & Yu, T.-H. (2004). A functional analysis of the 2000 Taiwanese and U. S. presidential spots. *Asian Journal of Communication, 14*, 140–155.

Wert, H. E. (2016). Hanging around us in plain sight: The great American political campaign poster, 1844–2012. *PS: Political Science & Politics, 49*, 59–70.

Wesleyan Media Project. (2012, October 24). 2012 shatters 2004 and 2008 records for total ads aired. Accessed 5/7/16: http://mediaproject.wesleyan.edu/releases/2012-shatters-2004-and-2008-records-for-total-ads-aired/

Wesleyan Media Project (2020, February 26). Presidential ad spending approaches $900 million. Accessed 4/15/20: https://mediaproject.wesleyan.edu/releases-022620/.

West, D. M. (1994). Political advertising and news coverage in the 1992 California U.S. Senate campaign. *Journal of Politics, 56*, 1053–1075.

West, D. M. (2001). *Air wars: Television advertising in election campaigns, 1952–2000* (3rd ed.). Washington, DC: Congressional Quarterly.

White, D. M. (1950). The gate-keeper: A case study in the selection of news. *Journalism Quarterly, 27*, 383–390.

White, T. H. (1961). *The making of the president 1960*. New York: Harper.

Wiese, D. R., & Gronbeck, B. E. (2005). Campaign 2004 developments in cyberpolitics. In R. E. Denton (Ed.), *The 2004 presidential campaign: A communication perspective* (pp. 217–239). Lanham, MD: Rowman & Littlefield.

Williams, A. P. (2005). The main frame: Assessing the role of the Internet in the 2004 U.S. presidential contest. In R. E. Denton (Ed.), *The 2004 presidential campaign: A communication perspective* (pp. 241–254). Lanham, MD: Rowman & Littlefield.

Wilson, R. (2020, October 23). Biden breaks all-time television spending record. *The Hill*. Accessed 10/26/20: https://thehill.com/homenews/campaign/522483-biden-breaks-all-time-television-spending-record

Winneg, K., Kenski, K., & Jamieson, K. H. (2005). Detecting the effects of deceptive presidential ads in the Spring of 2004. *American Behavioral Scientist, 49*, 114–129.

Wisconsin Public Television. (2001). *The:30 second candidate*. Accessed 3/8/05: http://www.pbs.org/30secondcandidate/timeline.

Wong, W., Sheeley, C., & Siemaszko, C. (2020, October 24). For second straight day, U.S. Covid cases reach new high. *NBC News*. Accessed 10/27/20: https://www.nbcnews.com/news/us-news/coronavirus-case-increase-sets-new-u-s-record-rising-over-n1244490

Wood, S. C. (1990). Television's first spot ad campaign: "Eisenhower Answers America." *Presidential Studies Quarterly, 20*, 265–284.

World Population Review. (2020). The 200 largest cities in the United States by population 2020. Accessed 4/15/20: https://worldpopulationreview.com/us-cities/

WSIU. (2002). *A broadcast technology timeline*. Available: http://www.wsiu.org/digitaltv/index.shtml

Yoon, R., & Snow, K. (2003, July 1). Dean leads Democratic competitors in second-quarter contributions: Former Vermont governor makes extensive use of Internet. *CNN*. Accessed 1//29/22: https://edition.cnn.com/2003/ALLPOLITICS/06/30/democrats.fundraising/999999

Zaller, J. R. (1992). *The nature and origins of mass opinion.* New York, NY: Cambridge University Press.

Zaller, J. R. (1997). A model of communication effects at the outbreak of the Gulf War. In S. Iyengar & R. Reeves (Eds.), *Does the media govern? Politicians, voters, and reporters in America* (pp. 296–311). Thousand Oaks, CA: Sage.

Zaller, J. (1999). The myth of massive media impact revived: New support for a discredited idea. In D. C. Mutz, P. M. Sniderman, & R. A. Brody (Eds.), *Political persuasion and attitude change* (pp. 17–78). Ann Arbor: University of Michigan Press.

Zimbardo, P. G., & Leippe, M. R. (1991). *The psychology of attitude change and social influence.* New York: McGraw-Hill.

2020 Democratic Party Presidential Debates. (2020). Accessed 7/14/20: https://en.wikipedia.org/wiki/2020_Democratic_Party_presidential_debates#:~:text=The%202020%20Democratic%20Party%20presidential,in%20at%20least%20one%20debate

2020 Democratic Party Presidential Primaries. (2020). *Wikipedia.* Accessed 7/14/20: https://en.wikipedia.org/wiki/2020_Democratic_Party_presidential_primaries.

2020 Republican Party Presidential Primaries. (2020) *Wikipedia.* Accessed 7/14/20: https://en.wikipedia.org/wiki/2020_Republican_Party_presidential_primaries.

2020 United States Presidential Debates. (2020). *Wikipedia.* Accessed 10/26/20: https://en.wikipedia.org/wiki/2020_United_States_presidential_debates.

Index

Agnew, Spiro 10
acceptance addresses
   acclaims 123
   candidate's character traits 55, 108, 122, 269
   Clinton, Bill 25, 51
   functional approach 67, 106–107, 116–117, 132, 134, 138
   as medium 81
   nominating convention 105–106, 161, 198–199, 222–223
   presidential messages 3, 42, 274
   topics 107–108
   Trump, Donald 131
acclaim
   on character 43, 61, 63, 94
   functional approach 44, 48, 116, 131, 168, 175, 177–178
   general goals 172
   incumbents 133, 183–184, 268
   news coverage 225–226
   PACs 87
   on policy 43
   Presidential debates 95
   primary vs general campaign 148, 156–157
   tv spots 123, 137
   vice presidential debates 96, 124–125
advertisements (television), *See* spots
agenda setting 19, 25, 27, 82, 93, 118, 121
   campaign message 223
   current events 219–221
   voter privileges issues 232–233
Alexander, Lamar 146
Anderson, John 12, 89, 92, 142, 192
attack
   advertisement campaigns 85–87
   anti- Trump PACs 30
   Bush on Gore 65, 107
   Bush's foreign policy 90
   campaign message 94–95, 270
   campaign phase 146–148
   challengers 131, 133
   on character 53, 61, 63, 95–96, 270

316 | INDEX

Clinton on Dole 60
coding themes 66
by direct mail 109
on Ford's leadership ability 130
functional approach 42–44, 47–48, 116, 131, 168, 175, 177–178, 180, 267–268
general campaign 155–157
general goals 172
image restoration options 136
levels 164
negative ads 41–42, 167
news coverage 225–227, 247
non- presidential campaign messages 184
on past deeds 183
on policy 43, 53
on vice presidential candidates 125
patterns 101
political advertising 199
primary campaign 158–159
surrogates, use of 123–124
tv spots 137
utterance function 170
voter privileges issues 39–40

Bauer, Gary 157
Benton, William 81
Biden, Joe
 acclaims and attack 94–95, 147
 as president 33
 clinching Democratic Nomination 151
 Covid- 19 management 28
 Electoral Vote support 30
 first debate with Trump 29
 general campaign 155
 television spot 87
 Trump nick naming 40
 as 2020 Democratic primary. in 2020 28
 Vice Presidency 11, 27, 35
blame, *See* responsibility
Bloomberg, Mike 11, 28, 147
Booker, Cory 147, 154–155
Bradley, Bill 66
Brady, James 52–53, 146, 208–209, 211
Brokaw, Tom 90

Brown, Jerry 145, 213
Buchanan, Pat 29, 127, 146, 157, 198–199, 201, 205–206
Bush, George H.W 7, 10–12, 17
 Buchanan as opponent to 146
 Clinton as opponent 239
 incumbents *vs.* challengers 126, 131
 issue ownership theory 118
 Operation Desert Storm 220, 222, 233
 political debates 89–
Bush, George W 2, 15–17, 21, 23, 29, 35, 39–40, 46
 Acceptance Address 106–108
 allegations 135–137
 attack on the opposition party 86
 battleground states., 161
 campaign resources 58
 character 51–53, 121
 different media portrait 78–79
 educational policy 241
 Electoral College votes 57
 functions and source of campaign messages., 124
 Gallup polls 263
 issue ownership theory 118, 121
 news coverage 204, 211
 opponent to Kerry 144, 261–262
 party affiliation 73
 party's nomination 127–128, 143, 145, 151, 157
 policy positions 56, 231–233
 political debates 198
 surrogate sources 125
 target audience 148
 TV spot 65–67
 uniting Democrat opponents 158
 vice presidency 132, 163, 192
 webpages 97
Bush, Jeb 11
Buttigieg, Pete 11, 28, 35, 69, 95, 147, 154–155

campaign phase
 arena 150
 in battleground states 161–162

contextual factors 162–164
nominating conventions 160–161
number of opponents 146–148
party of opponent 144–146
primary *versus* general 141–144, 154–159
state influence 150–154
target audience 148–149
voter knowledge 154
candidates
acclaims 38–39
attacks 39–42
defenses 42–43
difference from opponents 35–37
information to voters 37–38
Carson, Ben 11, 148
Carter, Jimmy 8
campaign messages 21
effects of the economy on voting 17
governmental experience:, 157
incumbents *vs.* challengers 126–131, 139, 143
Kennedy challenging 29
Maynard's questions 90–91
news coverage 144, 192
Reagan's debate with 89
slim margin 16
television advertisement 121
weak opponent 12
challenger
attack resources 129–130
direct mail, use of 110
election winning 126
Ford vs Carter 139
functional approach 102, 128, 132, 183
Kerry, John as 128
news coverage 214
non-presidential campaign messages 175–176
voter perceptions 234, 242
character
acceptance address 108
acclaims 38, 94, 172
attacks 39–42, 85, 95, 172

campaign messages 178, 180
direct mail advertising 110
functional approaches 43, 102, 104, 235–238, 267–268
general campaign 155–156, 159, 164
as major factor in campaign message 26
news coverage 189, 196–198, 200–215, 217–219, 223–228
nomination convention 161
non- presidential campaign 168–170
non-U.S tv spots 182–184
policy proposals 48–54, 60–61, 63–65, 70–72, 78–80, 84, 87, 103, 254, 277–278
posters 112
Republican and Democratic messages 121–122
Scandals 137–138
talk show appearance 111–112
through webpages 98–99, 101–102, 103
voter influence 23, 27, 35, 37, 46, 82, 93, 96, 134–135, 154, 229–230, 232, 241–242, 264–265
Chideya, Farai 91
Christie, Chris 11, 145
Clinton, Bill
attacking Dole's tax proposal 60
campaign message 222–223
character 52–53, 135–137
Dole's portrayal 26
function in Acceptances 106–107
general campaign 157
incumbents *vs.* challengers 126–128, 131, 143
media buys 57
news coverage 195, 203, 210
policy position 24–25, 51–52, 237, 272–273
political debates 89–90
primary campaign 12, 145–146
talk shows 110
target audience 148
television spots 64–66, 86
voter's choice 233, 239

Clinton, Hillary
   acclaims and attacks 67, 86
   advertisement expenditure 1–2
   direct mail advertising 108
   discussion on current state of affairs 19
   Facebook pages 101
   incumbents *vs.* challengers 126, 130–131, 145
   news coverage 247
   party nomination 151
   Sanders challenging 33
   as senator 41
   social media use 103
   spreading effect, ideas and messages 243
commercials (television), *See* spots
Cruz, Ted 3, 11, 60–61, 148, 183
cyberpolitics 99–100

Dean, Howard 2, 90, 97, 146, 151
debate
   general 84, 89, 92, 274
   primary 3, 27, 36, 84, 88–91, 95, 145–146, 148, 151, 158–159, 196, 254, 277
defend 42–44, 48, 87, 96, 131, 168, 172, 268
defense (national/military) 25, 55, 79–80, 117, 119, 159, 220, 235
deficit (balanced budget) 37, 272–273
delegates 27, 34, 105, 143, 148, 150–152, 208, 210, 212
Democrat (ic Party)
   context of discourse 142–155, 158–160, 163
   discourse source 115–122, 125, 127–128, 130–131, 135, 137–138
   functional approach 33–36, 38–41, 46, 55–56, 59, 67
   nature of political campaigns 1–3, 7, 9, 11–15, 19, 22, 24, 26–30
   news coverage 186, 192–193, 195, 198, 209–213, 215, 222
   non-presidential and non-U.S. discourse 173–174, 180
   role of medium 69, 73–74, 80–81, 86, 88–92, 94–95, 97, 104–106

   voter's role and election outcome 231, 235, 237, 239–241, 243–244, 246–247, 257–258, 263
Dewey, Thomas 88–89
direct mail advertising
   advantages 108–109
   common function 110
   face- to- face contact vs 109–110
Dole, Bob
   against President Bill Clinton 24, 26, 52, 127
   campaign phase 146
   general campaign 157
   incumbents and challengers 127–128
   negative advertisement 273
   negative attacks 12
   news coverage 195, 222–223
   talk shows 110
   tax policy 25, 60, 237
   tv ads 64–65
Dole, Elizabeth 157
Dornan, Bob 146
Douglas, Stephen 88
Dukakis, Michael 121, 128, 139, 157, 163, 192

Eisenhower, Dwight
   general campaign 157
   incumbents *vs.* challengers 126, 129–131, 135, 139
   news coverage 192
   second term in office 157
   television spots 81, 121, 139
election campaign
   effects on voters 10–11, 20–26
   limited effects model 6–10
   mass media's role in 4–5
   obvious and Subtle Effects 5
   political party affiliation 11–14

Facebook 100–102
Forbes, Steve 12, 146, 157
Ford, Gerald
   effects of the economy on voting 17

general campaigns 11–12
  incumbent vs challengers 127, 129, 132, 139, 143
  primary debates 89, 91
  vice presidency 10
front-runner 40127, 147–148, 158–159, 164
functional analysis
  acclaim 44, 48, 116, 131, 168, 175, 177–178
  advantages 64–67
  assumptions 34–39
  attack or criticizing opponents 42–44, 47–48, 116, 131, 168, 175, 177–178, 180, 267–268
  character 43, 102, 104, 235–238, 267–268
  defending attacks 42–43
  Democratic party 33–36, 38–41, 46, 55–56, 59, 67
  general campaign 55, 57–58
  news coverage 223–227
  primary campaign. 35–36, 39, 48, 58, 66–67
  policy vs character 60–64
  predictions of relative frequency 47–60
  Republican party 34, 36–41, 46, 51, 55–56, 58–60, 66–67
  television spots 86–87, 183, 189, 271
  voting choice 43–47
future plans 60–61, 64–65, 132–134, 137, 157, 176–178, 183–184, 269, 277–278

Gabbard, Tulsi 28, 69
general campaign 11, 178, 269
  context 144–146, 149–150, 154–157, 159–160, 163–164
  functional approaches 55, 57–58
  nature 11
  news coverage 198, 201, 204–205, 207–210, 214, 223, 227
  role of medium 77, 79–81, 83–84, 86, 89, 92–93
  sources 117, 139, 141
  general goals 60–64, 132, 157, 159, 171–172, 178, 180–181, 184, 268, 277–278
Gephardt, Dick 90, 144, 146, 152
Gillibrand, Kirsten 35, 154
Glenn, John
Goldwater, Barry 37, 89, 128, 157, 192
Gore, Al
  Acceptance statements 106–108
  campaign message 223
  electoral vote 57
  general campaign 157, 161
  incumbent administration 10
  incumbents vs. challengers 126–127, 132, 146
  negative information 65
  policy position 36, 56, 121, 231
  political advertising 125
  primary elections 151
  talk shows 78–79
  television spot 66–67
  vice presidency 53, 272
  vote choice 15–16, 21, 23
Gramm, Phil 146

Harkin, Tom 145, 150, 172
Harris, Kamala 29–30, 35
Harris, Kathleen 16
Hart, Gary 135, 137
Hatch, Orin
Humphrey, Hubert
  general election 89
  incumbent administration 10
  incumbents vs. challengers 126, 132
  mid- point of public opinion 36
  news coverage 212
  nominating conventions 105
  party's nominee 143, 157
  slim margin 16
  television spots 146
  vice presidency 192

ideals 56, 60–64, 116, 138, 171, 172, 178, 180–181, 183–184, 268, 277, 278
image. *See* character

image restoration discourse 135–136
incumbent 10, 17–18, 24, 48, 56, 85, 95,
    102–103, 110, 115, 126–134, 137, 143–
    144, 175–178, 180, 183–184, 214–215,
    233–235, 241–242, 268–269
Internet 96–97. *See also* World Wide Web
    webpages of candidates 97–99
Iowa 12, 39, 57–58, 83, 87, 141–142, 150–
    153, 162, 211, 214
issue
    knowledge 23, 58, 73, 82, 93, 127, 162,
        189–190
    party's 118–119, 121, 137, 149, 159
    position 7, 21, 25, 36–37, 70–71, 75,
        87, 96, 98, 119, 176, 189, 203, 211,
        235, 239
issue ownership 116–120, 122, 137,
    159, 173–174, 178, 184, 234, 237,
    241, 268

Jackson, Jesse 157
Johnson, Lyndon 89, 105, 192, 211

Kalb, Marvin 91
Kasich, John 3, 11, 38–39, 60, 64, 148
Kennedy, John
    assassination 126
    general campaign 89
    incumbents vs challenges 130
    most watched primary debate 254–255
    news coverage 212
    party's nominees 143
    personal traits 122
    radio debate 113
    slim margin 16
    talk shows 110
Kennedy, Ted
    general campaign 157
    incumbents vs challenges 127–128
    news coverage 192
    opposing re-nomination 29
    slim margin 16
Kerry, John
    approval rating 73
    battleground states 57, 162

campaign discourse 19
campaign expenditure 2
character 135
incumbent vs challengers 128, 144
nominee conventions 160
policy position 119, 237, 277
political advertising 125
primary campaign 151, 158
primary debates 146
public opinion polls 261–263
religious affiliation 74
Keyes, Alan 146, 157
Klobuchar, Amy 11, 28, 35, 39, 94–95, 147

leadership ability 34–35, 51, 60–61, 64, 70,
    93–95, 128, 130, 189, 200, 208, 235, 237,
    272, 277–278
Lehrer, Jim 52–53, 90
Lieberman, Joseph 36, 83, 144, 146, 277
Lincoln, Abraham 88
Lugar, Dick 146

Maynard, Robert 90
McCain, John
    Facebook pages 101
    general campaign 58
    incumbents vs. challengers 126, 128
    political attacks 67
    polling places 150
    primary campaign 35, 39–40
    voter perception 10
McCarthy, Eugene 211–212
McGovern, George 44, 128, 157,
    193, 210
media environment. *See also* news coverage
    change in use 76–77
    comparisons 112–113
    election information flow 71–72
    key aspects 74–75
    political campaign information 71
    political party affiliation 73–74
    presidential campaign 71–72, 80
    social security themes 79
    sources 75–76
    television advertisements 81–85

2016 campaign 76–77
  variety of differences 78–81
Mondale, Walter 128, 192
mudslinging, *See* attack

Nader, Ralph 4, 93, 142, 146, 198, 254
negative, *See* attack
news coverage
  accuracy 195
  agenda-setting 219–221
  bias 192–194
  campaign speeches 198–199
  content analysis 195–200
  framing 222–223
  functional analysis 223–227
  gatekeeping function 190–192
  limited effects model 219
  non-presidential campaigns 213–223
  of presidential primary
    campaigns 207–213
  policy vs issues 200–207
  political campaign 200–207
  presidential primary campaign 207–213
  primary and general debates 195–198
  priming 221
  television spots 199–200
  voter learning 185–190
New Hampshire (primary) 35, 57–58, 109, 142, 145–146, 150–153, 162, 208, 210–211
Nixon, Richard
  audience view on messages 254–255
  incumbents *vs.* challengers 126, 128–132, 135, 137, 143
  news coverage 193, 218
  party nominee 105
  presidential debate 113
  public opinion 36
  re-election campaign 44, 57
  slim margin 16
  television spot 139
  vice presidency 10, 89, 157, 192
  Watergate issues 10
non- U.S. debates
  general goals 178
  personal qualities 180–182
  tv spots 183

Obama, Barack
  Facebook/Twitter pages 101, 103
  general campaign 157
  incumbents *vs.* challengers 126, 130–131
  policy positions 243–244
  Republican's primary attacks 67
  Trump's criticism 18–19
  tv spot 3, 86, 108
  voter's behavior 10

past deeds 60, 64–65, 132–134, 137, 157, 159, 176–178, 183–184, 268–269
Pelosi, Nancy 86
Perot, H. Ross 89, 142, 146, 198, 203, 237
personal qualities 51–52, 55, 61, 64, 87, 121–122, 157, 167–168, 199–201, 204, 208, 216, 235–236, 277–278. *See also* character
  in non- presidential tv spots 172
  non- U.S. Debates 180, 182
policy 49–51, 53–54, 60–64, 70, 80, 99, 101–102, 111–112, 156, 168–170, 179, 182, 202, 204–206, 208–209, 224–226, 232, 236, 274, 277
Political Action Committees (PACs) 29–30, 86–87
political party, *See* Democrat (ic); Republican party
political party affiliation
  campaign discourse vs 116–119, 121–122
  Democrats vs Republicans 119–121
political party conventions
  acceptance addresses 106–107
  nominee's identity 105–106
political scandal 133–137
polls, public opinion 5, 9, 12, 15–16, 41, 48, 54, 56–57, 59, 70, 78, 85, 91, 95, 100–101, 118, 141, 147–148, 150, 152, 158–159, 161, 164, 184, 192, 194, 200, 202–204, 207–209, 211, 215–216, 218–219, 229, 260–265, 269

positive, *See* acclaim
posters 112
presidential debates
    function 93–95
    topics 95–96
primary campaign
    context 142–145, 147–149, 151–152, 154–155, 157–159
    functional approach 35–36, 39, 48, 58, 66–67
    nature 3, 11–12
    news coverage 207–212, 224, 226–227
    role of medium 88–89, 92, 105

Reagan, Ronald
    Acceptance Addresses 106–107
    general campaign 157
    incumbents *vs.* challengers 126–128, 131, 136–137, 143
    news coverage 192, 213
    party's nomination 145
    policy position 52
    political debate 89, 91–92
    primary campaign 12, 152
    slim margin 16
    voter behavior 8, 21
reliability, inter-coder 278
Republican (Party)
    context 142–146, 148–152, 158–159, 163
    functional approaches 34, 36–41, 46, 51, 55–56, 58–60, 66–67
    nature of political campaign 1–3, 7, 9–15, 21–22, 24, 26–30
    news coverage 188, 193–195, 198, 211, 213
    non-presidential discourse 167, 173–174
    role of medium 73–74, 80–81, 88–89, 92, 95, 101, 106–107, 113
    sources 115–122, 125, 127–131
    voter choice and election outcome 231–232, 235, 237, 240, 243–244, 246–247, 251, 254, 257

responsibility 87, 135, 136
Romney, Mitt 3, 101, 108, 128
Rubio, Marco 3, 11, 145, 148

Sanders, Bernie
    attacks through debate 94
    campaign discourse 33
    news coverage 247
    party affiliation and nomination 11, 35, 155
    social media use 103
    strategic reason to attack 147
    2020 Democratic primary candidate 28
    voter perception 69
Schumer, Chuck 86
Sharon, Ariel 90
Simon, Paul
social media 99–100
sources
    campaign aspects 115
    grounded theory analysis 121–122
    incumbency challenges 126–133
    issue ownership 116–121
    political party affiliation 116
    political scandal 133–137
    public opinion polls 118–119
    surrogates 123–125
    television spots 116
South Carolina (Primary) 36, 149, 153, 247
Specter, Arlen 146
spots (television) 3, 12, 20–21, 27, 29, 40, 42–43, 46, 51–52, 55–57, 60, 64–67, 75, 77, 79
    advantages 81–85, 119, 125, 163, 166
    attacks 130, 154, 167
    coding themes 131–133
    debates 88–95, 98, 155–158, 268
    functional analysis 86–87, 183, 189, 271
    message forms 104, 112, 116, 121–123
    negative 272
    news coverage 199–202
    primary campaigns 145–146, 149, 151
    topics 87, 95–96

U.S. non-presidential 168, 172, 174, 213–219
Stassen, Harold 88–89
Stevenson, Adlai 34, 81, 126, 192
Steyer. Tom 36, 39, 69, 154
straight-ticket versus split ticket voting 14–15

target (attack) 25, 39, 41–42, 47, 57–58, 66–67, 97, 108, 111, 147–149, 157–159, 186, 237–238, 261–262, 269
Taylor, Morry 146
television advertising
   political debates 88–93
   topics 87
television spots (TV spots), *See* spots
television talk shows 110–112
   emphasizing personalities., 111–112
Trump, Donald
   acclaims and attacks 60, 86, 148
   anti-Trump PACs 30
   approval rating 73
   baseless allegation 232
   as business man and media celebrity 69
   campaign spending 1–3
   character 270
   Covid-19 pandemic: management 29, 231
   debate viewers 88, 92
   electoral college win 16, 23, 57
   first debate 18–19
   fund-raising 141
   general campaign 149
   impeachment hearings 254
   incumbents *vs.* challengers 126–127, 129–132, 145
   issue ownership 120
   levels of attacks on opponent 40–42 95
   media preferences 83
   messages and ideas, voters view 243–244
   news coverage 154, 246–247, 259–260
   non-person-to-person campaigning 28
   party affiliation 11
   party nominee 34, 151, 157
   policy positions 24–25, 36–37, 39
   social media use 3, 74, 103–105
   tv spots 2, 87
   2020 election campaign 27
   voter choice 35
Tsongas, Paul 145, 210
2020 election campaign 27
   advertisement expenditure 29
   Covid-19 issue., 28–29
   federal election results., 30–31
   rise of Political Action Committees (PACs) 29–30
   top seven candidates, Democrats 28
Twitter 103–105

uncommitted (undecided) 5, 16, 44, 47, 59, 106, 121, 149, 219, 263
U.S. non-presidential campaign discourse
   functions and topics 168–170
   general goals and ideals 171–172
   incumbency in 175–178
   issue ownership in 173–174
   overview 165–168
   personal qualities 172
   tv spots and debates 178–180

vice president
   ascendency to presidency 8–9
   attacks 106, 121, 124–125
   audience views 88, 92
   battle ground states 161
   campaign messages 163–164
   debates 3, 22, 27, 29, 53, 89, 272
   functional approach 93, 95–96
   incumbent administration 10
   incumbents vs challenges 126–128, 130–132, 135, 146, 180
   news paper coverage 192, 247
   party nomination 35, 157
   policy position 36
   primary campaign 105
   primary phase of election campaign 11
   talk shows 79

television spots 51, 123
webpages 98
voting behavior
   cognitive response model 247–248
   decision-making 238–242
   elaboration likelihood model 248–249
   election outcomes 17–20
   favorable and unfavorable thoughts 250
   information processing 242–247
   mass audience 254–260
   motivation and involvement 249
   peripheral cues 250–251
   political party affiliation 232–238
   public opinion polls 260–264
   role of affect (emotions) in politics 251–254
   straight-ticket versus split ticket voting 14–17
   theory of affective intelligence 251–254
   thinking ability 249–250
   three key factors 230–232
voters' perceptions
   comparative decision 34–35
   competing vs preferable candidate 34
   of economy 18
   effects of campaign messages 20–26

Washington establishment 66
Wilson, Woodrow 108
   World Wide Web (Internet) 4, 70, 72–78, 84, 93, 108, 186–188, 255, 259
   social media and 96–105

Printed in the USA
CPSIA information can be obtained
at www.ICGtesting.com
CBHW072344130724
11570CB00012B/578